THE
CRIME
OF THE
CENTURY

MORNING AFTER

The alarm rang at five-forty A.M. in the bedroom of Judy Dykton; she was determined to get in some final licks for the neurology exam. She switched off the fan that had been working overtime against the summer heat and heard a noise that sounded like the whimpering of an animal, but paid no attention.

She walked to the basement of the town house, took some clothes that had been drying overnight, and returned upstairs. Again she heard a sound, and this time it was more distinct, like a little child crying or calling out. She opened a blind and looked out and saw a woman standing across the street, looking up at 2319, toward the crying voice. Opening the window, Judy could now clearly hear Cora's cry:

"Oh, my God, they are all dead!"

Cover photos of the nurses are (top, from left) Mary Ann Jordan, Nina Schmale, Patricia Matusek, Valentina Pasion, and (bottom, from left) Gloria Jean Davy, Suzanne Farris, Merlita Gargullo, and Pamela Wilkening.

"Fast-paced detective work and high drama in the courtroom combine to make *The Crime of the Century* a first-rate thriller."
—James R. Thompson, governor of Illinois 1977–1991

THE
CRIME
OF THE
CENTURY

RICHARD SPECK AND THE MURDERS THAT SHOCKED A NATION

Dennis L. Breo and William J. Martin

Skyhorse Publishing

For Julie

—Dennis L. Breo

For Dan Ward, John Stamos, and Lou Garippo for trusting me with the prosecution.

—William J. Martin

CONTENTS

"God, please instill in the hearts of the people the understanding of the meaning of this tragedy. I plead for a purpose, a worth in so disastrous a loss. Why this death? Its reason I do not know. But in the years to come it will show. I trust in this."

—A poem written by Gloria Jean Davy in 1963
after the assassination of President John F. Kennedy
and read at her own funeral in July 1966

INTRODUCTION
A SCREAM OF TERROR

The first alarm clock went off at five A.M. Corazon Amurao had been huddled under a bunk bed for two hours. Now she began to untie herself, working her hands back and forth to loosen the double knots of the bedsheet that bound her. Then she untied her ankles. Another alarm sounded. It was five-thirty.

Crawling slowly on her stomach, she emerged from her hiding place and with great effort moved under another bunk bed, from where she could peek out the open door. Nothing moved in the hallway. She stood up and began to walk to her own bedroom. She saw the body of one of her roommates lying on the bathroom floor. As she walked across her own bedroom, she stepped over the bodies of three more, covered with blood. She closed her door, fearing the killer might still be in the house.

She climbed onto her top bunk, opened the window, and screamed almost continuously for five minutes. There was no reply. Dressed in pajama shorts and top, she crawled out the window and jumped down to a ledge of the town house facing 100th Street on the far southeast side of Chicago. She stood there screaming for twenty more minutes before anyone came, a scream that shook terror into the very heart of Chicago:

"They are all dead! They are all dead! My friends are all dead. Oh, God, I'm the only one alive!"

It was July 14, 1966, and Chicago awoke on that hot and sticky morning to reports that eight young nurses had been brutally stabbed, strangled, and sexually assaulted. The killings took place as the victims were settling in for the evening in the safety of their own beds. This murder of innocents shocked the conscience of the nation. It seemed that a monster was on the loose, that a crazed killer who walked on ten-foot stilts bestrode a terrified city. Doors were locked, strangers were scrutinized, parents checked on their children.

The monster, who was flesh and blood, was little more than a mile due east of the murder scene, toward the lake, in the rough Calumet Harbor area of the Southeast Side. Richard Franklin Speck, twenty-four, a heavily pockmarked, tattooed drifter from Dallas, was sound asleep in a small upstairs room at the Shipyard Inn, a tavern-rooming house catering to seamen and steelworkers. A small black pistol was tucked under his pillow. A stale can of beer sat on his nightstand, next to a crumpled pile of dollar bills. What had started out as a twenty-five-dollar robbery had turned into a crime that will never be forgotten.

Speck had swept through the nurses' town house like a summer tornado, and his savage murders had changed the landscape of crime. Within a few weeks, Charles Whitman would take a rifle to the top of a tower at Texas University and kill sixteen; within a few years, Charles Manson would mastermind the "helter-skelter" killings in southern California. Speck's legacy to us is the banality of today's mass murders and serial killings.

This is how it all began.

PART I
THE MURDERS

CHAPTER 1

The Chicago thermometer hit 98 degrees on Sunday, July 10, 1966. It was the eleventh day in the past two weeks that the heat had been 90 degrees or higher, and the city was wilting from the oppressive stickiness.

In July 1966, the median annual salary in Chicago was $8,000. Truman Capote's best-selling story of the brutal murder of a Kansas family in their quiet farmhouse, *In Cold Blood*, could be bought for $5.95—in hardcover. The sporty car of the hour was the gas-guzzling Pontiac GTO designed by John DeLorean and sold for $3,000. The big stories on Sunday were the widening war in Vietnam and the growing race rift in the United States. American soldiers chased Vietcong units into Cambodia and reportedly killed 238 elite enemy troops. The Reverend Martin Luther King pinned a list of fourteen demands for racial equality on the City Hall door of Chicago mayor Richard J. Daley. The action followed a freedom rally that attracted a crowd of thirty thousand to Chicago's Soldier Field. King warned that there would be "many more marches this summer," and that "We'll fill up the jails, if that's what it takes to get black people out of the slums."

Meanwhile, Richard Speck was spending a quiet Sunday with his brother-in-law, Eugene Thornton, and his older sister,

Martha Speck Thornton. Gene Thornton was a railroad switch-
man who worked nights and who had once served in the U.S.
Navy. Speck's sister Martha was a registered nurse who had
worked in pediatrics before her marriage. The Thorntons had
two teenage daughters and lived on the northwest side of Chicago in an apartment described by neighbors as "disgustingly
neat." The Thornton home was a second-floor apartment at 3966
North Avondale, in a working-class neighborhood just west of
the Kennedy Expressway and not far from Wrigley Field, home
of the Chicago Cubs. The apartment was decorated with expensive furniture and Martha Thornton's crystal collection. The
small apartment was cramped, and Speck was forced to sleep on
his sister's sofa.

Speck had been living with the couple on and off since he
had boarded a bus for Chicago from Dallas, four months earlier.
Since then, Gene Thornton had tried to satisfy Speck's drifting
life-style by arranging for him to stay with relatives near Monmouth, Illinois, and by helping him find a commercial ship on
which to sail. At six feet one inch tall and weighing 160 pounds,
Speck was a muscular, outdoorsy type who had arms as hard as
a baseball bat. He had slicked-back dirty blond hair, light blue
eyes, and a pale, angular face with a prominent aquiline nose.
Some women found him attractive, and he might have passed as
moderately handsome were it not for the deep pockmarks that
pitted the sides of his face, and his occasional habit of staring
stupidly into space with his mouth half open. He often appeared
to be in a fog.

Speck had spent the weekend moping around his sister's
house. Martha Thornton, like Speck's four other sisters and one
brother, was a religious teetotaler, and Speck was not allowed to
drink in her house. Able to blend into his surroundings, Speck
always conducted himself as a perfect gentleman while staying
with the Thorntons. A fastidious man, he indulged his daily habit

of taking several showers and going through several changes of shirts. He left the house that weekend only to get a Saturday haircut, and to shoot a few games of pool in a nearby saloon. Speck had great dexterity with his strong hands, and he tinkered with his sister's TV set and used his carpentry skills to build her some wooden household furniture.

That Sunday another one of Speck's sisters, Erma Speck Holeman, and her husband, Kenneth, brought their son to Chicago to enroll at the Judson Bible College in Elgin, Illinois. The Holemans visited the Thorntons for Sunday dinner, and Speck was on hand, neatly dressed in black pants and a white short-sleeved shirt. He was mild-mannered and quiet, but preferred reading comic books to engaging his family in much conversation. He read with some difficulty, since he needed reading glasses, but he was too vain to wear them. All he offered in conversation was that he had his heart set on buying a new car. He told his two older sisters that he was going to ship out to make enough money to buy a new car.

Monday morning began with a bang. At one A.M., a heavy thunderstorm with tornado-force winds lashed through the Chicago metropolitan area, slashing a wide swath from the northwest to the southeast. The winds reached eighty miles per hour in suburban McHenry and at fifty miles per hour rattled the windows of the downtown Loop skyscrapers. Savage and vicious bolts of lightning lit up the night sky. Hail the size of marbles pelted the city and several funnel clouds were sighted, though none touched down. The torrential rains pounding down on Lake Michigan created a *seiche*, and tidal waves reaching six feet crashed against the lakefront, which had to be closed. The temperature dropped from 82 to 71 degrees in the two hours between one and three in the morning. Then, as the storm spent its fury, the sun rose and the heat began to build toward an eventual high of 93 degrees.

The Thorntons' hospitality and patience with Richard Speck were running out. Speck had spent most of the past two weeks with them, usually holding court on the back porch and telling tall Texas tales of how tough he was to the teenage suitors of his two nieces, Kendra and Tennessa. He kept a large hunting knife hanging in a sheath from his belt. His switchblade was always in his pocket and he often brought it out to flash the three-inch blades. Eugene Thornton, a brisk, no-nonsense man, and his bright, animated wife had seen enough of the lazy ways of their young visitor. On Monday morning, Speck was asked to toss his entire wardrobe into a tan vinyl suitcase and a small red-and-black plaid carrying grip. He had an assortment of polo and sports shirts and wash-and-wear slacks, and his sister had washed and neatly folded all his underwear shorts and T-shirts. Gene Thornton also gave Speck a black corduroy jacket. Speck left behind a souvenir of his stay: On a backyard tree, he had carved the year "1966" and his initials, "R.S." He added a few flourishes designed to resemble the logo of a gang to which one of his teenage buddies belonged.

Promptly at eight A.M., Martha and Gene Thornton loaded up their car and drove Speck to the National Maritime Union Hall (NMU), a hiring center for merchant seamen. The union building was located at 2315 East 100th Street, about an hour's drive from where the Thorntons lived. The hiring hall was only a few doors east of three nursing residences. Because of a dormitory-room shortage, nearby South Chicago Community Hospital had rented three small, boxlike, two-story town houses at 2311, 2315, and 2319 East 100th Street for its senior nursing students and for a few Filipino exchange nurses. The three town houses rented by the hospital were part of a row of six town houses fronting on the south side of East 100th Street. The other three were private residences, scattered between the nurses' quarters. In the middle town house, at 2315, the hospital had placed a housemother, to whom the nurses were required to report. The easternmost town house, 2319, was directly west across Crandon Avenue from the union hall, and the comings and goings of the "ladies in white" were a common sight to the seamen.

The previous Friday, Thornton had taken Speck to the NMU to obtain a seaman's card and to register him for a berth on a ship. For a few moments, Speck and Thornton had gotten their hopes up that Speck would be able to hire out on the *Flying Spray*, a cargo ship scheduled to sail to Vietnam, but the coveted berth had gone to a seaman with greater seniority. Speck was only a deckhand with temporary sailing papers. Now, Speck was back to renew his search for a job. He was embarrassed, though, to have to go into the hall carrying all his clothes in the two bags, and he pleaded with his brother-in-law to help him find a room. Thornton, however, was adamant, insisting that they try the NMU first. The two entered the building together and learned that two ships were listed on the hiring board. Thornton assured Speck that he would be able to hire out on one of them. Speck cajoled, "Well, if I don't ship out today, I'll just sleep on the beach." Thornton gave Speck twenty-five dollars and left him on his own.

Alone, Speck was a gathering storm ready to break. Unknown to the Thorntons, he was on the run from police in two states. Speck was the bad apple of a good family. His father died when he was only six, and Richard spent his formative years with a hard-drinking, hell-raising stepfather whose behavior he chose to mimic. While his six older siblings put down family roots near Monmouth, Illinois, the town 215 miles southwest of Chicago where Richard Speck was born, Richard and his younger sister, Carolyn, were shuttled off to Dallas to live with his mother and her new husband. In twelve years, the nomadic family would live at ten different Dallas addresses, all of them in poor neighborhoods. Speck's stepfather, Carl August Rudolph Lindberg, was a Swedish traveling salesman and professional drunk who had lost his left leg at the knee in an accident, and was forced to walk on crutches. His drunken tirades were in stark contrast to Speck's mother, the religious Mary Margaret Carbaugh Speck, who did not drink and who had raised her older children not to drink. Lindberg despised young Richard, told him often that he couldn't stand the sight of him, and refused to adopt him. Speck's mother was largely unsuccessful in trying to shelter her youngest son from Lindberg's drunken physical abuse.

Richard took his first drink of whiskey at thirteen after breaking into the secret liquor cabinet Lindberg kept hidden from his wife. On many occasions, he threatened to take Lindberg's crutches "and bash his head." Aping his hated stepfather, Richard dropped out of school at sixteen to work at various odd manual jobs. During his youth he ran with a fast crowd of older men, spending most of his time bragging, drinking, lying, and whoring. Along the way, he acquired a variety of cheap tattoos, usually drawn while he was dead drunk. During his Dallas days, he was arrested forty-one times for break-ins, burglaries, forged checks, robberies, and violence against women, spending almost two years in the penitentiary and many other nights in local jails. In the meantime, he had married at nineteen, fathered a daughter, and divorced four years later. He had been physically violent toward both his ex-wife and his ex-mother-in-law. His probation officer had once described him this way:

"When Speck is drinking, he will fight or threaten anybody— as long as he has a knife or gun. When he's sober or unarmed, he couldn't face down a mouse."

Although a young man, Richard Speck was, by July 1966, a total loner who usually sought out a twilight world inhabited by older hard-drinking men and women who, like him, were aimless and ambitionless. He was mad at the world and always looking for a chance to hit back. The Thorntons' Chicago home was a temporary sanctuary for him—a place in which the police were not yet chasing him.

In Dallas, the police were looking for Speck in connection with the burglary of a grocery store he had broken into on March 6. If caught, this would be Speck's forty-second arrest in his adopted home state, and would send him back to prison. The warrant for his arrest had forced him to pack all his worldly belongings into the large tan suitcase and the small red-and-black bag and board a bus for Chicago. His mother and his younger sister, his only protectors, had taken him to the bus station. They would no longer be around to take care of him, give him money, and bail him out of trouble. A return to his boyhood home of Monmouth was also out of the question, since Speck was a leading suspect in both the burglary-rape of an elderly woman and the murder of a thirty-two-year-old barmaid whose body was found in an abandoned hoghouse. Both crimes had been committed in April, and Speck had slipped out of town on April 19, arriving back at the Thorntons' Chicago home with the wildly fabricated story that a crime syndicate had forced him out of town.

Lying was a Speck specialty. He had an uncanny ability to give the events of his life a fictional twist that would keep him out of danger, and although his formal IQ tested at only 90, which is barely low-normal for an American adult, his criminal skills were much more highly developed. He had the natural gifts of animal cunning and charm. Speck's secret weapons were his gentle eyes and soft-spoken southern drawl, a disarming combination that usually put his male rivals at ease and his female victims off guard.

When he walked into that Chicago hiring hall on July 11, 1966, Speck had a growing hatred in his heart from his dismal status in life. Broke, friendless, homeless, and jobless, he was self-conscious about his disfiguring acne and suffering from low self-esteem. A loser in the major tests of maturity—failing to complete an education, find a job, and maintain a marriage—he was now separated from his family in Texas, Monmouth, and Chicago. Worse, he despaired of ever improving his propects.

He was also a potential killing machine, with his trademarks already written into the criminal ledgers of two states: He was an expert at breaking and entering, usually with the aid of a screwdriver or the sharp edge of a knife, and he always had one or the other with him. He had threatened women with knives before, often attempting or completing a rape, and he usually spoke gently and softly, assuring the women he meant no harm.

CHAPTER 2

Boredom ruled at the National Maritime Union, as the seamen whiled away the hours in the cavernous warehouselike building, waiting for a ship. The commercial shipping center of Chicago was only two miles east, at Calumet Harbor in Lake Michigan. In 1966, the Calumet Harbor area boasted many steel mills and shipping and ship repair docks. Times were good, and the area was a melting pot of nationalities; factory time clocks were often explained in eleven different foreign languages. The ethnic enclaves were noted for their wide-open saloons and nonstop, around-the-clock heavy drinkers. When the workers or their families needed medical care, they were usually referred to South Chicago Community Hospital, which was located one mile north of the union hall.

Richard Speck had been in this neighborhood before. In April, after his flight from Monmouth to the Thorntons, Speck had been driven by Gene Thornton to the Chicago headquarters of the U.S. Coast Guard, in the heart of the Calumet Harbor area. In order to apply, he was required to be fingerprinted on all ten fingers and to provide a two-inch-by-two-inch passport photo, which he obtained at a photography studio around the corner. In addition, Speck had supplied a statement from a physician under contract to the Coast Guard, documenting that he was physically competent to perform his shipboard duties. Once his application had been accepted, Speck was given a letter of authority allowing him to be employed as an ordinary sea-man on any U.S. merchant vessel weighing one hundred tons or more and engaged in trade on the Great Lakes. His application carried the name "Richard Benjamin Speck," his birth name, although he usually preferred to be known as Richard Franklin Speck. Both middle names came from his late father, Benjamin Franklin Speck.

Armed with the application, Speck was driven to the National Maritime Union on April 30 and found a ship right off the bat. He signed on as a deckhand with temporary papers aboard Inland Steel's ore-carrying ship, the S.S. *Clarence B. Randall.* The *Randall* sailed the Great Lakes with a crew of thirty-three, pick-ing up ore to return to Inland Steel in Calumet Harbor. Ports of call included stopovers in Michigan, Wisconsin, and Canada. Within four days of his enlistment, however, Speck had suffered an acute attack of appendicitis and had been taken by the Coast Guard to a hospital in Hancock, Michigan, for an emergency appendectomy. Once recovered, he had rejoined the *Randall* on May 20 and worked steadily until the night of June 14, when he was fired for getting into fights when drunk and for assaulting a ship's officer. His twenty-six days of continuous employment with Inland Steel were the longest he had worked in a year. His discharge papers were short and sweet:

"Steady drinker—warned on two occasions, but continues drinking. When drunk, is looking for trouble."

After his firing, Speck had spent a week living in a fleabag hotel in the seamy Calumet Harbor world before returning to the Thorntons. The men and women inhabiting the bars and transient rooming houses of the Calumet Harbor area in 1966 constituted a demimonde, a shadowy world in which ambition and time had little meaning. Most were blue-collar workers or unskilled laborers who slid seamlessly from flophouse to flop-house, bar to bar, drink to drink, and sexual partner to sexual partner. Usually, they were either looking for work, about to begin a new job, or freshly fired from an old job. They made just enough money to finance the next drinking bout, and in their own way they hung together. Speck felt completely at home. He took a room at the St. Elmo, named in honor of the patron saint of seamen. It was a Southeast Side version of Chicago's fabled Skid Row flophouses. The downstairs bar, Pete's Tap, was a dirty hillbilly dive where police were called regularly to break up fights. This joint reeked of stale beer and cloudy ciga-rette smoke that hung permanently in the air. It was Speck's favorite hangout.

Now, he was back on the Southeast Side, again looking for a ship. Speck spent the morning of July 11 at the union hall playing cards with other seamen. Bored with sitting around, Speck inquired about a room for the night and was directed to Pauline's, a rooming house located a few blocks away. It was operated exclusively for sailors by a kindly, soft-spoken Croatian. The Croatians ran many of the working-class bars, restaurants, and rooming houses in this tough shipping and steel neighborhood.

Speck visited Pauline's twice that afternoon. The first time he was told that no room was available, but he was allowed to leave his two bags and check back later. He was also granted permission to use the washroom, where he changed from a black polo shirt to a white one. Then he adjourned to a nearby bar, the Rafter Lounge, where he told bartender Michael Ger-bis that he was from Dallas and had to catch a boat at two-thirty P.M. It was already one-thirty P.M., and shortly later Speck announced, "Fuck it, I'm not going." He continued to drink until he returned to Pauline's at three-thirty P.M. "I got bad news for you," Pauline told him. "There's no vacancy. Nobody shipped."

Speck called upon his manipulative skills. Pauline's retarded son was in the room when she gave Speck the bad news. Ignoring what Pauline had told him, Speck engaged her in a conversation about her son. He took an empty cigarette pack and placed it in the boy's hand. When the boy threw it, Speck picked it up and returned it to the boy. A game was in progress, and Speck was friendly and sympathetic to the retarded boy. He spoke in a low soft voice. Pauline relented and told Speck he could sleep in the enclosed front porch.

Speck promptly changed into a striped shirt and headed off to Ann's Tavern in the neighborhood. Bartender Mary Crnkovic noticed that Speck had a knife in a leather sheath hanging from the left side of his belt. He was freshly shaven, perfectly sober, and "talked real nice." When Speck returned to Pauline's for the third time that afternoon, he learned that someone had now shipped out and he could have the man's room. This inspired him to hit the Southeast Side taverns, including his old hangout, Pete's. Drunkenly weaving his way back to the rooming house at twelve-thirty A.M., Speck waved to one of the seaman he knew on the front porch, complaining, "Damn, there's no action and no girls around here." Then, he went to bed.

Tuesday, July 12, was a scorcher, reaching a high of 100 degrees. On the city's near West Side, a young black boy opened a fire hydrant to get some relief from the heat and a crowd gathered. The police soon arrived on the scene to close the hydrant and disperse the crowd. A melee ensued and ten people were hurt, including one police officer. There were twenty-four arrests. Commenting on the incident, Dr. King announced, "This is the beginning of a long, hot summer." On the international front, Defense Secretary Robert McNamara told a press conference that he "anticipated" more U.S. air and ground forces would soon be needed in Vietnam. In Europe, Brigitte Bardot married German playboy Gunther Sachs. In Hollywood,

Frank Sinatra announced that he was engaged to Mia Farrow, who was thirty years his junior. On both East and West Coasts, adventurous young women were beginning to wear the latest look—miniskirts.

In the midafternoon of July 12, Richard Speck received an assignment to report to the *Sinclair Great Lakes*, a ship that was arriving in East Chicago, Indiana, a thirty-minute drive from the union hall. Saying that he was broke, Speck managed to bum a ride from Bargellini, a small, kindly veteran sailor who spoke with a pronounced Italian accent. On the way, they stopped at Pauline's, where Speck claimed his two bags. Bargellini and Speck arrived at the dock at five P.M.

Speck was unable to get the berth, however, because another seaman with more seniority had claimed the position. It turned out that the hiring hall had simply sent Speck out as a backup, in case the other man did not show up. After a meal aboard the ship, Speck was forced to leave. Sore about not getting the job, Speck was angry and disgusted. Bargellini gave Speck a ride back, part of it in the company of another seaman, George Mackey, who had just walked off the *Sinclair*. During the drive, Speck told Mackey, "Oh, hell, I'm going to New Orleans to ship out." In spite of Speck's anger, however, Mackey recalled him as "just another ordinary guy."

After dropping Mackey off, Bargellini began driving Speck back to Pauline's, but Speck said that he wanted to return to the union hall. Bargellini told him the hall was closed, but Speck insisted, so Bargellini dropped him off across the street from a Tastee-Freeze stand that was one block east of the hall. As Bargellini drove away at five-thirty P.M., he saw Speck cross the street toward the ice cream stand, which was frequented during summer by the student nurses from down the block.

As the disgruntled Speck walked past the union hall, he noticed some commotion in the alley behind the nurses' town house at 2319. One of the nurses, Pamela Wilkening, was being picked up for a blind double-date, and some of her class-mates had come outside to check the man out. As the nurses stood around the car, Speck had a chance to notice that one of them appeared to be wearing a yellow dress. While the nurses laughed and talked, Speck changed direction and headed east, away from the town house and in search of a gas station where he could drop his bags.

He first tried the Clark Service Station on East 100th Street, where he was refused by the manager, David Wilhelm. During the conversation, Wilhelm noticed that Speck had a tattoo on his left forearm inscribed, "Born to raise hell." Wilhelm joked, "Born to raise hell, hey?" Speck replied, "You bet. I've raised plenty in my time, too." Then, he continued walking east, carrying his two bags and a black jacket slung over one arm. He finally got permission to leave his bags at the Manor Shell Station on South Torrence. Then, he called Gene Thornton, explained his bad luck, and asked Thornton to come to the union hall the next day to use his influence to help Speck gain an assignment.

At eight-thirty that night, Speck walked into the Casino Lounge a few blocks from the gas station and ordered a breaded veal dinner. The food was slow in coming, and Speck got angry, asking the owner, Zika Djordjevic, "Who runs this place?" Djordjevic was a Serbian who spoke little English and left con-versations to his wife, who was not there. "None of your busi-ness," the Serb grunted. Speck jumped up and walked out of the restaurant, refusing to wait for the meal.

Speck didn't have money for another room, so he returned to the area of the union hall and slept there, perhaps on a bench in Luella Park, the small grassy area directly behind the three town houses where the student nurses resided. The park was separated from the buildings only by a metal fence, a cinder alley, and a paved parking area behind each town house. Speck had a troubled sleep. He had come close to shipping out, only to be rejected at the last moment. His rage was building.

Early on the morning of July 13, Speck arrived at the Manor Shell Station to claim his two bags. Station attendant Dennis Ryan noticed that he approached from the southwest—the direction of the nurses' town houses. Speck made some light conversation about the weather and referred to the ship he had missed. To midwesterners used to nasal twangs, Speck's soft Texas drawl was hard to pick up, but Ryan heard him say something about a "damn ship" or an "ammunition ship." Speck was allowed to use the station's rest room to wash up. He doused his head in water, slicked back his short hair, shaved, and dabbed on some of the Old Spice cologne he always kept in his carrying bag. Then, he headed back to the union hall.

It was going to be another hot day, again soaring above 90 degrees. The heat would help trigger full-scale race riots on the West Side, resulting in seven policemen injured by snipers and thirty-five arrests. Relief, at least for the weather, was predicted for July 14, when a "cool front" was expected to drop temperatures into the 80's.

Meanwhile, at eight-thirty that morning, another seaman, Sam Barger, sixty, a slender wrinkled man who walked with a limp and boasted a full head of gray hair, arrived at the hall and found Speck sitting with his two bags in front of the building, waiting for it to open. After a short conversation in which Speck again referred to his missing the ship assignment, Speck asked Barger to watch his bags while he went for a drink of water. Barger watched Speck walk the thirty feet or so southeast to the fountain in Luella Park, which was immediately behind the nurses' town houses.

Straightening up from his sip of water, Speck was staring directly at the large picture window of the back upstairs bedroom at 2319, where four nurses slept. It was a very short walk

from the fountain to the back door of the town house. Speck had
been in the neighborhood for three days now, time enough to
observe his prey. The nurses were brought to and from South
Chicago Community Hospital, which was located only a mile
away at 2320 East Ninety-third Street, by a hospital jeep. In
their leisure hours, some of the nurses would sunbathe in the
area directly behind the town houses, right across from Luella
Park. Some would stroll east down 100th Street—past the union
hall—to the corner Tastee-Freeze. Most wore shorts or light
summer dresses.

Within a few minutes, Speck returned from the fountain and
thanked Barger for watching his bags. When the hall opened,
Speck raised hell with the union agent, William Neill, for dispatching him to a job previously assigned to another seaman.
Neill recalled, "He was really pissed off, and I had to tell him
to drop it." Later that morning, Gene and Martha Thornton
arrived to console Speck about his missed assignment. He sat in
their car and talked for about thirty minutes, again managing to
coax twenty-five dollars from Thornton by saying that he was
prepared to sleep on the beach, "just in case a job didn't show
up." The car was parked directly across the street from one of
the nurses' town houses.

After the Thorntons left, Speck inquired as to where he might
find a room, and was directed this time to the Shipyard Inn, a
tavern-rooming house on South Avenue N, in the same Southeast Side area as the St. Elmo. The Shipyard Inn was consider-
ably more upscale, though, for the neighborhood. Now that he had
both money and a place to go, Speck promptly announced, "Fuck it!
I'm tired of waiting around for a ship." It was only ten-thirty A.M.,
prime time to find a job, but Speck left the union hall and walked to
a more comforting environment—Pete's Tap in the St. Elmo.

Bartender Ray Crawford recalls that Speck spent nine dollars
on drinks, but was unwilling to redeem the Benrus wristwatch

he had pawned for seven dollars a few weeks earlier. Speck pretended he had a $1300 check coming from his previous ship assignment, and that as soon as he got it, he would pay for the watch. He bragged that he was fired because he'd stabbed the first mate, another lie. Crawford described Speck as being relatively sober, and as "a very neat man, a very polite man, a very soft-spoken man."

Speck soon left Pete's to register at the Shipyard Inn, stopping first at the establishment's downstairs bar. Owner Agnes Budak, a bespectacled, portly, fashionably dressed Croatian, was told that the man at the bar was looking for a room and she approached Speck. Budak had the gruffness typical of a woman running an establishment catering to hard-drinking sailors and steelworkers and came quickly to the point: "By the night or the week?"

Speck replied, "I'm waiting for a ship, but I don't know when I'll get one. I'd better take it for a week." Speck was wearing dark wash-and-wear slacks and a red polo shirt. Budak noticed his tattoos. On his right arm she saw he had a knife with a snake entwined around it. But she inquired about one which struck her as looking odd. It was a skull with a pilot's helmet. "That's my mother-in-law," Speck joked. Beneath the skull was the word "Ebb," Texas slang for "Fuck you!" Capable of droll humor, during a Texas arrest Speck had once given the officer the name Ebb Dangler as an alias.

Budak took Speck to the second floor and showed him room 7, which he found acceptable. The room rented for ten dollars a week, and Speck paid her on the spot, plus one dollar as a deposit for two keys. The rooming house could be entered either from 100th Street, by first walking through the bar and then climbing the stairs, or with a key through a private outside entrance on the building's N Street side. When the transaction was completed, Budak gave Speck a receipt and he returned to the bar.

Later that afternoon, Speck returned to Pete's Tap and struck up a conversation with Harold "Fats" Christian, a twenty-six-year-old millworker and a resident of the St. Elmo. Christian was with his girlfriend, who happened to be married to someone else. Speck walked over, put his arm around both Christian and his girlfriend, and joked, "Is this your wife or your girlfriend?" He bragged to the girl about the $1300 check he had coming and how he was blackballed from the ship because he had stabbed the first mate.

Relieved of his immediate financial worries and uninterested in finding work, Speck was back to his old tricks. Bragging, drinking, and lying sure beat hanging out at the union hall waiting for a job.

CHAPTER 3

Ella Mae Hooper was a short, skinny mother of ten who was originally from Tennessee, where she dropped out of school in the eighth grade. She looked much older than her fifty-three years. She had a wrinkled face, stringy salt-and-pepper hair, dirty fingernails, skinny legs, and a Southern accent. She was a barfly who drank anything and everything. She fit in perfectly at Pete's Tap.

Ella Mae lived in the Calumet Harbor neighborhood with her daughter, Betty Hooper, but spent most of her nights with a man ten years her junior in a house that was an absolute mess. On July 13 she started her day by sleeping late and visiting a girlfriend, where she drank three cans of beer. She was wearing a cheap green housedress and tennis shoes, and carrying a large white imitation straw purse. After leaving her girlfriend, she took a bus to the Soko-Grad Tavern at Ninety-ninth and Ewing, which was directly across the street from Pete's Tap and only a few blocks from the Shipyard Inn.

She had come to the Soko-Grad, another Croatian operation, to get her gun. Ella Mae had obtained the .22 caliber black Rohm pistol for sixteen dollars from a mail-order house in West Virginia. The gun was Ella Mae's birthday gift to herself, and it was delivered to her by parcel post on March 10, 1966—her birthday.

She had subsequently pawned it to Sam Petrovich, owner of the Soko-Grad, and now, she told Sam, she wanted it back.

Sam offered to buy the gun for fifteen dollars, but Hooper replied, "I better take it. I might need it sometime." Paying him off, she put the pistol, which had six live cartridges in its clip, into her large straw bag and walked across the street to Pete's Tap. Several regulars were at Pete's, including Richard Speck, who was a total stranger to Ella Mae. She played the jukebox and had four or five beers at Pete's.

Mrs. Hooper was a habitué of the many taverns that adorned the commercial strip on the Southeast Side. After two or three hours at Pete's, she departed for the Ewing Tap and some more drinks. Next, she began walking east on 100th Street in the direction of the Shipyard Inn.

Suddenly, Speck, who had been following her from bar to bar, walked up behind her and asked, "Where are you going?" When she didn't reply, he added, "When I talk, I want answers."

Hooper did not respond and started to walk faster. Speck pursued, saying, "Let's go somewhere and have a drink. Let's go to the Shipyard Inn and have a drink."

"No, I want to go home."

"What if I force you to have a drink?"

"Nobody forces me to have a drink. If I want one, I just take one."

By now, the middle-aged woman and the pursuing young man had reached 100th Street and Avenue L, a short distance from Speck's room at the Shipyard Inn. Speck walked directly behind her and threatened, "You are going to the Shipyard Inn to have a drink. I have a knife stuck in your back. You don't see anybody around, do you? I could stab you right here and nobody would know who did it. Do what I tell you and I won't hurt you. All I want to do is ask you some questions."

The weather had turned cloudy, prelude to a sudden brief thunderstorm that would cool the night air. Speck repeatedly told Hooper that he would not hurt her if she did what he told her, "He must have said this twenty-five times," she would later tell investigators.

At one point, Speck asked, "Where do you think I'm taking you, somewhere to rape you?" He answered his own question: "I'm not going to rape you. If I can make you go to bed, I'm going to give you twenty dollars."

Hooper told Speck that she had ten or twelve dollars in her purse and he was welcome to have it. Speck haughtily answered, "I don't want your money. I have a check for thirteen hundred in my pocket." Speck took her to the side door of the Shipyard Inn, which he opened with his key, and had her walk up one flight of stairs to his room on the second floor. He opened the door to room 7 and told her to put her purse down. She put the purse on the dresser and sat on the bed.

Speck flipped open the tabs of two cans of beer and handed one to her over his shoulder. As they sipped their beers, Speck conducted a strange interrogation. He spoke with a Southern accent in a very slow and calm manner. He began by asking if she had an apartment, if she had kids, inquiring:

"Do you like young men?"

"I got nothing against young men."

"Would you like to live with a young man?"

"I hadn't thought of that."

"If I was to tell you to pull your clothes off and get in bed, would you?"

"Yes."

"If I let you out of here, would you tell anybody about this?"

"No."

"I'm a sailor and I make lots of money. If you want an apartment, I'll get you one. I'll give you two hundred dollars tonight, if you meet me up at Peck's to get you an apartment."

Ella Mae said she didn't know Peck's.

"Yes, you do. You go in there and drink all the time. That is the tavern before you came out of the last one."

"That's Pete's."

"Well, Pete's, whatever it is, there's where you better meet me if you want to live."

With that, Speck ordered Hooper to take off her clothes and get into bed. There followed a minute or two of automatic sexual intercourse. Speck had not touched her at any point before she got into bed.

Afterwards, Speck suddenly jumped out of bed, pulled up his pants, and ordered, "Get your clothes on." A bag was sitting on the dresser and Speck handed it to Hooper, saying, "Take this bag with you and do what I say and you won't get hurt." She took the bag. As they were climbing down the stairs, Speck said, "If you ever tell this, I'll kill you and your kids, if it takes me a hundred years.

"When we get outside the door, you just turn left. I'm going the other way. I want to go cash this thirteen-hundred-dollar check and go to a nine-thirty union meeting. You're going to meet me later tonight at Peck's and I'm going to give you two hundred dollars. Don't forget, if you don't meet me there at Peck's, you're in trouble. I don't like no woman to lie to me."

When they hit the sidewalk, Speck turned right, crossed the street, and walked into Kay's Pilot House, a restaurant-lounge. For Speck, it was time for a hamburger and a beer. When Hooper arrived at her daughter's home, she opened the paper bag and found three unopened cans of Hamms beer. She opened her purse to get the gun and put it in her basement. There was no gun.

CHAPTER 4

July was a happy time for the young student nurses. They were only weeks away from graduating and taking wing from the cramped and disciplined lives they had had to live for the past three years. There were thirty members in the South Chicago Community Nursing Class of 1966, and half were living in the town houses across from the seaman's hall. They offered more freedom than the hospital's nursing dormitories, but not much more.

The hospital's director of nursing education was Josephine Chan, a Filipino who ran the nursing program like military boot camp. Her "girls" were required to follow a strict code of conduct, and many referred to it as "living in a convent." Students were subject to a long list of rules and demerits, and violations brought various restrictions, including expulsion. For example, improper conduct or dress in the library brought five demerits; failure to keep rooms neat, three; use of the laundry washer on days other than designated, two. Any student who accumulated more than eight demerits in one month was required to appear before a judiciary board, which would mete out "a penalty to suit the misdemeanor." Minor penalties ranged from "written composition on designated subject" to grounding to the residence except for work duty. A barrage of memos reminded town house students that lights were out at one A.M., that no phone calls were allowed after one A.M., and that "dishes must be washed, dried, and put away one hour after meals." Town house Rule #1 was, "Students must not allow anyone into the town houses without the housemother being there." Rule #2 was, "All students in residence at the town house must take the jeep leaving at six-thirty A.M. If unable to take the six-thirty A.M. jeep, you must then plan on your own transportation." The typical work day was seven A.M. until three-thirty P.M. Still, seniors enjoyed additional privileges, including late leaves until twelve-thirty A.M. and overnights when not assigned to duty the following morning.

On July 13, 1966, there were five student nurses assigned to the easternmost town house, number 2319: Gloria Davy, Suzanne Farris, Patricia Matusek, Nina Schmale, and Pamela Wilkening. Also living there were three Filipino exchange nurses: Corazon Amurao, Merlita Gargullo, and Valentina Pasion. The eight young women lived in crowded dormlike surroundings, sleeping on bunk beds in the three upstairs bedrooms.

The three Filipinos were in Chicago as part of a program to recruit Filipino nurses to enter the U.S. as exchange visitors for up to two years. The program allowed the nurses both to improve their skills by learning American medical methodology and technology and to live in faraway and romantic places—like Chicago. For American hospitals, the program helped meet a shortage of nurses. South Chicago Community Hospital had an agent in Manila who recruited the three Filipinos living in 2319, and three other nurses. On May 1, 1966, the excited group of young women left Manila for Chicago. It was an eight-thousand-mile journey, but the psychological distance was even greater. When the Filipino nurses arrived at Chicago's O'Hare Airport, a bus from the hospital was waiting to take them directly to the town houses. For the next three months, that ride on the expressway was to be almost all they would see of Chicago and its cultural attractions. Their time was spent working on the surgical floor at the hospital and living in the town houses, where their time was spent writing long letters back home, cooking Filipino food, and doing laundry.

There was very little kinship between the Filipino nurses and the American nursing students. There was no friction, but there was no closeness, either. The American students were bonded by their three years of school together and their common interests; they wanted little to do with the clannish and homesick Filipinos. By July, the Filipinos had lived in the townhouse for only ten weeks. They had displaced some of the American nurses' friends, and were thought of as "spies" for Josephine Chan, the Filipino who was director of nursing for the hospital. The Filipinos stuck together, usually shopping at the nearby Grocerland to buy food to prepare their favorite home-cooked spicy dishes at the town house, while the Americans usually ate out or ordered chicken or pizza. Finally, the Filipinos were working nurses and were paid a living salary, while the Americans were still students and scraping by on nickels and dimes.

Among the Americans, Gloria Davy, Suzanne Farris, and Nina Schmale were part of the seniors' "in-group." Gloria and Suzanne both sported slender good looks, and their forceful and independent personalities had marked them from the start as student leaders. The sophisticated and well-dressed Nina was probably the most popular of the town house students. Stocky Pat Matusek and heavyset Pamela Wilkening were both earnest students who were dedicated to careers in nursing and who were well liked by their classmates.

All the Americans except Pamela were planning to marry in the near future. Suzanne Farris, in fact, had set aside Wednesday night, July 13, to go over her wedding plans with Mary Ann Jordan, another senior nursing student and sister of Suzanne's fiancé, Phil Jordan. Mary Ann, who lived at home with her parents, was the other charter member of the 1966 in-group, and Suzanne had arranged for her to spend the night at 2319, where three other residents—Gloria, Nina, and Pat—were all scheduled to be members of the Farris-Jordan wedding party.

Valentina Pasion, twenty-four, came from the tiny Philippine rural town of Jones City, 150 miles north of Manila. She was one of six children born to a schoolteacher and his wife, and the family was so poor that she had to wait two years to enter college while her older brother finished his education. Although shy and reserved, she had two admirers in Manila, a doctor and a dentist, and she wrote often to both. Once, she had sent the dentist a recording by American singer Jerry Vale, who was a favorite of theirs, and was teased for it by her friends in America. In response she joked, "It will be my first and last gift to him."

The Filipino nurses were paid $350 a month, and Pasion regularly sent more than half her salary back home. Her letters, too, often focused on money. "If I send you money, you will be able to fix the house," she wrote in one. She rarely complained, but once wrote to her younger sister, "Sometimes I can't help but shed tears. You know it's really hard to be a thousand miles from home." Another time she reported: "The weather is really terrible . . . but work is easier than in the Philippines . . . only the patients here are as big as water buffalo."

Merlita Gargullo, twenty-three, grew up on Mindoro Island, the oldest of nine children in a very poor family. Like Valentina, she was shy and reserved, but she had a beautiful voice and loved to sing and dance. She had taught her Filipino friends how to do the latest American dance crazes, the hully-gully and the jerk. She wrote home about how she was being treated at the hospital: "I receive such remarks as 'You're so pretty' . . . and whenever I meet male patients, the first thing he'll ask is, 'Do you have a boyfriend?' Well, I can't answer at once and if I didn't answer, he'll say, 'Do you want me to fix you up?' . . . One of the nurses here told me that it means he is going to look for somebody for me." Merlita, however, had boyfriends in the Philippines and was quite homesick. She had recently enjoyed a Fourth of July ceremony in Chicago and written home, "Well, it was a fine, dizzy, exciting, and wonderful weekend, but I still believe that there is no place like home."

Corazon Amurao, twenty-three, grew up in the tiny agricultural village of Durangao, a rough, rural area fifty miles south of Manila. She was one of eight children born to Ignacio and Macario Amurao, a superstitious and unsophisticated couple. Ignacio ran a small clothing store, but the family was dirt poor. Cora grew up as a bright, hardworking girl who enjoyed the simple pleasures. She was fun-loving, open, and a deeply religious Roman Catholic. Like Merlita and Valentina, her native language was Tagalog, a high-pitched and singsong Filipino dialect, but she and the others had studied English since the first grade and so spoke and understood it.

Pamela Wilkening, twenty, was known as "Willie" to her friends. She loved small children and fast cars. She often babysat for a woman next door to the town house and became very attached to the little girl, even attempting to teach her how to play the piano. Because she was so fond of her older brother Jack, she often followed him to his road races and watched him compete in the Porsche and Lotus racing cars he owned. Around her wrist, she wore a bracelet with an automobile racing insignia, a gift from Jack. She had once told a friend, "I want to be a nurse more than anything in the world." She joined all class activities and tended to blend in with her classmates. She was the class representative to the Student Nurse Association of Illinois, and had helped select the class motto (from a Robert Frost poem), "And miles to go before I sleep. . . ."

Gloria Davy, twenty-two, was the class golden girl. Gloria had always been a leader with an independent turn of mind.

In high school in Dyer, Indiana, she had been "Sweetheart of the Future Farmers of America." She had also been head of the cheerleading squad, written a column on teenagers for the local paper, and volunteered to work as a nurse's aide in Our Lady of Mercy Hospital. Before enrolling as a nursing student, she had attended Northern Illinois University in DeKalb. She was president of the Student Nurses Association of Illinois for 1965–66, and was considering joining the Peace Corps. A perfectionist, she would resew buttons that were slightly out of line on her blouses and jackets, and she looked forward to graduating and being able to custom-tailor her nursing uniforms. The ones provided by the hospital were always slightly off, in her opinion. In her free time, Gloria liked to study philosophy and write poetry.

Suzanne Farris, twenty-one, was especially fond of children, and had planned a career in pediatric nursing. She was high-spirited and liked Irish jokes and spontaneous pranks. She often said about herself, "Suzie is Suzie—and she's always Irish!" That past winter, she and two of the others at 2319 had put on some old bridesmaids' dresses they had saved, and for no particular reason had a sizeable "coming-out" party in the town house. This consisted of strapping on roller skates, putting classical music on the stereo, turning it up full blast, rolling up the rugs, and skating throughout the whole house. The production was such a noisy success that the girls were grounded for a week.

Although she lived at home, Mary Ann Jordan, twenty-one, was in on most of the fun and pranks played by her close friends, Suzanne Farris, and Pat McCarthy, who lived at 2311. She was a talented mimic and loved music and rock 'n roll. She was very athletic, not especially preoccupied with boys, and spent much of her free time with her youngest brother, who was retarded. The two often visited her friends at the town houses on 100th Street.

Nina Schmale, twenty-three, was very devout. Noting that her Catholic friends all wore religious medals, she had one made stating, "I am a Lutheran." She came from a prominent family in Wheaton, Illinois, and had studied chemistry at Elmhurst College before enrolling as a nurse. Her brother was a physician, currently completing a residency in pathology. She wanted to be a psychiatric nurse and hoped to work with children. During her free hours, she was inseparable from Peter McNamee, her boyfriend of seven years and the man she was engaged to marry. Nina was the nurse who, in the words of classmate Judy Dykton, "seemed to really have her act together. She was very mature and poised." She was also the girl whose memory brought the greatest delight to her classmates. One recalled, "She had a real dragged-out voice . . . It was just like she was sitting on a swing." The other nurses all admired Nina's relaxed bedside manner while giving patients baths. "She could toss wet washcloths across the patients into distant basins without ever spilling a drop," a nurse said in wonder. Another recalled, "She loved pets and once ended up with twenty-three seahorses because one of the pair of males she had bought turned out to be pregnant." A third recalled, "One day she came to me and asked for a mop. I asked her what for and she said, 'I had this glass, see. I threw it in my drawer. I forgot it had water in it!' " Before entering nursing school, Schmale had done volunteer work in a county home for the aged. After entering school, she continued to make regular calls on her elderly friends. When she visited, they would show her photos cut from magazines of beautiful girls they thought looked just like her.

Pat Matusek, twenty, was ecstatic when she returned to the town house that Wednesday after a visit home. The Matusek family was very close knit. Her younger sister, Betty Jo, suffered from scoliosis and her father, Joe Matusek, ran a neighborhood saloon, with the family living in an upstairs apartment. Her father had driven her back to the town house. Pat had just been accepted at Children's Memorial Hospital in Chicago and had become engaged to a male nurse, Robert Hinkle. They had spent that previous Sunday making wedding plans and going out to see the movie *Doctor Zhivago*. The couple liked to go to concerts and to swim together. Pat Matusek was a champion swimmer. She liked to do things her own way, and had decided to have her engagement diamond put into a special setting that was patterned after her grandmother's. Her thick, shiny hair was a special source of pride, and she brushed it every night with great care and precision.

July 13 was a typical day at 2319. Pamela, Pat, and Valentina had taken the day off. Corazon, Gloria, Suzanne, Merlita, and Nina had all taken the six-thirty jeep to begin their eight-hour work days. After their work was over, they took the hospital jeep back to 2319, arriving at about four P.M. Pam and Pat were out enjoying their day off, and the other American girls soon also left to do their own things. Cora and Merlita found Valentina already hard at work in the kitchen, whipping up her *pancit*, a Philippine dish of noodles, pork, and vegetables. Because the American nurses were not as neat, the three Filipinos had bought their own set of glasses and were planning to buy their own pots and pans as well.

At four-thirty, the Filipino girls sat down for their home-cooked meal. After dinner, the three went upstairs for a nap. Cora and Merlita were best friends and bunked in the northeast bedroom, with Cora sleeping on the top bed. Valentina slept in the large back bedroom. At about six, the three awakened and pursued their usual activities. Valentina watched TV in the living room; Merlita sat down at one of the living room desks, writing letters home; and Cora washed her nursing uniforms by hand in the upstairs bathroom. It was eight P.M. before Cora had finished washing her clothes and hanging them to dry in the basement. Then, she got her own paper and pen and joined Merlita at the writing desks.

As Merlita and Cora wrote their letters home for hour after hour, some of the American girls drifted back to the town house. Suzanne and Mary Ann stopped in the living room for about five minutes, dressed in Bermuda shorts. Mary Ann had her parents' car and the two were soon off for a prearranged meeting with Pat McCarthy, their nursing friend from 2311. Gloria Davy, too, had taken a late leave. She was out on a date.

At about ten-thirty, Cora locked the front door and went upstairs; Merlita had preceded her by five minutes. The hallway light was on and Cora glanced inside the big bedroom, noting that Valentina, Pamela, and Pat were all lying on their beds. The bedroom light was off. The door to the northwest bedroom was slightly open, but Cora did not look inside. Nina and Suzanne slept in this bedroom and there was an extra bunk for Mary Ann. Returning to her own bedroom, Cora found Merlita lying on the bottom bunk, dressed in white pajama shorts and top. Cora locked the bedroom door and was about to turn off the bright overhead light when Merlita asked her to wait. She wanted to say her prayers first. Cora climbed into the top bunk and closed her eyes. Moments later, she drifted off to sleep.

CHAPTER 5

Richard Speck arrived at the downstairs bar of the Shipyard Inn at eight-thirty P.M., wearing black slacks and a red polo shirt. Taverns like the Shipyard Inn and Kay's Pilot House across the street catered to the nearby factories and shipyards. In 1966, times were good, the factories worked three shifts, and the bars were usually crowded with hungry and thirsty customers.

The Shipyard Inn had three booths against the wall, with a pool table in the center of the room. A game was in progress. Patrick Walsh, a twenty-six-year-old construction laborer, had arrived at the bar accompanied by his brother, Jim, and U.S. Army Sergeant Richard Oliva, who was on leave from Vietnam. The Walsh family lived in the neighborhood. Patrick Walsh, a solidly built Irishman with slicked-back black hair, was a street-wise kid from the Southeast Side. He had broken his ankle three weeks before on a construction job and had a walking cast up to the knee on his right leg. This cast kept him from playing pool, but he sat at the large end booth and watched as Oliva, Jim Walsh, and his other brother, Michael, shot a round of pool.

While waiting for his shot in the game, Sergeant Oliva, an intent, muscular man with olive skin, noticed Speck enter the tavern. Speck went right to the bar and ordered a Jim Beam and Coke; moments later, Oliva's attention was distracted when he heard something fall to the floor with a large thud. He turned and saw Speck bend over to pick up a black switchblade. Speck took "his good sweet time" in doing this, slowly putting the knife back in his left-hand pants pocket.

Speck took his drink to the bar's middle booth, settled in, and looked over the crowd. Shortly afterwards, he strutted over to play the jukebox, and lifted up his polo shirt, which was hanging outside his black slacks. Oliva noticed that Speck was wearing a six-inch-long hunting knife inside a scabbard on the left side of his belt. Speck glanced slowly at the pool table and, in Oliva's opinion, was "showing" him the knife. Speck then dropped his red shirt down over his belt, played some rock 'n roll, and returned to his booth, where he continued to menacingly stare out at the scene.

When the Walsh brothers and Oliva concluded their game, Speck started up a game with Michael Compateso, a welder for the American Shipbuilding Company, which was located across the street. Compateso was on his twenty-minute break, and agreed to play. Speck concentrated on his shots, knew how to bank the ball, and won the game, despite the fact that Compateso was an experienced pool player and played often on the Shipyard Inn table. Speck then returned to his booth and continued to nurse his drink.

Moments later, Patrick Walsh looked up from his end booth and noticed that Speck was staring intently at him. This went on for several minutes, prompting Walsh to ask, "Do I know you from somewhere, or do you know me?" Speck said nothing, but continued to stare. Walsh propped himself up in the booth for a better look, and as he did, he saw Speck reach into his waistband and pull out a gun. Speck held the gun beneath the table of his booth and clicked the trigger.

Walsh swung his casted leg out of the booth, stood up, walked over to Speck, and looked at the gun, which was a black .22 caliber revolver. "What's the matter with you?" Walsh asked him.

"Nothing. I didn't know your leg was broken."

"You should watch who you pull a gun on, or some people might sneak up behind you."

Speck put the gun away. He asked Walsh how he had broken his leg, and Walsh replied that he had fallen off a scaffold at work. The two men then talked about construction jobs and construction unions. Speck offered to buy Walsh a drink, but he declined. Speck persisted, "I wish you would have a beer. I am sorry for pulling out the gun. I didn't know your leg was broken." Walsh declined again, and left to call his fiancée so that she could come and pick him up. He also asked his fiancée's brother, to come along and keep an eye "on this guy who pulled a twenty-two on me."

Walsh then went to tell his army buddy, "Rich, that goofball pulled a gun on me!"

"You want me to get him?" Oliva asked. "If you want, I will get him with the pool stick."

Walsh decided that since they were there to have a good time, there was no sense in starting trouble. He told Oliva, "Forget it! The guy seems like he's OK." Walsh rejoined Speck at the booth and told him that he was a fool for pulling out a gun in a place like the Shipyard Inn. "I have never seen you around here before," Walsh told Speck, "and you probably don't know what kind of a neighborhood you're in. Some of these people play rough, and you should really watch what you're doing."

Speck replied, "I got to watch out for myself."

A few minutes later, Walsh met his fiancée at the door, took her to the middle booth, and introduced her to Speck. She was a slender woman with flaming red hair. She and Walsh sat across from Speck in the booth and talked for about thirty minutes. As they talked, her brother sat at the bar to keep an eye on things. Speck told the couple that he had been on a barge, had an attack of appendicitis, and that the U.S. Coast Guard had taken him by helicopter to a hospital. He also talked about his divorce, and his ex-wife and child back in Dallas. Speck told Walsh he reminded him of a gang leader he had known back in Dallas.

As they talked, Speck took out his billfold to find the photos of his ex-wife and daughter and his seaman's card. As he did so, he spilled the second Jim Beam and Coke he had ordered. The fussy Speck cleaned up the mess and promptly ordered a new drink. He also insisted on buying a beer for Walsh, explaining, "Let me buy you one. I want to show you that I am sorry about pulling the gun." Walsh relented and allowed Speck to buy the beer. As the conversation continued, Speck referred to his ex-wife as a "son of a bitch. I am sorry I used that word, but that is what she is," he said, turning to apologize to Walsh's girlfriend.

Her brother came over to visit the booth while they were talking and brought with him a small puppy belonging to another patron. He showed the dog to his sister and Speck commented, "That's a nice-looking pup." Walsh later described Speck as "Not intoxicated and not acting goofy, except for pulling the gun, which was stupid. Spilling the drink had to be an accident, because he was not drunk or even high. He just kind of looked lonely, sitting there all by himself." His fiancée agreed that Speck was neither drunk nor high. She considered him "harmless."

At nine-fifty P.M., the young couple stood up to leave and join her brother outside at his waiting car. Speck accompanied them to the front door, where he was introduced by Walsh to Oliva. Walsh told Oliva, "Rich, I want you to meet Rich, Rich Speck. He's a good friend of mine." Walsh was amused by the fact that both men were named Rich. Speck shook Oliva's hand. He then patted Walsh's back and shook his hand, saying, "I'm sorry again about pulling the gun." Walsh replied, "Well, OK, take it easy."

A few minutes later, Speck managed to pick up a quick game of pool with Michael Walsh, Patrick's brother and a mechanic at American Shipbuilding. Speck won the game by sinking five balls in a row and running the table. "He played with such skill that he did not seem the least bit intoxicated," Walsh recalled.

Having practiced his signature characteristics of first demonstrating superior weaponry and then engaging in drink buying, handshaking and friendship seeking, Speck decided to try to further impress people by creating tales of his fictional exploits. Shortly after ten P.M., three employees from American Shipbuilding dropped in for their break, just as Speck was running the pool table on Michael Walsh. Speck struck up a conversation with the three strangers, explaining that he had just returned from Vietnam on a freighter carrying high explosives.

In great detail, Speck then wove a story about how he had been in a tough bar in Vietnam while carrying two .45's—one in a holster and one in his belt. Trouble developed, Speck claimed, when one man showed up with a can of gas and another one with a torch. Speck said that he feared that he would be incinerated, but U.S. Army personnel intervened to get him safely out of the bar. He concluded with a smile, "Next time, I want to be stationed somewhere peaceful—like Hawaii." Speck also told the three shipyard workers that on the way back from Vietnam, his freighter stopped at an island—"possibly Cuba"—and he had "a great time." Laughing and smiling, Speck said that girls were available for three dollars a night.

When the three coworkers left at ten-twenty P.M., Speck was standing at the bar, grinning widely, with one foot resting on the bottom rung of a barstool. Armed with Ella Mae Hooper's .22 caliber pistol and his own hunting knife and pocket knife, and lubricated with enough alcohol to be able to talk glibly to strangers, Speck was now ready for his night's work. He left the bar and returned briefly to his upstairs room. He grabbed his black corduroy jacket to cover the tattoos on his arms. He left behind the hunting knife, which was bulky and visible, and kept the gun and switchblade on his body. There was no public transportation heading west on 100th Street to cross the Calumet River Bridge and cover the one and a half miles from the Shipyard Inn to the nurses' town house at 2319 East 100th Street, and Speck did not want a cabdriver as a witness to his destination. It would take Speck, dressed all in black, only thirty minutes to walk from his dumpy room to the back door of the nurses' town house.

CHAPTER 6

The nurses' town houses were in an area of Chicago formally known as Jeffery Manor, a middle-class, white-collar community where almost half of all residents were children under eighteen. Although this quiet area was little more than a mile from the rough-and-tumble of the Calumet Harbor shipyards, it was a world away. The middle-class executives who worked in the South Chicago industrial complex of shipping and steel lived in Jeffery Manor. The neighborhood had a distinctly sedate middle-class texture, and the annual family income was a distinctly 1966 middle-class average of $8000. Most of the homes were neat single-family bungalows, and residents described the neighborhood as "the kind of place you can walk day or night . . . bicycle thefts are a bigger problem than muggings." Nevertheless, on all three town houses rented by the hospital, both the front and back doors were double-locked, with either a lock and chain or a deadbolt. The hospital's manual advised that the doors always be kept locked.

The six town houses fronting on 100th Street were flanked at both ends by three town houses built back from the street at a perpendicular angle to the others. In the middle of this horseshoe of boxy, buff-colored town houses was Luella Park, which was illuminated only by a few streetlights.

The town house at 2319 was very isolated. Behind it was an alley and the dark, empty expanse of Luella Park. The town house to the immediate west, 2317, shared a common brick wall, and on July 13, as the nurses knew, its residents were away on vacation. The common solid-brick walls between houses muffled noises, and the nurses living at 2315 were not likely to hear anything going on in 2319, nor were the other nearest neighbors around the corner on the southeast. At the front of the house was 100th Street, and across it was an elementary school and schoolyard that took up the entire block. On July 13, it was completely empty. To the immediate east was the empty union hall.

It was now about eleven P.M. While the nurses in 2319 slept, the ones in 2315 were hard at work. Sitting at the kitchen table just inside the back door were seven student nurses studying for final exams. The housemother, Mrs. Laura Bisone, a woman in her midfifties, was in the living room watching TV. She had just returned from a game of pinochle with neighbors who lived in the town house right around the corner from 2319, and she was now staying up to log in the girls who had taken late leaves. The nurses were required to report in to her to prove that they had returned by the required twelve-thirty A.M.

CHAPTER 7

As Merlita Gargullo prayed, and the nurses in 2315 studied at the kitchen table, Speck made his move. Springing from the shadows, he walked quickly across the soft cinders of the alley to the back door of 2319. Using the blade of his knife, he pried open the back window, slid the screen aside, and reached inside to unlock the door.

Moments later, Corazon Amurao was awakened by four knocks on her door, "done in a normal manner." The ceiling light was still on. A clock on the dresser showed the time to be eleven P.M. Cora unlocked the bedroom door and started to open it, only to have the intruder push the door open. Amurao, at five feet two inches and 98 pounds, was face to face with Richard Speck, six feet one inch and 160 pounds. He was standing in the center of the doorway and was illuminated by the bedroom light. Cora stared at him for a few moments and saw that he was dressed in black from shoulder to shoes. His short sandy hair was combed straight back, and his face was deeply pockmarked. She also saw that in his right hand, he held a small black gun. Cora lowered her head, turning away from it. It was the first time the young nurse had ever seen a gun.

Speck asked, "Where are your companions?" Then he grabbed her forearm. Her roommate got out of bed, and at gunpoint,

Cora and Merlita were walked down the corridor to the large bedroom at the rear of the floor. The nurses jokingly referred to the large back bedroom as the "ward" and to the two front bedrooms as the "semiprivates." The gunman turned on the light and found three women sleeping. In the meantime, Cora, Merlita, and an awakened Valentina Pasion rushed into a large walk-in closet off the bedroom's west wall. For five minutes, the three frightened Filipinos, all dressed in white shorts and tops, held the door tightly closed.

Soon, there was a knock on the closet door, and a female voice said, "Come out of the closet. He is not going to harm you." The three Filipino nurses emerged to find that Speck had turned on the light and awakened Pamela Wilkening and Pat Matusek. Cora also saw Nina Schmale for the first time. Speck had his left arm around Pamela's waist and with his right was pointing the gun at Pat and Nina. He turned off the bedroom light, and the only illumination in the room came from the lights in Luella Park through a gap in the bedroom drapes. Pamela was dressed in white shorts and a blue-and-white pajama top. Pat was in panties and a yellow nightgown. Nina's nightgown was brightly colored and sheer.

Speck motioned with the gun for the women to sit on the floor in front of the twin dressers under the large window looking out over Luella Park. They were told to sit facing him, with their backs to the window, pressed up against the dressers. Pamela was seated immediately to Speck's left. Seated next to her in a row were Nina, Valentina, Pat, Cora, and Merlita. Speck was standing, leaning against the double bunk just inside and to the right of the door. This bunk belonged to Pat, who slept on the top, and Pamela, who slept on the bottom. Next to it near the west wall was another double bunk, where Gloria slept on the top. On the south wall was a third double bunk, where Valentina slept on the bottom. Nina had been sleeping in the other "semiprivate" bedroom before the noise had awakened her.

As Speck made the nurses sit down in the upstairs bedroom, Suzanne Farris entered the town house from the back. She, Mary Ann Jordan, and Pat McCarthy had just driven Mary Ann's car into the paved parking area immediately behind 2319. Suzanne walked quickly to the kitchen house phone and called 2315 to check in. One of the studying nurses took the call and logged Suzanne in before curfew, prompting Mrs. Bisone, who was still in the living room watching TV, to complain, "If I'm in the house, she should check in with me." Suzanne quickly walked back out of 2319 to meet her two friends.

Upstairs, Speck was not aware of Suzanne's brief appearance. He heard nothing, due to the commotion he had created. Now, one of the American girls asked him, "What do you want?" Speck answered, "I want some money. I'm going to New Orleans." Cora had read about New Orleans in her history classes back in the Philippines, but this was the first time she had actually heard the city mentioned.

Speck sat facing the women, his back to the door and his face to the window. His legs were stretched out along the sliding closet that lined the east wall. The women were now in a sort of semicircle sitting around him. It looked a little like a powwow of Indians. Speck talked softly with a Southern drawl. His eyes looked "gentle," Cora thought.

"How did you come in?" one of the Americans asked. Speck answered, "Through the door." Pamela volunteered, "We are going to give you some money." Speck did not say anything, but he motioned with the gun, as if he did not want anyone to make a move. But he continued to talk to the women, and one of the American nurses giggled at something he said in his soft, soothing voice. Speck was smiling, always smiling. Another of the American nurses spoke up, saying, "We are going to give you some money."

Then, Speck asked each of the six, "How much do you have?" The women answered: "I have five dollars." "I have four dollars." "I have two dollars." Cora said, "I have ten dollars." Pat said, "It's on my bed," pointing to the upper bunk just inside the bedroom door. She stood up, took some money from her purse, and handed it to Speck who remained seated, the gun pointed at her. He took the money with his left hand and stuffed it in his pocket. Pat sat back down in the same position.

Pamela asked, "Can I stand up to get my purse?" She stood up, got the money, and handed it to Speck, who remained seated, his eyes and gun trained on her until she sat down again. This procedure was repeated for Valentina. Then Nina asked if she could get her purse. Speck asked, "Where is your purse?" Nina replied, pointing toward the door, "It's on my bed." Suddenly, Speck stood up and walked to the bedroom door, which was slightly open. He looked down the corridor, turned around, and told all the women to stand up.

At gunpoint, Speck marched the six in single file the few steps required to reach Nina's bunk. A sign on her bulletin board proclaimed, "Sleep well tonight . . . your National Guard is awake!" Speck took Nina's money. Then, he marched the six nurses back down the hall and ordered them to sit in the same positions. Speck counted them by waving and clicking his gun: "One, two, three, four, five, six."

Pamela, at five feet six inches and 160 pounds, was solidly built. Pat, at five feet six inches and 155 pounds, was a stocky, strong girl who kept in shape with swimming. Nina, at five feet seven inches, 130 pounds, was frailer than the other two Americans. Each of the Filipino nurses was petite, standing roughly five feet and weighing about 100 pounds. Now, the six nurses, three American and three Filipino, sat facing Richard Speck, wondering what he would do next.

It was eleven forty P.M., and Gloria Davy was sitting in a car outside the town house. She had just returned from a date with her fiancé, Robert Stern. Gloria was a tall, slender, dark-haired beauty and an outspoken leader. Bob, thirty-one, was an athletic, clean-cut young man who was vice president of a Chicago distillery company. They had just finished a dinner in Stern's apartment on South Shore Drive, celebrating both their engagement and the recent discharge of Stern's mother from the hospital. Mrs. Stern had been there too, and the trio had celebrated with champagne and steaks. Now, the couple was sitting in the car and listening to the music of Jay Andres's popular *Music 'til Dawn* show on WBBM, when their favorite song, "You'll Never Walk Alone," came on the air. The young lovers sang along with the lyrics:

> *When you walk through a storm,*
> *Hold your head up high,*
> *And don't be afraid of the dark.*
> *At the end of the storm,*
> *There's a golden sky*
> *And a sweet silver song of a lark.*
> *Walk on through the wind,*
> *Walk on through the rain,*
> *Though your dreams be tossed and blown,*
> *Walk on, walk on, with hope in your heart,*
> *And you'll never walk alone.*

As the lyrics died away the couple kissed, and Bob waited in the car while Gloria walked to the front door. When she had unlocked the door, waved good-bye, and entered the town house, Bob drove away.

Upstairs, Speck was still seated on the floor, eyeing his six hostages, when he heard a female voice. Gloria was calling Mrs. Bisone, the housemother, to check in. Then, slightly tipsy from the champagne, she began climbing the stairs. After hearing the voice, Speck walked back and forth on tiptoe from the bedroom door to the window looking out over Luella Park. As he heard Gloria begin to climb the stairs, he moved to the door, holding the knob. When Gloria put her hand on the knob, Speck opened the door for her. Surprised, she screamed in a low voice. Speck thrust the gun against her body and ordered her to sit down between Pamela and Nina. She became the seventh young woman in the bedroom.

Speck asked, "Do you have any money?" Gloria answered, "Yes, I have two dollars," adding, "Do you need coins? It might help you." Speck said, "No, I just want bills." Then, for five minutes or so, Speck talked in a very low voice to the American nurses. "Don't be afraid," he said. "I'm not going to kill you." As he reassured them, Speck again sat on the floor and casually smoked a cigarette. As he smiled and joked with the American girls, Cora, incredulous, was too frightened to pick up the banter.

Suddenly, Speck stood up and took the bed sheet off Pat's top bunk and began to slice it into long strips with his knife. It was the first time the women saw his black switchblade, and Cora noticed the shiny reflection of the three-inch blade. By now, the nurses were completely paralyzed by fear.

It took Speck only about five minutes to slice the bed sheet into three-foot strips, placing each ribbon around his neck. While he did this, he put the gun on the top bunk, within his reach. Then he squatted in front of Pamela Wilkening, who was seated closest to him, and began tying her ankles with the bed sheet. He tied the knots very tightly, first tying a strip of sheet completely around one ankle, knotting it once, and then looping the ends around the other ankle and knotting it twice. He then politely asked her to turn around and face the window, so he could tie her wrists. Placing her hands together behind her back, with the palms facing outward, he tied a strip of sheet completely around both wrists, knotted it once, and then looped it over one wrist and knotted it twice. He told her to turn around and face him, which she was barely able to do.

Speck needed only a minute or two to tie Pamela into a position of total helplessness. As he tied her, he kept his gun on the floor closely within reach. Then, still in a squatting position, he moved with a crablike crawl over to Gloria Davy and began tying her in a similar manner, the gun kept on the floor beside him.

"Why are you doing this?" Gloria asked. "We are student nurses." Speck smiled again, replying, "Oh, you are a student nurse." Since, after being tied up, Gloria was unable to obey Speck's command to turn away from the window and face him, he picked her up and placed her on Pamela's bottom bunk.

Speck was now on automatic pilot and he moved methodically from woman to woman, ritualistically tying each into helplessness. Several times, he promised, "Don't be afraid. I'm not going to kill you."

While he was tying Pat Matusek's ankles, the doorbell rang downstairs. Speck motioned for Cora and Merlita, the only two not yet bound, to stand up. At gunpoint, he followed the two tiny nurses down the stairs, walking on tiptoe.

CHAPTER 8

It was now midnight. Merlita went down the stairs first, followed by Cora, Speck's gun stuck in the small of her back. When they reached the front door, Speck pressed the gun harder into Cora's back and ordered her to open the door. She did, staring out at the emptiness of 100th Street. "There's no one here," she told Speck. Satisfied, he marched the two women back up the fourteen stairs.

The bell had been rung by Tammy Sioukoff, who was standing at the back door. Tammy, who lived next door in 2315, had worked the night shift and had just been driven home in the hospital jeep. As was her custom, she had been talking on the town house pay telephone with her boyfriend when she suddenly got hungry and decided to make a sandwich. Finding that there was no bread at 2315, she had put her boyfriend on hold and scooted out her back door to the back door of 2319, only a few steps away. Each town house had one downstairs house phone and one pay telephone for outside calls; the hospital had vetoed the nurses' request for upstairs phones.

Tammy peered through the back door and saw only that the living room was faintly lit by the night light of a hospital lamp and that a slight draft was rustling the living room drapes. She heard some footsteps on the second floor, but since she was in a hurry to resume her call and since no one had responded to her buzzing, she decided to scoot west on the alley to the back door of 2311. There was no bread in 2311, either, she was told. Tammy returned empty-handed to 2315, which was still a bee-hive of activity among the late-night students.

Meanwhile, Speck was back at work. He quickly finished tying Pat Matusek, and finally Cora and Merlita. When Speck tied Cora, she smelled alcohol on his breath. As he tied Merlita, Speck asked, "Do you know karate?" She did not reply. Before and after the buzzing by Tammy, Speck had frequently tiptoed to the bedroom window and peered outside through the drapes. As he talked to the nurses, he constantly clicked the gun, revolving the cylinder from chamber to chamber.

As Speck continued his routine, a car drove slowly into the alley behind 2319. Another senior nursing student, Kathy Emmons, who lived at 2311, was returning from a date in time to beat the twelve-thirty curfew. She had asked her boyfriend to drive slowly past the back of 2319 to see if anybody was up. Earlier that day, Kathy had borrowed a typewriter from Nina Schmale to type her boyfriend's term paper. The typewriter was in the car and she wanted to return it. Ironically, Kathy's boy-friend was a target shooter and had taught her how to handle a pistol. He had also persuaded her to carry one for protection. In her purse, Kathy was carrying a loaded Derringer, and she had the temperament to fire it if threatened. However, since all appeared dark and still in 2319, the two continued driving on down the alley to 2311.

It was now twelve-fifteen A.M., and in the upstairs bedroom of 2319 all seven women were tightly bound. Speck had the run of the house. He stood up and walked over to Pamela Wilkening. He untied her ankles, grabbed her forearm, pulled her to her feet, put the gun in the small of her back so she would not scream, and walked her out of the room. The door to the south bedroom was left only slightly open. Several strips of bed sheet were still wrapped around Speck's neck, as he walked Pamela down the hall to the northeast bedroom.

After one minute, Pamela could be heard to say, "Ah." It was like a sigh. Nothing was heard after this. Speck stuffed a wad of white cloth into her mouth and secured it in place with two strips of bed sheet. One was wrapped around her face and tied in a double knot at the back of her neck, the other wrapped around her neck and tied in a double knot over her mouth. Then, Speck spreadeagled her on the bedroom floor. Intent on rape, he ripped off the retaining strap on her sanitary napkin belt.

As Speck hovered over the prostrate body of Pamela, a debate was going on among five of the nurses in the back bedroom. The sixth, Gloria Davy, had fallen asleep. The Filipino nurses wanted to fight for their honor, to scream or to push a lamp out the back window or to do something. Cora had been raised in a rough rural hamlet where the natives carried the *balisong*, or "long knives," and she knew a criminal when she saw one. Speck, she thought, was up to no good and she urged her fellow hostages to fight.

Unfortunately, the lack of closeness between the Americans and the Filipinos got in the way of any joint action. The Americans overruled the Filipinos and called for calm. The American nursing students had all taken classes in "psych," and, in their minds, this situation was a little like handling an unruly patient in the emergency room. Unable to agree on a plan of action, the nurses remained silent.

There was a lot of talk going on at 2311, the westernmost of the three nurses' dorms. In an upstairs bedroom, Suzanne Bridgett Farris and Mary Ann Jordan had been talking for about an hour with Pat McCarthy, who lived in the room. The three were fast friends, and, flush with the prospects of their coming graduation and Suzanne's marriage to Mary Ann's brother, Phil, they were in high spirits. Although Mary Ann lived at home with her parents, she had decided to spend this evening with Suzanne to look through wedding books and talk about the upcoming wedding. Earlier that evening, Suzanne and Mary Ann had picked up Pat McCarthy, who had been at home on a sick day, and the three had driven to a nearby Burger King for hamburgers and Cokes.

At eleven-ten P.M., Jordan had parked the car at the rear of 2315, only ten minutes after Speck had entered. Suzanne had momentarily entered 2319 to call the housemother, then rejoined the others. Pat McCarthy had returned from home with an armload of books and packages and some clothes on hangers, and Suzanne and Mary Ann helped their friend carry her stuff inside 2311. The three had settled down for a long talk.

Shortly before the twelve-thirty curfew, Suzanne and Mary Ann asked McCarthy to sneak out and join them for the night at 2319. Feeling tired, McCarthy decided to stay where she was. Before the three said their good-byes, Suzanne walked into the adjacent bedroom to find some aspirin on the nightstand of Kathy Emmons. At exactly this moment, Kathy returned from her date and was irked to find Suzanne in her bedroom. "Sorry," Suzanne explained, "I have a splitting headache."

So did Kathy, it turned out. She had just thrown an engagement ring back in the face of her boyfriend after a sudden argument the couple had while sitting in his car in the parking lot behind 2311. The boyfriend had angrily peeled rubber pulling away from the alley. Now, Kathy was in no mood for pleasantries with her fellow nurses.

Shortly afterwards, Suzanne and Mary Ann decided it was time to go. Before leaving, they chatted a while with four other student nurses who were still studying at the kitchen table. Moments later, the girls in 2315 looked out the window and saw their two classmates heading down the alley. Since

Mary Ann was not supposed to be spending the night, she and Suzanne were anxious to avoid seeing the housemother, and they crouched low as they whizzed by the window of 2315, making faces and waving happily at their friends. They looked like twins, Suzanne dressed in bright floral-patterned Bermuda shorts and a solid halter top, and Mary Ann just the reverse. The tall, thin, dark-haired Suzanne was a "clotheshorse," and one of the brightest girls in the class. The auburn-haired, fresh-faced Mary Ann was the all-American girl and a talented softball and volleyball player. She was looking forward to staying in Suzanne's room, because she knew that Nina Schmale kept an air-conditioning unit there, the only one in any of the dorms. At twelve-thirty, they entered 2319.

CHAPTER 9

Suzanne and Mary Ann rushed up the stairs, where, through the open door of the northeast bedroom, they saw a gagged and spread-eagled Pamela Wilkening and a startled Richard Speck, the strips of bed sheet still around his neck.

The pair tried to run, but Speck blocked off a retreat down the stairs. The two then burst into the back bedroom, with Speck in hot pursuit. The gun was still in his hand. The other six nurses sat tightly bound. "You two come here," Speck said. Neither moved. Speck called in a louder voice, "You two come here."

At gunpoint, he herded the pair out of the south bedroom, closing the door behind him. He forced them to walk down the corridor to the northeast bedroom where Pamela was still lying, gagged and helpless.

The Irish girls fought, and the women in the back bedroom suddenly heard a yell, as if Suzanne and Mary Ann were resisting. Speck reacted violently. Lashing out powerfully with his switchblade, he killed them quickly and brutally. He stabbed Suzanne eighteen times, eleven in the front of her chest, seven in the back. Then, he took a white nurse's stocking and strangled her. He smashed Mary Ann's left eye with his knife, which he then plunged into her chest three times. Speck could take a while longer with Pamela, since she was helpless and gagged, and, with precision, he stabbed the prostrate victim in the heart. Within minutes, Speck had snuffed out the lives of three young nurses.

He took a light woolen blanket from the bed and tossed it over the faces and upper bodies of Suzanne and Pamela. Mary Ann was left uncovered, lying on her back, her face oozing blood. In her right hand, she clutched a strip of bed sheet. Speck closed the bedroom door and, moments later, the remaining six helpless women heard water run in the bathroom.

The cunning Speck was acting with calculated care. His next victim would see neither the blood on his hands nor the bloody condition of the friend who had preceded her. He returned to the large bedroom and pointed the gun menacingly at the remaining six. The engine of destruction was gathering momentum and there was nothing to stop Speck from continuing his repetitive, ritualistic killings. Now, he was also eliminating witnesses.

Speck walked over to Nina Schmale, untied her ankles, and led her at gunpoint from the room. He took her to the front, northwest bedroom, where she, Suzanne, and Mary Ann had expected to spend the night. After about one minute, she said, "Ah," just like Pamela.

It was now too late for the other nurses to do anything but try to hide, and all except Gloria Davy managed to change their positions on the bedroom floor. Gloria's blood-alcohol was at 111 milligrams, only slightly below the then-defined legal intoxication limit of 150, and she had fallen sound asleep on Pamela's bunk. The others, flopping about like beached fish, desperately struggled to find shelter.

Pat Matusek, a stocky woman, crawled between the two bunks on the north wall of the bedroom, lying on her stomach, facing the window. Valentina Pasion and Merlita Gargullo, both very small, fought their way to the west wall, on the far side of the bunk where Gloria normally slept. They were flat on their stomachs, facing the picture window overlooking a quiet Luella Park.

The tiny Cora turned on her side and then rolled backward on her stomach, rocking left and right for momentum, trying to maneuver herself under Valentina's bunk on the south wall of the bedroom. She got her body under the bed, but her head protruded. She banged her body up and down against the floor and the bedsprings, but she was unable to get all the way under.

The five women lay helplessly on the floor until Speck returned to the bathroom to wash his hands of blood. Then, for the second time, the terrified nurses heard the water run.

In the town house at 2315, the busy nurses were oblivious to what was going on next door. Tammy Sioukoff had been pressured to get off the phone with her boyfriend so a pizza could be ordered. She reluctantly agreed to end her call and to chip in for the cost of a pizza, which was ordered from Aldo's, two blocks away. The women had to pool all their money to come up with enough.

Their scheduled final examination was in neurology, and Judy Dkyton was rehearsing a mnemonic for the twelve cranial nerves. The cue was this nursery rhyme:

On old Olympus's towering top,
A Finn and German
Viewed some hops.

To signify:

"On (olfactory) old (optic) Olympus's (oculomotor) towering (tracheolar) top (trigeminal),

A (abducent) Finn (facial) and (acoustic) German (glossopharyngeal)

Viewed (vagus) some (spinal-accessory) hops (hypoglossal)."

Judy shared her memory secret with the others, and the nurses sat there reciting the nursery rhyme. Suddenly, Tammy thought she heard some strange noises coming from outside.

Tammy was the "exotic" member of the class of 1966. Her parents had fled Russia during World War II and her father had become a mechanic for an American construction company with global ties. She had grown up in Casablanca and Australia and had traveled widely, learning to speak fluent English, French, and Russian. In her application to nursing school, Tammy had stated that she wanted to be a "medical missionary." Nevertheless, she had been raised in a very protective, strict home and her enrollment in nursing school was a "first breath of freedom." She was small and attractive, with delicate facial features that were vaguely Asian. She did wear her hair in a modified beehive, the style of the day, but while most of the other students were just "so American," drawn to pizza and rock and roll, Tammy preferred classical music and the haunting Mideastern music of stylists like Nana Mouskouri. By contrast, the current musical offerings in Chicago ranged from the early Rolling Stones to the syrupy sounds of Pat Boone, Henry Mancini, and Andy Williams.

Among her closest friends were Gloria Davy and Nina Schmale, both of whom were curious and open-minded enough to appreciate her music, personality, and travels. Gloria, in particular, was a big fan of Tammy's music and would often borrow her albums for weekend trips.

Now, Tammy stepped into the alley to try to find out what it was she had heard. To her ears, it had been "an indescribable noise, an animalistic sound, like nothing human. It was not a gasp, but a scream." As she had earlier that night, she walked to the back of 2319, this time staring at the darkened downstairs rooms and the upstairs bedroom window. She listened intently, but now could hear only the steady whir of an air-conditioning unit. Nina's prized air conditioner was blowing cool air on per-spiring Richard Speck, who was now hovering over Nina herself.

Since she neither heard nor saw anything, Tammy returned through the open back door to rejoin her friends at the kitchen table at 2315. By now a delivery boy from Aldo's Pizza had arrived. Aldo's was about to close, so the order had been rushed. He had gone, however, to the wrong address. He was standing at the front door of 2319, only fourteen steps below Speck. He noticed that the drapes were drawn in the front windows and that a faint light was on in the living room. He heard nothing. Suddenly realizing his mistake, he neither knocked on the door nor rang the bell. Instead, he quickly cut across the lawn to the front door of 2315 and delivered the pizza to Carol Beneski. Mrs. Bisone reminded her girls that they only had ten minutes to fin-ish the pizza before lights out at one. Tammy and the others dug into the hot pizza.

CHAPTER 10

Speck was gone with Nina Schmale for twenty minutes. Then he returned to the large south bedroom, grabbed Valentina Pasion, who was still tightly tied, and placed her in sitting position out of the room. After a minute or two, Valentina was heard to say "Ah" much more loudly than two American women who had preceded her. It sounded like a scream.

Another twenty minutes passed, and the water ran again. Speck returned to the bedroom. Each time he returned, Cora noticed, he would tiptoe over to the window and stare out at Luella Park.

Speck now moved toward Merlita, and Cora, who was partially hidden under the bed only a few feet away, pressed her forehead against the floor. Speck did not bother to untie Merlita Gargullo either. He easily picked up the petite young woman and carried her from the room.

After about five minutes, Merlita was heard to say in her native Tagalog: *"Masakit!"* Cora knew what she meant: "It hurts!"

Speck was gone for about thirty minutes with Merlita, and, then, for the fourth time, the water ran. Before going to the bathroom to wash the blood from his hands, Speck had tightly closed the door to the northwest bedroom. Inside were three more dead bodies.

He next moved to Pat Matusek, who was cowering on the floor. "Are you the girl in the yellow dress?" Speck asked softly. Pat responded by asking, "Will you please untie my ankles first?" Cora, quiet and still, only a few feet away, kept her forehead pressed to the floor, suspending her furious attempts to get her head under the bed while Speck remained in the room. Then Speck resumed the march of death, and, after a few minutes, Cora could hear him say, "Lie down here." The voice sounded as if it were nearby. A minute passed, then in a louder voice Speck said, "Lie down here." When Pat did not respond quickly enough, Speck viciously kicked her in the stomach, knocking her on her back to the floor, her face underneath the bathroom toilet bowl, her arms tied behind her back, her feet protruding into the hallway. Speck was gone with Pat for thirty-five minutes, and there was silence. During that time, Cora had managed to get her entire head beneath the bunk.

Speck did not have to go far to wash his hands of blood for the fifth time. He had moved his killing field to the bathroom, which was right outside the large bedroom. He left Pat lying there, his seventh victim. The bathroom door was left open. Speck no longer needed to conceal his victims.

As Speck killed, life went on normally elsewhere. Less than seventy-five feet away, town house neighbor Mrs. Betty Windmiller was sound asleep. Since the night air had turned cool, she had shut off her air conditioner and opened a window. About one-thirty, neighbor Bill McCarthy returned from a date and circled the block twice before he found a parking space in the pavement behind the town houses. About three, neighbor Harry Levin returned home, parked his car behind the town houses, and noticed that two girls in 2315 were still studying at the kitchen table, giving him only a passing glance. As he retired to bed, Levin heard a loud "thump, as if someone had dropped something." Tammy and Leona were the last nurses to retire in

2315, shortly after three. Judy Dykton had drifted off an hour earlier, figuring, "If I don't get some sleep, I'll be shot for the test." The three had persuaded the housemother to let them stay up to prepare for their final exams. She had retired shortly after one; since all her girls had reported in, she had seen no need to make bed checks.

Meanwhile, at about two-thirty, Speck had returned to the large bedroom and sat down next to Gloria Jean Davy, who was still sleeping on her side on Pamela's bunk. He reached back with his left hand and forcefully slammed the door shut. Upon being awakened, Gloria said eerily, "I dreamed that my mother died." From her hiding place beneath the bunk, Cora looked up and saw that Speck had pulled off Gloria's jeans and underpants, and was on top of her. Cora put her head down, praying furiously, as she heard the bedsprings move.

She heard Speck ask, "Have you done this before?" After a few minutes, Speck asked softly, "Will you please put your legs behind my back?"

Cora kept her head tightly pressed to the floor as she listened to the bedsprings move for twenty to twenty-five minutes. Five minutes after the bedsprings had stopped moving, she looked up and saw that Gloria and Speck were no longer there.

Cora decided to take a big risk and to change her hiding place. She wanted to move from under the bunk in the center of the room to a spot near the far wall. She feared that Speck had already noticed where she was. With great effort, she crawled out from under the bunk on the south wall nearest the window. Then, terrified that Speck would return at any minute, she desperately crawled her way backward across the floor, rocking from side to side on her stomach, until she reached the double bunk on the west wall, the place where Merlita and Valentina had tried to hide. She wedged underneath the bunk, squeezing her way under farther and farther until finally her head was under. A wool blanket hung down from the bottom bunk, touching the floor and covering her hiding position. Speck was gone with Gloria for about fifty minutes, the longest time he was out of the room. Nevertheless, it was only barely enough time for Cora to crawl into her new position.

It was now a little after three-thirty A.M., and Speck returned to the large south bedroom for the final check. He turned on the light, the first time it had been on since he had awakened the nurses four and a half hours earlier. He picked up Gloria's purse and shook it back and forth, checking for any loose change. Cora, only a cough or a sneeze away from death, prayed to herself as she heard the coins jiggle. Speck took the coins and threw the purse under the bed, almost hitting Cora. Then, he turned off the light and walked out, leaving the door wide open. The bedroom was in a shambles. In the house there was silence.

Speck walked out the front door of the town house, leaving the door wide open as he stepped into the black night. Upstairs, the blood was congealing on the bedroom floors. Turning his back on the trimmed lawns and tidy bungalows of Jeffery Manor, Speck donned his black jacket and began his long walk back to the rough Calumet Harbor area of shipping and steel. Undoubtedly, he had been true to his fastidious nature and had managed to keep the blood spilled onto him at a minimum. He had brought plenty of T-shirts in his zipper bag for a fresh change.

At the intersection of 100th Street and Torrence Avenue, a few blocks east of the nurses' town houses, Speck may have been caught in the headlights of an approaching car. Tony Caprigalione was driving to work, and he almost ran over a man who looked like Speck. Caprigalione was the general yard master for the West Pullman Railroad, which was right across the street from the Shipyard Inn, and he was rushing to work. He swerved aside just in time to avoid hitting the man, who continued his walk.

The scene Speck encountered on his walk home was surrealistic. A few blocks west of the Shipyard Inn is the large bridge that offers the only way across the wide Calumet River. The area of 100th Street before the bridge is bleak and desolate, dominated by huge mountains of slag and salt. The slag was used by the steel mills; the salt was stockpiled by the city to fight winter snow. Rail tracks crisscrossed the area. The only building in sight was an enormous Commonwealth Edison substation whose power would soon be used to light the awakening city. Across the whole landscape arched the Chicago Skyway, where a few motorists were whizzing by.

Before stepping onto the bridge, Speck threw his bloodstained pocketknife into the river's deep, dark, choppy waters. After splashing the murky surface the knife floated for a brief moment before sinking to the muddy bottom. Speck took the unfired pistol with him back to room 7 of the Shipyard Inn. Before calling it a night, he had time for a sip of beer from the can he had left on his bedside table. He was sleeping shortly before dawn.

CHAPTER 11

The alarm rang at five-forty A.M. in the bedroom of Judy Dykton;
she was determined to get in some final licks for the neurology
exam. She switched off the fan that had been working overtime
against the summer heat and heard a noise that sounded like the
whimpering of an animal, but paid no attention. She walked to the
basement of the town house, took some clothes that had been drying overnight, and returned upstairs. Again she heard a sound, and
this time it was more distinct, like a little child crying or calling
out. She opened a blind and looked out and saw a woman standing across the street, looking up at 2319, toward the crying voice.
Opening the window, Judy could now clearly hear Cora's cry:

"Oh, my God, they are all dead!"

Judy grabbed a robe and hurried to the front of 2319, where
Cora was on the ledge, crouching low and crying. Judy walked
through the open front door and saw a nude Gloria Davy, lying
face down on the living room sofa, her hands tied behind her,
her head drooping off the edge of the sofa, a strip of cloth knotted around her neck. Judy ran to get the housemother, yelling,
"There's trouble in nineteen." Then, she returned to get Cora.
Mrs. Bisone threw on a robe and alerted her housemates. "Get
up, kids, the kids in nineteen are in trouble." She ran out the
door, just a few steps ahead of Leona Bonczak.

Cora was now off the ledge, and Judy found her standing midway down the stairs leading to the front door. She was afraid to come all the way down, wailing, "Everyone on the *sampan* has been killed." She warned Judy, "Don't come in, he might get you. He might still be in the house." Judy climbed up a few stairs, put her arms around Cora, and gently but firmly led her down, out the door, and over to 2315. Cora was clinging to her, shaking and sobbing. Both nurses were weak with shock and when they entered the living room, they slid down onto the carpet. Judy "could not keep her feet on the ground," she said later. She thought that "time was standing still."

In the meantime, Mrs. Bisone and Leona entered 2319, where they found Gloria lying on the sofa. While Mrs. Bisone went to the outside phone in the kitchen to call the hospital, Leona walked over to Gloria, touched her on the right shoulder, and called, "Davy!" There was no response. She then ran upstairs and found Pat Matusek lying on the bathroom floor. "Matusek!" she cried. No reply. She looked into the back bedroom and saw no one. She then opened the door to the front northeast bedroom and saw three bodies on the floor, covered with blankets and wrappings. She could not recognize who they were. Looking in the front northwest bedroom, she found three more dead bodies. She could not tell who the two lying on the floor were, but she did recognize Nina Schmale, spread-eagled on the bed. Leona's search took only a minute or two before she returned downstairs. She met the housemother and told her not to bother to go upstairs, since "nothing can be done. They're all dead." Bisone called the hospital again and screamed, "My God, all of my girls in nineteen have been murdered." Asked their names, she replied, "Don't ask me now, get me help! All we can see are blood and girls!"

Mrs. Betty Windmiller had been the first to hear Cora's cry and she alerted Robert Hall, a steel company foreman, who was out walking his dog. Both neighbors lived next to 2319, and now they began running back and forth, alerting other neighbors and trying to get the attention of passing motorists. Finally, a patrolman driving west on 100th Street heard the yelling and screaming and stopped. Mrs. Windmiller ran into the street and asked the policeman for help. It was Daniel Kelly, a handsome young Irishman who had been on the force for only eighteen months. Kelly radioed for assistance and wheeled around to the front of 2319. He was met by Mrs. Bisone, who told him breathlessly, "My girls have been murdered."

Mrs. Bisone and Leona Bonczak then left 2319 and returned to try to comfort the hysterical Cora. Pandemonium reigned, as most of the nurses were now awake and had converged upon 2315. A classmate asked, "What happened?" Judy Dykton replied, "You won't believe it, but I think that they're all dead over there." Another exclaimed, "Oh, no. Was it toxic fumes or something?" Leona Bonczak, who had conducted her own gruesome investigation, knew better. "They were all killed," she told her classmates.

Officer Kelly walked into the living room, where he found a body lying on the sofa. In an odd twist of fate, the rookie policeman recognized that it was Gloria Davy. Kelly had grown up with Davy, and five years earlier had dated her older sister, Charlene. In addition, Kelly's wife worked at South Chicago Community Hospital, and hours later the stunned policeman would realize that he knew most of the victims. Now, gun drawn, Kelly checked the basement and the upstairs to see if the killer were still around. Within minutes, he was joined by police officer Leonard Ponne, a young blond-haired, muscular patrolman. All they found were more dead bodies, all partially nude and covered with blankets and wrappings.

The hospital maintenance man arrived at the front door of 2319, prepared to take the nurses to work in his jeep. The policemen turned him away. Ponne then radioed communications central in the headquarters of the Chicago Police Department and called for reinforcements. Within seconds, the first of a fleet of squad cars was rushing toward the death scene. And the first of a series of news bulletins was going out to inform a disbelieving world about what had happened.

Kelly himself would soon be interviewed by WIND-Radio, Chicago, and report live from the scene. Like Speck, Kelly lost count of the dead bodies. He told the radio station:

"It seems as though seven females total—six on the second floor and one on the first—have been molested, strangled, and bound with nylon stockings. The majority of them were nude. . . . The only thing we can tell you is that they were student nurses and this was sort of like a student nurses' home here, where they were all residing. The (nursing) supervisor hasn't been contacted yet, so as far as identity we can't say. The bodies that have been found are the only ones in the building at this time. There may be more, but we don't have any information on this now. The downstairs was in an orderly condition. However, the bedrooms in the upper floors were in terrible condition. There is no indication of robbery, due to the fact that the dresser drawers and other things were closed."

This was Kelly's initial report. Years later, he would say that going through the town house was the most traumatic event of his life. "Words cannot describe it," he said.

The first homicide detective to arrive on the scene was Jack Wallenda, who entered 2319 at six-thirty A.M. Wallenda was a big, solid German shepherd of a man, but exceptionally polite and soft-spoken. He was a cousin of the "Flying Wallendas," the high-wire trapeze circus family. He worked the midnight shift with his partner, Byron Carlile, and this duo was among the very best homicide detectives on the police force.

Himself the father of eight and a devoted family man, Wallenda lived in the neighborhood and knew first-hand the values of the community. Although personally kind, loving, and loyal, he was also an experienced homicide dick with a hardened view of life, death, and human nature. He was profoundly shocked at what he found inside 2319.

In the living room, Wallenda found the nude body of Gloria Davy, lying face down on the sofa. Her hands were tied tightly behind her back, not with strips of bed sheet, but with pieces of purple-and-white cloth cut from her blouse. Tied tightly around her neck and knotted at the back was a strip of sheet. Wallenda noted, "The knots were tied very, very tight. They were all double knots and they were all done very professionally. I couldn't get my fingers between the cloth and the neck, and I had to cut the knots with scissors."

As he carried Gloria down the stairs, Speck had ripped off her blouse, and the stairwell was littered with buttons and fabric, as well as strips of bed sheet that fell from Speck's neck. Semen was recovered from between her buttocks, indicating that Gloria had been sodomized.

A size 38–40 white BVD T-shirt was found lying on the living room floor, wrinkled and wet with perspiration. Days later, police investigators would also find a white size 38–40 Hanes T-shirt wrapped up inside Davy's white underpants and purple-and-white slacks that were left in the upstairs bedroom. It too was wrinkled and wet, and also stained with blood. The fastidious Speck had brought plenty of extra T-shirts, anticipating the blood and sweat he would incur.

In the northeast bedroom, Wallenda found three bodies.

Lying on her back, hands tied tightly behind her, was Pamela Wilkening. There was a gag in her mouth, and one stab wound in her left breast, through her heart.

Lying next to her, face down, was Suzanne Farris. Tied tightly around her neck, double-knotted at the back, was a white nurse's stocking. She had eighteen stab wounds in her back and neck. A strip of bed sheet was wrapped loosely about her wrists, as if Speck might have tried to bind her before she resisted. Her face lay in a large pool of blood.

Lying next to Suzanne was her close friend, Mary Ann Jordan, who was on her back, a piece of bed sheet clutched in her right hand, as if she had tried to tear it from Speck's grasp. She had been stabbed three times in the chest, once in the left eye, and once in the neck.

In the northwest bedroom, Wallenda found three more bodies:

Nina Jo Schmale was lying spread-eagled on her bed, her wrists tied behind her back and her face covered by a pillow. Bound tightly around her neck was a piece of bed sheet, tied in two knots at the back. Her head was on a pillow, and another pillow was placed over her face, as if Speck had tried to suffocate her. Her nightgown was pulled up just below her breasts. Otherwise, she was naked. There were three superficial stab wounds in her neck, as if Speck had tortured her with a tattoo of knife pricks. Lying on the bed, above her head and resting against the wall, were two dolls.

Valentina Pasion was lying on her stomach on the floor. Her hands were unbound, with one arm underneath her and the other folded behind the small of her back. There was a deep, six-inch slash in her throat, so hideous that it exposed her voicebox. Her head lay in an enormous circle of blood.

Lying in an "X" position across Valentina's body was the body of Merlita Gargullo. Merlita was on her back, face up, her buttocks resting on those of Valentina, Merlita's wrists and ankles tied. Around her neck was a piece of bed sheet tied in two tight knots at the back, and there were four stab wounds in her neck, which was grossly dislocated.

Speck had dumped Merlita on top of Valentina and then thrown a blue flowery bed quilt over both bodies. The quilt was heavily stained with blood. The double bunks where Suzanne and Mary Ann had planned to sleep were neatly made and undisturbed. Nina's purse sat on the lower bunk; a large pocket watch hung on the wall next to it, suspended from the top bunk. Resting on a dresser was a blood-splattered nurse's cap. Above it was tacked the sign, "The emergency room—where the action is."

In the bathroom, Wallenda found Patricia Matusek, lying on her back on the tile floor, her hands tied behind her, her feet unbound. Around her neck was a piece of bed sheet tied very tightly and knotted twice at the back. She was wearing a yellow nightgown that had been pulled up to her breasts, and a pair of white panties that had been partially rolled down, exposing the upper region of pubic hair. She had a severe hemorrhage of the stomach, caused by a kick. On the floor were several towels and a white nurse's stocking that was soaked in blood.

As Wallenda was concluding his morbid inventory, housemother Bisone and the director of nursing, Josephine Chan, were allowed into 2319 to try to identify their nurses. However, Speck's devastation was so total that they could recognize only Gloria Davy, Pat Matusek, and Pamela Wilkening. The others would have to be identified by relatives and friends at the county morgue, after autopsy technicians had washed off the blood and restored the mutilated bodies as much as possible.

By now, people were beginning to flock to the scene. Neighbors, aroused by the activity, had crowded into 100th Street. Pushy reporters were on the scene, one of whom had removed the screen from the back window and stuck his head inside to try to see what was going on. Police soon managed to rope off the area, including a portion of the alley.

Eight patrol wagons arrived and the bodies of the eight nurses, draped with blankets, were carried out the front door of 2319 on police department stretchers, while the TV cameras whirred. Wallenda could only report, "Something has occurred, something very, very bad, but we don't know yet what caused it."

That job would fall to the Chicago Police Department and Commander of Homicide Francis Flannagan, and to Cook County Coroner Andrew Toman, both of whom were emerging from 2319 to meet the crowd and the waiting press. Toman had sealed off 2319, authorizing subsequent entry only to a parade of police officers, prosecutors, and crime-lab technicians.

Flannagan, a bald-headed, pipe-smoking Irishman who clicked his teeth when pausing between sentences and dressed in a rumpled fashion, was a man's man, charming in manner and courtly, engaging, and effervescent. He was loved throughout the department and possessed a rare wisdom born of his front-row seat in witnessing mankind's anger, greed, and passion. He looked over the growing crowd of spectators. The crowd was silent at first, but as he spoke and his listeners began to comprehend the enormity of what had happened, there were cries for vengeance. Flannagan knew that he and his men had to find the killer—fast. He said nothing more.

Toman was more direct. With shock visible on his face, he spoke to the crowd.

"It is the crime of the century."

PART II
THE MANHUNT

CHAPTER 12

Thursday, July 14, 1966

By early morning, Speck had already slid back into the seedy world of Calumet Harbor bars, to begin another day of bragging, drinking, lying, and whoring. At ten-thirty, fresh from several hours sleep, he strolled into his favorite hangout—Pete's Tap. He was wearing clean, neatly pressed slacks and T-shirt and was freshly shaven, smelling of Old Spice cologne. Hanging in a scabbard from his waist was a brown-handled, foot-long hunting knife. This was the same knife Speck had carried on his belt when he strutted about the Shipyard Inn before he set out to kill. Since he had not used the knife in the town house, he felt safe in brandishing it again.

Speck gave bartender Ray Crawford a ten-dollar bill and said that he wanted to get the watch he had left in pawn about a month earlier. It was a twenty-five-jewel, self-winding gold Benrus. Crawford gave Speck the watch and three dollars change, prompting Speck to order a glass of beer. Crawford, a former U.S. Army master sergeant, struck up a conversation with his customer. Suddenly, Speck reached down and removed the hunting knife, asking, "Ray, put this knife behind the bar. I don't want to be seen with it."

Crawford put the knife away, and Speck began a long story about how he had killed several people in Vietnam with this very knife. He also repeated his lie about having stabbed a first mate, this time saying it happened on a ship sailing from Vietnam. Then, standing up from his bar stool, Speck leaned over, retrieved the knife from behind the bar, and walked up behind Crawford, who was standing at the end of the bar. Putting his left arm around Crawford's chest, Speck took the hunting knife in his right hand and placed it at the bartender's throat, tilting the blade so that it touched the Adam's apple. "If I was gonna kill somebody, this is how I would do it," Speck said. Crawford pushed Speck away and reclaimed the knife, warning, "I don't go for that. I don't like to mess around with knives."

Speck treated the incident as a big joke and returned to his bar stool to strike up a conversation with another saloon regular, William Kirkland, who lived upstairs at the St. Elmo flophouse. Speck was sitting there, talking and laughing with Crawford and Kirkland, when two girls he had met during his earlier stay at the St. Elmo walked in—Judy Feather and Wanda "Boots" Hooper. Judy Feather was the stage name of the young woman, who was a go-go dancer at a local bar; she and Speck had once had sex together. Hooper was divorced from Zack Hooper, a son of Ella Mae Hooper. Speck stood up and strutted over to the jukebox, where he bent over the machine, choosing hillbilly tunes. The girls were playing the nearby bowling machine. Neither Feather nor Hooper had seen Speck for weeks and Feather asked, "I thought you left town." Speck answered, "I changed my mind."

Returning to the bar, Speck told Crawford that he had a $1300 check coming the next day, inquiring, "Can you cash it for me?" Crawford replied that he did not have that kind of money on hand. Speck asked him for his knife back, and then sold it to Kirkland for a dollar. Wanting Kirkland to know what a valuable piece of weaponry he was buying, Speck explained that he had bought the knife from a soldier in Vietnam, where he had sailed on an ammunition ship. While returning to the United States, Speck added, he had gotten drunk and stabbed the first mate in a fight. The knife, with its seven-inch blade, had actually been given to Speck by his brother-in-law Gene Thornton, who obtained it during his days in the navy. New-found friends Speck and Kirkland then walked across the street to the Soko-Grad tavern. Kirkland noticed that Speck appeared nervous and gulped down two beers in fifteen minutes.

While Speck whiled away the hours drinking, the manhunt and media blitz were well under way. With racial violence begin-ning to erupt, Chicago was already a jittery city. Now, Speck's murders had pushed the race riots to the bottom of the front page. EIGHT NURSES ARE STRANGLED read the big, black headline in the early edition of the *Chicago Tribune*. The subheads added, "Student building invaded by sex maniac . . . Report hospital aides raped."

These were the last days of big-city "front-page" journal-ism and Chicago's four dailies, two published in the morning, two in the afternoon, would demonstrate an insatiable appetite for reporting the story. The murder of the nurses was the big-gest crime in the U.S. since 1949, when ex-serviceman Howard Unruh had taken a midday walk onto the sidewalks of Camden, N.J., and gunned down thirteen people in twelve minutes. Unruh told police, "I'd have killed a thousand if I'd had enough bul-lets." He was found insane and committed to a mental institu-tion. Now, the murder of the nurses was bringing back memories of Chicago as the home of Al Capone, the mastermind of the St. Valentine's Day Massacre of 1929. Capone's men, disguised as federal agents, had lined up seven members of a rival gang and mowed them down from behind with machine guns.

The manhunt for the nurses' killer had begun immediately. At six-thirty A.M., patrolman Leonard Ponne took down the first statement from a hysterical Corazon Amurao. Cora's initial description was marked by her heavy accent and hesitancy with the English language, and by her hysteria. Ponne himself was shaken by what he had seen. The description of the event was this:

"One white male, approximately 25 years old, 6 feet tall, short or crew-cut hair, no hat, wearing a black waist-length jacket, dark pants. . . . At about 11 P.M., offender had knocked on her bedroom door. When she opened door, offender was standing with a gun in one hand and a knife in the other hand . . . Offender tied nurses up and made them sit in a circle in the room. Offender stated, 'I won't hurt you, I want money to go to New Orleans.' "

At six-fifty, Detective Byron Carlile arrived at 2315 to take over the interview with Cora. Carlile worked the midnight shift with his partner Wallenda. He was a big man with broad shoulders, short gray hair, dark-rimmed glasses, and a craggy, weathered face. He had seen it all and was smooth and classy, possessing a profound understanding of the motives that drive people. He suggested that they move to an upstairs bedroom for privacy, and a grateful Cora quickly agreed. To provide emotional support, she was accompanied by Tammy Sioukoff and Josephine Chan. Carlile obtained the additional details that the killer spoke in a soft drawl and had blond hair. Cora emphasized, "I really want to help."

The descriptions were relayed to communications central of the Chicago Police Department. Cora was taken to South Chicago Community Hospital, where she was placed under police guard and heavy sedation. In the meantime, grief-stricken parents and relatives of the nurses were assembling at the Cook County Morgue to identify the victims. Wallenda recalls, "Hardened men broke down and cried. What could we tell the parents? I knew Joe Matusek, who ran a saloon at 108th and Michigan. And knew Suzanne Farris and Mary Ann Jordan from the hospital emergency room. We simply didn't have any answers. How could we?"

The nearest Chicago police station, Area 2, was located at Ninetieth and Cottage Grove, about one mile from the murder scene. Homicide Commander Flannagan and Deputy Chief of Detectives Mike Spiotto had decided that Area 2 burglary should be involved in the manhunt, since there was a possibility that a "known burglar" might have been the perpetrator. This instruction was relayed to Sergeant Victor Vrdolyak, the acting lieutenant for the burglary unit, and his deputy, Sergeant Michael Clancy. Vrdolyak, an ambitious, bright Croatian whose father owned a tavern on the Southeast Side, was a big, muscular man who combined high intelligence and a dry wit with exceptional street savvy. He was given to wearing twin brown leather shoulder holsters carrying magnum-force firepower. He was also given to aggressively taking over a case, if he could. Clancy was an ascerbic, tough, no-nonsense stocky Irishman who wore glasses and had thinning gray hair.

The homicide and detective commanders advised Vrdolyak and Clancy that since few people knew about the nurses' residences, the killer must have either lived in the area, had business in the area, or been in some way a "hanger-on" who became aware of who lived in 2319. They provided Cora's description of the killer and added that he apparently had started out looking for nothing more than money to get to New Orleans.

Vrdolyak and Clancy relayed this information to their detectives, who were told to begin the hard grind of ringing doorbells and asking questions.

Thursday was a day off for burglary detective Edward Wielosinski, but he knew that his Area 2 colleagues needed all the help they could get. The blond, boyish Wielosinski was a cop's cop with a natural instinct for people, and he knew the Southeast Side like the back of his hand. By 1966, Wielosinski had been on the police force for sixteen years. He had heard about the murders on his car radio while returning home from his moonlighting job as a security guard. He tried to drive to the scene, but he couldn't get past the crowd. Instead, he turned his car around and showed up for the eight-thirty A.M. roll call at Area 2 headquarters. Sergeant Vrdolyak read off the murderer's description: "Six feet, one hundred sixty pounds, short blond hair, black coat, Southern drawl, wanted money to go to New Orleans." Wielosinski and two other burglary detectives, Edward Boyte and John Mitchell, went to work.

They began their investigation on foot and quickly proceeded to the intersection of 100th Street and Torrence Avenue. The trio figured that since Torrence Avenue provided the quickest exit from the city on foot, and since 100th Street provided the best way to hitch a ride east to Indiana, the murderer might have walked this route to try to get out of the city.

This intersection was also the location of a Shell gas station, which Wielosinski knew to be a popular hangout for the neighborhood punks. He suggested to Boyte and Mitchell that they check it out. At eight forty-five, the three burglary dicks walked into the station and asked attendant Dennis Ryan if he had seen anybody matching the suspect's description. Ryan thought a moment and replied, "Well, yes, there was a guy who came in early on the morning of July thirteenth to wash up and get some bags he had left at the station. He had a soda and ate a candy bar and made some small talk. He spoke with a real Southern drawl and appeared plenty pissed off. He mumbled something about a 'damn ship' or an 'ammunition ship.'"

Wielosinski had been in the merchant marine, during World War II and he knew that there was a seaman's hiring hall across from the scene of the murders. At nine A.M., Wielosinski, Boyte, and Mitchell fought through the crowd gathered around the town house and entered the National Maritime

Union building to talk to the Chicago Port Agent, William Neill, to see if he recalled anyone answering the description just provided by Ryan. Neill wanted to be helpful, but nothing rang a bell. Finally, he suggested that the only seaman answering the description was a man named Peter Crowell, who had shipped out on July 11 aboard the *Flying Spray*, a ship bound for Vietnam. Neill offered to cable the ship to see if Crowell was aboard.

The detectives returned to the streets and revisited the Shell station. This time, Ryan suggested, "Why don't you talk to Dick Polo. He talked to this guy, too." Polo, the manager of the station, was the man who on July 12 had given Speck permission to leave his bags. He was now home sleeping, having worked through the night. Mitchell called Polo's home from the station and insisted that he be awakened. Polo recalled Speck and volunteered, "Well, I assumed the guy was a sailor. He had two bags, he was looking for a room, and he was very upset about something. I referred him to a rooming house at Ninety-fourth and Commercial and allowed him to leave his bags overnight."

Encouraged by developments, Wielosinski called headquarters and requested reinforcements, so that two two-man teams could split up and canvass the nearby hotels and rooming houses. Boyte and Mitchell were one team, and Wielosinski was paired with the meticulous and tenacious Eugene Ivano.

The teams split, and, a few moments later, Wielosinski and Ivano checked out the Clark Gas Station at 2416 East 100th Street, which was west of the Shell station and only a few blocks from the town house at 2319. The attendant, David Wilhelm, recalled that "Yes, a man who appeared to be a sailor came here about five-thirty or so on July twelfth and wanted to leave two bags overnight. He appeared disturbed and loitered around and made me so nervous that I finally had to ask him to leave, refusing to keep his bags. He appeared pretty upset about something, and said he hoped to 'ship out in a few days.' He also had some funny tattoos on his arms."

At ten-thirty A.M., about the time a refreshed Speck was walking into Pete's Tap, Wielosinski and Ivano returned to the Maritime Union Hall. "A second gas station attendant has placed this stranger in the area," Wielosinski said. "Did Peter Crowell miss a ship or did some other seaman miss a ship? This guy was complaining about a 'damn ship' or an 'ammunition ship.' "

Suddenly, Neill snapped his fingers and began rifling through his wastebasket. "Wait a minute," Neill said. "On July twelfth, in the morning, a ship berthed in Indiana Harbor requested two seamen, when only one was required. Two seamen were sent from the hall. One was hired, and the other returned the next morning disgusted and mad. This guy has a Southern drawl, like a hillbilly, and he fits the description. He's tall. I finally had to tell him to quit blowing steam and settle down, that he'd get another ship."

Incredibly, Neill reached down and fished out of his wastebasket a duplicate of the assignment slip that had dispatched Speck to the *Sinclair Great Lakes*. The slip provided the name, "Richard B. Speck." The address provided was that of the Thorntons, his sister and brother-in-law, and read, "3966 N. Avondale, telephone: AV 3–2830."

With this information, Neill was able to retrieve the entire union file on Speck. He informed Ivano and Wielosinski that Speck had been fired from the *Clarence B. Randall* for assaulting a ship's officer, and that he also had several tattoos on his arms. The description on file perfectly matched the ones provided by Ryan and Wilhelm of the disturbed stranger who had visited their gas stations.

Wielosinski and Ivano passed this information on to Sergeant Clancy in Area 2, suggesting that he check the Chicago Police Department's Bureau of Inquiry Section. Clancy made the check, but Chicago police knew nothing of Richard Speck.

For the next four hours, the four burglary cops pounded the pavement, knocking on the doors of nearby rooming houses in search of a "Richard Speck." At two P.M., the four returned to Area 2 headquarters to meet with Commander Flannagan, who had overall responsibility for the case. He told them to "stay with the case. We've got our hands full as it is."

In the meantime, technicians from the Chicago Police Department crime lab and from the lab's identification section were hard at work inside 2319 checking for possible fingerprints.

While the cops chased leads, Speck and Kirkland were still drinking. They were at the Soko-Grad when the TV broke in with a more accurate report about the murder of eight nurses. For the first time, Speck learned that he had left a survivor. He said to Kirkland, "It must have been a dirty motherfucker that done it!"

The two returned to Pete's, where Speck kept up his storytelling, excitedly jabbering away. He confided to Kirkland that he had a "pig" Puerto Rican girlfriend he kept at the Shipyard Inn. Speck launched into a long anecdote about his brother-in-law, Gene Thornton. In this fiction, Speck related how he had stolen a fifth of whiskey from Thornton's home one Sunday while Thornton and his sister were at church. "I got good and smashed," Speck explained, "and my brother-in-law threatened to call the police and have me jailed. Well, I handed him the phone and said, 'Is this what you want?' When he said, 'Yes!' I hit him over the head with the receiver. His face was covered with blood. My sister gave me eighty-five dollars and said, 'Get the hell out of here!' So, I packed my bags and here I am."

Speck had shrewdly taken an experience rooted in fact—how he had once stolen liquor from his *stepfather*—and transformed it into an excuse-making fiction, in this case to explain why he had money.

By noon, Kirkland had seen enough of Speck, who seamlessly relocated to Eddie and Cooney's Tap, a few blocks north of Pete's. Here, he ran into another drinking buddy—Robert R. "Red" Gerrald. Speck and Gerrald, fellow hillbillies, had worked together and drunk together while sailing on the *Clarence B. Randall* back in April of that year. Gerrald had a slender build, big nose, and close-cropped red hair. He wore a perpetual puppy-like sad expression, and on this day was well on his way toward a monumental drunk.

Speck ordered a hamburger, took only two bites, and pushed it aside. "I have a bad hangover from last night," he explained. Gerrald thought that Speck seemed "calm, but nervous." The two continued to drink beers, with Speck occasionally suggesting that they "walk over to Bond's, so I can buy some new clothes." The drinking got in the way, however, and the two moseyed only a few blocks farther north to the Ebbtide Inn.

While drinking at the Ebbtide, Speck and Gerrald heard the bartender and two customers discussing how the nurses had been murdered. Speck spoke up, "It must have been a sex maniac to have done something like that." Then, persuading Gerrald to join him, Speck decided to return to the Shipyard Inn. Speck tried to call a taxi, but was unable to get through. Frustrated, he gave the bartender a dime and asked him to make the call, adding, "Thank you, sir." A Commercial Cab arrived at the Ebbtide to take Speck for the short ride back to his room at the Shipyard Inn. Slowly, he was beginning to run.

At two-ten P.M., Speck and Gerrald arrived at the Shipyard Inn bar, where Speck switched his drink from beer to Jim Beam and Coke. He went up to his room to switch T-shirts. When he returned, Gerrald was on the verge of a boozy collapse and wanted to return to his rooming house "to straighten up." Speck suggested that Red go to his room instead, and handed him the key. First, though, Speck laid another alibi on his drinking buddy.

Speck said that he had picked up a girl the night before and that she had stayed with him all night. He embellished the story with the detail that she had first told him she wanted ten dollars for her favors, but "she got drunker than I did and I ended up getting it for nothing."

Red went upstairs, but was unable to get the key in the lock and had to return to ask Speck for help. Finally, the door was opened and Red managed to lie down for forty minutes or so to try to stop his head from "slithering around." Gerrald noticed that the bed had been slept in. Speck remained in the bar and ordered another Jim Beam and Coke.

As Gerrald slept off his hangover and Speck sipped his drink, Sergeant Clancy sat in Area 2 headquarters only a mile away. At three P.M., he picked up the phone and dialed AV 3–2830. Gene Thornton answered the call, and Clancy attempted a ruse. "This is Mr. Olsen at the National Maritime Union," Clancy said, "and we have an assignment for Richard Speck. Is he there?"

Told that Speck was not there, Clancy persisted, "Well, can you locate him? He needs to get in touch with us immediately, if he's going to ship out." Thornton understood the opportunity, adding, "Thanks for calling. We need to get this guy on a ship and out of our hair. I'll see what I can do." Minutes later, the phone rang at the Shipyard Inn and was answered by the day bartender, a bespectacled, jolly plump man who looked like he could easily pass for Santa Claus. "Richard Speck?" he announced.

Speck took the call and was told by Thornton to call the union hall about a job. Moving to the saloon's pay telephone, Speck called the hiring hall and asked to speak to Mr. Olsen. William Olsen, the deputy port agent, had been rehearsed by Clancy in what to say to lure Speck to the union hall. Detectives Wielosinski, Boyte, and Mitchell were at his side, staking out the site for Speck's arrival. In his nervousness, however, Olsen was too clever by half:

"We have a ship for you," Olsen told Speck. "It's the *Sinclair Great Lakes* and we'll hold the assignment open until you come on over here."

Speck, however, knew full well that the *Sinclair Great Lakes* had already shipped out. Mumbling in a slurred voice, he replied, "Well, I'm up in the Loop"—the city's downtown business district—"right now at Ruth's Place. I'll be there in about an hour."

The killer had a different destination in mind, however. Quickly spinning out new stories, he first called Gene Thornton and thanked him for the call, adding, "I turned the job down because it was only good for one day." Speck returned to his room, roused Red from his stupor, and told a new story. "I've been given an assignment on the *Sinclair Great Lakes*, but I have to go to my sister's to get some money." He quickly tossed his clothes into the tan suitcase and plaid zipper bag, left the room with the suitcase, and asked Red to bring down the plaid bag.

Returning downstairs, Speck took his tan suitcase out the side door and placed it on the curb. Then, he went back inside and told the bartender, "I've just been given a job on a ship docked at Indiana Harbor"—in nearby East Chicago, Indiana—"and I'm going to have to check out." He did not ask for a refund on his one week's rent, but he was given a one-dollar refund for the key. Next, Speck went to the phone, and called the Commercial Cab Company. Asked his name, he replied, "Johnson." Asked his destination, he said, "North Side." Gerrald reappeared and was told by Speck to wait for the cab, too. He took the plaid bag and walked out the tavern's side door, where he sat on the curb, holding his aching head in his hands.

Still acting cool and collected, Speck decided that he had time for one final game of pool while he awaited his escape vehicle. Since no one else was there, he played by himself. As the balls clicked about the pool table, three Chicago police vice officers from Area 4 headquarters walked into the Shipyard Inn, which was one of their stops in a canvass of Southeast Side taverns favored by sailors.

The three officers were all dressed in plain clothes. They were looking for Richard Speck, but they did not yet have the name. All they had to work with was the initial description given by Corazon Amurao earlier that morning, as the identification of Speck's name by Eddie Wielosinski and his burglary colleagues from Area 2 had not yet been passed on to the officers from the 4th District, who were assisting in the manhunt.

The three detectives "looked the place over pretty good," according to the bartender, who was asked if he'd seen anyone fitting their description of Speck: "White male, about twenty-five, six feet one inch tall, a hundred sixty pounds, slender build, with a blond crew cut." Speck was only ten feet away, lining up a pool shot. The bartender replied, "No, doesn't ring a bell with me."

At three thirty-five P.M., Matthew Hogan, a driver for Commercial Cab, walked into the front door of the Shipyard Inn and announced, "Commercial." Speck, who by now was sitting at the end of the bar, only a few stools away from the policemen, raised his hand and said, "Just a moment." Hogan walked back out the front door, and, moments later Speck slipped out the side door. He again roused Red, and helped load him and the bags in the cab.

A mile away, at the union hall, detectives Clancy, Wielosinski, Boyte, and Mitchell sat waiting for Speck, a vigil they would continue until the hall closed. Speck, however, was long gone.

CHAPTER 13

Matthew Hogan was a career bartender who just happened to be driving a cab between bartending jobs. A burly, strong man, Hogan was alert and streetwise. He noticed that Gerrald was dead drunk and an absolute mess. By contrast, Speck was clean and neat, with his hair combed and his face freshly shaven. He appeared sober. Nevertheless, Hogan thought Speck was acting fishy.

Speck told the driver, "Don't worry about him," gesturing toward Gerrald. "He'll be OK." Speck then asked Red where he wanted to go and was told, "Eddie and Cooney's." Speck directed Hogan to drive to this tavern, which was a few blocks north of the Shipyard Inn. On the way, Speck repeated his alibi to Gerrald: "I've got a job on the *Sinclair Great Lakes* and have to show up at the dock right at seven A.M. tomorrow. But, first, I need to get some money from my sister." Gerrald got out of the cab with these words ringing in his ears.

Speck stretched out in the backseat, calmly smoking a cigarette, and told Hogan, "Take me to the North Side, the poor side of the North Side." Hogan replied, "Where do you want to go? I need an address."

"The worst place, the scummiest place. I hate to admit it, but that is where my sister lives."

"That's not good enough. I need a street."

"Do you know where the beatniks hang out?"

"You mean Old Town?"

"Yes, that's it."

It was now midafternoon, and the sun was bouncing off Lake Michigan as Hogan drove his bright red-and-yellow Commercial Cab over to Route 41, where he turned left and proceeded to drive north on South Shore Drive to Lake Shore Drive. With the shimmering lake and sailboats on the right and the city's parks and skyscrapers on the left, the route along which Hogan was taking Speck is one of the most beautiful drives in the world. Speck, however, was still in his own interior world, telling stories:

"I just got into town this morning at four," Speck told Hogan, "and I went over to see my good buddy, Red. When I knocked on his hotel room door, I saw that he had a broad with him and they were both stinkin' drunk. I drank some whiskey with them and got on a good buzz, and finally Red asked if I wanted a woman. I said, 'You bet!' He went next door, knocked, and came back with a broad for me. I shacked up with her." The only description Speck provided of this mythical "broad" was that she "smelled bad."

As Speck was winding down his alibi, Hogan turned west onto Randolph Street and bisected the city's Loop before again turning north on LaSalle Street, a major thoroughfare that ran north into the Old Town district. Hogan next turned west on Division, and as the ride continued he looked back at Speck and said, "We're about running out of Old Town."

Speck, who didn't have a clue as to his whereabouts, peered out the window and saw the Cabrini-Green housing projects, a grim, all-black concrete ghetto. "This is starting to look familiar," replied Speck, who then directed Hogan to let him out at a parking lot at 1160 North Sedgwick, right in front of one of the Cabrini-Green residential towers. He added, "Yes, that is the building my sister lives in."

The ride cost $5.90, and Speck handed six one-dollar bills to Hogan, who then drove out of the lot, observing in the rearview mirror that Speck was standing there in the bright sun, his two bags at his feet, stretching and nervously looking around. It was four-twenty P.M., and Speck was twenty miles from the Shipyard Inn. He figured that the trail of a white man would go dead in a black ghetto. However, another eyewitness had him in her sights.

Fannie Jo Holland, who lived on the 11th floor of the building, was staring out the window, watching her husband walk east on Division Street to go to work. Although she lived in a public housing development, Fannie Jo Holland was a classy lady. An attractive, bright, well-spoken black woman, she was a college graduate with a degree in English. A devoted wife and mother of four young children, she also kept a neat, homey apartment. She always watched her husband leave for work, to wave good-bye and to throw him his cigarettes or keys, in case he forgot them.

Now, she was astounded to see a white man with two bags get out of a cab in the middle of a parking lot for an all-black building. Noticing that the red-and-yellow markings were not those of a city cab, she stared long and hard. Speck, she noticed, waited until the cab had driven out of sight before he picked up his two bags and walked to the edge of the parking lot. Then he bent over, opened his suitcase, and removed something. Straightening up, he looked around in all directions and then walked about twenty steps north to Division Street, constantly looking around in all directions. He was wearing dark slacks and a white T-shirt. In the bright sun, she could see dark blue markings on his arms, which she realized looked like tattoos.

Speck had taken the pistol from his suitcase and put it in his waistband. Then he walked four blocks east on Division to its intersection with Dearborn. At this point he was standing near

Rush Street, the "Street of Dreams," a one-block strip cluttered with singles bars. Only a few steps away was Butch McGuire's, America's original singles bar. It was now late afternoon, prime time for other Chicago men the same age as Speck to hit the street of dreams in search of business and romantic opportunities. Instinctively, Speck turned away and headed south on Dearborn. He walked six long city blocks, constantly looking left, right, up, and back, before finally breathing a sigh of relief. Rising above him at 648 North Dearborn was a flophouse—the Raleigh Hotel.

The Raleigh had been built with a high sense of promise back in 1882. It was constructed only eleven years after the famous Chicago fire had gutted much of the downtown area, and Swedish-born architect Lawrence Gustav Hallberg designed the Mentone Apartments, as they were originally called, to be one of the city's first luxury high-rise apartment buildings. The original eight-story building was designed in striking red and green terra-cotta stones, and contained only twelve large apartments, each of which included eight or nine rooms and offered handsome views of Lake Michigan, one mile to the east. Every convenience was provided, and the residences included a library, parlor, walnut woodwork, flocked wallpaper, and separate kitchen and service entrances.

As the decades slipped by, however, the apartments were broken down into smaller units and converted into a transient hotel, initially catering to the theatrical profession. In 1952, a fire swept through the building, uprooting 125 residents, many of whom were displaced people from Europe who spoke no English and were left homeless. By 1966, the Raleigh was a full-fledged flophouse, located midway between the city's bustling downtown Loop and the fashionable near North Side. It was only a few blocks from the fortresslike Merchandise Mart and the block-long prim granite headquarters of the American Medical

Association, but it was also only a short walk removed from the seamy street life of North Clark Street, one block to the west. It was now Richard Speck's kind of place.

At four forty-five P.M., Speck walked in the Raleigh's front door and went to the registration office run by Otha Hullinger. She was a heavyset loquacious woman in her midfifties whose entire body and jowls shook as she talked. Her short, wispy gray hair was combed tightly back, and she wore thick black-rimmed glasses. She lived in the hotel, and much of her time was spent tinkering with various cooking utensils designed to keep her on a special diet. She was smart in the way of most hotel clerks and was not easily fooled.

Speck was very calm and polite and asked to register for one week, handing her a ten-dollar bill to cover the rent (nine dollars) and key deposit (one dollar). He registered under an alias, David Stayton, using the name of one of his Dallas friends. Hullinger asked him where he was from.

Speck replied, "I'm from the North Side, but I had a big argument with my brother-in-law, who threw me out of his house because I drink too much." Asked if he was working, Speck said, "No, but I will be." Asked how he was going to get by in the meantime, he said "Don't worry, my sister will see me through." Mrs. Hullinger inquired further about the sister, and Speck provided her correct name and address—"Mrs. Martha Thornton, 3966 N. Avondale."

Speck was wearing black shoes, tight-fitting black pants, and a white sport shirt under a white jacket. Before entering the hotel, he had changed into the new shirt, and a jacket to mask his tattoos. Speck took the elevator up to room 806, on the hotel's highest floor. For his nine dollars he got a small room with bed and mattress, sink with hot and cold water, nightstand, and small refrigerator. Speck dumped his two bags on the floor; he was settled in.

At about eight that evening, he returned to the lobby, told Hullinger he was going out to eat, and politely asked if he might buy her something, perhaps a hamburger. Hullinger replied, "Why, thank you, but I'm on a diet and I can't eat hamburgers and I don't care for any coffee." Speck walked out the door, cut west a few steps to one of the many greasy spoons on Clark Street, and returned shortly with a little brown paper bag with two cups of coffee, one of which he insisted on giving to Hullinger. He also handed her a few packets of sugar. He called his sister, Martha Thornton, so she wouldn't worry about him. "I have a room down here on Clark Street," he lied to her, "and I'm going out drinking with Red."

As Speck did favors for Mrs. Hullinger and courteously reassured his sister, the Area 2 burglary detectives were huddling on the other side of town, wondering what to do now that Speck had failed to show up for the stakeout at the union hall. At seven P.M., Sergeants Clancy and Vrdolyak met with Homicide Commander Flannagan and Deputy Chief of Detectives Spiotto, and were told to keep their men on the case.

The burglary cops split into three three-man teams and fanned out to make a thorough search of all taverns, hotels, and rooming houses on the Southeast Side known to cater to merchant seamen. They put special effort into trying to find the "Ruth's Place" that Speck had mentioned when calling the union hall for his assignment. At midnight, they gave up. There was no "Ruth's Place."

Speck was back in the bars, only this time it was on the North Side. Only a few feet west of the Raleigh Hotel was North Clark Street. Its one-mile strip between 500 North Clark (Grand Street) and 1200 North Clark (Division) was a highway of sin and lost souls. It was only five blocks west of fashionable Michigan Avenue, but its denizens were living light years away. The Clark Street strip offered a variety of choices: The Pink Twist

Inn, the 661 Club, otherwise known as the Liberty Inn, the Club Erin, the Queen's Paradise, and the Shamrock. All were on the order of Pete's Tap in physical amenities: a carpet of beer foam, a fog of stale cigarette smoke, and a background stench of puke. The clientele, many of them ex-cons, was even worse: alcoholics, drug addicts, panderers, pimps, and prostitutes, all of a rich multiracial mix—black, Hispanic, American Indian, and white. Speck was at home.

He spent most of the night of July 14 at the Pink Twist Inn on North Clark Street. Bartender Jerry Bohne recalls that Speck came in at about ten P.M. and remained until three A.M., drinking at least five or six Jim Beam and Cokes served by Bohne, who was not the only bartender. Speck spent most of his time by the jukebox, standing all alone and drinking.

Elsewhere in the city, racial riots were in full fury. On the night of July 14, six policemen were shot and wounded, along with an uncounted number of civilians, as the city police fought rioters. By midnight, at least 118 persons had been arrested, and the police began carrying machine guns, shotguns, rifles, and tear gas, in addition to pistols and nightsticks, to combat roving gangs of vandals, looters, and snipers.

The Chicago Transit Authority shut down bus and elevated lines, and police blocked off main streets. In one violent incident, more than a hundred policemen exchanged shots in an hour-long encounter with snipers in two high-rise buildings at Lake and Wood streets, only a few miles from the Pink Twist Inn. Chicago police, now working twelve-hour double shifts with all leaves canceled, had more on their minds than Richard Speck. Throughout the city, there was an unspoken tension between blacks and whites. To the all-white middle-class neighborhood of Jeffery Manor and to much of the rest of the city, it seemed that the world was going to hell. And now, there was a mad killer on the loose, a killer who was assuming mythic proportions.

This mythical monster remained slouched against a saloon jukebox until closing time. Then, he struck up a deal with a hovering prostitute. Speck and the hooker walked the short block from the dive to the flophouse.

Friday, July 15

At about three-fifteen A.M., Speck used his key to unlock the front door of the Raleigh Hotel. He entered the lobby in the company of a black prostitute. Sitting inside the Raleigh's front door was an elderly night clerk, Algy Lemhart. Lemhart lived in the hotel in room 209 and was on night duty in case anyone tried to rent a room very late at night, in which case he would push a button to release the locked front door. Now, he was face to face with Richard Speck and a companion whom Lemhart later described as "a colored girl, about age thirty and five feet six inches tall and a hundred twenty or thirty pounds. She had medium-brown skin, big dark eyes, kind of high cheekbones. She was wearing blue shorts about six inches above the knees and white tennis shoes. She had a scarf on her head."

The woman was not drunk, but Richard Speck was. He talked "cracky," Lemhart thought. A belligerent Speck said that he had rented room 709. As the elderly Lemhart left to check the registration book, Speck and the prostitute stepped onto the elevator. Before the door closed, Lemhart heard the woman say, "Richard . . . ." Lemhart discovered that 709 was empty, but decided it was not worth the bother of awakening the temperamental Mrs. Hullinger to find out which room Speck had actually rented. About thirty minutes later, the prostitute stepped off the elevator and told Lemhart, "He is asleep now. I left him. He seemed nice, but when I got up to the room I saw that he had a gun."

Lemhart asked the man's name and was told, "Richard . . . I don't know the last name." Adding that she had not taken anything, the prostitute walked into the night. When Mrs. Hullinger arrived at her desk that morning, Lemhart told her about the man with the gun and provided a description. Hullinger believed the description matched that of the man she knew as David Stayton, and she called the police.

At eight-thirty, Officer Robert Ratledge, a tall, quiet, balding man, arrived at the Raleigh with his partner, Clarence Shuey. Both were from the 18th District Police Station, which was located only a few blocks away on Chicago and Clark, within spitting distance of all the joints. The two officers were told that there was a man with a gun and were escorted to room 806 by the Raleigh porter, who carried a passkey.

Officer Ratledge knocked three times, and, getting no response, put his head next to the door and listened for sounds. Nothing. The porter unlocked the door and stepped back into the hall. The two policemen entered to confront Speck, who was dead drunk and sound asleep, a black pistol protruding from the left side of his pillow. Speck was fully dressed in slacks, shirt, and socks.

Ratledge took the gun and put it in his right pocket. He then awakened Speck. "Why have you got a gun?" Ratledge asked.

Opening his eyes wide, Speck replied, "Where is the girl?"

Told that the girl was gone and had reported to the night clerk that he had a gun, Speck said, "I don't have a gun or a knife or a weapon of any kind. The girl had a gun and she must have left it." He then gave an entirely false description of the girl: "Puerto Rican, about five feet three inches, kind of short and dumpy. Wore glasses."

Asked where he met the woman, Speck stood up and walked over to his small window. Looking out at Clark Street, he pointed to the Liberty Inn, a few buildings away from the Pink Twist Inn, on North Clark, and said, "I think it was that place. I like hillbilly music and they have a little hillbilly group there. That's where I met her, then I brought her right over here." The Liberty Inn had only a two A.M. license.

Reaching into his pockets, Speck pulled out two crumpled one-dollar bills. "That girl took about ten dollars from me, he added. "I must have really tied one on." Ratledge asked his name, and Speck responded, "Richard Speck. My wallet is on the dresser." Ratledge picked up the wallet and found a seaman's card with the name Richard Speck" and a small passport photo. At the time the name meant nothing to Ratledge, or to most Chicago police officers.

"Why have you got one name up here and another down there?" Ratledge asked.

"The last ship I was on, well, I won a lot of money in a dice game and there were two guys from that ship who were pretty mad at me. They were after me, wanted to beat me up, so I changed my name."

Ratledge pressed him about the gun, and Speck said repeatedly, "I never carry a gun. The girl had the gun. I'd seen it in the bar, and I guess she just left it here."

The interrogation had now lasted fifteen minutes. There were six cans of beer on Speck's dresser, two empty and four full. Speck asked the officers, "Would you two like a beer?" After the officers turned down a warm beer, Speck countered by offering to buy them some hot coffee. "I have enough money for us to get some coffee, if you want coffee."

Ratledge noted that Speck "was very calm, very friendly, and very sure of himself. He spoke slowly, he never hesitated in his speech, and he never stumbled over any words. He understood everything that I asked, I never had to repeat any questions, and he always looked me directly in the eye. He never appeared upset by the questions."

Asked how long he would be staying in the area, Speck said, "Well, I'm paid up for the week, and I'll probably be leaving after that." The policemen then said that they were leaving. Speck followed them to the door, saying politely, "Take it easy!"

During the elevator ride down, Ratledge told the porter, "He's harmless."

CHAPTER 14

Speck wandered downstairs about ten on that morning of Friday, July 15 to confront an angry Otha Hullinger. "I told you when you checked in," she said, "that no lady friends can go to the room, unless you check with me first. You brought one anyway, when I was sleeping." Speck said softly, "Ma'am, I am sorry. I was just drunk. It won't happen anymore."

Policeman Ratledge had seized Speck's gun. However, he was working a double shift and to avoid the necessary paperwork he decided not to inventory the gun at police headquarters. He wrote that the report of a gun was "unfounded." In police language, this meant that no gun had been found in Speck's room.

Corazon Amurao and the Area 2 detectives were also having a busy Friday morning. At about seven, Sergeant Clancy and Detectives Boyte, Ivano, Mitchell, and Wielosinski had resumed their stakeout of the union hall. When agent Neill arrived to open the doors at eight, Clancy pressed him to try to obtain a photo of Speck. Neill suggested that the National Maritime Union headquarters office in New York might have one.

This was not good enough, given the urgency of the manhunt, and Clancy decided to first exhaust all local possibilities. He and Ivano drove to the U.S. Coast Guard office on South Ewing, which was only a mile away, two blocks south of Pete's

Tap. The two detectives were in luck. The Coast Guard came up with a two-inch-by-two-inch photo of Speck, a similar one for Peter Adam Crowell, another suspect, plus two others. Speck had been photographed and fingerprinted on April 25, 1966, before he shipped out to the Great Lakes on the *Clarence B. Randall*. Sergeant Clancy called headquarters with the good news and was informed that Deputy Chief Spiotto had just left for South Chicago Community Hospital to interview Corazon Amurao. He was directed to rush to the hospital and give the photos to Spiotto.

At nine-thirty, Cora met with Spiotto, Carlile, Wallenda, Homicide Detective Joe Gonzales, and a police artist. Gonzales showed her an album of a hundred large "mug shots" of known burglars and sex offenders from the area. She identified one as appearing "similar." Clancy suddenly arrived and gave Spiotto the four loose photos. Spiotto, a bald, sharp-featured, gum-chewing tough cop, was dedicated and capable. He remained remote from the men under him and was not beloved like Flannagan, but he was aggressive and bright. He handed the four small photos to Cora.

Wallenda was standing right beside Cora. "The minute she looked at Speck's photo, I knew that he was the one. I don't want to say Cora looked scared, but she stiffened and sat bolt upright. One thing you learn from being a cop is that the blacks and the Orientals don't show shock as readily as the whites. Cora looked shocked."

She gasped. "That is him! The hair is longer . . . it is the same hairline." The police officers were as excited as Cora over the identification. Tears welled up in Wallenda's eyes.

Cora and the police artist were left alone to develop a sketch of the killer, drawn from her memory. The police artist never saw the photo of Speck. Despite Cora's accented English and unfamiliarity with colloquial terms like "crew cut" and "pockmarks," she tried to explain to the police artist how the killer looked. Cora's words guided the artist's hands as he drew only one sketch, producing a likeness that prompted a nod of approval from the distraught and exhausted nurse. At eleven-thirty, Spiotto notified Area 2 that the survivor had identified a photo. Richard Speck was now the prime suspect. Another check was made at the Bureau of Inquiry, but there was no Chicago rap sheet on Speck. His identity was still known only to the burglary and homicide cops of Area 2 and to top brass.

The Chicago Police Department asked the FBI to obtain Speck's fingerprints from their Washington headquarters as soon as possible and to rush them back by plane. Several major air carriers were on strike, but the FBI was asked to pull out all stops. Commander Flannagan directed the Area 2 detectives to intensify their efforts to find Speck, and Sergeants Clancy and Vrdolyak sat down to decide how best to deploy their men.

The stakeout of the union hall was continued, and it was decided to begin additional ones at the Shipyard Inn and the home of Mrs. Martha Thornton. Then, working feverishly, a fifteen-man force began to chase Speck backward in time. Within a matter of hours, Speck's movements of the past week and months began to fall into place for the pursuing police officers.

Speck was traced to Pauline's rooming house and from there to the Shipyard Inn, where it was learned that he had left by taxi the previous day. Commercial Cab dispatchers and driver Matthew Hogan cooperated, and the officers learned that Speck had been dropped off at the Cabrini-Green housing project, on the North Side. By one-thirty, Vrdolyak was driving around, circling the Cabrini-Green complex, and checking possible points of departure. At the same time, Clancy was introducing himself to Martha Thornton, who provided a comprehensive rundown of Speck's travels since boarding a Dallas bus for Chicago in March. Whatever her feelings might have been to learn that her brother was a suspect in the mass murder, Martha Thornton kept them to herself. She and her husband cooperated fully with the police investigators.

At two-thirty that Friday afternoon, Vrdolyak and Clancy were radioed to return to headquarters. Red Gerrald was in custody. The dazed Gerrald readily admitted to having spent much of the previous afternoon with Speck.

By now, the search for Speck was well under way. The Thornton home was guarded by a two-man delegation headed by Detective Carl Edenfield, a polite, soft-spoken, neatly dressed gentleman who was able to put the Thorntons at ease with his kindness and understanding. An alert had been sent to all shipping docks and marine hiring halls, authorizing a "stop order" for any man resembling Speck's description. Extra police officers carrying rifles were dispatched to the area near Cabrini-Green.

At five P.M., the phone rang at Area 2 headquarters. Edenfield told Vrdolyak that Speck had just called his sister, saying that he "was down on Clark Street, drinking with Red." With Edenfield at her elbow, Martha Thornton had pleaded with her brother to "come on home and sober up." Speck had declined.

After calling his sister, Speck strolled into the Raleigh lobby and sat down with Mrs. Hullinger and the hotel porter to watch the TV. The big news was the search for the slayer of eight nurses. Speck offered to repeat his coffee courtesy for Mrs. Hullinger, who again refused. Speck walked out the door, and returned minutes later with a little brown bag and two cups of coffee, insisting that Mrs. Hullinger take one.

He also handed her the evening paper—the *Chicago American*. Dominating the front page was the police artist's sketch of the killer. Even with clear skin and a crew cut, it bore an eerie similarity to Speck. Chicago Police Chief Orlando Wilson had decided to risk the wrath of civil libertarians and to use the power of the press to help apprehend the killer. The sketch had been given to all the papers; the *American* was the first to run it.

Speck said softly to Mrs. Hullinger, "That is terrible about the nurses, isn't it?" She replied, "It certainly is." Glancing at the front page, she added, "The killer looks a little like a Filipino. He sure does, doesn't he?" Speck agreed, then blurted out, "Oh, give me that paper back!"

Mrs. Hullinger then left to clean her electric broiler and prepare one of her diet specials. Speck was left with the porter. "This is terrible about the fellow killing those eight girls," Speck began. "It looks like a Mexican or somebody was the one who done it." The porter agreed, and then added, "I was just out and I see that the police are out looking for somebody. I was walking a few blocks from here and some police were out with their rifles. Something is going on wrong in this neighborhood. This neighborhood is pretty hot."

Speck said, "I think I'll go upstairs." He took the paper with him. The porter later described Speck as calm, saying he took the news about the police being out with their rifles "just as calm as a lamb."

By now, Clancy and Vrdolyak had decided to mount an all-out surveillance of the hillbilly joints and flophouses in the North Clark Street area. About seven P.M., a small army of detectives assembled at the police traffic headquarters on North Clark, hard on the north bank of the Chicago River and only five blocks from the Raleigh Hotel. Broken down into two-man teams, the detectives were given their marching orders: To hit every saloon, restaurant, rooming house, and hotel in the immediate area and inquire about Richard Speck. Each team carried a duplicate of Speck's small passport photo. Accompanying one of the teams was Red Gerrald, who could offer positive proof of Speck's identity. At seven-fifteen, the dragnet began.

By now Speck had left the Raleigh and was three blocks away, drinking at the Pink Twist Inn. At about eight, he walked out; the police arrived fifteen minutes later. Speck had crossed to the other side of Clark Street, where he struck up a conversation with two winos who were drinking on the corner, passing a bottle of muscatel back and forth.

The West Side race riots had closed down the bars on Chicago's Skid Row, which was located a mile southwest of the Raleigh. Among the many Skid Row residents forced to move north to find their cheap booze were the two men Speck began talking to—Claude Lunsford and Shorty Ingram. Both were day laborers who stayed at the Starr Hotel on West Madison, in cubicles renting for ninety cents a night. The two men, both in their forties, were drinking under a large awning above the Erie Clothing Store, an establishment that bought and sold cheap clothes and knickknacks. Ingram was interested only in getting drunk. Lunsford was a little more interesting.

Lunsford was a one-eyed hobo. He had lost an eye in a boiler room accident years ago and had descended into drink and divorce. One of his chief concerns was to not further embarrass his family, and, in his own peculiar way, he retained a sense of pride. For that reason, he went by the names Bill Brian and William Miller.

The two older alcoholics offered Speck a drink, and the three got to talking. Lunsford mentioned that he had come to Chicago from Dallas on a freight train, and that he was an accomplished hobo. As the police patrols walked by, Speck stood on the sidewalk and listened intently to Lunsford. He wanted a crash education in catching freight trains. "How long are you staying in Chicago?" Speck asked.

"I don't know. I might stay five minutes and catch a freight out."

Speck decided he would join Lunsford at the Starr Hotel, and asked the two to wait "while I pick up my bags." Returning to the Raleigh, Speck went directly to his room and repacked a few items from his portable wardrobe into a shopping bag. He fastidiously put a piece of red cloth over the top of the shopping bag, carefully tucking it in all the way around, so that nothing showed.

A little after nine, Otha Hullinger and Algy Lemhart, the night clerk, were sitting in the Raleigh lobby. Lemhart had just arrived for work. They looked up and saw Speck walk through the lobby, carrying the shopping bag and the plaid grip. He was wearing black slacks and shoes and a white sport shirt with a blue design. Speck smiled and said, "I'm going to the laundry on Clark to wash my clothes."

About fifteen minutes later, the Chicago police entered the Raleigh lobby. Detective Joe Nolan showed Mrs. Hullinger Speck's photo and asked if she recognized it.

"Oh, my God," she said. "It's him. It's Richard. He just left."

CHAPTER 15

Speck and his two new buddies, "One-Eye" Lunsford and Shorty Ingram, walked through the police dragnet and headed southwest toward the Starr Hotel in the heart of Skid Row. Along the way, Speck disposed of his shopping bag of clothes, transferring the few items he would need into his small plaid bag. He reassured Lunsford and Ingram that he would take care of them, "because I have a gun here in my grip, and I know how to use it." He added, "Let's leave tonight and go to Dallas. I used to live there."

Lunsford asked Speck a few questions about Dallas neighborhoods and concluded that he was telling the truth. He was also thinking. "The more I watched him and the way he talked, why, the more I wanted to get away from the guy. He jumped from one sentence to another, one subject to another, never finishing one thing before he got onto another. And his mouth was funny. It was always half open. He had kind of a fish mouth."

Still, Lunsford and Ingram were both too drunk to avoid Speck's sudden attentions. When they arrived at the Starr Hotel, Speck signed the register for one night under the name, "David Stayton." He was assigned to room 548, a few steps down from where Lunsford was staying in room 584. Lunsford was registered under the name, "B. Brian."

Registration procedures at the Starr were loose. "In Skid Row, you don't bother to ask the other guy's name," Lunsford noted, "because most of the time he wouldn't tell you the truth, anyhow." The Starr night desk clerk followed the credo, "This is Skid Row and if you start asking customers questions, well, all of a sudden you don't have any customers."

With the Starr Hotel, Speck had hit absolutely rock bottom. It made the St. Elmo seem like a palace. The great grid that marks the city of Chicago begins at Madison and State, which is zero-zero. To the east lies the lake, and every 800 number in any direction from State and Madison measures one mile. In 1966, if you were to move west on Madison from State, you would first encounter Dearborn, Clark, and LaSalle streets, all dominated by skyscrapers and all centers of the city's commercial clout. Four or five blocks farther west, however, was Skid Row, home of life's losers. Chicago poet laureate Carl Sandburg called it "The Boulevard of Forgotten Men," a refuge for derelicts, drunks, and itinerant workers. Census takers never even bothered to count the residents of Skid Row.

This was Speck's new neighborhood. The blinking red neon sign over the entrance proclaimed, "Starr Hotel, Fireproof Rooms." At the Starr, men lived like animals confined to cages. Its floors were filled with the noise of men coughing and making other sounds of illness; the next most common sound was the clank of empty beer cans hitting the cement floor. On July 15, 1966, the Starr had 350 male tenants, who paid eighty-five or ninety cents a day for cubicles separated by plywood partitions. The five-feet-by-seven-feet cubicles contained only a cot and mattress, footlocker, and stool. Each cubicle was covered on top with rusty chicken wire to allow ventilation of the fetid air and to prevent thefts or sudden attacks from neighbors. Still, veteran roomies knew how to lean over the cubicle wall, reach a stick through the chicken wire, and prod pants and other clothing items off the hook on the cubicle door and then pull them under the door, which was raised several inches to increase ventilation.

Speck's cubicle in 548 cost an extra nickel. For that, he got a tiny vent that allowed filtered sunlight to pass through a square of greasy glass blocks embedded in the drab olive wall.

Now, the three odd fellows, Speck, Lunsford, and Ingram, sat out on the fifth-floor fire escape of the Starr Hotel and worked their way through a fifty-cent bottle of wine. A few miles to their west the city was in flames from the racial riots. Lunsford soon sent Ingram out to get another bottle of wine, but didn't ask Speck to help pay "because he wasn't drinking very much. He was pretty sober, and all he wanted to talk about was catching a freight out of town." Speck never told Lunsford his name, and Lunsford never bothered to ask.

As the new friends drank cheap wine on their flophouse fire escape, Lieutenant Emil Giese, commander of the police department's fingerprint identification section, was setting out from his home toward central police headquarters on South State, only three miles from the Starr Hotel. Giese was the department's leading fingerprint expert. Earlier that day, he had been told that some prints were being flown in from Washington and that he should make himself available to "get right on it." By five P.M., however, the prints had not yet arrived and Giese went home, leaving word that he should be called immediately if the prints arrived.

The call had come at nine P.M. from his watch-mate, Sergeant Hughie Granahan, who was on night duty. Giese, the father of ten children, did not own a car, despite moonlighting on a second job. He took the subway. When he arrived at headquarters, Granahan was waiting to show him a ten-fingerprint card of Speck that the FBI had flown to Chicago from its headquarters in Washington, D.C. The prints had been taken by the Coast Guard in Chicago but were subsequently acquired by the FBI. It took a major effort by the FBI because many of the nation's airlines were on strike. An agent turned the Coast Guard fingerprint card over to a pilot for American Airlines, one of the few carriers not on strike, and asked him to deliver it to Chicago on his next flight. The FBI also forwarded Speck's long police record in Dallas. Also on file at FBI headquarters and subsequently sent to the Chicago Police Dept. were two other ten-fingerprint cards of Speck taken in Texas by the Dallas sheriff's office and by the Huntsville branch of the Texas Dept. of Corrections. The three fingerprint cards had three different names. The Dallas prints listed the name as "Richard Franklin Lindbergh." The Huntsville prints read "Richard Franklin Speck." The Coast Guard prints read "Richard Benjamin Speck."

Giese and Granahan sat down at adjoining desks. Their task was to try to match Speck's prints with any of the "latent prints" (invisible to the naked eye) taken from the nurses' town house at 2319 by crime lab technicians. By using standard techniques, it had been possible to "lift" the latent prints from various surfaces in the town house. By Friday night, the technicians had found thirty-three prints at 2319. Five of the thirty-three prints were too smudged or lacking in detail to be compared against other inked impressions. Of the twenty-eight remaining prints found suitable for comparison, eighteen did not compare with anyone whose inked impressions were tried. Of the ten latent prints that had been positively identified, two belonged to patrolman Dan Kelly, and eight to the nurses. That left two prints yet to be compared.

Giese and Granahan asked Ray Heimbuch, chief of the photo section, who was also working overtime, to make some enlargements of the two remaining unknown prints. Then, they poured some coffee and bent over the prints with magnifying glasses.

As the Chicago police studied his fingerprints, Speck begged Lunsford to help him catch a train out of town—right now. "No," Lunsford said, "let's get some sleep and work tomorrow and then maybe we can catch a train." With that, Lunsford, Ingram, and Speck left the fire escape, returned to the narrow fifth-floor hotel corridor, and walked back to their cages. Before retiring, Lunsford made a point of walking over to Speck's cubicle and saying, "Don't call me before six tomorrow morning. I don't want to get up any sooner than that." Speck agreed. Then, Lunsford asked the night clerk to awaken him at five A.M. He wanted to avoid seeing Speck again.

Saturday, July 16

By five A.M., Giese had hit pay dirt. He had proven ten points of identification between Speck's right middle finger on the Coast Guard print and a print taken from the inside of the town house door.

Bleary-eyed, Giese called over to Granahan: "Hughie, this one looks very good. I think that I have a match." Granahan, in turn looking very closely at the comparison, agreed.

Giese was now in the happy position of being able to give the detectives the good news. He called the home of Homicide Commander Flannagan, awakening his wife. "He's not here," she said. "He's on the streets working on the murders." Giese reached Flannagan on his car radio at five-fifteen with the message: "Chief, we've got a match on the prints." Within minutes, Flannagan passed the news on to the weary officers who were still staking out Clark Street.

Wielosinski recalls the reaction of the hardened coppers:

"Tears. We were running out of steam, and, then, to get this news, well, it was a helluva feeling, something else. Once the prints matched, that was it. This is the guy, and everything else stops. We thought that Speck was a goner. Once the guys found him and positively identified him, well, we didn't think that he would come out alive. Feelings were running pretty high."

At the time, though, Wielosinski and his colleagues needed some rest. They adjourned to the nearby Holiday Inn at Ohio Street and Lake Shore Drive, where everything would be on the house. "We told them who we were and what we were doing," Wielosinski recalls, "and they couldn't do enough for us." Enough was a quick shower, a soft bed, and later, a big breakfast, over which Wielosinski exclaimed, "SUMBITCH! We did it!"

About the time the detectives got the good news from Giese, Speck was breaking his promise to Lunsford. It was only five A.M., but he awakened Lunsford by kicking on his door and pleading, "Let's hurry up and catch that freight."

CHAPTER 16

Lunsford put Speck off by saying, "Meet me down in the lobby in a few minutes." Then he tried to avoid his pesty pursuer by walking one block west to a restaurant, where he ordered a cup of coffee. Speck, carrying his plaid bag, soon tracked him down, pleading, "Let's get that freight and get out of here." Lunsford countered, "Look, let's work this one more day and then we'll have enough money to eat and get by on."

Like many roomers at the Starr, Lunsford did day labor to finance his drinking bouts. The hiring agency, Lake Shore Employment, was right across the street from the hotel, and it needed laborers to work at McCormick Place, the city's giant convention center on the lake. Speck accompanied Lunsford to Lake Shore to register for a job, but got nervous and fidgety. "I'm not feeling so hot," Speck said. "You go ahead and work, and I'll see you tonight. I'm going to sell this bag to make some money." Lunsford took a bus to McCormick Place; Speck faded back into the shadows of Skid Row.

At nine A.M., Lieutenant Giese turned his findings over to his senior fingerprint identification specialist, Burton Buhrke. Giese was an intensely loyal supervisor. He figured that the Speck case would be Buhrke's swan song, and he wanted him to have the credit. "Take over," Giese told Buhrke. "It's your case now." As

Giese was taking the subway home, Buhrke helped nail down the fingerprint identification.

He got a second match, this time between Speck's right index finger and another latent print from the inside of the town house door. In the meantime, two crime lab mobile unit technicians returned to the town house and found a new print at the bottom of the inside of the door to the south bedroom. Instead of lifting the print, the technicians called Burton Buhrke to the scene, where he compared Speck's fingerprint cards with the new print. Once he had established that the print matched the middle finger of Speck's left hand, Buhrke preserved the print and removed the entire door for possible use in court.

On Saturday morning the first funeral was held, for Gloria Jean Davy. A requiem mass was offered in St. Joseph Church, in Dyer, Indiana, her hometown. Her parents were Arline and Charles Davy. Her father, a handsome, polished man, was a successful sales executive. Gloria had four sisters and a brother.

Sitting behind the bereaved parents and siblings was an honor guard of Gloria's classmates from South Chicago Community Hospital. Dressed in their white uniforms and nurses' caps, they offered a striking contrast to the mourners in black. The hospital had offered a ten-thousand-dollar reward to anyone supplying information that would lead to the arrest of the killer.

The Reverend Ambrose E. Switzer tried to explain the loss with a poem Gloria herself had written in 1963 after the assassination of President John F. Kennedy. At the age of nineteen, she had written:

"God, please instill in the hearts of the people the understanding of the meaning of this tragedy. I plead for a purpose, a worth in so disastrous a loss. Why this death? Its reason I do not know. But in the years to come it will show. I trust in this." She was buried in Holy Cross cemetery in Calumet City, Illinois.

Meanwhile, it was a tired, tense, but relieved group of people who gathered at one that afternoon at a walnut conference table in the large second-floor office of Cook County State's Attorney Daniel P. Ward, in the Criminal Court Building on South California Street. Sergeants Clancy, Vrdolyak, and John Murtaugh, and detectives Carlile, Pete Velesares, Wallenda, and Wielosinski had been sent by Chief Orlando Wilson to obtain a warrant for Speck's arrest from the State's Attorney's office. The police delegation was met by Ward, criminal division chief Louis Garippo, and an assistant state's attorney, William J. Martin.

With their coats off, shoulder holsters showing, and emotions in check, Carlile, Vrdolyak, Wallenda, and Wielosinski gave a long recitation of the pursuit of Speck, concluding that the trail had gone cold at the Raleigh Hotel. State's Attorney Ward decided that Garippo and Martin would work together to question Speck if he were captured. Everybody in the room feared that Speck had escaped and, if found, would not come out alive.

Carlile and Martin adjourned to a nearby office to prepare the warrant for Speck's arrest. Carlile, who had done this type of thing hundreds of times, sat down at the typewriter. Suddenly fearful, the hard-eyed copper said, "Oh, hell, I'm afraid to do this. If I make a typographical mistake, the SOB may go free!" Martin took his place and pecked out the simple arrest warrant.

Daniel P. Ward, a legal scholar and former law school dean, was very concerned that Speck's legal rights be scrupulously observed, and he emphasized this to everyone in the room. One of the detectives told Ward that Police Chief Wilson had scheduled a press conference for that very afternoon to name the killer. Ward was a member of the American Bar Association's Committee on Free Press—Fair Trial, and he knew that an overzealous press could jeopardize a fair trial and conviction. He grabbed the phone to call Wilson at police headquarters and to give him the

circumspect guidelines for public dissemination of news about a
suspect.

"This is State's Attorney Ward," he told the answering officer. "Please put me through to Chief Wilson."

There was a long pause, then the response: "He's giving a
press conference right now. Oops, wait a minute, he's just finished." Wilson had gone the other way. He had decided to let
the news media publicize Speck as the killer and help track him
down. At the press conference, a grim-faced Wilson had held up
a photo of Speck and named him as the killer. Reciting Speck's
description, tattoos, and long police record, Wilson concluded:
"As far as I'm concerned, there's no question that he's the murderer." It was too late for Ward to do anything about it.

An all-points alert was issued for Richard Speck. The FBI said
he was the most wanted man in America. Within hours, his name
and photo were on all the front pages and TV screens of America.

In the meantime, Speck had sold his plaid bag at a Skid Row
junk shop and had money to finance another drunk. There was
no problem finding liquor. Sid's Junction, right next to the Starr,
offered a "large glass of tap beer" for a dime. Harvey's, below the
Starr, offered package goods, including a pint of California muscatel wine for forty-nine cents.

By midafternoon, Speck had bought several papers, all with
his name and photo on the front page, and had taken them back
to the Starr along with a pint of San-Clar muscatel. He made
one last effort to hide his identity, telling a hotel employee that
he had lost his key and gaining entrance to room 584—where
Lunsford was registered under the name "B. Brian." The rent
was paid three days in advance. In this desolate cubicle, rented to
another man with an invisible identity, Speck tried the ultimate
escape: suicide.

At about five P.M., he walked to the community washroom
at the end of the hall and broke the bottle of wine he had just

finished drinking. Using the jagged glass, he slashed the inside of his left elbow and his right wrist. Then he returned to 584, leaving behind a trail of blood. He fell back upon the cot in the cubicle and lay there, his left arm dangling over the side of the bed and staining the newspapers scattered on the floor.

He would find no pity from the roomers of the Starr Hotel. The first to encounter him was George Gregrich, the roomer in 582, who had been out all day on a job. He had returned to Skid Row at about six, cashed his check, and returned to the Starr with a six-pack of Budweiser and a half-pint of Jim Beam.

Gregrich was a serious drinker and was oblivious to most everything else. He returned to his cubicle, dropped his stash of booze, and walked to the community shower, stepping over the trail of blood left by Speck. After showering, Gregrich returned to 582, took a sip of whiskey, and opened a can of beer. He then settled in with the day's racing form. "I wanted to see who was running," he recalled. "Even though I didn't play it, I still liked to follow them up."

Speck heard the commotion coming through the thin plywood partition, and there followed a conversation:

Speck: "Please get me a drink."
Gregrich: "Get it like I do. I worked all day, and I had to walk a mile to get my drink."
Speck: "I need a glass of water. Won't you please come over and see me?"
Gregrich: "How the hell did you get in there? Listen, like I told you before, you can certainly go out and get yourself a glass of beer or drink whatever you want."
Speck: "I got a story to tell you. I did something bad."
Gregrich: "I don't want to hear no part of your story. I don't know you. Leave me alone. I just got through working and I'm tired."

Speck: "Please come to my room."
Gregrich: "Are you sick?"

There was no reply. Ten minutes later, Speck again asked for water and Gregrich told him, "I'm not leaving this room. If you want any water, you know where it's at."

Speck continued to beg for water, and Gregrich went downstairs and told the desk clerk, Bill Vaughn, "If you don't get this guy out, I'm going to put him out."

When Gregrich returned to his room, Speck continued to plead with him, saying on three occasions, "I did something bad. I want to tell you."

Gregrich asked, "What did you do so bad?" There was no reply.

Speck then resumed his pleas for water, begging Gregrich to come to his room. Gregrich cut him off: "I know you hillbillies all got a good story to tell. I don't want to hear your story." Gregrich then went downstairs to complain a second time about Speck. By this time, Gregrich had killed the half-pint of whiskey and four cans of beer. He left the hotel to resupply, buying two quarts of Budweiser and another half-pint of Jim Beam, returning to the hotel about eight o'clock. The man in 584 was the least of his concerns.

In the meantime, Claude Lunsford had finished his day of work at McCormick Place and returned to Skid Row at about six-thirty P.M. He promptly went to the Blue Ribbon to cash his check for $8.47 and to buy a bottle of Bud. Then, he moved over to Sid's Junction, where he drank two more bottles of beer. As he drank, Lunsford noticed the front page of the paper that was being read by the man sitting next to him. He thought the face looked familiar.

Lunsford walked into the Starr Hotel to go to his room. He passed the open door of 582 and was asked by Gregrich: "Don't you have the same room?" Lunsford said, "Sure."

Lunsford unlocked the door and found Speck, lying on the cot, covered with blood. "What happened to you?" Lunsford asked. Standing up with great effort, Speck replied, "I fell into the window."

The window was glass brick and Lunsford knew that it could not possibly have cut anyone. Lunsford said, "See you later," closed the door, and beat a hasty retreat. He walked down to the Silver Dollar restaurant, where he found an early edition of the Sunday *Tribune* lying around. He ordered a cup of coffee and stared long and hard at Speck's photo, which the newspaper had enlarged and run over three columns in the center of the front page. Lunsford had normal vision in his one good eye.

The newsprint made Speck's hair look black, and Lunsford recalled it as dirty blond. After fifteen minutes, he walked over to the Lake Shore Employment Agency and asked the owner, Louis Novinson, "Say, what was the color of the hair of that guy I was with this morning?"

"Dirty blond," Novinson said.

Moving outside, Lunsford asked another day laborer, George Hanson, to read him the description of Speck, as published in the *Tribune.* When Hanson was through reading, Lunsford told him to keep the paper. "I don't need it no more," he said.

Lunsford then walked very slowly toward the LaSalle Street commuter station a few blocks away. He didn't want to get involved, but he thought that he should do something. Thinking that he looked too "beat up" to use a phone in any respectable place, Lunsford chose the anonymity of the pay phone at the train station. He deposited a dime, dialed the operator, and asked to be connected with the police emergency number. The operator promptly put him through to the Chicago Police Department's hot line.

A police officer answered and Lunsford said, "The man you're looking for is in room 584 of the Starr Hotel with blood all over." Pushed for his name, Lunsford said that he did "not want to get involved, but my initials are C.L." After making his call to the police, Lunsford walked down to the Ram Hotel a few blocks away and registered for the night. He then settled into his new surroundings with a six-pack of beer, turned on the TV, and watched the Miss Universe pageant.

Protocol for the multimillion-dollar telephone system required the police dispatchers on duty to carefully log all incoming calls and then radio a police car to go to the scene. The police never sent a car.

CHAPTER 17

Sunday, July 17

At midnight, as Gregrich was sitting on his cot and sipping his last quart of beer, Speck staggered against his open door, forcing it to slam against Gregrich's left knee. Jumping up, the roomer shouted, "What the hell's going on?"

Speck fell to the floor, covered with blood. Not wanting to mess up his own cubicle with Speck's blood Gregrich reluctantly helped him back to 584. He then pushed the elevator emergency button to summon help.

The emergency buzzer was answered by the elevator operator, who rushed to the fifth floor, where he saw a crowd of roomers gathered outside room 584. Speck had remained a loner to the end, and no one had the foggiest notion who he was. Someone said, "We got a man bleeding to death here." The elevator man rushed down to the basement and got the hotel's night handyman. He took one look and said to call the police.

At twelve-ten A.M., a call went out from the police communications center to patrolman Michael Burns and his partner Eugene Krause to investigate an "injured man" in room 584 of the Starr Hotel, on West Madison. Burns, a balding heavy man who wore black horn-rimmed glasses and walked with a lumbering gait, was a career wagon man, having spent the last twenty-five years in this depressingly routine work. He and Krause had begun their twelve-hour shift at two P.M. on Saturday and were nearing the end of their long night. They were called to the Starr six or seven times a week to transport injured or sick roomers, so to them, this was just another night.

The coppers were told there was a man bleeding to death in 584. As was customary, they asked the name and were told "B. Brian." Arriving on the fifth floor, they found a semiconscious Speck, who said only one word: "Water." The roomers told them that there was broken glass at the end of the hallway. Burns and Krause believed this was just another case of a "drunk falling on some broken glass." While Burns left to get a stretcher, Krause said that he needed something to make a tourniquet. A leather belt was found, and using his nightstick, Krause wrapped the belt tightly around Speck's upper left arm to stop the bleeding.

The officers then carried Speck, mattress and all, out of the cubicle and put him on the stretcher, requiring help to maneuver the stretcher down the narrow hallway to the elevator. This was another routine hospital run with an injured drunk, and it was only a ten-minute drive from the Starr to the gigantic Cook County Hospital on the city's near West Side. Within this medical complex is the Cook County Morgue, where the bodies of the eight nurses had been taken for identification.

The coppers asked the Starr's elevator operator to come along to hold the tourniquet, so they wouldn't have to bother. While Krause drove the paddy wagon and Burns sat shotgun, he sat in the back with Speck, holding the tourniquet. Since he appeared nervous, the coppers occasionally looked back into the wagon and told him to "hold the nightstick tightly." Otherwise, they concerned themselves with more pressing topics, like the fact that Mayor Daley had persuaded Illinois governor Otto Kerner to call up the National Guard to put down the race riots.

They never bothered to check the *Police Bulletin* on their dash-board, which contained a description and photo of Speck.

The Starr Hotel soon resumed life as usual. Gregrich told anyone who would listen, "That guy really bugged me . . . he really bugged me." One roomer volunteered, "He was here about four months . . . kinda stuck to himself . . . I think that he's a lumberjack."

In a trash can at the end of the corridor was a broken San-Clar California muscatel wine bottle. Remaining behind in room 584 were the last of Speck's clothes and his black wallet with the Coast Guard ID photo and seaman's card. Arranged neatly on a stool were his toilet articles: a toothbrush, a tube of Gleem tooth-paste, a pack of Gillette razor blades, a bottle of Old Spice after-shave, and a smeared bottle of Max Factor Signature cologne.

During the short ride to the hospital, Speck asked for water about fifteen times. He said nothing else. At the emergency room, the police reported, "Patient, B. Brian, had been drinking and evidently fell on a broken bottle causing lacerations of both arms." Then they left and returned the elevator man to the Starr. They had done their job.

In the meantime, Speck was in shock. The first nurse to help him was Geraldine Gorski, R.N., who was working the night shift in the ER. She was a tall, young, blue-eyed blonde. When the police had removed their makeshift tourniquet, the blood spurted and Gorski put a compress over the cut on the crease of Speck's left elbow and wrapped it with an Ace bandage. She did the same on his right wrist. Then, she used scissors to cut open his blood-splattered T-shirt and check for any additional wounds. She lowered his trousers to do the same. There were none. She wheeled the gurney into the hallway and directed, "Emergency . . . take him to trauma." She saw Speck as "a clean-shaven young boy with muscular arms and tattoos." She had removed from his pants' pocket a key with a plastic tag and the name "Starr Hotel"—well known to hospital emergency room staff as a notorious Skid Row hotel—causing her to wonder, "This is not the kind of guy who belongs in a flophouse."

At twelve-fifty, Speck was taken to the trauma unit on the hospital's third floor, where he would be helped by six more nurses, including Shirley Azares, who was a Filipino working at County under the same exchange program that had brought Cora, Merlita, and Valentina to South Chicago Community Hospital. Without medical help, Speck would have died within an hour. When he arrived at trauma, his pulse was very weak and his blood pressure was a very low 70/50 (normal is 120/80). His eyes were closed and his skin was pale, cold, and clammy. Nurse Kathy O'Connor asked him what his name was and what had happened. There was no response. Following normal procedure, O'Connor slapped Speck a few times in the face, trying to rouse him. He did not respond. The nurses immediately started an intravenous solution of dextran and saline and an intravenous infusion of blood to restore his blood pressure.

The physician on duty in the trauma ward was Dr. Leroy Smith, a first-year resident in orthopedic surgery. A boyishly handsome, eligible young bachelor and man-about-town, he came from a socially prominent family in Long Beach, Michigan. Smith was new to the trauma unit, and had been scheduled to have this Saturday off before trading shifts with his roommate. Having begun a twenty-eight-hour shift at eight A.M. on Saturday morning, he was scheduled to stay on duty until Sunday noon.

A few hours before meeting Speck, Smith had taken his dinner break at The Greek's, a popular restaurant directly across from the hospital. A stack of newspapers had been dropped off near the door, and while eating, Smith had idly read about Speck and his tattoos, including the trademark "Born to raise hell." He had been paged to return to the emergency room. Nurse

O'Connor, a short, spunky brunette with big blue eyes and a wry sense of humor, told him that the pace was picking up; a stabbing victim and a man in shock from loss of blood were now in trauma. Smith folded the *Chicago Tribune* under his arm and returned to work to treat a patient whose hospital name tag read "B. Brian."

As the doctor started to examine Speck, he thought that the patient "looked very familiar, as if I had just seen him." I had brought the *Tribune* back to my office right off the trauma floor, and I asked Kathy O'Connor to go get it. She thought that I was crazy, but she did it, anyway. I checked the photo and the story and I held the paper next to the patient's face. Except for the acne, this patient named B. Brian was a dead ringer for the photo of Richard Speck.

"His arms were caked with blood and I was so excited that I used saliva to begin to scrub the blood off. As I removed the blood from the left arm, I saw the 'B' first and then the rest of 'Born to raise hell.' In my mind, this was definitive. Speck's blood pressure was 70/50 and mine must have been 270/150. The adrenaline was really pumping. I called Kathy over to the side of the room, away from the patient, and said, 'You're not going to believe this. . . .' Then I returned to the side of Speck, who was beginning to come out of shock, and I said, 'What's your name?' I grabbed him by the back of the neck—there's a major spinal-accessory nerve there near the trapezius muscle—and I squeezed hard, real hard.

"I repeated, 'What's your name?' He answered: 'Speck. Richard Speck.' Then, he gasped, 'Water . . . water.'" Smith found himself muttering, "Did you give those nurses any water?"

Then he instructed the nurses, "Let's get busy and not let this man die." Speck kept repeating, "Water, I want water . . . I am sick." O'Connor asked how he had hurt himself and Speck said, "I did it to myself." Another nurse let some ice shavings drip into Speck's mouth. Smith told Nurse O'Connor to call the police.

Patrolman Alan Schuman was outside the trauma unit, guarding another patient. Within two minutes, he responded to Smith's summons. "You're not going to believe this—" Smith began. Schuman replied, "Bullshit! Don't bullshit me!"

It was one A.M. when Schuman relayed the news to his commanders. Five minutes later, there were fifty police cars converging on the hospital. The reporters quickly followed. By one-thirty, police were swarming the trauma unit. Speck was placed in leg irons and chained to his hospital gurney. Three FBI agents appeared, but were asked not to interrogate him. By one-fifty, Chicago Police mobile crime lab technicians had arrived to fingerprint and photograph Speck and take custody of his clothing.

The police asked Smith not to question Speck about the murders until a representative from the state's attorney's office and a court reporter arrived. Smith said, "Fine, I'll just ask him medical questions." Assistant state's attorney Bill Martin arrived at two A.M. Also on hand by then was the supervising surgeon, Dr. William J. Norcross, who asked Smith to brief him. Informed of Speck's capture, Norcross told Smith, "Well, we have a patient to worry about. How's he doing?"

Smith reported that Speck might have severed an artery and that he required surgical exploration and repair of the inside left elbow. The cut on the right wrist, Smith added, was no problem. No vessels had been severed and the cut had easily been repaired with four stitches. Smith had also noticed a superficial scratch on Speck's chest that was about two and a half inches wide. The scab indicated that it was about three days old and that it could have been inflicted by a fingernail.

It took two hours to prep Speck for the exploratory surgery. During this time, the police stayed in the background, only asking what the doctors intended to do. Smith replied, "We're going to try to move him to surgery as fast as possible."

At three, Nurse O'Connor administered atropine as an anesthetic and antispasmodic and morphine as a pain reliever, and Speck was wheeled up to the eighth-floor surgical suite. Trailing behind were twelve policemen and the representative from the State's Attorney's Office, Bill Martin. Smith scrubbed for surgery and took Speck into the surgical suite, where an anesthesiologist and surgical nurse were waiting. By now, Speck was becoming lucid. Before the general anesthetic was given, the following conversation took place:

Smith: "Hey, man, where you been?"
Speck: "In a flophouse."
Smith: "What have you been eating?"
Speck: "I haven't been eating . . . I haven't had a damn thing to eat. Just been drinking cheap wine. Hey, Doc, can I ask you a question?"
Smith: "What?"
Speck: "How long is this going to take?"
Smith: "About an hour. Have you ever had surgery before?"
Speck: "Once, for a busted appendix. Say, are you going to get the ten-thousand-dollar reward?"

Smith remained mute, offering no further conversation. Around them in the OR, there was deadly silence.

Smith told Speck that he needed to pass a tube down his throat. Speck replied that this had not been necessary during his appendectomy and he didn't want it done.

Smith: "If you don't cooperate, I will have to cut your damn arm off."

Speck: "I don't give a damn. Cut it off. How about some water, Doc? How about some water?"

Smith: "No water until after surgery."

The tube was passed down Speck's throat, sodium pentobarbital was administered for anesthesia, and surgery was begun upon Speck's left arm. While Smith proceeded with his surgical repairs, Norcross gave hell to Martin and the policemen, asking them to leave the area because they were not in surgical attire. As this debate was intensifying, Speck temporarily came out of the anesthesia, sat bolt upright, and screamed, "I'm scared, I'm scared." Throwing his legs off the operating table, he began to wrestle with Smith over the surgical scalpel, a reaction not uncommon in patients who have been drinking.

Six policemen rushed into the OR to subdue Speck, breaking the sterile environment and enraging the two other surgeons operating on other patients. Speck was subdued, the anesthesia was turned up, Speck went back under, and Smith continued with the operation. The surgery proved routine. Smith found that Speck had missed the major artery inside the left elbow, merely making a superficial laceration of the brachiocephalic vein inside the left elbow. The vein had a seventy-five-percent tear in the wall and had collapsed. Smith quickly repaired it with five nylon sutures.

The doctors and nurses of Cook County Hospital had saved the life of Richard Speck.

PART III
THE INVESTIGATION

CHAPTER 18

Bill Martin sat anxiously outside the surgical suite awaiting Speck's recovery. His immediate assignment was to make sure that no one tried to extract a drug-induced confession from the suspect, or do anything else that might jeopardize the state's prosecution. Martin was only twenty-nine, but he was the right man in the right place and things were now moving very fast.

Only the day before, Martin had stopped by his office to finish a brief due to be filed before the Illinois Supreme Court. After going four years without a vacation, he had been looking forward to taking off the next two weeks, although he didn't plan on getting much rest. Among other things, he was going to be painting his parents' house. Walking toward his office, he had been stopped by Lou Garippo, the chief of the criminal division. "Stick around," Garippo said. "Area Two is coming in. They know who killed the eight nurses. Mr. Ward is on his way." Martin stuck around. However, he believed that Speck had fled the city or, if caught, would not be taken alive. He didn't think his vacation was in jeopardy. Even when Martin's boss, State's Attorney Dan Ward, announced that Martin and Garippo would be on a special alert the rest of the weekend, Martin believed his phone was not going to ring.

It rang shortly after one A.M. on Sunday, July 17. Garippo was on the line, explaining that Ward had directed him to report to

Cook County Hospital for a possible interview with the murder suspect. However, Garippo continued, his bad back had flared up and he had difficulty standing up. Martin would have to make the trip, instead; a car was on its way. Showering quickly, Martin threw on a suit and climbed into the backseat of a waiting squad car. The West Side race riots were still smoldering, and one of the police officers in the front seat cradled a shotgun on his lap.

News of Speck's arrest had spread quickly, and the main lobby of County Hospital was filled with reporters and TV cameras. Strong-willed surgeon William Norcross knew that he would have his hands full protecting his notorious patient. Referring to Jack Ruby's shooting of Lee Harvey Oswald, he told Martin, "We don't want another Dallas incident here." Martin agreed that Speck should be moved without the glare of klieg lights, and he and Norcross asked police brass Frank Flannagan and Mike Spiotto to meet the press in the lobby and announce that Speck would remain at County until further notice. As the reporters swarmed about the lobby during the press conference, Speck was placed in an ambulance at a secluded rear exit. This was the first of a long series of dodges to protect the integrity of the prosecution's case from the news media.

At four-fifty A.M., young resident Dr. Leroy Smith got into the ambulance with Speck and three police officers for a short drive to the Cermak Memorial Hospital, which was the medical facility for Chicago's nearby House of Corrections complex. The complex, which had been rebuilt in 1961, included the massive Criminal Court Building and the County Jail. Dr. Norcross and Bill Martin made the trip in separate cars. Speck's only conversation during the ten-minute ride was a request for water. After Speck was admitted to the jail hospital, Smith was released to return to his duties as a lowly medical resident, albeit one who was about to become world famous. Others remained behind to begin grinding the wheels of justice. At six A.M., Detective

Byron Carlile arrived with the warrant for Speck's arrest. It had been kept under lock and key at Area 2 headquarters. Speck was formally arrested and placed in "soft restraints" (leather) in room 324, where he was the only patient. Carlile and Martin were allowed to see him briefly.

> **Carlile:** "Hi, Dick, how are you?"
> **Speck:** "OK."
> **Martin:** "Have you been treated well?"
> **Speck:** "Yes."
> **Martin:** "I am Assistant State's Attorney Bill Martin and this is Detective Byron Carlile."
> **Speck:** Unintelligible grunt.
> **Carlile:** "Would you like some water?"
> **Speck:** "Yes." (Water was furnished by an orderly.)
> **Martin:** "How do you feel now?"
> **Speck:** "Sleepy and dopey."

The meeting was over. Both Speck's medical condition and his constitutional rights were being scrupulously guarded. Martin was very mindful of a recent ruling by the U.S. Supreme Court, which held that a suspect could not be interrogated unless he first gave a full and knowing waiver of his right to legal counsel. Under the direction of Chief Justice Earl Warren, the High Court had begun its revolution in protecting the rights of criminal defendants in the famed 1966 *Miranda v. Arizona* ruling. Mirandizing, as it came to be called, began with the immortal line, "You have the right to remain silent." Carlile and Martin left, and two detectives remained outside 324 to guard Speck.

Miranda was one concern; the news media was another. Later that morning, State's Attorney Ward went on the radio and said, "A warrant has been issued for the arrest of this man. This is a matter under investigation and there will be no statements made by this office at this time. I don't know when a statement will be given, if any. Under these circumstances, we will conduct ourselves properly, in accordance with the ethics and the requirements of the law. There will be an ethical observance of the requirements of the law."

Ward knew full well that prejudicial press coverage could jeopardize the prosecution of Speck. However, keeping the media at bay was easier said than done. The world was waiting for news about Speck, and the news media were determined to try to deliver it. It started immediately. The Sunday *Chicago Tribune* screamed in big black type: NAB KILLER SUSPECT! The front-page photos were not of heroic police officers but of the Starr Hotel's staff members and Speck's coresidents, as well as Cook County Hospital's Leroy Smith and Kathy O'Connor. Speck had made them all bit players in his continuing drama.

In the meantime, the preparation of the Speck case had to begin without delay, and Bill Martin more or less fell into the job. He walked to the nearby Criminal Court Building, which was known simply as "the building," because it was here that "real" lawyers worked on "real" cases—criminal cases. In 1966, Martin was one of thirty assistant prosecutors—all male—who were assigned to the Criminal Courts detail. They were a rough-and-tumble crew whose frequent shouting in the halls made their second-floor location sound more like a fraternity house than a law office. All night-call assignments were posted above the urinals in the men's room. Martin bounded up the marble stairs two at a time in a rush to reach his office. It was going to be a busy Sunday.

The challenge of bringing Richard Speck to justice belonged to the Cook County State's Attorney's office, the chief prosecuting agency in Chicago and surrounding Cook County. Each of the 102 counties in Illinois has an elected prosecutor, known as the State's Attorney because he or she prosecutes offenses against state laws within the county. The Cook County State Attorney's Office, or SAO, of 1966 was a superior team headed by two splendid leaders—Daniel Ward and his chief deputy, John Stamos. Much as police chief Orlando Wilson had reformed the Chicago police force in the wake of convictions of policemen for aiding and abetting a burglary ring, so had the Cook County SAO been reformed by Ward and Stamos in the wake of the madcap administration of their predecessor, Benjamin S. Adamowski.

Daniel Patrick Ward had been the respected and reserved dean of Chicago's DePaul University Law School when Mayor Richard Daley persuaded him to run in 1961 as the Democratic Party's blue-ribbon candidate for State's Attorney against the Republican incumbent Adamowski. Ward was a former Assistant U.S. Attorney and seemed the perfect choice to derail Adamowski. He did. The lantern-jawed Ward was both articulate and erudite and was an imposing figure both physically and intellectually. He came to the office possessed of a magnificent grasp of legal history and a magical command of language. It was his rock-solid belief that above all else a prosecutor "must strike hard blows but fair blows."

Ward set out to hire the best and brightest young attorneys he could find, and many of them were assigned to the crown jewel of the reinvigorated office: the criminal division headed by John Stamos. The pay was modest and the hours long (and uncounted), but the assignment offered a young law-school graduate a rare opportunity to develop quickly into a trial attorney. A tour of duty as a Cook County assistant state's attorney (ASA) was the legal equivalent of a medical or surgical residency at Cook County Hospital. The young lawyers hired in 1961 and 1962 had developed into savvy veterans by 1966. Bill Martin had been part of this transformation.

By 1966, Ward's chief deputy, forty-two-year-old John Stamos, had been promoted to First Assistant. A tall man with pronounced Mediterranean features, sad bloodhound eyes, and dark black hair, Stamos knew the office inside out and had an impressive record of winning difficult cases. He also was a first-rate raconteur who told nonstop Homeresque tales about zany old-time criminal attorneys. Perpetually armed with a cigar, his trademark was to park the stogie on the ledge above a courtroom door as he entered and to reclaim it upon leaving. As tough as he was entertaining, Stamos brought fear to the hearts of his young assistants when he stabbed the air with his cigar and ordered, "Do the right thing!"

Excitement crackled in the air that Sunday as Ward and Stamos assembled their team of prosecutors to hand out assignments to begin the investigation of Richard Speck. After a long day, Ward decided to take Garippo, who was working in spite of his back troubles, Stamos, and Martin to dinner at Schaller's Pump, a popular pub located in the South Side Irish enclave of Bridgeport only a few blocks from the home of "da Mare"—Richard J. Daley. After Stamos had loosened the group up with a few larger-than-life tales, Ward expressed his opinion that the demands of the Speck case could not be allowed to interrupt the daily demands on each assistant state's attorney to handle his courtroom's two-hundred-plus active felony files. At the time, the SAO was responsible for more than four thousand indictments and seventeen felony trial courts. Ward made it clear that after the *blitzkrieg* investigation of Speck during the first few days, most of the investigators would have to return to their usual assignments. Only a small permanent team would be left to prepare the Speck case for trial.

Stamos and Ward believed that "doing the right thing" meant suppressing their own ambitions and letting their young assistants prosecute the celebrated Speck case. They thought their obligation to run the office overrode the opportunity to run one case that would require at least a year of intense effort. This

was an odd philosophy for two Cook County political officials
to follow. In July 1966, Ward was a candidate for the Illinois
Supreme Court and Stamos hoped to be the Democratic candidate to succeed Ward as State's Attorney. For these two political
candidates, the Speck case might have been considered a dream
come true. Ward and Stamos, both of whom were little known
outside legal circles, would have become household names. In
addition, Stamos had a personal interest, living as he did only
three blocks from South Chicago Community Hospital and having grown up near the steel mills and shipyards of the Southeast
Side. Nevertheless, Ward and Stamos had decided that it was
their responsibility to administer the office, not prosecute cases.

The older prosecutors had taken Martin under their wing,
and they were now entrusting him with his biggest assignment. There was no ceremony, but Martin clearly understood
that he was in charge of the Speck case. Still running on sheer
adrenaline and anxious to begin to carry out the assignment
he had just been given, he was unable to eat. Quietly excusing
himself from dinner with his colleagues, Martin headed back
for "the building."

Still ringing in his ears were Stamos' cautionary words about
fame: "Do the right thing. Do your job and forget about everything else—and that means the press. Today's headline wraps
tomorrow's garbage." Martin had heard this advice before. In
1964, while conducting a grand jury investigation of a call
girl ring, Martin had become excited about the likelihood of
announcing indictments to the press. Stamos had told him, "Son,
a week from now no one will remember if you were the pimp, the
patron, or the prosecutor. All they will remember is that you had
something to do with whores!"

Martin and all the police and prosecutors involved in investigating Speck and his crime would have a press vocabulary of
exactly two words: "No comment." This felt natural enough to

the young assistant attorney. He was still speechless over the fact that he'd been given the assignment of prosecuting the biggest criminal case in Chicago history. He hoped that he was up to it. It would be a long time before he would get around to painting his parents' house.

CHAPTER 19

Youth is the major export of Ireland. Shortly before the turn of the century, a feisty twenty-two-year-old angrily quarreled with his parents over his refusal to play the fiddle at a family gathering. He fled the family's small farm in County Limerick, stowed away on a freighter bound for New York, and kept right on running until he arrived in Chicago—penniless. The barrel-chested immigrant worked as a laborer until he joined the U.S. Army and fought in the Spanish-American War of 1898. Subsequently, he became a fireman, and with his own hands built a two-story yellow brick apartment house on the West Side of Chicago. He was Bill Martin's grandfather, and his traits of independence, hard work, and never backing down from a fight were family traditions.

In the Irish immigrant tradition, Bill Martin was born on the second floor of the two flat, where his parents lived above his grandparents. After World War II, Martin's parents followed the wave of westward emigration to the nearby leafy suburb of Oak Park, the boyhood home of novelist Ernest Hemingway and a community featuring numerous landmark homes designed by famed architect Frank Lloyd Wright. Martin attended Fenwick, an all-male Catholic high school run by Dominican priests who demanded discipline and hard work. He was an Honor Roll student with two passions—journalism and ice hockey.

Having been editor and publisher of his own two creations, *The Hockey Herald*, and *The Hockey Review*, since the seventh grade, he was amply prepared to edit the school newspaper, *The Wick*. He also learned to play a scrappy game of hockey by practicing for frostbitten hours on frozen ponds fed by the Des Plaines River. At five feet two inches and 100 pounds, Martin had chosen his sport wisely. He was too short to play basketball, was good-field, no-hit in baseball, and was too small for the powerhouse Fenwick football team. Ice hockey would be Martin's game; he loved its chaos, speed, and violence, and the chance to excel based on sheer determination. He practiced his skating and puck-handling for hour after hour, bringing tears to his eyes from the cold and wind. He never let himself stop. He became good enough to play in the rough-and-tumble Illinois Amateur Hockey Association and even drew a scholarship offer from a small college in Massachusetts. He decided to stay closer to home.

In 1954, Martin became the first member of his family to attend college when he enrolled at Loyola, an urban university on the North Side of Chicago hard by the elevated lines of the Chicago Transit Authority. After majoring in political science, he planned to acquire a master's degree in American civilization and then pursue a career in journalism. However, a close college friend talked him into giving Loyola Law School a try. Law school proved to be a good match for Martin, who created and edited the *Loyola Law Times*, a quarterly journal of legal opinion, made the national moot court team, and was voted the outstanding law student in his class.

His first journalistic assignment in law school was to develop an article on the Cook County Public Defender's Office. As part of this assignment, he met and twice interviewed Public Defender Gerald F. Getty, the man who would later be appointed to represent Richard Speck. In these early meetings, Martin formed the impression that Getty was an enormously talented criminal-defense lawyer who was unselfishly dedicated to defending the down and out, whatever their crimes. Martin liked Getty and decided to make him a role model.

Graduating in 1961, Martin remained ambivalent about a legal career. He skipped that fall's bar examination in order to work for the Chicago Commission on Human Relations, analyzing the real estate sales patterns and practices in racially changing neighborhoods. A modest and self-effacing man, he had long since taken his godawful pink Ford coupe and had it repainted a basic black, right down to the white sidewall tires.

After a few months of this work, though, the memory of how difficult it had been to acquire a legal degree persuaded Martin to give the law a try, after all. In spring 1962, he passed the bar exam and became licensed to practice. Martin again looked up Public Defender Gerald Getty, this time with the intent of finding a job. Martin was a committed liberal who believed fervently in the cause of the poor and in upholding the Bill of Rights. He was accorded two more interviews with Getty, an amiable, courtly man who brewed tea for his guest and made pleasant conversation. Getty was courteous, but Martin was not invited to join the Public Defender's staff.

In desperation, Martin turned to his law school dean, John C. Hayes, to enlist his help in becoming an assistant public defender. The dean could not help, but offered an alternative. Newly elected Cook County State's Attorney Dan Ward had asked each Illinois law school to nominate its outstanding student for an assignment as an assistant state's attorney. Hayes told Martin he would gladly nominate him. Martin recoiled. At the time, he thought that becoming a prosecutor was entering into a pact with the devil. He asked for time to mull things over, but eventually rationalized that since Getty was not going to hire him, being a prosecutor was the next best thing to prepared him to become a better criminal-defense lawyer.

Things moved quickly. Martin soon found himself sitting before a man who would become one of his mentors. First Assistant State's Attorney Ed Egan.

"So, the Dean thinks you are the outstanding student at Loyola?" Egan began with a trace of sarcasm.

"No, sir, I'm afraid I'm the only one who asked for the recommendation," Martin meekly whispered.

"Well, you start tomorrow in the Municipal Division, the police court at Forty-eighth Street and Wabash. Uphold the Constitution and don't take any money."

Egan administered the oath of office and on June 16, 1962, William J. Martin became a duly authorized Cook County assistant state's attorney. He was one of 152 ASA's who were divided between Civil and Criminal Divisions.

The Civil Division, which was housed in downtown Chicago at the Civic Center, represented county officials in civil cases such as real estate property tax matters and tort claims. The Criminal Division was a pyramid of units with its apex being the Felony Trial Division in the Criminal Court Building of the House of Correction complex at Twenty-sixth Street and California Avenue on the Southwest Side. Apprentice prosecutors called the Felony courtrooms the "Big Top." Beneath Felony were the divisions for Appeals, Juvenile, Municipal, Suburban, and Traffic. The bottom of the pyramid was the misdemeanor division where minor crimes—punishable by no more than one year in the county jail—were prosecuted in makeshift courtrooms located at police stations.

The Criminal Division looked down on the Civil Division as a boring haven for paper pushers; the Civil Division thought of the Criminal Division as a place for legally illiterate macho hip shooters. The State's Attorney relied upon his First Assistant and Chief of the Criminal Division to keep this unruly law firm together. The successful working of the SAO required its three top officials to give up the glamor of personally trying cases in favor of effectively supervising the 152 assistants, any one of whom could create a political disaster through mishandling of a sensitive case.

Martin started at the bottom of the pyramid—the misdemeanor division. An introverted, shy man, Martin doubted his ability to speak before a courtroom of strangers. And, like all law school graduates of the 1960's, he didn't have the foggiest notion of how to try a case, since law schools of that era did not teach courses in trial procedure. It was with great apprehension that he drove on his first day to the courtroom at Forty-eighth and Wabash, deep in the heart of the crime-ridden South Side.

This first courtroom was on the second floor of an old and dirty police station. Hopelessness oozed out of every brick. The court came complete with a gruff police sergeant who kept track of police paperwork and witnesses and, in Martin's early days, effectively tried the cases for the frightened young prosecutor. Martin was so afraid of speaking in public that he thought he had chosen the wrong career. During his first week, Martin convicted a man who had stolen four dollars' worth of food, including some bread, from a supermarket. During his presentencing remarks, Martin told the court about the man's four-page criminal rap sheet, which included dozens of jail sentences for petty thefts.

"What's the State's recommended sentence?" the judge asked coldly.

Martin paused and fidgeted. He was sympathetic to the poor man's desperation in having to steal bread. At the same time, he recalled what Anatole France had said about the majesty of the law, that the law must forbid rich and poor alike from sleeping under bridges.

"Judge," he finally said, "the State has to recommend two days in jail." Martin avoided looking at the defendant.

The judge, incredulous at Martin's bleeding-heart liberalism, boomed out: "Two days! I'm ordering 364 days in the House of Correction" (the maximum sentence for petty theft). He slammed down the gavel.

For Martin, the summer of 1962 was long, hot, and educational. After two weeks at Forty-eighth Street, he was promoted to the branch courts in the central police headquarters on South State. By now, Martin was able to open his mouth in the courtroom. The South State operation was the home of Gun Court, Gambling Court, Women's Court, and Paternity Court. The daily lineup included men and women charged with carrying concealed weapons, operating illegal "numbers" rackets, gambling, minor sex crimes, prostitution, and quarreling neighbors. These sweltering courtrooms, always filled with wall-to-wall people, were on the building's upper floors, and the windows had to be opened for relief from Chicago's sticky heat and humidity. Regularly wafting through the open windows was the clackety-clack of the nearby Wabash Avenue elevated trains. Trials were often halted in midsentence while the "El" trains roared by.

The first judge there with whom Martin worked escaped from the wretchedness of the crowd swarming before him each and every morning with a bottle of vodka. As the courtroom filled, the judge retreated to his chambers and the washroom with his bottle. To Martin's ear, the sounds escaping from the washroom suggested that the judge both drank the vodka and used it to gargle. Anything to get the taste of court out of his mouth. Anxious to be rid of the lawyers and witnesses hounding them to begin court, the clerks attempted mightily to wean the judge from his morning ritual. Nothing worked. The judge retreated to his private preserve, consoled himself with the vodka, and often stared out the window at the Illinois Central

Railroad tracks below. If he caught sight of the Panama Limited, he would patiently count the number of cars it carried.

It was usually late morning before the judge ascended to the bench. Even then, he frequently retired to his chambers for additional swigs of vodka. He never allowed himself to be rushed and court dragged on until seven P.M. or later. The other courts were usually done by two P.M. Midway through the lazy afternoons, the judge would experience vodka-triggered flashbacks to his navy days. Suddenly, he would sit bolt upright and announce, "The smoking lamp is lit." With that, he would light up a cigarette and proceed to chain-smoke as he dispatched the press of paternity cases. Legal arguments were alternately interrupted by the clack of the El trains and by the terrible hacking cough of the judge.

On weekends, Martin and the other police court prosecutors were sent to the Criminal Court Building for what was jokingly called "Holiday Court"—a place to handle the flood of humanity that had been arrested Friday and Saturday nights. This holiday duty introduced Martin to his first real courtroom, replete with all the trappings of the majesty of the law. The weekday trials in the police courts were "stand-up benches," so named because everyone stood up during the trial. There were chairs neither for the witnesses nor the jurors, nor were there jury boxes. In Holiday Court on the weekend at the massive Criminal Court Building, Martin for the first time saw courtrooms outfitted with the full appurtenances of justice. One Sunday, a veteran bailiff pulled Martin over to the imposing jury box. "Some day soon," she said, "you'll be standing here arguing to twelve people." Martin fidgeted. He was still trying to master the art of a stand-up bench. The thought of arguing to a jury—twelve strangers—seemed a feat beyond his imagination.

By the time "summer school" ended, Martin was no longer shy in a courtroom. Assistant state's attorneys were on their own, and necessity forced them to develop the basic skills of a trial lawyer: stand up to the judge; argue the law vigorously; object strenuously when your opponent crosses a legal line; cross-examine like a dog digging for a bone. Knowledge came quickly, and with knowledge came confidence. Martin now had his sights set on the Big Top, the rooms in the Criminal Court Building where prosecutors tried suspects for armed robbery, burglary, rape, and murder. First, though, he had to survive a few tests.

In October 1962, his boss, Ed Egan, told Martin that he was being transferred to the Appeals Division. Martin was reluctant to leave the gritty trial division for the ivory tower of writing briefs to the Illinois Supreme Court, but a vacancy had to be filled and Egan was not concerned about his underling's feelings on the issue. So Martin joined five other lawyers working out of cubbyholes on the second floor of the Criminal Court Building, right next to the library. This six-man brief department was a haven for the SAO's scholarly elite. Its two star members were James R. Thompson, later to become the governor of Illinois, and Marvin E. Aspen, destined to become a federal judge. Thompson and Aspen had helped draft the 1961 Illinois Criminal Code.

The brief writers played an important role in the march of justice. After reading the court reporter's transcript of a felony trial and the brief of the defendant asking the Illinois Supreme Court to reverse the conviction, the Brief Department lawyers would write the state's brief in rebuttal, using citations about past cases pulled from musty library shelves. This lonely and tedious work forced Martin to patiently study what his colleagues actually did during a trial—question by question. It turned out to be a wonderful experience. Most Illinois lawyers only visit the state's highest court on the day they are sworn in as members of the bar. The brief writers went to Springfield, Illinois, the state's capital, every other month to deliver thirty-minute arguments before the seven justices of the Illinois Supreme Court. Egan kept Martin in the appeals division for eighteen months—long enough for him to make more than thirty oral arguments before the state's highest court.

During this period, Martin survived two potential derailings. The first involved legendary comic Lenny Bruce; the other, Chicago Mayor Richard Daley.

Lenny Bruce, an iconoclastic genius given to blue-language performance, had been sentenced to one year in jail for the alleged obscenity of his comic routine at Chicago's Gate of Horn nightclub. The State's brief on appeal was assigned to Martin, whose liberal conscience was deeply offended. Martin did not believe that Bruce's act was obscene, and he certainly did not believe that Bruce deserved to go to jail. Martin asked that the assignment be given to someone else. Though Martin feared that this act of conscience might cause his demotion, he was pleasantly surprised. The refusal earned him the respect of his superiors.

Later, Martin was summoned before Mayor Daley, who was looking for an administrative assistant. Martin had been recommended for the job by one of his law school professors. Since Daley wanted unquestioned loyalty, he never chose as a close adviser anyone who had existing political connections. Since Martin had no political contacts, he met this qualification. Martin had three short meetings with Daley, and the charismatic mayor and city leader made the young prosecutor feel as if he were the center of the universe. He also offered him the job.

Many of Martin's colleagues would have killed for this assignment, but Martin felt differently. Signing on with the mayor would make his future contingent upon a political machine. Martin reasoned that soldiering on in the obscurity of the brief department, sustained by the promise of eventual experience in the trial division, would give him employable

skills independent of any political figure, no matter how charismatic. Although Martin declined the offer of working for the
mayor, it still required the direct intercession of State's Attorney
Dan Ward to keep Martin as one of his 152 assistants. Daley, it
turned out, liked Martin's independence and spunk, and Ward
had to talk the mayor out of hiring him away from the State's
Attorney's Office.

Persistence paid dividends in April 1964, when Martin was
promoted to the Big Top courtroom of Judge Walter P. Dahl,
a burly, crew-cut, gruff ex-Marine with the proverbial heart
of gold and the patience of a saint. Dahl was a judge's judge:
instinctively bright, compassionate, scrupulously honest, and
gifted with an exquisite sense of fairness. He also took pains
to gently teach trial skills to the young prosecutors and public
defenders assigned to his court. Trying cases before Dahl gave
Martin the chance to attend "graduate school," taught by the
best of the flamboyant defense lawyers who were then part of a
dying breed.

Driven by pride of performance, the earnest young prosecutor supplemented this courtroom education by touring each
section of the Chicago Police Crime Laboratory. Through first-
hand observation, he became familiar with the techniques used
to examine documents, lift fingerprints, identify firearms, and
make microscopic examinations of fibers. The scientists who
ran the labs were delighted that a prosecutor would take a special interest in their esoteric work, and they willingly shared
the secrets of their trade. Martin was beginning to understand
the complexity of scientific evidence. He was also fascinated by
demonstrative evidence—maps, aerial photographs, scale mod-
els, and scene photographs—and studied how these exhibits
were prepared by the crime lab. He learned that these exhibits
draw jurors into a case and enable them to better follow the live
testimony.

Bill Martin's self-education also included a study of psychiatry and the insanity defense. In 1964, he prosecuted a man who had committed armed robbery. Testifying for the defense was psychiatrist Marvin Ziporyn, M.D., who told the jurors that the robber did know the difference between right and wrong, but was unable to control his criminal actions because of an "organic brain syndrome." This was the first time Martin had heard of such a condition and he checked with his supervisor, Louis Garippo, chief of the criminal division. Garippo, it turned out, had started a collection of transcripts of Ziporyn's testimony. With amazing regularity, the psychiatrist was known to diagnose criminal defendants as being insane due to what he termed an organic brain syndrome.

Martin's psychiatric education moved to the graduate level in early 1965. On January 2 of that year, an eighteen-year-old University of Illinois freshman named Harrison Crouse was home on Christmas break visiting his family in their expensive tri-level home in fashionable Wilmette, a suburb north of Chicago. Crouse took his father's rifle and proceeded to shoot his mother as she cooked dinner, his father as he worked in the basement tool room, and his fourteen-year-old sister as she was writing a letter in her bedroom. Martin was on night call when the murders occurred, and he and a court reporter raced to the police station to obtain a confession.

When Martin spoke with Crouse, he found him strangely calm. A well-intentioned physician had given him a sedative. Informed of this, Martin decided to skip the questioning because he believed that any confession would run the risk of being thrown out as drug-induced. In the weeks that followed, Martin interviewed Crouse's neighbors and high school and college classmates and teachers. Their unanimous opinion was that Harrison was a wonderful boy with no psychiatric problems. So, when the defense attorney proposed that an impartial psychiatric panel be appointed to evaluate Crouse and report expert findings that would be *binding* upon both the State and the defense, Martin did not object. Firmly convinced that any panel would find Crouse competent to stand trial and legally responsible for the three murders, Martin jumped at the chance to have the defense bound by these findings.

One month later, the psychiatric panel unanimously reported that Crouse was not competent to stand trial because of a minor irregularity in the recording of his brain-wave activity. The lesson for the stunned Martin was painful but clear: Don't paint yourself into a corner by agreeing to be bound by the findings of a panel of psychiatrists. Instead, insist on the right to present *nonpsychiatric* evidence of sanity.

Martin's next exposure to the insanity defense happened in Watseka, Illinois, a small town surrounded by cornfields ninety miles south of Chicago. Roy Harper, an elderly man, had shot and killed his young wife. Wayne Clemens, the Iroquois County State's Attorney, believed that Harper would claim he was insane, and had prevailed upon Dan Ward to send down an ASA from Cook County. Martin got the assignment. Arriving in Watseka, Martin proceeded to interview everyone who knew Harper and to compile a Crouse-like biographical study of the defendant, with special emphasis upon whether or not the murderer had exhibited any evidence of insanity *before* the crime.

Martin had learned that if the claim of insanity exists only for the precise time period of the murder, it is a convenient claim of "insanity" that will not be easily accepted by a jury. To prevail, the prosecutor will have to demolish expert or psychiatric claims of insanity by calling in rebuttal witnesses who knew the defendant before the crime and who could document a lifelong pattern of normal behavior. If presented effectively, the words of ordinary people can counter the testimony of psychiatrists hired by the defense. Harper's attorneys decided not to risk the insanity defense before a small-town jury, doubting they'd get away with it. However, for Martin, it was another useful experience in developing a murderer's biography as the means to overcome a claim of insanity.

In early June 1966, State's Attorney Ward had assigned Martin to present a lecture on the requirements of the *Miranda* ruling to the entire office. Later, Martin repeated the lecture to police supervisors, concluding the talk by handing out *Miranda* warning cards he had prepared.

Two years of nonstop trial experience in the Big Top, supplemented by all he could learn in his spare time, had transformed Martin from a shy young man with a law degree into an adroit, seasoned, and steely prosecutor. By July 1966, Martin was ready to do battle with the man who had once declined to hire him, Public Defender Getty, who at age fifty-three was almost twice as old as Martin.

Bill Martin was ready to prosecute Richard Speck.

CHAPTER 20

Monday, July 18

It was Martin's job to reunite Corazon Amurao and Richard
Speck in a courtroom, and it would not be easy. Speck, a brutal
killer, had to be treated with great care legally for fear of having
him set free on a technicality. Cora, the surviving eyewitness,
had to be treated with great care psychologically for fear of having her repress her memory of the night of terror. Martin had
to both write Speck's biography and record Cora's memories,
and both Speck and Cora had to be shielded from the reporters.
Martin and everyone involved in the case were on edge.

Speck was entitled to be brought before a court with all due
speed, and Martin's boss, Dan Ward, was sensitive to a possible
claim that Speck was being held incommunicado and in leather
restraints at Cermak Hospital when he should have immediately been brought to court. Ward insisted that Speck face a
judge so that he could be advised of his legal rights and have
a lawyer appointed to defend him. In the Chicago of 1966, a
murder defendant was first taken before Judge Daniel J. Ryan
in the Felony Court for a preliminary hearing, to see if enough
evidence existed to hold the defendant for an investigation by
the grand jury.

The problem was Dr. William Norcross. The fiercely independent surgeon did not believe his patient was well enough to be taken to a courtroom. Norcross was not only fending off Ward, he was also being forced to stonewall the hundreds of reporters who were camped out on the front lawn of his hospital. To appease the reporters, Norcross agreed to hold two daily press conferences. At one P.M. on Monday July 18, Norcross faced a forest of cameras mounted on tripods and a sea of reporters surging forward from the hastily arranged lawn chairs on which they had been asked to sit. The veteran Chicago crime reporters on hand included Ray Brennan, Edmund J. Rooney, Art Petacque, and Bob Wiedrich. In addition, there were representatives from the major U.S. dailies and TV networks and from foreign nations, including Australia, Canada, France, Ireland, Japan, West Germany, and, of course, the Philippines. The reporter for the *Manila Chronicle* referred to the murders as the "Chicago Massacre." Others picked up on Coroner Toman's description: "The crime of the century." All were in a feeding frenzy for nuggets of news as Norcross walked out on the lawn to meet them.

Bald-headed and bow-tied, Norcross held up a single sheet of paper in his muscular surgeon's hands as he quickly explained that Speck was "anemic," was being kept in "isolation in soft restraints," and was unable to attend court. With that, Norcross turned his back and walked away from the frustrated reporters.

Awaiting Norcross in his first-floor hospital office were Bill Martin and a court reporter. Ward had ordered Martin to put Norcross and the Cermak staff psychiatrist, Albert Feinerman, "on the record" as to their reasons for not allowing Speck to go to court. Ward advised Martin, "Find out if they'll let the court go to his hospital room to advise him of his rights." Norcross was adamant that Speck's physical exhaustion precluded any legal proceedings and that the emotional trauma of any proceedings, whether in a courtroom or a hospital bed, would be physically harmful.

Norcross said, "Mr. Speck, who is currently in a state of physical exhaustion, is in no condition to comprehend or respond in a responsible fashion to any legal proceedings."

"How long will this condition last?" Martin asked.

The surgeon smiled and responded, "As my residents will tell you, I often state that a surgeon is an observer, not a prognosticator. Since Mr. Speck's medical condition can change in either direction at any time, such a prognostic statement is not indicated and will serve no useful purpose."

Martin turned to Feinerman and repeated the first question.

The staff psychiatrist responded, "I would say that Speck has intellectual impairment based on impaired memory, poor contact with reality, and disorientation. He would not be able to fully comprehend involved questions and his replies would be erratic, unpredictable, and, very likely, inappropriate."

Martin relayed these unbending medical opinions to Ward, who remained concerned about protecting Speck's legal rights. Ward telephoned Public Defender Getty and asked him if he would come down from his third-floor office in the Criminal Court Building to Ward's office on the second floor. Within minutes, Getty was sitting across from Ward's desk.

"Gerry," Ward began, "this fellow Speck doesn't appear to have any money. If his family doesn't hire a lawyer for him, you may want to be prepared to be appointed to defend him." Getty nodded solemnly. He realized he was about to begin the toughest case of his career. Returning to the third floor, Getty began to mobilize his own team of veteran trial lawyers. Speck, who only weeks earlier had pawned his watch to get drinking money and who had set out to rob the nurses of a few dollars in pocket change, would have the benefit of a million-dollar defense. The public defender's office was the equivalent of a large, specialized law firm, and if Speck had been billed at the usual hourly rates of most large legal firms the cost would have been astronomical.

Speck's legal case would feature an amazing cast of characters, and even as Ward and Getty talked, two of these characters were sitting in a nearby office. Experienced police investigators know that highly publicized crimes bring kooks out of the woodwork, often "hysteric confessors" who want to claim credit for the crime, but all such reports have to be checked. Garippo and Stamos were taking separate statements from a husband and wife who had arrived at the Criminal Court Building that morning to claim that Speck was innocent.

The couple, both of whom were unemployed, said that a man they were sure was Speck had spent the entire night of July 13 in their apartment on the city's north side. They reported that they had taken a homeless and hungry person into their home and that when they later saw Speck's photo in the newspapers they realized that he was this same man who had spent the night of July 13 at their home. There is a temptation to turn away volunteers telling incredible stories, but when it came to Richard Speck, nothing could be left to chance. The couple was interviewed by the two highest-ranking lawyers working for Dan Ward. Garippo and Stamos, both expert cross-examiners, gently probed the story to the point of collapse. Although the wife and husband contradicted each other on major points and had no factual basis for believing that their homeless guest was Speck, their names and addresses were recorded and later turned over to the public defender.

While strangers came out of nowhere to try to help the defense, the prosecutors hit the road. Martin chose Sergeant James R. Reilly, a scholarly vice officer, to lead a team of undercover investigators into the seamy streets and saloons of North Clark Street near the Raleigh Hotel, to pin down pimps and prostitutes on the identity of the mystery prostitute who had accompanied Speck to his room in the Raleigh in the early morning hours of July 15.

Assistant State's Attorney Bill Nellis was assigned to direct a team developing Speck's biography. A law school classmate of Martin, Nellis was tall, thin, and brilliant, and had inexhaustible energy and an insatiable zest for detail. He and his team of investigators wrapped up their work in Monmouth, Illinois in time to catch the Monday red-eye flight to Dallas to research Speck's years in Texas.

In one of the few instances where the press helped the prosecution, Martin had learned from news reports that Speck had spent the last week of June 1966 in Hancock, Michigan, visiting Judy Laakaniemi, one of the nurses who had helped him recuperate from his appendectomy. Martin put ASA Ken Gillis in charge of two police sergeants and a court reporter, and dispatched them to Michigan to gain Laakaniemi's perspective on what Speck was like only weeks before the murders.

Also on Monday, the remaining funerals were held. By coincidence, this day was the feast day for St. Camillus, the Roman Catholic patron saint of nurses. Mourners overflowed area churches to pay their final respects to Suzanne Farris, Mary Ann Jordan, Pat Matusek, Nina Schmale, and Pamela Wilkening. Chicago Archbishop John Patrick Cardinal Cody conducted the mass for Merlita Gargullo and Valentina Pasion, whose bodies were then flown back to the Philippines.

Alone of the nine nurses, Corazon Amurao would have a chance to see Speck again. On Monday morning, a team of doctors and nurses from South Chicago Community Hospital brought Cora to Cermak Memorial Hospital. For purposes of identification, Martin wanted to have Speck stand in a lineup with five other men of similar dress and size and have Cora view all six. Arrangements were under way to bring five men similar in appearance to Speck to the hospital. Norcross, however, insisted that his patient could not possibly stand the physical strain of being placed in a police lineup for identification. The confrontation was postponed.

However, Byron Carlile did show Amurao the revolver that Detective Ratledge had removed from Speck's room at the Raleigh Hotel and had finally inventoried. Although Cora was still frightened by the prospect of seeing Speck again, she betrayed no emotion, and responded tersely to questions. Deputy Chief Spiotto asked her, "Did you ever see this before?"

Cora: "Similar."
Spiotto: "When?"
Cora: "That night with the man."

This was the end of the questioning. Police did not want to pressure Cora's fragile psyche. By noon, she was returned to the security of the hospital.

Spread-eagled by soft leather restraints in his hospital bed, Speck himself spent a fitful and restless day.

Tuesday, July 19

Norcross again met the waiting press at a one P.M. news conference, and reported that Speck had developed an infection in his left arm, a frequent complication after intravenous medication is administered. He then returned to the hospital, where Corazon Amurao was being allowed to make a "medically supervised" visit to Speck's room to try to identify the killer, who sprawled dejectedly on his narrow cot.

Cora was brought to the jail hospital at one-thirty P.M. The plan was that Norcross and a Cermak nurse would accompany Cora, who was wearing her white nursing uniform, and Spiotto on a visit to Speck's room. Norcross told Cora, "Do nothing unusual . . . you are just a nurse making rounds with me." When they entered 324, Speck was with the hospital psychiatrist, Dr. Albert Feinerman. Norcross and Spiotto entered the room first, followed within minutes by Cora and the other nurse. Feinerman was still talking to Speck when Cora entered.

Cora remained in the room less than three minutes, not saying one word. She then walked out with the nurse, followed by Norcross and Spiotto. When she got ten feet from Speck's room, Cora said, "That is really him." Then she started to collapse. Detectives Carlile and Wallenda, both big burly men, were alertly walking next to her and kept her from falling. The detectives took Cora to Norcross's office, and after she regained her composure, she was ready to talk. Looking directly into Spiotto's eyes, the stoical Cora made clipped and precise answers to his questions:

> **Spiotto:** "Did you ever see this man before?"
> **Cora:** "Yes."
> **Spiotto:** "When?"
> **Cora:** "The night that it happened to the girls."
> **Spiotto:** "How did you recognize him?"
> **Cora:** "His face. When I opened the door, he was there. I am positive."
> **Spiotto:** "Anything else?"
> **Cora:** "His voice. He spoke softly."

By now, Dan Ward had found a way to protect Speck's legal rights, despite the suspect's inability to come to court and Norcross's refusal to allow the court to come to him. Ward had decided that he personally would appear before Judge Ryan at Tuesday's scheduled two-thirty P.M. arraignment to present Norcross's testimony that Speck was medically unfit to appear. He would also request that Public Defender Gerald Getty be appointed to represent Speck. Hobbling on crutches from a recently broken ankle, Ward came into court to carry out his responsibility.

Shortly after Ward, Martin, and Dr. Norcross arrived in Ryan's court on the fourth floor of the Criminal Court Building, the doctor was paged to take an urgent phone call in the judge's chamber. When he emerged moments later, he was asked to testify about Speck's medical status. Norcross told the judge, "It is inadvisable that any proceedings take place that may, in any way, excite the patient." Martin cut in to ask Norcross to precisely describe Speck's present condition. Norcross's answer shocked everyone in the jam-packed courtroom.

"The problem," he said, "is one of determining exactly whether the patient is or is not having a heart attack."

The phone call Norcross had taken in chambers was from the Cermak Hospital cardiologist who had reviewed the electrocardiogram (EKG) given to Speck earlier in the day after he had complained of chest pains. After reviewing the tracings of Speck's heart rhythms, the cardiologist reported to Norcross that he could not rule out a heart attack. Ward asked Judge Ryan to adjourn the case until an additional medical report could be made the following afternoon. Before granting the request, Ryan appointed Getty to represent Speck.

Anxious to talk to his new client, Getty convinced Norcross to allow him a medically supervised three-minute visit with Speck later that afternoon. Getty found that Speck was too out of it to have a meaningful conversation. Speck did, however, tell Getty he was glad to see him, a courtesy he did not extend to his brother, Howard Speck, who had arrived from Monmouth, nor to his brother-in-law, Gene Thornton. Speck refused to see either one of them and refused a visit from a minister.

At his five P.M. conference, Norcross told the reporters that there was an "eighty-percent chance" that Speck had suffered a heart attack. Speculation ran rampant that the brutal killer of eight would evade justice by succumbing to a fatal heart attack brought on by the awareness of the enormity of his crime. Martin began to wonder if there would be any need for the detailed investigation he was beginning.

His feelings were mixed. If there were no case, he could take a vacation, spend time with his family, and paint his parents' house. However, without a case, there would be no presentation in public of the proof of Speck's evil deeds. Martin was bothered by questions about the 1963 assassination of President John F. Kennedy that were never answered because Lee Harvey Oswald had been killed before the evidence about the assassination could be publicly tried. Vicious rumors were already spreading about Speck's murders—that he must have had accomplices, including Cora; or that he must have dated one of the nurses—rumors that could be effectively repudiated only in a public trial. If Speck were to die from a heart attack, the investigation would be stopped and the victims' families and the public at large would be denied the full knowledge and catharsis that comes from a public trial. Since Speck was still breathing, Martin had no choice but so continue the painstakingly thorough investigation of who Speck was and what he had done.

As this drama unfolded, the prosecution team assigned to track down Judy Laakaniemi ran into a roadblock. The nurse had hired a local attorney who was now telling the investigators that she was "psychologically unfit" to be questioned at this time.

Wednesday, July 20

Luckily, Martin didn't have long to worry about Speck escaping a trial. At that afternoon's court appearance, Norcross testified that Speck had improved slightly and that his EKG and blood workups indicated that if he'd suffered a heart attack it was a mild one. Norcross added that the problem might also be a minor heart condition. Judge Ryan appointed two eminent board-certified Chicago cardiologists to examine Speck and report back to the court. He then adjourned the case pending the medical reports.

Meanwhile, back in Michigan, prosecutor Ken Gillis was stopped by a local radio reporter who asked him if he had been given any reason for Judy Laakaniemi's refusal to talk. Gillis replied, "No valid reason," explaining that the reason given—that she was psychologically unfit—was contradicted by the fact that she was continuing to work as a nurse.

Gillis stepped up his efforts to contact the nurse, and finally resorted to driving ninety miles to ask her mother to convince Judy to cooperate. The mother had no interest in helping the prosecution. At nine o'clock Wednesday night, the tired team went to Laakaniemi's home, but she refused to open the door. "Judy," Gillis said, "I think that you are making a big mistake." The police sergeant with him added, "You'll regret this for the rest of your life." Rebuffed, the two left.

While Gillis and his team were being snubbed in Michigan, other investigators were turning the Raleigh Hotel upside down in search of evidence. This flophouse, where Speck had made his home the night after the murders, was destined to be a jinx for Martin and his team.

Already, faulty police work had cost the prosecution the use of the gun Speck had used to frighten his victims. The anonymous tip by an unknown prostitute that a man had a gun in his room was not a sufficient legal basis for the police to enter Speck's room. The Fourth Amendment to the U.S. Constitution prohibits entry into a person's home without a valid search warrant. The few narrow exceptions to this prohibition did not apply to the use of a passkey to enter a hotel room solely based upon the word of an anonymous source. Speck's home in the Raleigh, room 806, was no less his castle than a mansion on the

Gold Coast, and a man's castle cannot be legally breached upon the word of an unknown and uncorroborated informant.

This was too bad.

The gun that officer Robert Ratledge had seized from under Speck's pillow—and subsequently inventoried—was later traced from its serial number directly to Ella Mae Hooper, from whom Speck had stolen it. Corazon Amurao subsequently identified the gun as "similar" to the one Speck waved about in the town house. Speck had slept with this gun under his pillow at the Raleigh Hotel. The .22 caliber pistol was real evidence. It would have graphically demonstrated to a jury how and why Speck was able to subdue his captives. Regrettably, however, Ratledge's seizure of the gun was incontestably illegal.

Also at risk was the evidence of Speck's comportment on the morning of July 15, only twenty-four hours after the murders. Speck was clear-headed, engaging, and logical in his banter with Officer Ratledge, whose testimony of this conversation would have been a compelling rebuttal to a claim of insanity. However, were it not for Ratledge's illegal entry into Speck's room, he would not have observed Speck's evident sanity the day after he murdered. Along with the gun, Ratledge's potentially key testimony was seriously in question.

Martin, however, knew that the Raleigh Hotel had other evidence that could be seized with a valid search warrant. Otha Hullinger, the Raleigh night supervisor told the police that Speck did not have his tan suitcase or black jacket when he slipped out of the hotel that Friday night in search of a "laundromat." The suitcase and whatever secrets it might hold were still sitting in room 806.

Assistant State's Attorney Joel Flaum did the factor and legal work necessary to prepare a valid search warrant. Using Sergeant Vic Vrdolyak as his witness, Flaum appeared before a judge in the early evening of July 20 and presented sufficient probable cause to have a search warrant issued. Then, warrant in hand, Flaum and Vrdolyak sped to the dilapidated hotel to enter room 806.

They found Speck's tan vinyl suitcase, still overflowing with the portable wardrobe that was testimony to his fastidious need to constantly change into clean clothes. The suitcase contained the black corduroy jacket, twelve men's shirts of various styles and colors, three pairs of slacks, three pairs of shoes, seven pairs of socks, two pairs of work gloves, and one BVD T-shirt, size 38–40. The T-shirt was stained with blood. Tucked under the mattress were the July 15 editions of the *Chicago Tribune*, the *Chicago American*, and *Chicago Daily News*, all displaying big bold black headlines about the murders.

At ten that night, Flaum and Vrdolyak returned to the Criminal Court Building to meet with Bill Martin. Vrdolyak was beaming as he turned over the bloodstained T-shirt. However, Flaum, only twenty-nine and on his first criminal investigation, seemed to Martin to be strangely distressed about what appeared to have been a successful search and seizure. His pained expression starkly contrasted with the happy policemen in the room, who were thrilled with the recovery of the bloodstained T-shirt. After all, it was a perfect match to the size 38–40 BVD found in the living room of the town house the morning after the murders. Eventually, Flaum motioned for Martin to step outside with him. Once they were alone, Flaum said, "I'm not sure how the blood got on the T-shirt. Something may have happened when Vic (Vrdolyak) opened the suitcase."

In 1966, the state of the art of blood testing allowed typing only as to basic blood groups. If the blood on this T-shirt were found to be of the same type as one of the nurses, it was one more bit of evidence connecting Speck to the crime scene. However, the odds were strong that almost anybody's blood, including

Vrdolyak's, would be of the same basic type as one or more of the nurses.

In 1963, a federal judge in Chicago had ordered the release of a man sentenced to death for the rape/murder of an eight-year-old girl in central Illinois. During his closing argument, the impassioned prosecutor had waved the little girl's bloodstained shorts in front of the horrified jurors. Subsequently, however, a microanalyst testified for the defense that the "bloodstains" were actually "red paint." Both Flaum and Martin were aware that the federal judge had reversed the conviction and that the case was now before the U.S. Supreme Court. Drops of police blood could set Speck free.

Martin asked to see Vrdolyak alone. The Croatian sergeant was strong-willed and physically imposing. Martin patiently explained to him the story of how a killer went free because bloodstained shorts turned out to be paint-stained. "Vic," Martin finally asked, "do you know how the drops of blood got on the T-shirt?"

Vrdolyak hesitated. He was as astute as he was tough and had quickly picked up on the drift of Martin's warning. "Yeah, I know. I cut my finger opening the suitcase. It's my blood." Martin replied, "I want you to print that in bold letters on your report when you turn the shirt over to the crime lab." One month later, the Chicago Police crime lab microanalyst told Martin, "I'm sure that the blood on the T-shirt from the Raleigh would match the blood type of the victims, but I didn't test it. You know why? The copper's report says he cut himself opening the damn suitcase!"

The prosecution was well rid of the bloodstained T-shirt, but, unfortunately, the other evidence might now have to be sacrificed as well. Again, this was too bad. The Raleigh search warrant for the seizures of July 20 was legally sound. The black jacket connected Speck to the scene of the crime because it matched Cora's description of how he was dressed when he came to her door. The three newspapers tucked under the mattress proved a consciousness of guilt. Martin, however, was reluctant to use the suitcase evidence at trial. He worried about a counterattack by Getty that a policeman's blood on the T-shirt was part of an effort to frame Speck.

The Raleigh jinx continued. Sergeant James Reilly had exhausted all leads in his search for the mystery prostitute. Although many prostitute-pimp teams came forward either to try to claim a reward or to harass their competitors, nothing checked out. The leading suspect passed a lie detector test. The mystery prostitute had walked out of Speck's room onto Dearborn Street before dawn on Friday morning and disappeared forever into the darkness.

All the powerful real evidence from room 806 at the Raleigh Hotel—the prostitute, the gun, Speck's banter of sanity with policeman Ratledge, the newspapers, the black jacket, the T-shirt, and other clothing—was at risk of never being shown to a jury.

In the meantime, on July 20, the State's star witness and the key to any jury conviction, Corazon Amurao, was being reunited with her mother and cousin. For the terrified young Filipino, the visit was a godsend. For the State's Attorney's Office, it was a security nightmare. The visit was made possible by a fierce competition between the *Saturday Evening Post* and *Life* magazines for the right to give airline tickets to Marcario Amurao, Cora's fifty-year-old mother, and Rogelio Amurao, twenty-seven, Cora's cousin, to fly from Manila to Chicago. *Life* had offered the Amuraos two free round-trip tickets to Chicago with one condition: that a *Life* photograper be able to "discreetly" photograph the emotional reunion between mother and daughter in Chicago. The *Post*, imposing no such condition, won out and paid for Marcario and Rogelio Amurao to fly to Chicago via Honolulu and San Francisco. Cora's father, Ignacio, was not well enough to make the trip and stayed behind in Durangao to care for the other children. The *Post* asked only that Cora "think kindly of it" *when*, not if, she decided to sell her account of the sensational murders.

The unquenchable thirst of the media for Cora's extraordinary eyewitness account of the night of horror was on a collision course with Speck's right to be tried in a fair and impartial atmosphere. As Martin well knew, Cora's account of what had happened in the town house needed to be told first to a jury, not to a magazine. What Cora needed, Martin thought, was an environment free of prying reporters. The *Post* had compounded this problem by requiring that a safe haven be found for three persons instead of one. Cora, her mother, and her cousin were living in a small room at South Chicago Community Hospital, which was a crowded and unpleasant place for them and a difficult place for the prosecution to effectively guard.

Cora's untold story of the murders was easily worth hundreds of thousands of dollars to magazines, and probably even more in performance rights from Hollywood. Any such offers, which would provide lifetime financial security for the poor Amurao family, was something the State's Attorney's Office could not begin to match—or stop. To threaten Cora with contempt proceedings, to jail her for endangering the fairness of the trial process, would conflict with her First Amendment right to free speech. Trying to enjoin a magazine from publishing the story would mean going afoul of the constitutional proscription against prior censorship. More important, trying to jail Cora would not have been the best way to start the prosecution of Richard Speck. After what Cora had been through, who could blame her for telling the story to enable her family to rise above its poverty?

Cora's mother would be no help in making the decision. Marcario Amurao, whose inscrutable expression was carved in stone on her Malaysian face, was unsophisticated and terribly superstitious. Only an inch taller than her diminutive daughter, she was experiencing severe culture shock in Chicago, which was light years away from her tropical shanty in the primitive, rural town of Durangao. Rogelio Amurao, Cousin Roger, was small at five feet two inches and 120 pounds. He had a round smiling face and understood and spoke English, although with a heavy Tagalog accent. He had completed four years of a five-year mechanical engineering program at a Manila university when he was asked to drop everything to fly with his aunt, Marcario, to Chicago. He and Cora had grown up together in Durangao and were very close. However, he did not have the sophistication to deal with the controversy swirling about his cousin. Only Cora herself could decide whether or not she would sell her story to the highest bidder.

Thursday, July 21

In the first days of its investigation, the focus of the State's Attorney's Office was to reconstruct the life of Speck. Martin figured that there would be ample time later to get to know Cora, who at least was safely under police guard in the hospital room. He saw no need to protect Cora from a visit from Philippine Consul-General Generoso Provido, who arrived at her hospital room at six P.M. on Thursday, July 21. The consular official encouraged Cora to sell her story, setting the stage for a subsequent international incident.

At the same time, the beleagured State's Attorney's investigators in Michigan were running into more problems. On Thursday morning, Gillis found out that he had been sued for slander for his comment to the radio reporter that there was no "valid reason" for Judy Laakaniemi's refusal to be interviewed. The slander suit was widely publicized in Chicago, where the frustrated reporters were hungry for any news relating to the

Speck case. Gillis and his team were quickly recalled to the safety of Cook County. Stamos sardonically told Martin, "Speck's only been locked up a few days and now they're trying to lock up our lawyers!"

On Thursday night, the court-appointed cardiologists examined Speck and concluded that he had not suffered a heart attack. The problem was pericarditis, an inflammation of the sac surrounding the heart muscle, a condition caused by a virus. Speck was expected to make a full recovery, and the State was free to take its case against him to the grand jury.

CHAPTER 21

Monday, July 25

Confident that Speck was both physically healthy and legally well-represented, State's Attorney Dan Ward presented the case against him to the Cook County grand jury on July 25. The grand jury is a unique Anglo-Saxon institution, dating back to the thirteenth century when it was created as a means of protection against the arbitrary and capricious accusations that might otherwise have been made, and sustained, by the British monarchs. The gist of the idea then was that before any British citizen could be forced to stand trial on a serious charge, the twenty-three ordinary members of a grand jury had to listen to and be convinced by enough evidence to "indict" him. The grand jury returned a "no bill" if the case was weak and a "true bill" if the case was strong.

By 1966, in Cook County, Illinois, the grand jury was little more than a historical artifact. The twenty-three grand jurors, who were regularly selected and empaneled from among the county's three million residents, almost always returned indictments after hearing the evidence presented by the prosecution. The institution was still useful, however, because it allowed the prosecutor to gather sworn testimony in secret and before trial, without the barrier of cross-examination. The defendant also gained by being provided a transcript of this secret testimony. If a witness's grand jury testimony differed from his trial testimony, the defense could exploit this inconsistency on cross-examination.

Since 1929, the Cook County grand jury had convened in ornate fourth-floor chambers in the Criminal Court Building that featured cream-colored marble walls set off by black marble Roman columns. The effect caused one architectural critic to describe the grand jury room as resembling a "feverish dream out of the Arabian nights." While the decor was grandiose, the business was down-to-earth. By 1966, thousands of indictments for murder had been issued from this baroque room.

The State presented enough of its case against Richard Speck to the grand jury to result in eight separate true bills for murder. Moments later, hobbling on crutches and with his great shock of silver hair blowing in the summer breeze, Dan Ward met the waiting press. Without elaboration, he somberly announced the return of eight indictments for murder. Asked if the State would seek the death penalty, Ward, zealously guarding Speck's right to a fair trial, steadfastly refused to comment.

The State's concern over protecting the rights of the accused was prompting national debate and a backlash of public opinion. Truman Capote, author of the best-selling true-crime book *In Cold Blood*, told a Congressional committee that recent U.S. Supreme Court decisions were "paralyzing" the efforts of law enforcement officials. Editorials in the Chicago press thundered that it was crazy that Speck, a cold-blooded murderer, should have to be treated as if he had just arrived from Mars. On the other hand, U.S. Attorney General Nicholas Katzenbach said that the Chicago prosecutors were not being "overcautious" with Speck. "This is what the law now requires," the nation's top-ranking law enforcement official told the National Press Club.

Despite their skittishness, the prosecutors refused to cave in to a horror scenario being painted by the *Chicago Sun-Times*. In a screaming front-page "exclusive," the tabloid daily reported that Speck's indictment might be thrown out because it published his middle name as "Franklin," as opposed to the middle name given on his birth certificate, which was "Benjamin." First Assistant John Stamos said, "I refuse to believe that any argument over the middle name can obscure the fact that we have the right man."

That right man was recovering nicely from his heart problem. The alert Speck saw that his guards were making notes of his every movement. Martin had directed that a diary be kept of whether or not Speck exhibited bizarre behavior as he recovered in the jail hospital. Speck decided that two could play this game.

On July 24, after returning from the bathroom, Speck informed a note-taking guard: "I shitted two times and farted twice. Write that down." Continuing in this belligerent style, Speck later said to the same guard after he examined Speck's food tray: "Stop fucking with it. I don't have no gun in it." The next day he told the note-taking guard: "Hey, man, I wiggled my left toe. Hey, Officer, I scratched my left forearm with my right finger." Later, Speck asked "permission to go piss. I promise to shake twice." When he emerged from the bathroom, Speck said, "I'm sorry. I shook four times."

When Speck was first asked at the jail hospital for his occupation, he quickly replied, "Bum." When psychiatrist Albert Feinerman first approached him later on that same day to conduct an initial psychiatric appraisal, Speck shrugged him off with the curt dismissal, "I don't talk to nobody."

Speck decided to spend his time lolling in bed, smoking cigarettes, and reading true-crime and detective magazines. By July 29, Dr. Norcross believed that Speck was well enough to be transferred from the hospital to the Cook County Jail, a building one short block away. The transfer was treated as if it were a top-secret military maneuver. Nobody wanted a repeat of the Jack Ruby shooting of Lee Harvey Oswald in the basement of the Dallas city jail. Sixty armed deputies were stationed along the one-block route. Sprawled on the floor of the back seat, Speck was quietly driven from the hospital to the jail in an unmarked squad car.

That took care of any would-be assassins. Now, there remained the matter of the reporters. Norcross called a press conference on the hospital lawn and read a statement to the reporters swarming about him, emphasizing that Chicago was determined to avert an incident like the one in Dallas. He informed the disappointed reporters that even as they had been listening to him, Speck had been secretly transferred to his new home in the infirmary of the nearby jail.

Upon his arrival there, jail warden Jack Johnson found him to be "very friendly." Clearly, the enormity of his evil had not diminished Speck's cunning capacity to ingratiate himself when he thought it would serve his ends. He had acted "very friendly" in the town house, too.

As Speck recovered, the nonstop demands of the first weeks were shaping what came to be known as Team Speck. Bill Martin was slowly putting together the small permanent team that would be with him for the duration. Martin's resolve was galvanized during a midnight visit to the scene of the crime.

At midnight, July 26, he and three other Assistant State's Attorneys, George Murtaugh, Joel Flaum, and James Zagel, decided to see for themselves what the lighting inside the town house at 2319 had been like on the night of July 13–14. Escorted by detectives Carlile and Wallenda, the prosecutors explained their business to the two uniformed police officers who sat in a squad car guarding the town house entrance. The front door was still sealed with thick yellow tape. Wallenda cut the seal with his pocketknife and the five men entered the town house.

The lights were left off as the men slowly walked in the inky darkness up the stairwell to the second-floor bedrooms. Although he was accompanied by two armed detectives, Martin momentarily felt an eerie fear that the killer still stalked the upstairs. As they walked about, it was hard to believe that eight young women had lived and died in this small, boxlike building. But the proof was still lying at their feet. The northwest bedroom reeked with the stale odor of congealed blood. It was the commingled blood of Valentina Pasion and Merlita Gargullo, and it formed a large pool in the center of the floor.

The group next walked to the large south bedroom. Martin looked out the window and noticed that the water fountain in Luella Park was only a stone's throw from where he stood. Although it was a hot, muggy night, Martin suddenly shivered. As he walked about the town house, his heart hardened. Nothing, he resolved, would be left to chance in building the State's case against the killer. He was not alone in this resolve. The midnight visit jolted the police and State's Attorney's Office investigators into a new sense of purpose. When it came to bringing Speck to trial, all future dealings between police and prosecutors would be marked by unprecedented loyalty and respect. When the six men walked out the door into the darkness, they walked out as a team.

Team Speck consisted of four prosecutors, Martin, Murtaugh, Jim Zagel, and John Glenville, plus the many police officers who would be assigned to the State's Attorney's Office to facilitate the investigation and trial.

James Block Zagel came to the Speck assignment with impressive academic credentials. The holder of a bachelor's and master's degree in philosophy from the University of Chicago, he was a 1965 graduate of the Harvard Law School. He had joined the Cook County State's Attorney's Office only eight months earlier, where he had been working in the Brief

Department. Though a rookie, Zagel was extraordinarily bright and a consummate legal scholar. Olive-skinned, slender, and addicted to tennis, he had been blessed with an inquiring, skeptical mind, and he stared intensely out at the world through black-rimmed glasses. Among other interests, Zagel was fascinated with psychiatry, and he quickly became the resident intellectual of Team Speck.

The next man to sign on did not fit the classic mold of young Turk prosecutors. Missouri-born John F. Glenville, fifty-one, the father of five children, had been admitted to the bar in 1935, one year before Bill Martin was born. After spending twenty-two years as a distinguished special agent of the FBI specializing in complex criminal prosecutions, he retired in November 1965. The next day, he joined the State's Attorney's Office. Trimly built with thinning gray hair, Glenville wore glasses and an easy smile. Though he was nearly twice the age of his colleagues, Glenville did his job with soldierly loyalty and team spirit.

The third member was George J. Murtaugh, Jr., who went by the nickname "Duke." A second-generation Irishman from Chicago's South Side, Murtaugh stood a thin six-feet tall and looked every inch the basketball star he had been at St. Rita High School in Chicago and St. Mary's College in Winona, Minnesota. A boyish-looking twenty-six with close-cropped black hair and sparkling blue eyes, Murtaugh walked on the balls of his feet, always appearing to tip forward. Disarmingly candid, Murtaugh had an uncanny ability to understand and handle people. He knew when to be blunt and when to be diplomatic, and had enjoyed a meteoric rise in the State's Attorney's Office since being sworn in barely a year earlier.

William Martin, the leader of Team Speck, was a mixture of fire and ice. Like the scrappy, competitive hockey player he had trained himself to be, Martin was both earnest and energetic. A short man with clear, fair Irish skin, Martin hid his penetrating blue eyes behind thick glasses. He was diligent, quiet, unflappable, and hard to read. Some called him inscrutable, but everyone recognized his air of command and competency. He looked like an altar boy with his fresh-faced innocence, and dressed like a banker with his three-piece suits. By 1966, Martin had already acquired the reputation of being a brilliant young prosecutor. His devotion to the Speck case would fall just shy of mania. Married and the father of four young children, he tended to be careful and thoughtful, in contrast to the mercurial Murtaugh. His courtroom appearances were marked by a spare, understated elegance that was almost chilling in its devastating effectiveness.

The many Team Speck strategy sessions tended to be intense, informal, spontaneous. His mind detailed as a dictionary, Glenville would calmly puff on a pipe and search for answers. Though the youngest member of the team, Zagel was always dogmatic and frequently right. Murtaugh expressed his views with earthy brevity and the energy of a caged lion. Martin, always pacing the floor, dropped his grim courtroom demeanor for a self-deprecating sense of humor.

Glenville worried about the time lapses that slipped into his detailed chronologies. Zagel worried about missing time for tennis. Murtaugh worried about having to put off dinner. Martin worried about everything. He knew that he would have to make the tough decisions alone, and he constantly reminded his colleagues, "If we win this case, no one will remember us. If we lose this case, no one will ever forget us."

CHAPTER 22

Monday, August 1

Electricity was in the air as the city braced for Speck's first appearance in a Chicago court.

On guard were fifty armed policemen, lining every inch of the route Speck had to cover as he was led in handcuffs down the hundred-yard distance of the "boulevard," the underground tunnel connecting the jail with the Criminal Court Building. He was then taken by armed guards into a steel-barred elevator that sped him to the bullpen behind the fourth-floor courtroom of Judge Alexander J. Napoli.

Speck was getting used to special attention. In jail, one cook had been assigned solely to prepare his food and deliver it to the police sergeant who maintained a twenty-four hour guard over Speck's private room in the Cook County Jail infirmary. Still a little weak from his medical ordeals, Speck was assigned to the infirmary and checked daily by a physician. Nobody wanted him to be poisoned by a vigilante cook.

Judge Napoli, the long time presiding judge of the Criminal Court, was cherubic-faced, soft-spoken, and scholarly. Napoli had given strict orders that anyone entering his courtroom was to be thoroughly searched, including the families of the slain nurses. At precisely ten A.M., a column of deputy sheriffs opened the back door to the courtroom, and Speck slouched into the crowded room. He was dressed in the dark blue suit he had bought in Dallas and brought with him to Chicago, neatly folded in his tan suitcase. Since he had little use for it during his forays to Monmouth, Michigan, and the Southeast Side of Chicago, he had left it behind at the North Side apartment of his sister, Martha Thornton. She had brought it to the jail for him. It would become his one and only "court suit."

Throughout the trip from his jail bed to the courtroom, Speck had been furtively darting his eyes hither and yon, searching around corners for strangers. John Stamos explained, "This type of furtive behavior is typical of a hardened criminal. Speck knew that there might be eyewitnesses to his crimes and if they were around he wanted to get a look at them." In his later court appearances, Speck would stare intently at the female spectators, but during this first day in court he was clearly bewildered. Standing in front of Judge Napoli, his handcuffed hands held in front of him, he stared resolutely at the floor, refusing to look up.

Napoli asked, "Are you Richard Franklin Speck? You will have to speak up so I can hear you."

Speck, his face still riveted on the floor, replied softly, "Yes."

State's Attorney Dan Ward interjected, "Let the record show that the defendant answered in the affirmative."

The judge then inquired as to Speck's worldly estate. "Richard Franklin Speck," Napoli began, "will you look at the court, please, and answer a few of my questions. Do you have a bank account of any kind?"

"No."

"You do not? Do you own any real estate of any kind?"

"No."

"Do you own any stocks or bonds of any kind?"

"No."

"Do you have finances of any kind or any assets of any kind?"

"No."

"You are not in a financial position to hire a lawyer as your own counsel, is that correct?"

"Uh-huh."

Speck had arrived at Cook County Hospital after his suicide attempt with about ten dollars in his pocket. This was now the sum of his worldly goods and he was using it to buy cigarettes and soft drinks.

Since the case was now at the Felony Trial level, Napoli reappointed Getty to represent Speck and assigned the trial of the case to Judge Herbert J. Paschen. Speck was escorted to the lockup behind Napoli's court to await transfer to the prisoner's elevator that would take him to the lockup behind Paschen's court on the seventh floor. The entire episode before Judge Napoli had taken about five minutes. The crowd stirred, filing out of Napoli's courtroom, and began to mill for the public elevators that would take them to Judge Paschen's court, Speck's second stop of the day.

In a *cause célèbre*, the selection of the trial judge is critical. The terrible engine of criminal law can jump the track if the trial judge is not intellectually and temperamentally suited to the demands of high-profile litigation. The best umpire is needed for the seventh game of baseball's World Series; the best judge is needed for cases like Speck's.

Herbert Paschen was the right judge.

At sixty-one, Paschen was six-feet-one-inch tall and solidly built. He stood ramrod straight, wore black horn-rimmed glasses, and sported a full head of thick white hair. He looked, in fact, like a movie star. A man who spoke in an authoritative and firm voice, the judge preferred to reason with attorneys rather than try to intimidate them. The grandson of a German immigrant who founded a hugely successful Chicago construction company,

Paschen had graduated from the Northwestern Law School in 1928. During the next thirty-two years, he had enjoyed immense success as an attorney and judge, and also as a politician in Chicago's mighty Democratic machine under Mayor Daley.

In 1956 he was elected treasurer of Cook County, and in 1960 he was the Democratic Party's candidate for governor of Illinois. However, a flap over a $29,000 "flower fund" in the treasurer's office forced him to withdraw from the gubernatorial race. Even though a subsequent bar investigation found him completely blameless, Paschen had turned his back on politics and was concentrating on being a good judge. Paschen believed that every defendant coming before him was entitled to the fairest possible trial. A prosecutor regularly assigned to Paschen's court once said, "If you can't get a fair trial before Judge Paschen, you can't get a fair trial, period." One public defender who frequently worked with him added, "Judge Paschen is a law man. He will rule on the law, not on his own emotions." Cultured and genteel, Paschen loved gardening and travel, and was devoted to his wife, Helen, and their two children and six grandchildren. When he gave fatherly advice to young lawyers, he liked to refer to himself as "Grandpa."

At eleven A.M., Speck shuffled out of the seventh-floor lockup, his eyes still riveted on the floor, and was led before the silver-haired patrician who would now control his fate. The prisoner's greasy hair was combed straight back from his narrow, pockmarked, sallow face with its large nose. At Speck's side stood fifty-three-year-old Gerald Getty, the Public Defender and a man who, like Paschen, had been disappointed by the surprises of Chicago politics. In Getty's case, though, the disappointment arose from not being appointed a judge— dashing a lifelong ambition. Getty had subsequently thrown his considerable talents and energy into running the Public Defender's Office.

A dapper dresser who wore his red hair combed back in a pompadour, Getty had been a public defender since 1946 and chief of the office since 1955, supervising thirty attorneys and four investigators. He was a Chicago native and had graduated from Mt. Carmel High School and De Paul Law School, also Mayor Daley's alma mater. Getty hid his shrewdness behind an easygoing folksy style. He was very good at working with the press and prided himself on having never lost a client to the electric chair. Getty had tried 402 death-penalty cases and not once had his defendant been sentenced to death. Speck, of course, posed a major challenge to this unbroken record of success.

He was getting this chance because of an act of conscience that had cost him a judgeship. When Daley had appointed Getty as Public Defender in 1955, the all-powerful mayor had made the pledge, "If you're out there a while and you do a good job, we'll make you a judge." Getty had the Circuit Court in mind. However, the mayor later revoked his promise because he disagreed with Getty's independence in handling a politically sensitive 1959 case. Gerald Getty would never become a judge. Now, determined to do a good job for a notorious client, Getty stood beside Speck and pleaded his client "Not guilty." Martin watched Getty carefully. He had never tried a case against the ingenious Public Defender. In fact, the last time Martin had seen Getty was four years earlier when Martin had wanted the job of Assistant Public Defender. Martin still didn't know why Getty hadn't hired him.

The appearance before Paschen, like the one before Napoli, only took about five minutes. Getty requested time to file some preliminary pretrial motions and Paschen concluded the perfunctory arraignment by scheduling August 18 as the date for Getty to file the motions. Speck shuffled back to the lockup. His eyes had remained on the ground throughout the proceedings.

Had he looked back and up at the ornate courtroom, he would have seen an impressive sight befitting the magnitude of the charges. The double entrance oak doors to the courtroom were framed in black marble. The cream-colored marble walls were paneled in dark antique oak, in contrast to the gleaming golden oak of the spectator benches. The lawyers' tables were trimmed with brown rosettes and set off with high-backed mahogany-brown leather chairs. The spectator benches were called "the hard seats," to distinguish them from the soft chairs in which trial participants sat.

The ceiling was a wondrous sight with its various panels hand-painted in a wild color scheme that intermingled pale blue, vermillion, and Paris green. The basic idea was an imitation of the Acropolis in Athens, but it was open to anyone's interpretation. Judge Paschen's chambers were entered through a leather-covered richly decorated swinging door that opened into a spacious office. The private bathroom and shower were encased in seven-foot-high, dark gray marble.

The entire Criminal Court Building, in fact, was a study in garish architectural eclecticism. One critic observed, "As you go from room to room you never know if you're in an Egyptian tomb or a Hollywood set from the 1920's." For the lawyers who plied their trade here, though, the decor was a historically rich backdrop for the drama of their work.

Now, Richard Speck was being added to the building's rich history. His initial appearance over, he was led down the tunnel and returned to his dingy room in the jail infirmary.

As keenly anticipated as it was, Speck's dramatic appearance in court was pushed to the bottom of the front page in the August 2 headlines. As Speck stood before Judge Paschen, college student Charles Whitman climbed to the observation platform atop the twenty-seven-story administration building tower on the campus of Texas University in Austin. Whitman carried with him a footlocker packed with an arsenal of weapons and provisions of food and water. Opening fire with his automatic weapons, the berserk rifleman killed sixteen and wounded thirty-one, including students, young children, and a pregnant woman. Wounded victims lay for hours in the 98-degree heat before police snipers shot the crazed killer.

Before beginning this rampage, Whitman, aged twenty-five and just a few months older than Richard Speck, stabbed his wife to death and shot and killed his mother. He left behind a note saying that he wanted to spare them the "embarrassment" of what he was about to do. The crime seemed out of character for Whitman, who had been an altar boy, a newspaper boy, an Eagle Scout, a scoutmaster, a U.S. Marine, and a model husband. His father was a hard-working and successful plumbing contractor and his mother was known for her church work. Whitman himself was a driven success and was thought of as a solid family man. Somehow, he snapped.

Subsequently, it was learned that Whitman had warned the campus psychologist that he was under intense internal pressure. The psychologist described Whitman as "oozing with hostility." Only thirty days before ascending the tower, Whitman learned that his parents were separating. He also was found to be in hock for heavy gambling debts. Most significantly, an autopsy found that he suffered from a brain tumor the size of a pecan, which was causing him excruciating headaches.

Whatever his reasons for snapping, though, why had Whitman decided to kill perfect strangers? Were the heavily publicized Speck murders a factor in his lashing out against society?

Chicago psychiatrist Jules Masserman, M.D., an expert in the criminal mind, was asked this question by the *Chicago Tribune*. His answer: "Maybe."

Elsewhere, American B-52 bombers continued to cross the DMZ and pound North Vietnam. Lynda Bird Johnson, daughter of President Lyndon Johnson, and actor George Hamilton attended a rehearsal for the marriage of her sister, Luci Baines Johnson, to Pat Nugent, a student at Marquette College in Milwaukee. Lenny Bruce, the comedian Martin refused to prosecute, died of a drug overdose.

CHAPTER 23

The State's case depended upon its eyewitness, Corazon Amurao, and protecting her ability to testify was Martin's biggest worry. Martin had no idea how Cora would react to pressure, and she certainly was under pressure. At age twenty-three, Cora was a sheltered young nurse only three months removed from a rural hamlet in the Philippines, and already she was being forced to make some big decisions. Josephine Chan, the director of nursing at South Chicago Hospital, was a woman with the temperament of a Marine sergeant, and she was pressuring Cora to return to her nursing duties so she would not become "spoiled." Cora was also caught in a conflict between the consular officials of the Philippine government, who wanted her to sell her exclusive story, and the State's Attorney's Office, which wanted her to remain silent until after Speck's trial. Martin decided to take a crash course in Philippine history and to get to know the eyewitness who was the heart and soul of his prosecution.

On May 1, 1966, Cora had left her world of the Orient to make her first plane trip, a long transoceanic flight to Chicago. Chicago was, in every way, a long way from the Philippines. Christened for King Phillip II of Spain, the 7,100 islands of the Philippine Archipelago were under Spanish rule for 333 years until the U.S. defeated Spain in the Spanish-American War of

1898. The "Pearl of the Orient," as the archipelago is known, sits at the crossroads of the Pacific Ocean and the South China and Sulu seas. By 1966, its population was a human menagerie of different peoples, and its culture was a blend of Malay, Madrid, and Madison Avenue. The country looked as if it had spent three hundred years in a Spanish convent and the last fifty years in Hollywood.

Cora grew up in the tiny agricultural village of Durangao in Batangas Province, fifty miles south of Manila. She was born on March 26, 1943, the apex of the occupation by the Japanese Imperial Army. The American troops had surrendered at Corregidor in May 1942, and the Bataan Death March soon followed. However, by the time Cora was two years old, the resurgent U.S. forces had demolished the Japanese Armada in the Battle of the Bismarck Sea and had captured Guadalcanal after a ferocious battle. As promised, General Douglas MacArthur would return in triumph to Manila in 1945.

Although the Philippines were granted independence on July 4, 1946, the American influence continued to grow. When Cora began the first grade of school in her tiny village, English was taught as the second language. Her native language was Tagalog, an Austronesian language that means "native to the river." The language has a seventeen-letter alphabet with three vowels and is notable for its complexity. To foreign ears, it sounds singsong and high-pitched.

In 1966, the Tagalog were the second largest cultural/ linguistic group in the Philippines and were the dominant group in and around the capital city of Manila. For more than five hundred years, the Tagalog had served as mediators for the Chinese, Spanish, and Americans, helping these foreigners adapt to the island's basic Indo-Malayan social patterns. At the same time, they sharply resisted any alien economic and political control. In the countryside, the Tagalog were mainly farmers who grew rice in diked, flooded fields. The principal cash crops were coconut and sugar cane. In urban Manila, the Tagalog were the leading force in education and finance.

Batangas Province is close to the Verde Island passage between the islands of Luzon and Mindoro. Although it rests on volcanic land, the province is picturesque with rolling hills, gentle slopes, clear mountain streams, and lush valleys dotted with palm trees. Coconut, mangoes, rice, and sugar flourish in the year-round tropical climate. Cora's father, Ignacio Amurao, ran a small clothing store in Durangao, while his wife, Macario, struggled to raise eight children in their primitive agricultural community. Cora grew up as a bright, hard-working girl who enjoyed the simple pleasures. She was fun-loving, open, and deeply religious.

In 1959, Cora left her small village to study nursing at the bustling Far Eastern University in densely populated Manila. She graduated, passed her licensing examinations, and became a registered nurse in 1964. She then left Manila's urban sprawl to work for eight months at San Sebastian General Hospital in Lipa City. This town, located on a 1,000-foot plateau that provides an invigorating cool climate, was known as the "Rome of the Philippines" because of its baroque cathedral dating to the seventeenth century and its many churches, convents, and seminaries. While in Lipa City, Cora was courted by Romeo Reyes, her first boyfriend. The romance cooled when Cora began to doubt Romeo's long-term commitment. She returned to the Far Eastern University as a staff nurse and worked for a year in Manila. During this time, she learned from agents representing American hospitals that Filipino nurses could enter the U.S. as exchange visitors for up to two years. Excitedly, she signed up and flew to Chicago.

In 1966, the ties between the Philippines and the U.S. were very close. The Philippines were the site of several strategic

American military bases, and the U.S. was a strong supporter of Ferdinand Marcos, who had been elected president in 1965 and was solidly entrenched in power. Because of the military importance of the islands, the Philippine Embassy in Washington, D.C., was influential, and there were Philippine consulates in major American cities. In Chicago, Consul-General Generoso Provido was the ranking consular officer. As the representative of Marcos's government, Provido was responsible for the well-being of all Filipino nationals in Chicago. In 1966, this responsibility included a nurse population that numbered 325 at Cook County Hospital alone.

On July 15, 1966, the day after the murders, Provido was allowed to see Cora briefly in her private room at South Chicago Community Hospital. The consular official told her that he was there to help her. On Thursday night, July 21, Provido offered his help when he visited Cora with a Filipino attorney, who practiced law in Chicago and whose father still lived in the Philippines. Provido was convinced that Cora was about to choose from among a bonanza of competing financial offers for her exclusive story, and he saw a consular duty to her as a Filipino citizen to help her pick the best. With Provido's blessing, the Filipino attorney told the Amuraos about the services he could provide them in negotiating the most lucrative deal from among the many offers, and assured them that they would need a Filipino attorney knowledgable in the wily ways of American commerce. He was thoughtful enough to bring a contract that would pay him twenty-five percent of any royalties earned from Cora's story. In handing the twenty-five-percent fee agreement to Cora, the attorney graciously told her, "You don't have to sign it now. We'll return tomorrow at eleven A.M." Later that night, Provido began to have misgivings about the twenty-five-percent fee. He called Cora to inform her that if she thought the fee was "a little high," she should ask the attorney to reduce it when they returned in the morning. Word of the contract reached hospital officials, who notified First Assistant John Stamos. The fair-minded Stamos said that the hospital should arrange for Cora to have independent legal advice without any fee. The hospital agreed, setting the stage for a showdown.

Cora chose as her own attorney John P. Coghlan, who also represented South Chicago Community Hospital. An ex-prize-fighter, Coghlan was an intrepid and robust trial attorney who had fiercely represented his clients during decades of defending celebrated cases. While his common sense and fatherly manner would endear him to Cora, his courage and tenacity would enrage Provido and his consular assistants.

Coghlan arrived at the right time—ten A.M. on Friday morning, July 22. Upon Coghlan's arrival, hospital officials called Provido and told him that Cora had an attorney and did not need the Filipino attorney he had brought to her the previous night. Philippine Vice Consul Rosalinda DePerio jumped in her car and sped from the Loop consulate offices to the hospital, where she met the Filipino attorney, who had also rushed to the hospital to protect his hefty fee. Citing "doctor's orders," the hospital's executive director refused to allow either DePerio or the attorney to see Cora. DePerio hotly disputed this excuse, since she had twice visited Cora earlier in the week. The hospital director stood firm, however, and Rosalinda DePerio called Provido to come to the hospital and resolve the impasse.

While DePerio and the attorney cooled their heels waiting for the consul-general, Coghlan continued to meet privately with Cora and set the stage for a confrontation with the government of the Philippines. After Provido arrived, Coghlan emerged from Cora's room and the two men met in the hallway. The brawny, stubborn Coghlan towered over the elfin diplomat. In a booming baritone, Coghlan told Provido, "You can't see her. You have to talk to me." Provido argued that his government had a treaty with the U.S. that guaranteed him the right to see Filipino nationals at any time and the right to arrange for their legal representation. In spite of this impressive claim, the old prizefighter would not back down.

Shaking off this alleged breach of international law, Coghlan refused to let the consular officials enter Cora's room. When the hospital administrator backed Coghlan's position, the enraged Provido and DePerio and the disappointed attorney had no choice but to leave.

Returning to the consulate, Provido called the Philippine Embassy in Washington, D.C., and was assured that he had an absolute right to see Cora whether she liked it or not. The embassy added that it would carry Provido's complaint to the U.S. State Department. The next morning, July 23, Provido called a press conference to allege that the U.S.-Philippine treaty had been violated. State's Attorney Dan Ward dispatched a court reporter to transcribe his remarks. Everyone wondered what Provido would do next, and they didn't have to wait long. Charging that Cora was being held incommunicado, Provido had the attorney file that very day a writ of habeas corpus demanding that Cora be made available to him.

In reply to this legal summons, John Coghlan produced a written statement, signed by Cora, stating that he was her personal attorney; that he was authorized to appear on her behalf to oppose the writ; and that any judicial proceedings affecting her and instituted by anyone other than Coghlan were unauthorized.

This was only half of it. Coghlan also released a further statement from Cora, reading:

"It is my desire to make it clear that the memory of dear colleagues is of such a character that I do not want to have it tainted by the acceptance by me of money or other personal benefit."

Signing these sweeping documents in the face of enormous pressure from her own government and in the face of the enormous sums being offered by America's pocket-book journalists was an act of great courage by the young nurse. The Amurao family, simple rural people, were risking the wrath of President Marcos and throwing away a windfall of instant wealth.

The international incident was still simmering, though. On Monday, July 25, Provido telephoned Daniel Ward to complain that he could not meet with Cora. Ever the canny lawyer, Ward asked Provido to state his position in writing. As anticipated, Provido responded by immediately dispatching a letter citing the relevant sections of the Consular Convention between the United States and the Philippines:

"Consular officers of either High Contracting Party shall, within their respective districts, have the right to interview, to communicate with, and to advise nationals of their country; to inquire into any incidents which have occurred affecting the interest of such nationals; and to assist such nationals in proceedings before or relations with authorities in the territories of the other High Contracting Party. . . ."

The treaty was quite clear in giving Provido an absolute right, sanctioned by international law, to see Cora. The U.S. State Department began working feverishly behind the scenes to end the impasse. As the incident played out, diplomacy was exercised on both sides. The consular officials distanced themselves from the earlier efforts to help Cora get rich. Once Cora had made it clear that she would not sell her story, Coghlan relaxed his ban against consular visits.

On July 29, the Philippine Embassy in Washington, D.C., sent former ambassador Amelito Mutec to Chicago, and he was allowed to visit Cora for fifteen minutes. Afterward, he made a conciliatory statement: "I wanted to see if she were being held against her wishes as some had reported. It is not true." This visit was followed by an August 4 visit with Cora by Jose Naldo, the Labor Attaché from the Philippine Embassy. After his visit, Naldo telephoned Martin to ask three worrisome questions:

"Could financial arrangements be made to allow Cora's mother and cousin to return to the Philippines immediately and come back to Chicago at the time of the trial? Could Cora herself stay at the Philippine Embassy in Washington until the trial? Could Cora return to the Philippines by the end of December?"

Martin, a Midwestern boy who was receiving a crash course in international diplomacy, invited Naldo to a dinner in his honor to discuss these questions. Put in charge of arranging the "State Dinner" for Señor Naldo was Assistant State's Attorney Jim Zagel, whose previous entertainment experience had been confined to occasionally buying a witness a cheeseburger. Zagel rose to the occasion, however, and reserved a window table at Café LaTour, a pricy French restaurant located forty stories above Lake Shore Drive. Accompanied by Joel Flaum and George Murtaugh, Martin picked up Naldo and drove him to the Outer Drive East, the high-rise building that was crowned by Café LaTour. Zagel stood smiling in the lobby. All was in order to put the distinguished visitor in the elevator and treat him to a memorable dinner above a magnificent nighttime view of Chicago and Lake Michigan. Naldo, alas, suffered from a medical condition that prevented him from taking an elevator to any great height. One of his associates pulled Martin aside to explain the snafu. While the group stood around and made small talk, Zagel ran to a phone and arranged for a proper table at the Red Carpet, an elegant restaurant located on the first floor of a nearby North Side brownstone.

Once settled in for dinner, Naldo grilled the four young prosecutors about American criminal procedures and about what evidence had been developed against Speck. The prosecutors, in

turn, emphasized the overriding importance of Cora's cooperation and continued presence in Chicago. Accepting the prosecutors' unyielding position that a successful case required Cora to
be in protective custody, Naldo returned to the embassy without breaking off diplomatic relations with the U.S. The international incident subsided, and with it the potential legal disaster
of Cora's story being sold to the highest bidder.

It was now Martin's job to begin to learn that compelling
story. He knew that he would need an interpreter to help Cora
learn to trust him.

On July 23, while Consul-General Provido was holding his
press conference to complain that Cora was being held hostage,
an important meeting was taking place in an office at South
Chicago Community Hospital. Bill Martin and his colleague,
Joel Flaum, were meeting with John Coghlan and a petite, styl-
ishly dressed dark-haired woman whom they hoped would help
bridge the gap between the State's Attorney's Office and the surviving eyewitness to the murders. Martin had asked Flaum to
find a Filipino translator who would act as both interpreter and
companion for the Amurao family. Working with the U.S. State
Department, Flaum located Myrna Foronda, a native Filipino
fluent in both English and Tagalog and the holder of a degree
in philosophy. Foronda was highly motivated, intense, sophisticated, and shrewd. She was planning to stay in the U.S. and was
hoping that her husband, a licensed physician who was also a
Filipino native, would be granted permanent-resident alien status.

Foronda agreed to work with the State's Attorney's Office.
Her instructions were to visit with Cora and try to establish a
rapport that would allow her to obtain Cora's detailed account
of the murders, as rendered in Tagalog. Foronda's first visit
with Cora was to be that very Saturday afternoon, a time at
which Cora was caught in a crossfire of conflicting advice from

Provido, Coghlan, hospital officials, and her fellow Filipino nurses. However, since Myrna Foronda was introduced to her as a representative of the men whose only objective was to gain justice for her slain colleagues, Cora decided to trust her. For the next three days, Foronda met with Cora in her small hospital room and gently probed for the nurse's account of the night of terror. After the third day, on July 26, Foronda had compiled a spiral notebook containing twenty-two pages of handwritten notes and town house diagrams. At seven P.M. that night, she was driven to Martin's office, where he was having dinner—a carton of skim milk and a peppermint patty.

Foronda handed the notebook to Martin, who, wide-eyed with wonder, slowly read the dramatic report. When he finished, Martin knew without a shadow of a doubt that Cora's account was a convincing and thorough narrative of the mind and method of a mass murderer, an account that was unique in the annals of criminal justice. Foronda, an intelligent professional interpreter, betrayed no emotion over the contents of her translation. She had been sworn to secrecy when she took the assignment and kept whatever feelings she had about the crimes to herself. Martin thought that Cora's eyewitness narrative was a devastating rebuttal of any claim that Speck was insane at the time of the crimes. The way in which he first lulled the girls into submission with a combination of charm and gun-clicking, and then the precise and purposeful way in which he hid each violent murder from the girl to be murdered next by closing the bedroom doors and washing his hands of blood, was more macabre than anything in *Macbeth*, a work with which Speck certainly was not acquainted. Martin, on the other hand, was acquainted with *Macbeth*, and the image of Speck's cleansing himself of the blood of the nurses began to haunt him.

The notebook was a gold mine. The story it told would not only help prove that Speck was the murderer, but would prove in graphic and powerful detail precisely how he had killed. Although excited about this breakthrough, Martin still worried. For Cora to speak in Tagalog to Myrna Foronda in the quiet of her hospital room was one thing; telling the world in a crowded courtroom with Richard Speck staring at her might be quite another.

Martin sealed the notebook in an envelope, put the envelope inside a folder, and placed the folder in a locked filing cabinet to which only he had the key. No copies were made and the Foronda notes would remain locked in this special hiding place. If those notes got to the press before trial, the prosecution would have great difficulty in finding a jury untainted by the sensational publicity of Cora's eyewitness account of a mass murder. After locking up Foronda's explosive report, Martin made his midnight visit to the town house. With Cora's description, as detailed in Foronda's notes, still ringing in his ears, the prosecutor felt an eerie chill as he retraced Speck's movements in the upstairs killing fields.

Bill Martin met Cora for the first time on Saturday morning, July 30. Myrna Foronda was there to break the ice for what might have seemed a light conversation about American TV, hospital food, and how "Mama," and "Roger," as Cora's mother and cousin would come to be known to their protectors, were adjusting to life in the United States. In fact, the conversation was anything but light. Throughout the small talk, the worried Martin was acutely afraid of making a mistake that would cost him the testimony of the key to his case.

The next afternoon, Martin returned with Foronda and Detective Jim Georgalas to take Cora on a sight-seeing trip on Lake Shore Drive. Georgalas, forty-four, was tall, slender, and handsome. A native of Chicago's West Side, he had spent four years in combat in the Pacific Theater of World War II, including one year in the Philippines as part of General MacArthur's recapture of the islands. He had worked as a redcap for the Rock Island Railroad during the last great days of rail travel. After joining the Chicago Police Department in 1953, he had served as a homicide detective before being assigned to the State's Attorney s Office in 1962.

This odd group of strangers gathered at the hospital and proceeded north on the Drive to Montrose Harbor on the North Side of the city. Only six years older than Cora, Martin found her to be endearingly unsophisticated and childlike in her openness and enjoyment of simple pleasures. The cultural differences between the twenty-three-year-old Cora and a twenty-three-year-old American girl were striking. Cora laughed easily and without pretense.

On the next Friday, August 5, Martin, Foronda, and Detective Georgalas returned to the hospital to take Cora, Mama, and Roger for a drive to Milton Olive Park, a grassy area adjoining Navy Pier at the lakefront just north of the Loop. The park had just been named in honor of the young black man who was one of Chicago's first soldiers to be killed in the Vietnam War. This was Mayor Daley's way of demonstrating solidarity with President Johnson, who was already beginning to take heat for the unpopular war.

As the group enjoyed a picnic of fried chicken, Cora frankly described her hopes and fears. In a memo Martin wrote the next day to Stamos and Ward, he summarized Cora's predicament this way:

> "1. Cora wants her mother and cousin to stay with her until they can return to the Philippine Islands together.
> "2. Cora does not feel well enough to work in the hospital at the present time. She is frightened of making mistakes.

"3. Cora wants to leave the hospital and the Southeast Side. She would like to live with her mother and cousin in an apartment in a different neighborhood.

"4. Cora does not want to see any representative of the Philippine government.

"5. Cora is frightened to be anywhere without a police guard."

It was only that afternoon that Martin learned how Josephine Chan was pushing Cora to return to work, believing that the work routine would take Cora's mind off the case. She also believed that Cora must not be coddled or pampered. As he ate his picnic lunch, Martin wrestled with the nagging questions of how Cora, her mother, and her cousin could best be kept occupied during the many months before trial, and whether Cora should be forced to continue working. The answers were not in any law book.

Martin decided to seek advice from an unusual source—William H. Haines, M.D., the director of the Criminal Court Behavior Clinic since 1941. A short, stocky tree trunk of a man with gray hair, shaggy white eyebrows, and a raspy voice, Haines had finished his training in psychiatry in 1933 and was board-certified in both neurology and psychiatry. An avid student of criminology, Haines had examined thousands of criminal defendants. Somewhat of a character, he always testified in a blue suit, unshined shoes, and a tie spotted with his last meal. Asked about how he conducted his complex and revelatory inquiries into the criminal mind, Haines would reply tersely: "My examination consisted of questions and answers."

The quirky, older psychiatrist and the serious young prosecutor had become good friends. They both were regulars at Reback's Pharmacy, an old-fashioned drugstore on the southeast side of Oak Park, where they drank milk shakes at a marble-topped table and talked about psychiatry and the law. Mostly,

Martin respected Haines's integrity. On Sunday morning, August 7, Martin called Haines to ask if he could stop by the doctor's house. "Come over," was the crisp reply. Martin had never called Haines's home before. Haines knew that the reason for the visit must be important. Martin rang Haines's doorbell thinking that, maybe, Josephine Chan was right. Maybe, he *was* treating Cora too tenderly. Perhaps, the best thing was to put her back to work.

The two sat in Haines's study, surrounded by floor-to-ceiling bookcases and the Sunday papers that were strewn all over the coffee table. Martin described his dilemma to Haines, thinking that the crusty tough-minded doctor would be the last person to put up with coddling anybody. Suddenly, Haines interrupted Martin's fumbling questions: "There's no way on earth," Haines said, "that you can be too kind to this girl. She has been through a trauma that defies description. It's crazy to make her work in that hospital. She should not have to work or worry about anything until this case is over."

Sensing that Martin was surprised by this advice, Haines became uncharacteristically talkative and emphatic: "Look, if you're not careful, this girl can lapse into psychosis or a situational reaction that will put her in a sanitarium. She can repress her memory of that night and never be able to talk about it."

Martin suddenly realized the danger of his position. He asked Haines if he thought Cora was becoming too dependent upon her interpreter, the strong-willed Myrna Foronda. Haines cut through the uncertainty: "You should be grateful," he said, "that she is relying emotionally on someone connected with you. You should make the interpreter a part of your office for this case."

Haines's final words cinched the outcome. "Don't worry about spoiling the girl," the psychiatrist said. "That's impossible. She can't have too much kindness." Never before had Haines been so loquacious and emphatic. As Martin walked out the door, he was formulating an unorthodox solution: Cora, Mama, and Roger would have to be moved—without delay—from the hospital to a safety zone.

Monday, August 8

The day after listening to Dr. Haines's advice, Martin had a plan ready to "kidnap" the Amurao family and take them away from the stifling and frightening atmosphere of their hospital room and hide them in a fifteen-acre resort located on Lake Michigan in Highland Park, a suburb twenty-five miles north of Chicago. The Moraine-on-the-Lake Hotel had a spectacular natural setting, with its main lodge nestled in heavy woodland and its rooms facing a private sandy beach just beyond a large outdoor swimming pool. The resort had been built in the grand manner during the 1920's on Sheridan Road, then the major thoroughfare between Chicago and Milwaukee.

Martin reserved two large adjoining suites on the third floor of the main lodge, using fictitious names for the Amurao family and Jim Georgalas and Jack Wallenda, the two police officers he had chosen to guard them around the clock. Wallenda, the father of eight children, had been a sergeant in the U.S. Army Tank Corps from 1944–1946 and had fought in the Philippines during the invasion of Mindinao. Myrna Foronda's presence was a blessing because Cora had come to depend upon her as a translator and companion, as well as a trusted fellow Filipino who could help her deal with the State's Attorney's Office.

Martin had the right translator and the right guards and had chosen what appeared to be the right day. Cora had been under pressure all day from Josephine Chan to resume working as a nurse, and Consul-General Provido had used a meeting with Roger to try to wrangle a visit with Cora. She was upset with the hospital and ready to leave.

At nine o'clock that night, Martin and two detectives arrived at the hospital. They waited for more than an hour as Myrna Foronda met alone with Cora, Mama, and Roger. Although Cora wanted to leave, she was nervous and frightened. It didn't help that her mother had climbed under the covers of her bed, frightened to venture farther into the strange world she had entered only a few weeks earlier. Badly shaken by the ordeal of being rushed to Chicago, Macario Amurao did not want to leave the security of the only room she had come to know in Chicago.

Finally, shortly after ten P.M., Foronda escorted the Amuraos to the waiting cars in the hospital parking lot. The two detectives climbed into an unmarked police car with Macario and Roger Amurao. Martin, Myrna, and Cora got into a second unmarked police car. There was no luggage. Then, under cover of darkness, the two-car caravan began its forty-mile journey along the lakefront from the hospital's location near the Indiana border to the Moraine-on-the-Lake Hotel near the Wisconsin border. The last stretch of the trip from Evanston to Highland Park was on Sheridan Road, which was pitch dark, hilly, and punctuated by sharp curves.

By the time the cars pulled into the unlit drive to the hotel at eleven thirty-five P.M., Mama was hysterical. She found herself in an alien land, left with strangers in the scary blackness of a darkened woods with lake surf pounding furiously in the distance. Jumping out of the car, she dropped to her knees and sobbed uncontrollably. In Tagalog, she told her fellow Filipinos of her superstitious belief that the moon was a bad omen.

Macario Amurao wanted to take her family back to the Philippines—right now. Speaking agitatedly in Tagalog, Cora and Myrna tried to calm the terrified woman. After much coaxing, Mama got up off the ground and agreed to enter the hotel. Once settled in their suite the three Amuraos met for two hours with Foronda and Martin in a dimly lit parlor next to a screened-in porch that shielded them from the buzzing night insects. The

Amuraos poured out their fears in Tagalog to Foronda, who translated them rapidly to Martin.

Money appeared to be the big Problem. Cora had sent most of her $350-a-month salary back home to Durangao to help out her two younger sisters through college and to help pay the medical expenses of her ailing father. Leaving the hospital meant giving up this salary. Mama was further worried about a debt she owed to a close relative. Roger was worried because he had left behind his job and his wife of three months.

The family decided that the only possible solution for these financial concerns was to return to the Philippines. Every fiber of Martin's being told him that he could not allow this to happen. He explained that the State's Attorney's Office had the funds to assist witnesses in protective custody. He made it clear that the State's Attorney's Office would stand by them and see that their obligations in the Philippines were met. It was almost two A.M. before the mollified Amurao clan agreed to spend the night at the Moraine-on-the-Lake.

As the Amuraos retired to their suite, Martin began his long drive back to his two-bedroom apartment on the West Side of Chicago. He couldn't help but wonder how a family with the debts of the Amuraos could refuse the fortune that awaited the sale of Cora's story to the *Saturday Evening Post* or *Life* or the movies. Uprooted from her home, Cora's mother had gnawing financial worries that had driven her to a panic attack. Nevertheless, Cora was steadfast in her refusal to profit from the tragic deaths of her friends. She asked only that her family's meager debts be paid while she stayed in America awaiting the trial. Martin could not comprehend how the impoverished and pressured Cora could make such an unselfish decision.

With admiration and gratitude he realized that Corazon Amurao was a remarkably decent and moral young woman. He was delighted to have her on his side.

CHAPTER 24

Working fourteen-hour days that ran together, Bill Martin widened his investigation and each day, it seemed, brought surprises that were both good and bad for the State's case.

On the night of July 27, Martin was paid a visit by Detective Byron Carlile, who brought a disheveled Claude Lunsford, also known as "Bill Brian" and "One-Eyed Jack," and a very boozy-woozy Shorty Ingram. Lunsford said that he was the man who had the receipt for the room in which Speck had been found at the Starr Hotel. Although Lunsford did not appear to be prime witness material, Martin thought that he had to be interviewed just like any other kook who turned up on the State's Attorney's doorstep. Former FBI agent John Glenville had been given the difficult assignment of interviewing the Skid Row residents who had any connection with Speck during his brief stay at the Starr Hotel. In his patient style, Glenville talked with One-Eyed Jack and Shorty Ingram and reported their story back to Martin: that Lunsford met Speck on Friday night and found him bleeding Saturday night in Lunsford's cubicle at the Starr Hotel. The punch line, Glenville reported, was that "Lunsford claims to have dialed the police emergency number at nine-thirty P.M. on July 16 and told the police, 'The man you want is in room 584 of the Starr Hotel.'"

Impossible, Martin thought. Lunsford must be a hallucinating wino. Martin was about to send One-Eye and Shorty back to Skid Row when Glenville suggested, "The police communications center keeps tapes of the emergency number calls. Why don't we get the tapes to see if anything's there?" Martin chuckled. "How can there be a tape, John? We know the police dispatcher didn't send a car to the Starr at nine-thirty. The desk guy didn't call until after midnight." He tossed Glenville's interview notes on the desk and said, "We've got too much to do to bother with these guys. Send them on their way." Martin believed that the police department had a million-dollar, state-of-the-art communications system that infallibly dispatched police cars to all emergency calls.

Glenville's obsession with detail won out over Martin's trust in police science. The next day, Glenville obtained the tapes and again walked into Martin's office. "Bill," he said, "there's something here you may want to hear." Martin listened impatiently to frantic voices on a scratchy tape. There, amidst a long series of taped calls to the emergency number, he heard the unmistakable and crystal-clear voice of Claude Lunsford calling at nine-thirty on Saturday night, when the manhunt was at its peak, and telling the police that the man they wanted was in room 584 of the Starr Hotel. He refused to give his name but had added, "My initials are C.L."

Dumbfounded, Martin demanded to know why the call was not answered. The police dispatcher had prepared a dispatch computer card but, mysteriously, a squad car was never assigned to make the run. To the embarrassment of the police department, this mystery was never solved.

Claude Lunsford was called back to Glenville's office, this time to make a written statement. To Lunsford's surprise, he was now treated as if he were a knight of the realm, not a knight of the road. John Glenville's dogged persistence gave the State a potentially pivotal witness to Speck's attempt to escape from Chicago, an attempt that betrayed his consciousness of guilt.

On July 29, during a final search of the town house's south bedroom, Detective Jack Wallenda found a size 38–40 white Hanes T-shirt wadded up inside Gloria Jean Davy's purple-and-white slacks and white panties. The T-shirt was the same size as the 38–40 white BVD T-shirt that had been found July 14 in the town house living room all wrinkled and wet with perspiration. It was also the same size as the 38–40 white BVD T-shirt removed from Speck at Cook County Hospital and the size 38–40 white BVD T-shirt found in Speck's suitcase at the Raleigh Hotel. Concluding their search, the police locked the town house up for good.

On August 7, the twenty-four surviving members of the South Chicago Community Hospital Nursing Class of 1966 were graduated at Arie Crown Theater at McCormick Place on the lakefront. The ceremony was conducted as a solemn memorial in honor of their six slain classmates. The diplomas for Gloria Jean Davy, Suzanne Farris, Mary Ann Jordan, Pat Matusek, Nina Schmale, and Pamela Wilkening were posthumously presented to their parents, while their brothers, sisters, fiancés, and other loved ones looked on.

One member of the Class of 1966 had been expelled he day before she was scheduled to graduate, and her story had momentarily shaken the State's Attorney's Office. Sherry Noreen Finnigan was not an exemplary student, but nothing she did deserved the dirt that a neighborhood newspaper tried to throw on her. The magnitude of the Speck case brought out the best in most people and institutions and the worst in some, but few actions were as despicable as those of the *Daily Calumet*, a small Southeast Side newspaper. In screaming page one headlines, the paper proclaimed that Sherry Finnigan had dated Richard Speck! If true, this jeopardized the prosecution, because Speck might have innocently left his fingerprints on the bedroom door while visiting Finnigan.

Stockily built at five feet five inches and 145 pounds, Finnigan was the daughter of a glass worker at the Libby Owens Plant in Ottawa, Illinois, a small town on the banks of the Illinois River. She had started her nursing education in Joliet, but had been dismissed because of poor grades. She was accepted at South Chicago Community Hospital, where she improved her grades and, in the fall of 1965, moved into the town house at 2319 East 100th Street to share a bedroom with Pam Wilkening.

Sherry Finnigan and Pam Wilkening became fast friends, but when Sherry wanted to indulge her wild streak she usually paired up with another student who lived in the town house, Roberta Spurlock. In March 1966, Sherry and Roberta signed out for "overnights" to go with their boyfriends to Wisconsin. They were scheduled to return to work at seven A.M. the following Monday. The girls failed to return. Later that morning, Sherry called nursing director Josephine Chan to report that the car in which they had been traveling had "blown up and ended in a ditch." Continuing this fiction, Sherry said that while both she and Roberta were "scratched and shaken up," they had hitchhiked home from Wisconsin without seeking medical attention. Chan ordered her two senior students to report to the South Chicago Community Hospital emergency room for an examination, but they refused. Chan was angry. The same two girls had only a few months earlier made a similar weekend trip to Springfield, and had excused their late return because a different car allegedly "blew up." While Chan fumed, Sherry and Roberta decided to press their luck. They did not hold the strong-willed Chan in the same awe as did their classmates. Two days later, the two took another "overnight" and again returned late to their nursing duties. This was the last straw for Chan. On March 9, 1966, she expelled the two students from the town house but allowed them to remain in school.

This expulsion saved their lives.

Sherry and Roberta rented a nearby apartment and continued to attend classes. Sherry had been dating a Southeast Side steel worker who was married with four children. In the spring and summer of 1966, the pair were together so often that their neighbors thought they were married. On the morning of July 14, as the bodies of her former roommates were being discovered, Sherry was having breakfast in the hospital cafeteria. She raced to the town house and tried to comfort Pamela Wilkening's parents. Distraught over the deaths of girls she considered sisters, Sherry became terrified that the mass murderer might still be lurking on the Southeast Side. That night, her married boyfriend took her to Pete's Tap, the fleabag joint that Speck had often frequented and where he had spent the morning after the murders. By the time they arrived, however, Speck had relocated to the Raleigh Hotel on the city's near North Side. While sitting at the bar, Sherry was approached by a callous stranger who idiotically asked, "Hello, nursie, how does it feel to be alive?" Her boyfriend pushed the man away. Sherry was shaking.

A few days later, Sherry received an even bigger jolt. The *Daily Calumet* ran scurrilous stories suggesting that she had dated Speck. This fire was put out when Assistant State's Attorney George Murtaugh sat down with Sherry in the kitchen of her cluttered apartment. Sherry told Murtaugh that she was two months pregnant by her married boyfriend, a fact which he confirmed. She said that the stories in the *Daily Calumet* had destroyed her nursing career, and indeed, the school would kick her out the day before she was supposed to graduate. Murtaugh was able to establish that Sherry had not lived in the town house since March 9, did not know Richard Speck, and absolutely had never dated him. The false *Daily Calumet* headlines were eventually used only to wrap garbage, but Sherry Finnigan, too, had been sucked into the malevolent whirlpool of events set into motion by the crime of Richard Speck.

Finnigan's classmate, Tammy Sioukoff, also knew well the feeling of being traumatized by Speck's crime. Sioukoff, who lived next door to the victims' town house, had almost lost her life when she went to the back door of 2319 to try to borrow two slices of bread. The memory of that night continued to haunt her. She recalls, "After the murders, we nurses were simply terrified. I moved back to the nursing dorm until graduation and I insisted on sharing a room with another nurse, Leona Bonczak. We were all scared of our own shadows. We couldn't go to the bathroom at night unless we went together. We couldn't fall asleep unless we heard the footfalls of the Pinkerton guard hired by the hospital to walk the corridors to protect us. Leona was the most traumatized of all because she had actually seen the dead bodies. We took long walks together to try to comprehend what had happened. Incredibly, there were sickos within the hospital itself who would call us on the house phone and we would hear a male voice saying, 'I'm going to finish off the rest of you the same as Speck did.' We received letters saying we were 'whores.' I mean, we weren't allowed to smoke, to swear, to stay out late, we all were very religious, we were trying to help and heal, and, now, we were being called 'whores.' "

On August 9, as Corazon Amurao splashed about the swimming pool of the Moraine-on-the-Lake Hotel, Richard Speck was transferred from his bed in the Cook County Jail infirmary to a small, greasy, steel-barred, maximum-security cell in the jail basement. For security reasons, the warden wanted to isolate him from other prisoners and Speck's new home was on death row, only a few steps from the electric chair.

That same morning, Martin awoke to the unsettling thought that his investigation was almost one month old and the murder weapon—Speck's switchblade—had yet to be found, despite an intense search. Detectives had gone over both sides of 100th Street from the town house to the Shipyard Inn with a fine-tooth comb, spending hours on their hands and knees in roadside bushes. Scuba divers with large flashlights had plunged to the bottom of the Calumet River near the 100th Street bridge, but the silty blackness of a river bottom constantly churned by huge ocean-going ships limited their vision to only a few inches.

That night, Martin sat down with several members of Team Speck for their regular ten P.M. dinner at the Wagons, a rustic steakhouse near the Criminal Court Building. The order of the night—every night—was what the police fondly called "a piece of meat," a thick juicy steak. Rugged six-foot three-inch detective Byron Carlile, the oldest member of the team, was an energetic and intelligent warhorse who loved water and boats. A highly determined man whose stubbornness knew no boundaries, Carlile was not satisfied with the scuba divers' futile search. "I think that we should drag the river bottom with a magnet," he told his fellow steak-lovers.

Burglary detective Eddie Wielosinski, the man who had cracked the case by alertly picking up the first clues to Speck's identity, took up the challenge. "I know the river, Byron," Willow said. "I'll go with you." Wielosinski had worked as a boatman for the Army Corps of Engineers in 1943 on a survey of the Calumet River. He was a man who knew his objective and would systematically remove every obstacle in his way.

Carlile and Wielosinski were perfect shipmates. The next morning, using a borrowed fourteen-foot aluminum powerboat, they methodically navigated the waters near the 100th Street bridge. As Wielosinski piloted the small boat, Carlile dragged a large, heavy magnet across the river's bottom twenty-six feet below. The routine lasted for three and a half hours and Carlile became arm-weary from pulling the magnet with a rope from bank to bank. In the end it yielded only a few nails and a lot of muck.

The two detectives were ready to give up when, fifteen feet from the south overhang of the bridge, in the middle of the river, Carlile pulled the magnet up for one last look. Sticking to it was the usual flotsam and silt—and a black-handled switchblade.

Wielosinski sped the boat to shore, jumped into his squad car, and raced to the crime lab with the knife still stuck to the magnet. The crime lab examination found that blade number 1 of the pocketknife was 2¾ inches long and inscribed "Improved Muskrat Knife." Its tang read "Shrade Walden, N.Y., USA," the manufacturer. The tip of this blade was broken off, possibly when Speck jimmied the screen off the window at the rear of the town house. The blade was speckled with flecks of human blood, but they were too minute to identify by blood type. Blade number 2 was 2³⁄₁₆ inches long and was flecked with traces of blood that were too minute to categorize as human or animal. Embedded in the blade receptacle were deposits of clothing fibers containing stains testing positive for blood, but again too small to categorize as human or animal.

Finding the knife in the Calumet River, one block from the Shipyard Inn, connected it circumstantially to Speck, but Wielosinski wanted to make a direct connection. Calling the manufacturer, he obtained the names of Chicago stores that carried the knife. The murder weapon, he was told, cost $4.75 and was usually bought by hunters. Wielosinski turned the town upside down, but was unable to find a witness who recalled selling an "Improved Muskrat" switchblade to a pockmarked drifter.

Martin worried that the $4.75 murder weapon, like the sixteen-dollar gun, might never be introduced into evidence.

CHAPTER 25

During the month of August, Corazon Amurao played in the sun at her lakeside hideaway, talking only to her family, her police guards, her interpreter, and Bill Martin. Richard Speck stayed in a Death Row cell, talking only to his guards and the jail psychiatrist.

Jim Georgalas and Jack Wallenda, the police detail guarding the Amuraos, were determined to make the time at the Moraine Hotel a calming interlude during which Cora, her mother, and her cousin could adjust to life in protective custody. Martin wanted her to learn to trust again. In the bright sunlight of these August days, Cora enjoyed the peacefulness and natural beauty of her new surroundings. Her privacy was complete: she even used a secret passageway to walk to the swimming pool. Each day, a Chinese restaurant in Highland Park sent food that was reheated in the hotel kitchen and brought to the Amuraos' suite by the hotel manager himself. The layout of the adjoining suites on the third floor was such that the police guards had total command of the entrance. Security arrangements were ideal, and the presence of the two affable detectives was a constant reminder to Cora that she was being protected every minute of the day.

With their upbeat, good-hearted natures, the policemen soon won the confidence of the Amurao family. Learning a few words of Tagalog, they joked with Macario—always respectfully called "Mama"—about life in the Philippines, and told tall stories about their own exploits in the islands during World War II. Myrna Foronda brought her husband and six-year-old daughter to stay in the suite's extra bedroom. Paul Foronda, an easygoing physician who had grown up in a province near the Amuraos' home in Durangao, was gentle and soft-spoken. When Bill Martin visited, sometimes with his four young children, he splashed around in the swimming pool with the Amuraos and Forondas. Cora enjoyed teasing Martin's daughters, Colleen and Vicki. Occasionally, Cora would play a mean game of badminton against Martin and punctuate her winning shots with bursts of laughter. The mass-murder survivor was becoming relaxed—swimming, sunbathing, singing, and even joking with her protectors. After a week of commuting from his office in the gritty neighborhood of Twenty-sixth Street to the peaceful charm of the Moraine, Martin believed that he had gained enough of Cora's trust to have a serious talk with her about the future. On Saturday afternoon, August 13, he sat down with her and Myrna Foronda in the Amuraos' parlor and came quickly to his main point: "Cora," he said, "we need for you to be with us until the trial is over. That may not be until six months from now, or even longer."

Cora answered him in halting English: "I want to stay until the trial is over, but I need Mama and Roger to stay with me." She added that the two policemen had been able "to make me feel safe, and I do not want to go anywhere without their protection." Martin nodded his understanding, and Cora continued: "I love nursing, but when I tried to go back to work at the hospital I was very frightened that I would make a mistake. I was very nervous. I do not want to go back to South Chicago Community Hospital."

Cora began to sob softly as she told Martin of her other concerns. "I do not want to live far from Myrna," she said emphatically, adding, "I want Roger to stay with me and Mama, but I want Roger to be happy. He needs to work. Can you help him get a job?" Knowing that it would be a headache to find employment for Roger Amurao, Martin said nothing. Then, he explained what he expected from her.

Martin began by telling her that Consul-General Provido might renew his pressure to see her. Cora became visibly upset at this possibility and began to jabber rapidly in singsong Tagalog to Myrna. Martin was worried. Cora then said, in forceful English, "I am not ready to see those people." Foronda added that Cora was also afraid to let the consular staff know of her reluctance to see them because she feared retaliation against her family in the Philippines. Martin assured Cora that he would do everything possible to protect her. Looking directly at her and noting how frail she appeared, Martin broached his main concern—the need to prepare her to testify. He had yet to speak one word to her of the crimes committed by Richard Speck.

"Cora," Martin said, "I have to prepare you to testify. This means that you have to know the questions I will ask you when you take the witness stand. I have to know your answers to these questions."

Cora winced. "This is very painful to me," she said softly.

"I know it will be," Martin replied, "and I'll try to make it as easy for you as I can. But we have to be able to go to trial and this means that we must do this as soon as you feel able."

Mindful of Dr. Haines's warning, Martin decided that now was not the time to push. Instead, he asked to meet alone with Roger to see how he could help the young draftsman. Still too shy to bond with the entire group, Roger spent most of his time in the suite, napping, watching TV, or playing a Philippine version of Scrabble. Roger desperately wanted a job to support his new wife. Beyond that, after only three weeks in Illinois he had already decided that he wanted to live permanently in America.

"I want to stay with Cora and Mama until the trial is over," Roger said, "but I have to work."

With these requests to ponder, Martin left the Amuraos and the Moraine Hotel for the long and winding drive back to his small office in the Criminal Court Building, where he sat down at his L.C. Smith manual typewriter. He had used this now beat-up machine to get through both college and law school, and he planned to use it to get through the Speck trial. Pecking out a six-page, single-spaced confidential memo to Dan Ward, Martin described his mounting logistical problems:

> "1. Find a secure place for Cora, her mother, and Roger to live anonymously under unobtrusive twenty-four-hour police protection. Any residence must be close to Myrna Foronda.
>
> "2. Shield Cora from Philippine government officials without indicating that it is Cora's desire not to meet with them.
>
> "3. Find a job for Roger without revealing his true identity.
>
> "4. Do all of the above in absolute secrecy."

Martin concluded the memo with a reference to John Stamos's oft-stated famous dictum: "Big cases, big problems."

Ward's handwritten response was prompt and pointed: "Do whatever has to be done."

Jack Johnson, the outgoing and popular warden of the Cook County Jail, worried that his most notorious patient, Richard Speck, might be a suicide risk. When Speck was transferred from Cermak Hospital to the jail infirmary on July 29, Johnson told Dr. Marvin Ziporyn, his part-time psychiatrist, to see Speck immediately.

During the next six months, Ziporyn would spend more than one hundred hours talking to Speck, and the two would become a true odd couple: Ziporyn, a highly literate psychiatrist, was also an internationally known concert violinist and lover of art; Speck, who could barely read and write, was, in the words of one jail guard, "a complete physical, social, and moral slob." Nevertheless, they would become friends of sorts.

Ziporyn supplied Warden Johnson with brief summaries of his sessions with Speck, and both Getty and Martin would later subpoena these reports. Martin knew that Ziporyn was prone to finding criminal defendants not responsible for their actions, and he was concerned that Ziporyn had been given full access to Speck.

Ziporyn was a strict "determinist," subscribing to the belief that free will is an illusion and that human conduct is predetermined by heredity and environment. He would spend much of his one hundred hours with Speck trying to convince the killer that he was neither legally nor morally responsible for what had happened in the town house. Martin followed Ziporyn's accounts of his meetings with the mass murderer with great interest.

During Ziporyn's first visit on July 29, Speck told the psychiatrist that at age ten he had fallen ten feet from a tree and landed on his head. "My sister thought that I was dead." Speck drawled. He added that at age fifteen he had run into an awning and "rammed a steel rod into my brain." Referring to the night of the murders, Speck told the psychiatrist that he "was drinking heavily with two sailors who invited me to their room. I joined them for a 'fix.' I don't know what it was. I took it in the vein. I also took six 'red birds' " (amphetamines). Speck claimed to have passed out from eight P.M. July 13 until eleven A.M. the next morning, when he awoke and again started to drink. He said that he had heard about the murders, but did not make a connection with himself. When he later heard his name mentioned as the killer, Speck recalled "I was too drunk to really feel anything." He claimed to have taken a bottle of sleeping pills, "but that didn't work." Speck told Ziporyn he had no idea why he attempted suicide and said that he did not know whether he had committed the murders or not.

On August first, Ziporyn reported, Speck was "irritable, moody, and withdrawn." When Ziporyn asked him directly what the nurses had done to trigger his murderous rage, Speck replied, "What, me? Get mad at women? No way." He added, "I don't even remember what those girls looked like."

On August 6, Ziporyn wrote, Speck was "quite sociable and rather amiable." He offered the psychiatrist a cigarette and a candy bar. Under questioning, Speck steadfastly denied any and all recollection of the murders, explaining, "If you were to let me go free tonight if I told you the details, I couldn't do it." At the same time, Ziporyn noted, Speck did not dispute the idea that he was the murderer. Ziporyn thought that Speck was "desperately eager to be accepted and liked," and he felt that a "rapport" was developing between the two.

On August 8, Ziporyn found Speck "interested in nothing—don't care about nothing." The psychiatrist felt that Speck would soon talk "extensively" to him.

As a world-class liar, Speck would over the months weave a web of deceits for his confidant, friend, psychiatrist, and, in time, biographer. It came as no surprise to Martin that by early August, Ziporyn already had a working diagnosis of Speck: "Chronic brain syndrome, associated with cerebral trauma."

Thursday, August 18

This was the first day of pretrial discovery, the effort by the defense to learn the State's evidence and to probe the contours of the prosecutors' case. Appearing before Judge Paschen, Public Defender Gerald Getty did what criminal defense lawyers always do. In a series of motions, he asked the State to produce a list of all the witnesses it might call; to produce copies of all fingerprints found in the town house; to provide copies of all reports by the crime lab; and to display to the defense copies of all the photographs and physical evidence the State had accumulated during the investigation.

In a bold move, Getty called for the court to appoint an impartial panel of psychiatrists who would decide two questions: Was Speck competent to stand trial? Was he insane at the time of the crimes? Getty told the court why he wanted an impartial panel: "We want to get away from the spectacle of psychiatrists battling psychiatrists. In our representation of this defendant, we are only seeking objective truth, whatever it may be."

He suggested that the State and the defense each submit the names of three psychiatrists and one psychologist for Judge Paschen's approval, and that this impartial panel would then have the authority to conduct whatever examinations and to retain whatever additional experts it felt necessary to determine the two key issues of competency and sanity. Further, Getty moved, the defense and the State would make available to the panel any relevant information, and the panel members would have full access to examine Speck and submit him to diagnostic tests.

The kicker was that all evidence on Speck's competency to stand trial and his sanity on July 13–14 "would be limited to that offered by the panel members and any who worked under their direction."

This roll of the dice had been hotly debated in Getty's office, and the Public Defender had won out. He had told his assistants, "We'd better have a panel, and we'd better trap them into taking a panel. Let's offer it in open court. If they reject it, then it's on the record."

Getty believed that the senseless, unprovoked, and vicious murder of eight women had to be the work of a madman and that any psychiatrist would agree. The trap he was setting for the State was to limit the evidence on Speck's mental condition to the opinion of the panel. Certain that the panel would find Speck insane, Getty wanted to prevent the State from using the powerful evidence it had accumulated in Dallas, Monmouth, Chicago, and Michigan while writing Speck's "biography." This evidence, told in the words of the ordinary people who had known Speck, made a convincing argument that his lawlessness was that of a hardened criminal, not of an insane man. In a public-relations coup, Getty seized the judicial high ground by seeking the court's *imprimatur* for an "impartial" panel. He also believed that he was taking no risk. If the State refused to accept the panel, Speck could refuse to talk to prosecution-appointed psychiatrists, and in that case any examination of his mental condition would be performed only by experts chosen by Getty.

The fifty-three-year-old Gerald Getty was at the top of his game. Dwarfing Martin and the other Assistant State's Attorney's in experience, Getty had tried 425 jury cases, one third of them murders, and had performed the nearly impossible feat of winning fourteen consecutive juries. As widely reported in the press, he had defended 402 death-penalty cases and had never lost a client to the electric chair. Jurors identified with Getty's folksy, smiling approach, his self-deprecating sense of humor, and his utter lack of pomposity. He would deliberately mispronounce big words like electroencephalogram ("electro-in-ceff-io-gram") and repetitious ("Rep-pew-tishous"), this comfortable old-shoe style masking a penetrating mind and a hard-nosed competitiveness. Getty had enlisted most of the battle-scarred assistants in the Public Defender's office to help on this celebrated case, and the defense was fielding a significantly bigger team than the State.

Martin had known from the start that Gerald Getty would be a very dangerous adversary and now, like a general throwing his crack troops into a massive attack early in the war, Getty was committing himself to the total victory of an insanity acquittal. He was betting that Richard Speck would be found "not guilty by reason of insanity." Martin was surprised by the request and asked for a two-week continuance to think things over. The motion for a court-appointed psychiatric panel was continued until September first.

Surrounded by twelve armed guards, Speck had sat through this court appearance looking as if his mind were a million miles away. Upon being returned to his jail cell, Speck told his guard, "You ought to see how all those cops in court were fighting to get their picture taken with me."

While deferring action on Getty's request for psychiatric evidence, Martin decided to respond promptly to his request for physical evidence. Since the morning of July 14, the crime lab's Sergeant Louis Vitullo had been examining every shred of the bed sheets, blouses, T-shirts, and other objects recovered from the town house, searching for three primary substances: blood, hair, and sperm. Vitullo placed each of the hundreds of pieces of evidence that had been analyzed into neat rows of clearly marked containers. This grim exhibit, organized in the lab's library, offered silent testimony to the victims' violent deaths. Team Speck Attorneys Martin, Murtaugh, Glenville, Nellis, and Zagel spent two full days in respectful silence, examining and cataloging these images of death.

Valentina Pasion's fingernail scrapings included traces of human blood—undoubtedly that of Richard Speck. In a futile effort to repel the killer, Pasion had inflicted a three-inch scratch on his chest, the scratch that Dr. LeRoy Smith had observed while treating Speck at Cook County Hospital. Pasion's blood-stained blouse contained a strand of human head hair that was microscopically similar in pigment, pigment distribution, scale structure, and diameter to the sample of Speck's hair taken at the hospital.

A minute cotton swab, stored in a jar, represented the rectal swab taken from Gloria Jean Davy. It tested positive for semen and was a lasting testament to the defilement Gloria had endured as she had been forced to lie face down on the living room couch, her hands bound behind her. Saliva was found on the front of her bra. The comforter from the couch was now wrapped in plastic and contained, in Vitullo's phrase, "plenty of sperm."

One box contained a harmless-looking strip of bed sheet, once forty-five inches long and three inches wide. It had been cut into three smaller strips, which had been used to make the plug that was shoved into Pamela Wilkening's mouth to stifle her screams. One strip had been balled up and shoved inside her mouth; another had been looped around her neck and tied in a double knot over her mouth; the third had been looped around her mouth and tied in a double knot at the back of her neck.

Another container held a bloodstained white nurse's stocking. Speck had used it to tie a double knot around the neck of Suzanne Farris and strangle her to death. Her gaily colored and bloodstained blouse was riddled with tiny slits that matched the wounds in her back where Speck had repeatedly stabbed her.

Other exhibits included more bloodstained nurses' stockings and strips of bed sheet; the shift worn by Nina Schmale, found hiked up to her breasts riddled with three bloodstained slits matching the wounds in her neck where Speck had stabbed her; the yellow nightgown worn by Pat Matusek; and the forlorn piece of bed sheet found tightly clenched in Mary Jordan's right hand after she had tried to wrest it away from Speck.

Viewing the evidence of what Speck had done exhausted Martin emotionally and, like the midnight visit to the town house, personalized his awareness of the incredible horror and inhumanity of Richard Speck's crime. "God, this was a brutal crime," he said to himself. The inspection enabled Martin to file a seventeen-page, single-spaced "Catalog of Photographic, Documentary, and Tangible Objects, as Arranged for Inspection by the Defense," at the next court appearance on September first. The list described in detail the terrifying meaning of every exhibit. Martin then made good on his earlier pledge to Getty to let the defense see more of his case than was required under Illinois law. Martin had told the Public Defender that all the physical objects gathered during the police investigation would be produced for the defense to view at the Chicago Police Department crime lab. There would be no trial by ambush. The State's evidence had literally been put on the table. In late September, Getty and three assistants were able to spend five days examining the grisly exhibit and grappling with their own thoughts about the events it dramatized.

This took care of Getty's motions for the physical evidence. In regard to the psychiatric panel, Martin would make a counterproposal. The case of Harrison Crouse—the University of Illinois freshman who murdered his parents and sister and got off because of an irregularity in his brain-wave activities—had taught Martin a painful lesson: Don't put all your eggs in one basket. He didn't want to give up his ace in the hole—the nonexpert Dallas-Monmouth-Chicago-Michigan testimony he was compiling to prove that Speck was sane. There was no way he would agree to limit the evidence of Speck's mental condition to a panel of "experts."

During the brief ten-minute September first appearance, Martin told Judge Paschen that the State would agree to have a panel, but added, "We cannot allow the panel to usurp the judicial function of determining competency and sanity. The question of criminal responsibility is not solely for psychiatrists." In other words, if Getty would agree that neither side was *bound* by the panel, Martin would go for it.

Convinced that any panel would find Speck insane and that the testimony of psychiatrists would make any nonexpert evidence worthless, Getty decided to give in on what appeared to be a minor concession. He agreed that either side could offer any evidence it wanted of Speck's mental condition, including the testimony of lay witnesses. He figured he could sit back and wait for Martin to sweat after the impartial panel of experts concluded that Richard Speck had been insane the night he entered the town house.

During this skirmish, Speck swayed back and forth as he stood before the judge, flanked by two guards and the court bailiff. His back was to the spectators who had waited for hours to be frisked before the guards would allow them to enter the courtroom. Jail officials had recently received five letters and two phone calls from people who said that they would kill him. Informed of the threats, Speck seemed unperturbed.

The court session was concluded after the state corrected the indictments against Speck. The coroner's pathology protocols for Valentina Pasion and Merlita Gargullo had been inadvertently reversed in the crowded morgue, a doleful reminder of the impersonality of a homicide investigation. The mistake in identifying the two bodies at the morgue was grim testimony that a murderer robs his victims of dignity even in death.

Judge Paschen set September 9 as the date for each side to submit its three psychiatric experts, ending the proceedings. The handcuffed Speck was taken by elevator to the basement of the Criminal Court Building to enter the "boulevard" for another long walk back to his Death Row cell. Elsewhere in the world, the U.S. Senate voted 66–21 to authorize a call-up of military reserves for the widening war in Vietnam.

CHAPTER 26

The battle lines were shaping up. Martin hoped to use Cora's testimony to prove that the cunning Speck murdered in cold blood. Getty hoped to use the findings of the psychiatric panel to prove that Speck was not responsible for his actions because of insanity. This meant that Cora would have to be relocated to a permanent home in Chicago and that Speck would have to talk to a long parade of psychiatric experts.

Three restful weeks at the Moraine-on-the-Lake had enabled Cora to distance herself geographically and psychologically from Southeast Chicago. However, the danger of her being identified at the Moraine was increasing each day, and Martin believed that it was time to find her a new home, a place where she could live securely until the trial. He chose the Sheridan-Surf Apartment Hotel in the heart of the city. This residence hotel was located three and a half miles north of the downtown Loop and only a few blocks west of the lake, near the busy intersection of Sheridan Street and Diversey Avenue. This Chicago neighborhood, popularly known as "New Town," was ethnically eclectic, and a Filipino family would not attract attention. With the confidential aid of the Chicago Real Estate Board, Martin rented two adjoining apartments at the end of the hall on the fifth floor. The move was made on August 28, a lazy Sunday. The police detail took up residence in a one-bedroom unit next to the new two-bedroom home of the Amuraos. The hotel's population was large and diverse enough that the five new residents were not noticed. To Cora's relief, the hotel was close to the neighborhood where Myrna and Paul Foronda lived, which was a key reason why it had been chosen.

Sergeant Frank Lassandrella, an electronics expert, installed a buzzer system to enable Cora to alert the police officers if a stranger came to her door. Since the officers' door opened into the hallway, they could readily intercept any unwanted visitors. During the seven months the Amuraos would live in the hotel, the alarm was used only once—when a Democratic precinct captain rang Cora's bell to register her to vote! An alert detective quickly stepped into the hallway to conspiratorially tell the unwitting visitor, "Look, pal, I've got a lady friend up here. There's no need to register her." The security arrangement worked so well that during the entire year this celebrated case was in the headlines, the press would come up with only one photo of Cora—a telephoto shot taken on July 19 when she entered Cermak Hospital to identify Richard Speck.

By September 8 the same two detectives, Jim Georgalas and Jack Wallenda, had stayed with Cora and her family nonstop around the clock for a full month. The detectives were affectionately known to the Amuraos as "Jacques" and "Jeem." However, this duty had been hard on their families, and Martin decided that he needed another two-man detail to alternate forty-eight-hour shifts. He knew the new duo must be carefully chosen to keep the Amuraos at ease. A national talent search could not have turned up two better guardians than Sergeants Steve McCarthy and James Concannon, two charming, lovable Irishmen, both in their fifties. McCarthy, who was born in a small village in County Clair, Ireland, came to America with a rich brogue when he was only nineteen, facing his new world with gentle eyes, a kind smile, and rich good humor. He was employed as a construction, freight, and iron worker before joining the Chicago Police Department in 1941. His police career was promptly interrupted by World War II, as McCarthy joined the U.S. Navy and served from 1942–1945 in the Pacific Theater aboard a tanker that hauled gasoline to combat zones. After the war, he returned to the police department and patrolled the Southwest Side of Chicago until, in 1961, he was assigned to the State's Attorney's Office, where his constant side-kick would soon be fellow Irishman Concannon. A Chicago native, Concannon spent ten years as a cook for the Campbell Soup Company before joining the navy in World War II, where his service included the invasion of Borneo and a stint at Subic Bay in the Philippines. He had once visited Bantangas Province, home of the Amoraos. He joined the Chicago Police Department in 1946 and worked as a detective until he joined the State's Attorney's Office in 1962. A craggy-faced, deep-voiced man, Concannon inspired affection and confidence. McCarthy's brogue carried a singsong lilt remarkably similar to Cora's Tagalog; Concannon's speech featured the sharp nasal twang of a lifelong Chicago South Sider.

The cover for the security operation was "Independence Insurance Adjustors," a fictitious firm "run" by Jack Wallenda's cousin and allegedly headquartered in North Olmsted, Ohio. "Assignments" were mailed by the cousin to the hotel—envelopes filled with newspaper clips. Business cards were printed for the four insurance investigators in the names of Pappas, Sarna, Moore, and Payton. The hotel desk clerk was told that their prospering Ohio firm had been forced to assign them to Chicago on a rotating basis.

Cora's new home in Chicago would be warm, loving—and secure. During the next seven months, she would be introduced by her police guards to the Chicago she had never seen. The "Amurao Squad" of Wallenda-Georgalas-McCarthy-Concannon decided that the best way to bridge the cultural gap was to keep Cora, Mama, and Roger entertained, happy—and tired. "Our strategy was to keep them on the run," said fun-loving Sergeant Concannon, and the police detail dreamed up more activities than the busiest tour guide.

Weekday shopping safaris gave Cora and Mama a chance to see the treasures of American department stores, ranging from the upscale Marshall Field to the bargain basement Kmart. Grocery shopping was done in the city's Chinatown area, where the Amuraos often selected live crabs and fifty-pound sacks of rice to be loaded into the trunk of the officers' unmarked squad car. Fall offers by far the best of Chicago's otherwise witches' brew of weather, and the group spent the golden weekend days of September, October, and November visiting such Chicago area landmarks as the Morton Arboretum, the Brookfield Zoo, and the Shedd Aquarium. A special favorite were apple-picking expeditions into the rural countryside of northern Illinois. The tiny Amuraos would hop onto ladders and excitedly pick a bushel basket of fresh apples.

All three Amuraos were devout Catholics and every Sunday began with mass at a neighborhood church. Evenings were spent bowling, playing miniature golf, dining out, and playing penny-ante poker. Speaking in his distinctive brogue, McCarthy named the poker game "penny for penny." The busy schedule provided many moments of camaraderie and humor between the Filipinos and their American hosts, not to mention a few moments of mild unease.

On one shopping visit, the unsophisticated Mama took a liking to a Rolex watch at Marshall Field and excitedly began jabbering and pointing, asking in Tagalog to have a closer look. Quick on his feet, Jim Concannon used elaborately acted-out sign language to steer her, instead, toward a Timex, explaining as best he could, "It keeps time better, very much better."

The Amurao clan became addicted to the live crabs they could purchase in Chinatown and cook in their apartment. The delicacy was always washed down with home-brewed rice tea. The Americans were less entranced with the crab cooking, and when the pungent odor of cooking crab blanketed the hallways, they would complain to each other that the "stink" was ruining their own delicacy—an oven-broiled "piece of meat."

Ever superstitious, Mama usually slept on the floor of the apartment, using a fifty-pound sack of rice as her pillow. In this way, she could make sure that the precious rice would not be stolen. With the secret help of the Illinois State Employment Office, Rogelio Amurao was recreated as Roger Tano and given a job as a draftsman at U.S. Steel, making him very happy. He knew that he was becoming Americanized when he was asked to join the company's bowling team.

One Sunday, as mass was ending at Old St. Mary's Church, which was located a few blocks from police headquarters, a *Tribune* reporter spotted Concannon, who was an old friend. After quickly signaling McCarthy to take Cora for a walk around the block, Concannon chatted amiably with the reporter.

"What brings you down here, Jim?"

"I was over at the headquarters."

"Hey, do you know where the girl is hidden?" the reporter then asked, referring, of course, to Cora.

"Gee, I think they took her to California."

On another occasion, Concannon, a staunch family man, ran into a relative while escorting Cora around Brookfield Zoo. Fearful that Cora's identity would be discovered, Concannon brusquely brushed off the surprised relative, who later told friends, "I don't know what's with old Jim . . . I caught him sneaking around with some young Oriental babe."

A favorite place for dining out was Jimmy Wong's, a popular Chinese restaurant located on the north side of the city. The police detail's expense diary indicates that most meals were reasonably priced, but occasionally there was pheasant under glass. Most nights ended with the Amuraos family and their police protectors playing "penny for penny." Cora usually won after McCarthy secretly slipped her his best cards.

As this relaxing routine between the Amuraos and the police detail settled into place, Chicago was again jolted by a brutal murder. The killing took place on Sunday, September 18, at five in the morning, in the unlikely place of Kenilworth, Illinois, a superexclusive lakeside Chicago suburb that was only a few miles north of the Sheridan-Surf. Valerie Percy, twenty-one, daughter of Charles H. Percy, the Republican candidate for the U.S. Senate, was bludgeoned and stabbed to death in her second-floor bedroom of the seventeen-room Percy mansion known as "Windward." The killer gained entrance into the lakefront mansion with the aid of a glass cutter that was used to jimmy open the beachfront French doors. Then, with the aid of a flashlight, the killer climbed to the second floor, entered the girl's bedroom, and swiftly and savagely beat her to death, while the rest of her family slept soundly on the same floor. Despite an intensive investigation involving thousands of leads, the Percy murder was never solved.

For the second time in only two months, Chicagoans feared that a vicious killer was walking their streets. Martin was worried that Cora's psychological recovery from her trauma might be reversed if she found out that the daughter of a prominent politician had been murdered in her own bed only a few miles from the Sheridan-Surf. He and the police detail tried to keep the terrible news from her, but the publicity was so massive that Cora was soon made aware of it. Although he feared the worst, Martin was pleasantly surprised to learn that the Sheridan-Surf detail was accomplishing its mission. Cora took the news of the murder in a stoical fashion, reporting that she felt confident and safe with her four loyal policemen. Still, Martin thought it wise to delay a serious talk with his eyewitness. He was acutely aware of the danger of causing her severe psychological damage if he sought the details of the murders before she was ready to share them with him.

Martin, in fact, was preoccupied with psychological issues. On September 9, Judge Paschen announced the names of the six experts who would probe Speck's mind. Three had been selected by the Public Defender, three by the State's Attorney's Office.

Getty's three choices to help determine Speck's competency and sanity appeared to be brilliant ones—psychiatrists Roy R. Grinker, Jr., Hervey M. Cleckley, and Edward J. Kelleher. Their credentials were impeccable, and their track records seemed to assure that they would find Speck insane. All three could fill volumes with their clinical experiences, but Martin noticed that Grinker and Cleckley had very limited exposure to the criminal mind. They were not used to working with murderers.

Grinker, the director of the Institute for Psychosomatic and Psychiatric Research at Chicago's Michael Reese Medical Center for the past twenty years, was a highly regarded psychoanalyst whose own psychiatrist father had been analyzed by the guru himself—Sigmund Freud. Grinker had been a practicing psychiatrist since 1921 and had done his postgraduate training during the heyday of psychoanalysis in the cities of Hamburg, London, Vienna, and Zurich. During World War II, he had been an army colonel in the African Theater and had supervised the psychiatric services to American, British, and French troops. As the chief editor of *The Archives of General Psychiatry*, an associate professor at the University of Chicago Medical School, and a full professor at the University of Illinois Medical School, Grinker had spent a lifetime as a student and teacher of psychoanalysis. And, Martin mused, diagnosing Speck must be a psychoanalyst's dream. In addition to his professional credentials, the beardless, bespectacled, red-haired Grinker had a strong round-faced look that made him come across more as a scholarly business executive than as a disciple of Freud. Grinker, in short, appeared to be an ideal witness for the defense.

Hervey Cleckley deserved co-star billing with Grinker. A clinical professor of neuropsychiatry at the Medical College of Georgia in Augusta, Cleckley had written the ground-breaking best-seller, *The Three Faces of Eve*, a study of multiple personalities that had been made into a hit movie starring Joanne Woodward. A former Rhodes Scholar and a diplomate of the American Board of Psychiatry and Neurology, Cleckley was a gracious southerner who wore an easy smile and spoke plainly without hiding behind jargon. The crown jewel of Cleckley's medical literary achievements was another best-selling book, *The Mask of Sanity*, which was a study of the sociopathic personality. This credential was especially important because under Illinois law sociopaths (or psychopaths; the terms are interchangeable) were legally responsible for their actions. If Speck were diagnosed as a sociopath, his insanity defense went out the window. The shrewd Getty had uncovered theories about sociopaths in Cleckley's many writings that led him to believe that Cleckley would not find Speck to be a sociopath, thus opening the door to finding him legally insane, and not responsible for the murders.

Getty's third choice, Edward Kelleher, was director of the Psychiatric Institute of the Municipal Court of Chicago, where over the past twenty-six years he had conducted an average of 1,200 psychiatric evaluations a year. A compactly built, outgoing man with tufts of white hair protruding from the sides of his head, Kelleher was an adept witness who was known to be willing to testify that a criminal defendant was mentally ill. Getty had been especially encouraged by this Kelleher quote to reporters immediately after the murders: "This is probably the greatest single sex crime in history."

Martin thought that Getty looked positively smug when he presented his choices to Judge Paschen. For his part, Martin, with the help of Jim Zagel, had looked for experts with strong clinical experience in diagnosing criminal defendants—experts who would not be fooled by Speck's convenient amnesia. The prosecutors avoided psychoanalysts and psychiatric theoreticians in favor of clinicians who had extensive experience in dealing with malingerers and hardened criminals—people like Richard Speck. Martin's three choices were psychiatrists Groves Blake Smith and Vladimir G. Urse and, a surprise choice, surgeon William J. Norcross, Speck's former attending physician.

Groves Smith was the director of the psychiatric division of the Illinois Prison System, the perfect clinical credential for detecting malingerers. Smith examined more than two thousand convicts every year. The slickest and shrewdest cons the Illinois prison system had to offer had not been able to fool Smith with feigned symptoms of mental illness. Martin especially liked his quote, "Mental illness is not a faucet that you turn on and off."

A board-certified psychiatrist for almost fifty years, the short, round Smith looked like Santa Claus without a beard. He had begun his career with a pioneering two-year psychiatric study of one thousand jailed defendants awaiting criminal trial in New York. The vast majority, he had found, were not mentally ill. Devoted to public psychiatry, Smith ran a residential school in his hometown of Alton, Illinois, for 350 emotionally disturbed and handicapped children.

Vladimir Urse, director of the Cook County Hospital Mental Health Clinic, was responsible for the hundreds of mentally ill poor people who passed through the portals of the giant hospital. A former army lieutenant colonel, he had been chief of the psychiatric service at the military's famed Walter Reed Hospital.

Urse's full head of slicked-back gray hair and matching moustache gave him a courtly European appearance. A direct, pragmatic man, Urse spoke in an authoritative plain fashion.

Smith and Urse had the experience to detect a bogus claim of insanity, or so Martin and Zagel believed. For their third choice, the prosecutors picked the only physician who had had the benefit of extensive daily contact with Speck during the two-week period immediately after his capture. This physician, of course, was Bill Norcross, a superb surgeon who had enjoyed a close rapport with the killer. Speck had bummed cigarettes from Norcross and jokingly referred to him as "Dr. Zarkov," a reference to the scientific genius in the movie serial *Flash Gordon*. Five psychiatrists were more than enough, Martin and Zagel figured. Norcross would balance the panel.

Judge Paschen authorized the six experts to consult whatever electroencephalographers, neurologists, and psychologists they found necessary. He ordered the panel to answer the two separate questions of (1) Speck's competency to stand trial, and (2) his sanity during the time of the murders, and allowed both sides the right to offer evidence to contradict the panel's findings. The panel was to report in secret as quickly as possible and long before the setting of a trial date. Its findings, whatever they might be, were to be made known only to the prosecution, the defense, and the court. Acting on his own, Paschen also appointed Dr. William Haines, Martin's adviser on how to treat Corazon Amurao, to examine Speck and advise the court separately from the panel's findings.

Meanwhile, a few miles west of the courtroom, black activists were mounting a huge civil rights march through the streets of the ethnic enclave of Cicero. Cicero's Bohemians, Poles, and Slovaks were out in force with their distinctly redneck attitude toward blacks. Illinois National Guardsmen with drawn bayonets were on hand to assure order. Mayor Daley angrily told the

City Council that the racial unrest was being caused by liberals in the media who were encouraging the "haters, kooks, and psychotics."

The psychiatric panel went right to work, and, during September and October, a steady parade of neurologists, psychologists, and psychiatrists visited a seemingly cooperative Speck in the Cook County Jail. The only way the experts could repeat anything damaging that Speck might tell them would be if Getty decided to use Speck's words as part of an insanity defense. Although Speck knew that his words to the panel members could not be used against him as admissions of guilt, he consistently claimed that he had no memory of entering the town house.

Chatting with professional men like Grinker and Cleckley was a far cry from bellying up to the bar at Pete's Tap, but Speck followed his usual behavior—spinning fanciful tales for the learned gentlemen. In addition to these new guests, Speck was continuing his twice-a-week visits with Dr. Ziporyn. It was enough to make a man feel important, and Speck's behavior with the jail staff demonstrated this new attitude. On September 13, fellow Death Row inmate Mike Clancy asked Speck about his case. Speck replied that he was getting tired of his heavily guarded court appearances, adding, "There are only two kinds of good guards—a dead guard and a dying guard." On September 18, Speck demanded two plates of food from the jail cook, and when this was not immediately forthcoming called the cook a "cocksucker." On October 2, angry that a guard had taken his TV section to check for hidden contraband, Speck rushed toward the jail bars with a cup of hot water and threatened to throw it in the guard's face.

The appointment of the panel gave Martin and Zagel a chance to provide the psychiatrists with the extensive biography of Speck that the State's Attorney's Office had compiled. Martin decided to share the biography with the six panel members and

Dr. Haines. Crammed into bulging three-hole notebooks, the biography included Speck's arrest, employment, medical, and school records, as well as detailed statements from his relatives and acquaintances in Dallas, Monmouth, Michigan, and Chicago. Cumulatively, these records gave no evidence that Speck had ever demonstrated insanity during his twenty-four-plus years before the murders.

One crucial period was missing from this detailed summary of Speck's life—the period from eleven P.M. on July 13 until three-thirty A.M. on July 14. Since the definitive account of this period existed only in Myrna Foronda's notes of her interviews with Cora—an account that Martin would not risk duplicating—he gave the panel members the next best thing. Using a scale model of the town house that had been built by the FBI, Martin gave each of the six panel members a separate factual recitation of Cora Amurao's narrative of what had happened during those missing hours in the murderer's life. Each psychiatrist, after interviewing Speck at the county jail, was next taken to Martin's office in the nearby Criminal Court Building for the briefing. The panel members were able to get the benefit of this inside information because of Judge Paschen's order allowing both prosecution and defense to give the psychiatric experts confidential information that would not have to be shared with lawyers for the opposing side. Thus, Getty and his staff also were able to meet privately with the panel members and furnish them with privileged information not disclosed to the State.

Armed with this expansive background information from both sides, the psychiatrists conducted their examinations of Speck in the privacy of the jail's eye-examination room.

On September 29, Speck was taken to the police psychiatric institute at the 1121 South State headquarters for a test of his brain-wave activity. Dr. Kelleher was in charge of administering the electroencephalogram. The cold-blooded killer was very jittery about undergoing this exam, but Kelleher managed to calm him down. Consistent with the usual protocol, the sedative Seconal was administered to induce a light sleep. Speck's brain-wave activity was measured both when he was awake and when he was asleep. Later, Speck left the building with a jacket draped over his head to foil the waiting photographers.

The pockmarked, tattooed, low-IQ ex-convict and drifter was still worthy of worldwide media attention and remained a riddle to much of the world. However, he was much less of a mystery to the State's Attorney's Office, whose investigative team, headed by Bill Nellis, had written his biography, the biography of a man who, indeed, was "born to raise hell."

CHAPTER 27

Speck's story is that of a man spoiled rotten by his mother, abused by his alcoholic stepfather, and haunted by his failures in school, marriage, and employment. A coward without a knife, he would prove to be a killer with one. While Martin practiced his prosecutorial skills in Chicago, Speck practiced his criminal skills in Dallas. Like a ball player in the minor leagues training for the trip to the majors, Speck served a long apprenticeship in crime, usually talking his way out of trouble with the cunning of a born liar. In effect, he had been rehearsing his techniques of violence against women long before he walked into the nurses' town house.

Ironically, though, Speck came from a family of God-fearing, law-abiding people. The decisive difference for Richard Speck was that as the seventh of eight children, he was the one son who never really had a father figure. His own father, to whom he was very close, died when Speck was only six, and he would later learn to violently hate his stepfather, an alcoholic lunatic who frequently abused him.

Richard Benjamin Speck was born on December 6, 1941, in Kirkwood, Illinois, a sleepy decrepit little village located a stone's throw from Monmouth, in the central part of the state. Kirkwood is a tiny town that time forgot, consisting of a few ramshackle barns, falling-down fences, and a gaggle of small houses loosely flung around low hills. The Burlington Northern Railroad runs through this town on its way to Burlington, Iowa, a quaint antebellum town that lies across the wide Mississippi. The only prominent buildings in Kirkwood are the Methodist and Presbyterian churches.

Speck's parents both came from the small farming villages of west-central Illinois. His father, Benjamin Franklin Speck, was born in 1895 in Oquawka, Illinois, to parents of German descent. His mother, Mary Margaret Carbaugh Speck, was born in 1903 in Kirkwood to parents of Dutch-Irish descent. The two were married in 1921 in Monmouth. The Speck family was poor, and raising eight children in those tough times tested the family's mettle. Benjamin Speck was an honest, hardworking man who earned money as a farmer, logger, and packer for Western Stone Ware in Monmouth. Mary Margaret Carbaugh Speck was raised by a foster family, after her own mother died while delivering her. That foster family had helped found the United Presbyterian Church, and Speck's mother was imbued with the church's values, which she in turn imposed upon all her own children. One rule was no alcohol, and Mary Margaret Speck argued violently with her husband on the one occasion when he broke his abstinence by having a beer at a fish fry. She ruled her household with an iron fist.

Richard Speck was so much younger than his two older brothers and four older sisters that the only family members he was ever close to were his mother and his younger sister, Carolyn, born in 1943 as the eighth and last Speck child. The first traumatic event in Speck's life was the death of his father in 1947, at the age of fifty-three, when Richard was only six years old. A few years later, Speck's mother took a train trip to Chicago that would be eventful. Proving that love is blind, the religious mother of eight met and fell in love with a hard-drinking hell-raiser named

Carl August Rudolph Lindberg, who had been born in Texas in 1898 to Swedish parents. Lindberg's arrest record began in 1925 with a forgery and included multiple arrests for drunken driving. When drinking, Lindberg was prone to instability and violence. He was in every respect the total contrast to Richard Speck's hardworking, sober father. Nevertheless, Speck's mother married Lindberg on May 10, 1950, in Palo Pinto, Texas.

While his mother was settling into her new life in Texas as Mrs. Lindberg, Speck lived for a few months in Monmouth with a married sister so that he could finish third grade. Sara Madeline Speck Thornton was married to Earl Thornton, an uncle of Gene Thornton of Chicago. She recalls that her little brother was a "very good boy" who pulled his little red wagon on the Monmouth sidewalks, had many childhood friends in the neighborhood, and liked to play baseball. That year he began wearing glasses for mildly poor vision. When school ended, Richard and his younger sister, Carolyn, joined their mother and Lindberg to live in the rural Texas town of Santo. The only few years of happy home life that Richard Speck would ever know were at an end.

In Illinois, Richard Speck's four sisters and brother, Howard, put down roots. In 1952, Richard's other brother, Robert Coleman Speck, was killed in an auto accident near Monmouth at the age of twenty-three. Richard Speck, destined to be the bad boy of a decent family, would take a different path from his siblings.

Speck spent his first year in Texas in Santo, where he completed the fourth grade. The Lindbergs then moved to Dallas, and Speck's nomadic lifestyle began. Unlike his earlier life in Illinois, where Speck had been very close to his natural father, the Texas years were marked by chaos, despair, and violence. Speck's stepfather, Carl Lindberg psychologically abused Speck with insults and threats. The impressionable young boy had to adapt to the fact that his mother apparently loved this alcoholic bully who had absolutely no use for him. It was a very destructive influence on the young Richard Speck. Speck struggled through grades five through eight in the Dallas public school system. His eighth-grade teacher described him this way: "He was sort of sulky, but he didn't talk back. Evidently, he'd been taught at home not to talk back. He was a loner. He didn't have any friends in class. He seemed sort of lost. It didn't seem as though he knew what was going on. I don't think that I ever saw him smile. I wasn't able to teach him anything. I don't think anybody could get through to him. He seemed to be in a fog."

Among many eccentricities, Speck had a deathly fear of being stared at and refused to recite in class. But soon that threat would be lifted. In the fall of 1957, Speck enrolled in Crozier Technical School. He earned no credits that semester and even managed to flunk physical education. When the second semester began in January 1958, Speck did not return. His formal education was over.

In the meantime, Speck's criminal education had begun on October 17, 1955. Speck and two friends were riding their bicycles through a used car lot when the owner chased them away. In retaliation, Speck set fire to some rags lying in the lot. The three police officers who arrested him found a scrawny, pimply-faced thirteen-year-old who stood five feet nine inches and weighed only 110 pounds. He was released to his parents.

In 1963, Lindberg separated from Speck's mother, and drifted to California. By December 1965, Lindberg suffered from cerebral arteriosclerosis, or hardening of the blood vessels supplying the brain, and he returned from California to the care of a daughter living in Dallas. By this time, Richard Speck was well into a life-style that eerily resembled his stepfather's behavior. Seeking male figures with whom to bond, Speck began as a young teenager to run with a tough older crowd whose lives centered on booze, drugs, fighting, easy women, and cheap tattoos. His forty-one Dallas arrests include numerous citations for disturbing the peace, drunk and disorderly conduct, and fights in movie theaters and on the streets.

When he was only nineteen, Speck walked into an apartment occupied by three young women and made idle talk with them. Later, he walked off with their jewelry and with money taken from their billfolds. One month later, Speck and a friend grabbed a fifteen-year-old boy on the street and cut him under the eye and kicked him. That same year, the police found Speck crouching in the yard of a residence that he was about to burglarize at three in the morning. Speck cavalierly told the police, "I always carry a screwdriver."

There was a Mrs. Richard Speck. In 1961, Speck met Shirley Annette Malone at the Texas State Fair in Dallas, when Shirley was only fifteen years old and a freshman in high school. At the age of nineteen, Speck was sexually experienced and had been treated for five separate bouts of gonorrhea. Shortly after they met, Shirley became pregnant. Speck's mother told her son that since Shirley was pregnant it was best that he marry her. Mrs. Lindberg met Mrs. Malone the night before the wedding ceremony, although neither set of parents attended the wedding, which was conducted on January 19, 1962, before a justice of the peace in Dallas County. The newlyweds initially set up home with Speck's mother.

The Specks' tumultuous marriage was marked by frequent changes of address in East Dallas, because of Speck's drinking and nonpayment of rent. For roughly half the four years they were married, Speck was either in jail or in the penitentiary. By July 5, 1962, when Shirley gave birth to their healthy daughter, Robbie Lynn Speck, the doomed lovers had already separated. At the time of her daughter's birth, Shirley had no idea of her husband's whereabouts, though she thought that he was working on a 7UP truck. Actually, when his daughter was born, Speck was serving a twenty-two day term in jail in McKinney, Texas, for disturbing the peace during a drunken spree with friends. He later refused to pay the bills for his daughter's birth and also refused the opportunity to donate blood to help pay for the bill.

While in jail, Speck indulged one of his real passions, acquiring three new tattoos rendered in India ink by a jail artisan. Etched on his right shoulder blade was the name "Shirley." Etched on the front of his upper left calf was the inscription "West Texas Dickie Bird." Above it was drawn the body and wings of a bird having for its head an erect penis. Etched on his left forearm was the phrase "Born to raise hell." The three helped round out his collection. Speck explained, "All the fellas I ran around with had tattoos." Speck acquired most of his while drunk.

Ida Malone described Speck as a cruel, irresponsible, unstable, and violent husband to her daughter. Mrs. Malone said she thought that Speck's mother was a "wonderful person, one of the nicest people I have ever met. The only thing she ever did wrong was try to buy Richard out of trouble." She added, "When Shirley was pregnant, Speck would park in front of the house in his convertible and neck with other women. He would laugh at Shirley, who was sitting on the front porch. He told her that there wasn't much she could do about it. He inflicted this cruelty on Shirley at least six times." Ida Malone said that Speck displayed repeated violence toward her daughter, and, on one occasion, even hit his own daughter, Robbie Lynn, in the stomach. She said, "One time, Richard threw a knife at Shirley and hit her in the leg. Then, he beat her up. He would beat her both when he was drunk and when he was sober. I saw the marks on Shirley's arms, hands, and neck. Once, he put a knife to her throat." When he was home, Speck was also known to force his wife to have sex with him four or five times a day.

Not content to simply terrorize his wife, Speck also turned his violent attentions toward his mother-in-law. Speck and

Albert Malone did not get along, and Speck once told Ida Malone that if she wanted her husband killed, he would be glad to push Albert into the lake when he was fishing. In 1964, Ida and Albert Malone divorced, and Speck stepped up his attentions. One day, Speck was in Mrs. Malone's home and found a photo of her in a bathing suit. He promptly told her, "Hey, I've got a pretty good-looking mama-in-law and if I wasn't married, I'd make a date." He took the photo with him and that evening passed it around to several men in a bar. He also supplied Mrs. Malone's telephone number. That night, Ida Malone received several explicit calls from strangers asking her to go out. She said she did not date.

In July 1965, Speck twice attacked Mrs. Malone with guns and knives. On the first occasion, he showed up at her University Park home with Robbie Lynn and another man who was armed with a gun. Speck himself carried both a .22 and a .32 pistol. He boasted that he had a third gun in the car and that five additional guys were waiting on the corner, all carrying guns. Straddling her lap, he twisted her arm around her back and announced, "I'm going to kill you." Having terrified her, he left, yelling back, "Now, you tell that SOB ex-husband of yours what I did and see if he'll do anything about it."

Two days later, Speck returned alone with a switchblade and stuck it in Mrs. Malone's face. She picked up a two-by-four and told Speck, "I'll make you eat that knife!" Speck cursed her and fled. Emboldened, Mrs. Malone signed a complaint against Speck to University Park police. No arrest was made.

The Malones had seen enough of Speck. In January 1966, Shirley Malone filed for divorce and the decree was entered in that March. Speck did not contest the divorce. The following day, she married Tinker Frazier, a pipe fitter she had met while working as a waitress at the Joe Dobbs Coffee House. Despite Speck's many claims that she had been "messing around" with other men, thus deserving the beatings he gave her, Frazier was the only man Shirley ever dated after separating from Speck. Shirley kept their daughter; Speck kept his tattoos. Before the divorce became final, Speck visited Shirley and begged her to reconsider. While there, he also tried to borrow her car.

One memory stuck in Ida Malone's memory. Once, she and Speck were discussing the assassination of President Kennedy in Dallas. Speck was sitting in bed, with his feet folded underneath him. He told her that he had been taking dope and "was high as a kite." He added: "One of these days I am going to get my name in the paper. It won't be a small item. It will be the entire front page."

Despite a spell in prison, Speck's violence would go way beyond Shirley and Ida Malone. On November 10, 1962, Speck was arrested for howling and yelling in Dallas's Major Theater. According to the manager, "he was trying to fight all the men and hug all the women." In 1963, Speck stepped up his criminal activity to include forgery and the burglary of a food store, where he and two buddies made off with beer, cigarettes, and three dollars in cash. These were felony offenses, and he spent time at the Dallas county jail before going to the Texas Department of Corrections at Huntsville. Speck was confined to the Texas penitentiary system from September 16, 1963, until January 2, 1965, when he was released on parole.

He adapted well to this regimented life. One of Speck's penitentiary buddies was David Wayne Drake, a convicted burglar who played basketball and dominoes with Speck. He said that Speck "liked basketball, but was kind of clumsy." He recalls Speck "as a pretty good ole boy . . . he was an easygoing guy who never got in a hurry and was just real calm all the time . . . he never bothered nobody. He got along real well and was what we call a 'good convict.' " Drake added, though, "Penitentiary-wise, you don't really get that well acquainted . . . in the pen, you can't tell that much about a man. If he was in the world, that would be different, but down here a man acts completely different than he does in the free world."

As part of the diagnostic workup, the Texas Department of Corrections obtained information from a past employer and from Speck's mother. The employer was the 7UP Bottling Company, where Speck had stolen another employee's payroll check, forged his signature, and cashed it at a grocery store. The company reported: "Richard Speck worked here from August 24, 1960, until July 19, 1963, as a laborer. He was careless, troublesome, and, yet, was hardworking. We would not rehire him. He was dishonest." This was the longest period of employment in Speck's life.

Speck's mother, a graying, slender, slightly stooped woman, recalled a rosy picture of the young Richard. "Richard always loved fishing and swimming—anything to do with water," Mrs. Lindberg recalled. "Whenever I couldn't find him, I would always go to the pond and there he'd be. He always brought home every fish he caught, and I cooked them—as long as he cleaned them first. He got his sportsmanship from his father, who he resembles physically." She displayed an overwhelming desire to protect her youngest son. She wrote to the corrections board that "Richard was always punished when he did wrong and always had to be home by nine P.M. He always paid board and helped with household expenses until he was married. He was interested in all kinds of electrical work."

Asked how he got into trouble, Mrs. Lindberg was expansive: "Richard's trouble started with his stepfather. He disliked Richard very much and told him he hated him and couldn't stand the sight of him. This left a mark on him during his years of growing up. He didn't have the companionship of a father. He sought his security with older boys, and this led him to drinking and running around. His stepfather drank very heavily. When he worked at 7UP, all the men were older and he ran around and drank with them. This is Richard's trouble—drinking. He is not an alcoholic, but he drinks on weekends with the men. He has always gotten into trouble when drinking and he has never gotten into trouble when not drinking. Our family has always been very close to Richard, and he is very loving, kind, and considerate toward us. Richard will stay with me at my daughter's house [Carolyn Speck had also married] until he gets a job and gets straightened out. We will help him, his wife, and baby, in every way we know how."

Similarly, Carolyn Speck Wilson was fiercely loyal to her brother and strongly antipolice. She said Speck loved animals and children, recalling, "Our house looked like a menagerie, with Richard always bringing home stray cats and dogs that later became pets. A sister could not have asked for a better brother. As children, we did everything together. I was a tomboy and loved doing the things he did—climbing trees, fishing, and swimming."

Speck himself professed to be ready to go straight when released. He had taken an interest in carpentry and claimed that he was anxious to return to work and support his new family. He added that he had been a devout Baptist since age eight and attended church regularly.

The psychologist at the Diagnostic Center of the Texas Department of Correction, however, made the accurate appraisal. Speck, the experts concluded, was dull and slow, was likely to relapse, and should be kept in maximum security because of his emotional and social immaturity. His rating for rehabilitation was described as "poor."

Rehabilitated or not, Speck was back on the streets. On January 4, 1965, two days after his release from Huntsville, Speck told his parole officer, Lewis Bramblett, that he would do nothing that would put him back in prison. Speck said that he was interested only in regaining his driver's license, finding a job, and having a happy home life with his bride of three years, Shirley Annette Malone Speck, and their young daughter, Robbie Lynn.

Five days later, at two-twenty in the morning, Sarah Wadsworth returned from a bowling outing and parked her car behind the Dallas apartment building where she lived. As she walked toward her building, a man sprang from the shadows, wrapped his left arm around her neck, and placed a long, curving knife against her throat. The man was Speck.

"If you scream, I'll kill you!" he said to her.

Wadsworth screamed and fell to the ground. She screamed again, and a man came running out of a nearby apartment, shouting, "Are you all right?" Speck ran from the parking lot. Two Dallas police officers responded within minutes and drove around the neighborhood seeking a man of Speck's description. The officers saw Speck cut down an alley and walk through an apartment gangway to another street. When Speck saw the police car, he changed directions and started walking faster. Speck was arrested, and a carving knife was found in the nearby shrubbery.

Speck told the officer, "I just left my girlfriend's house," and he gave a nearby address. Confronted by the officers with both the knife and Sarah Wadsworth's description, Speck fell silent. He smelled of alcohol, but was not staggeringly drunk. A few days later, Wadsworth positively identified Speck in a police lineup. Speck told a detective that he was broke and his motive was robbery. After sitting in the Dallas jail for four days on a charge of aggravated assault against a female, Speck dreamed up an excuse.

In this new version, Speck related how he had gone to downtown Dallas for the evening and was planning to return home by bus, when a casual acquaintance and another man picked him up in a car. Then, he alleged, the two men suddenly demanded money from Speck, who just happened to notice a foot-long knife on the floor of the car. In this new story, Speck grabbed the knife and ordered the men to let him out of the car. He took the knife and a bottle of wine with him from the car. Speck told Bramblett that he couldn't remember clearly what happened next, but that he did remember grabbing a woman in the parking lot with the intention of robbing her, because he had been unable to find work. The last thing he remembers, he told his parole officer, was that he ran from the parking lot. Speck was adamant that he had no intention of raping the woman. He added that he had no other recollection of the incident until "I came to in the county jail . . . If I hadn't been drinking, I wouldn't have done it." Bramblett found Speck to be subdued and remorseful.

What Speck was really demonstrating was his phenomenal animal cunning in knowing what to admit, what to deny, and when to claim amnesia based upon drink or drugs. First, he denied grabbing Wadsworth at all. When this did not work, his next line of defense was to admit to the less serious offense, robbery, rather than rape. He then steadfastly claimed a drug-shrouded amnesia to cover the inconsistencies of his stories.

Speck was sentenced to 490 days in jail for the assault on Sarah Wadsworth, with the sentence to run concurrently with a sentence for his parole violation. However, due to a bureaucratic slipup, Speck was required to serve only the time for the parole violation. He was released from Huntsville on July 2, 1965, about 300 days early.

After his second release from Huntsville that summer of 1965, Speck started to let people know that he was proud to be an ex-convict. Alvin Ray Wrenn, a Dallas barber who cut Speck's hair and often visited Speck's favorite Dallas bar, Ginny's Lounge, recalls: "He wanted everybody to know that he'd been in prison. I would have a roomful of people waiting in my barbershop, and Speck would brag that he was just out of the pen and tough as nails. One night, I bought a bottle of beer for a woman at Ginny's Lounge. Turned out it was Speck's wife, Shirley. Several customers warned me, 'Boy, do you know what you're doing? That's Richard Speck's wife, and you better not buy her no bottle of beer. He's mean, he'll kill you.' "

During that summer of 1965, Speck was employed as a driver for a meat company. Speck had six driving accidents during the three months he worked for the Patterson Meat Company. His supervisor, Jim Becker, found Speck a "very likeable fellow" when sober. When drinking, Becker added, Speck was "sometimes nasty, other times silent, in a shell." Becker was also a customer of Ginny's and recalls one occasion there when he saw Speck with a white-handled, blue steel .22 caliber pistol. Speck proudly showed Becker the gun, explaining that he carried it as "an equalizer."

The bartender at Ginny's was Nancy Simms, a stocky twenty-nine-year-old ex-professional wrestler who used various aliases and had a minor police record in Louisiana, New York, and Texas. By any name, Nancy was a formidable woman and quite capable of standing up to Speck, whom she met in October 1965. Nancy was divorced and living alone with her three children at the time, and was having trouble finding a baby-sitter while she tended bar. This was during one of the many periods Speck was both unemployed and separated from his wife. Speck's mother knew Nancy and called one day on Speck's behalf, asking if he might be allowed to move in with the bartender early that December. She agreed, and Speck stayed with her on and off for several months. He was good to her three children, often taking them on all-day fishing expeditions at a nearby lake, but she ran him off when he quarreled with her ex-husband. The relationship was nonsexual, though Speck would later falsely tell psychiatrists that Simms was simply "an old whore," and that her ex-husband had bashed Speck's head because he had "screwed her."

Nancy Simms offered some insights into Speck's character: "Speck," said Nancy Simms, "was lazy and drank too much, but he would occasionally go three or four days without drinking. However, once he sipped a beer, he would not stop until he was drunk. When he was not drinking, he was a nice, sweet person. When drinking, he was aggressive, belligerent, and a trouble-maker. He was very jealous and possessive, and he talked a lot about his many fights. He always carried a large pocketknife. He always did whatever he wanted to do whenever he wanted to do it without any thought of the consequences. Speck would do stupid things to hurt other people, and would always be sorry afterward. He was always sorry afterward, but while he might give a damn about what he had done, he always knew exactly what he was doing while he was doing it. Speck thought that he did not have to work or face consequences, because he believed that his mother would always give him money and take care of him and bail him out of trouble."

One of Speck's bosses, Huby Patterson, owner of the Patterson Meat Company, said, "Speck was a hard worker, when he applied himself. He'd handle those hundred-pound boxes the way most people would handle a ten-pound box. He was a like-able, social guy, but he didn't seem to care if the sun came up." Patterson fired Speck when he suddenly stopped showing up for work. Speck spent much of his nonworking time in Dallas at his favorite hangout, Ginny's Lounge. The owner, Virginia Norris, said Speck was a regular customer who was known for always having a knife with him. She said that Speck was extremely jealous about his wife, Shirley, and "didn't want any-one talking to her when she walked in. If someone did, Speck would create a scene."

Speck targeted Ginny's Lounge for his next brush with trouble. In January 1966, shortly after Shirley Malone sued him for divorce, Speck began to argue with forty-year-old Curtis

Robinson. Speck pulled his switchblade and stabbed Robinson several times. Both combatants were taken to Parkland Hospital, where Speck complained that his head, left chest wall, and thumb were hurting. However, his X rays were negative and he walked out of the hospital charged with aggravated assault. Speck's mother hired an attorney and the assault charge was reduced to disturbing the peace. Speck was convicted of the lesser charge and fined ten dollars. Refusing to pay, he spent three days in jail.

This would be the last time Dallas police would have Speck in custody, though it was not the last crime Speck would commit in Dallas. With forty-one arrests under his belt at age twenty-four, Speck still had one more Dallas burglary left in him. On March 5, 1966, he bought a 1954 Plymouth. The next evening at eleven P.M. noise was heard at the rear of the A & M Grocery and Market in Dallas. When police arrived on the scene, they found a screwdriver at the point of entry of the grocery's rear door. More than seventy cartons of cigarettes had been stolen. Speck left the scene with the cigarettes stashed in his trunk and set up shop minutes later in a parking lot, where he began to sell the contraband. By the time police arrived, the car had been abandoned.

Tracing the car to Speck, police went to his last known address, the residence of his sister, Carolyn. They were told that he had not lived there since October 1965. An arrest warrant for the burglary was issued in Speck's name on March 8, 1966. An arrest would mean another prison term. Speck decided it was time to leave Texas. On March 9, his sister, Carolyn, took him to the bus depot in Dallas. Carolyn had tears in her eyes; Richard had a growing hatred in his heart. There's a passage in the Talmud that says, "If you don't know where you're going, any road will take you there." The bus departed for Chicago.

His first stop was the Chicago home of the Thorntons, who had no idea he was on the run. He stayed only a few days, however, deciding to return to his boyhood home and look up the rest of his family. At first, he moved in with Elmer Johnson and his wife, Gertrude, both of whom were friends of the entire Speck family. Speck's brother, William Howard Speck, thirty-five, a Korean War veteran was a carpenter and recommended his younger brother to another carpenter in town, Oscar Neil. Speck signed on for a one-month payroll period. Howard Speck was also a very close friend of Monmouth police chief Harold Tinder whose force included only two part-time detectives to protect the 11,000 citizens of Monmouth. Tinder described Howard Speck as one of the "nicest people you could know." Richard Speck was something else; after working the mean streets of Dallas, Richard Speck would find Harold Tinder and his two deputies to be easy pickings.

Speck started out as a good worker, sanding plasterboard for Neil. Occasionally, he would tell Neil that he wanted "to make enough money to bring my mother to Monmouth." Soon, however, Speck began to skip work in favor of visiting various Monmouth taverns and chain-drinking Schlitz beer and chain-smoking Kool filters. On March 25, Speck left the Johnsons' and moved into the Christy Hotel in downtown Monmouth. He stayed almost a month, alternating occasional visits to his family with constant visits to saloons.

Erma Clair Holeman, the oldest of the eight Speck children, lived with her husband, Kenneth, in nearby Galesburg, Illinois, where they ran a family business, the Galesburg Tire and Vulcanizing Company. Speck showed up one day for a fifteen-minute visit and asked for ten dollars. His sister gave him the money, as well as "quite a talking to."

She recalls: "Richard was the bad apple in our family. The only other tragedy we had in the family was when my younger brother, Robert, skidded off an icy road near the bridge coming into Monmouth and killed himself. He was only twenty-three.

At first, we six older children resented Richard and Carolyn because our parents spoiled them so much, but we came to love them. Richard was constantly with his father. However, after Dad died in 1947 and Mom moved to Texas in 1950, we began to lose touch with Richard and Carolyn. The next time we saw them was a few years later, during a summer vacation. They were cute kids, but loud, and they were becoming worse and worse in being spoiled. You couldn't help but like Richard, though, because he had such a nice personality."

In 1960 the Holemans visited Dallas, and Speck's sister concluded, "Richard simply had no discipline. We older kids were all raised to believe that liquor was evil and that strict discipline was good. Now, Richard was allowed to go out every night and he was drinking. He was working for a pop company to make money. I didn't approve of the way he was living." She added that although Speck "always appeared meek, he also gave the impression that he was unloved."

In 1966, when Speck visited Galesburg, his older sister was still disapproving. "Richard felt bad because I didn't invite him to my home, but I didn't want him in my home," she said. "I thought that a person of his age should have been working and taking care of his wife and child. He didn't know how to work hard." She had also heard that Richard had been in trouble in Monmouth. "We all had reliable names up there in Monmouth and we didn't want to be embarrassed."

Summarizing her own view of Speck, as well as the view of all of the five older children, she said: "To be very frank, we didn't know him."

Speck worked only two carpentry jobs for Neil, one lasting three days and the other four. After this spurt of employment, he'd had his fill of sanding plasterboard. The saloons were more to his liking. Friendly and ingratiating on the surface, Speck was able to strike up barroom conversations, but he could never

connect on a deeper, meaningful level. And, as always, his bragging and lying were only one step away from violence.

One favorite saloon was the Palace Tap in Monmouth, where
the barmaid, Jane Boon, found him "spooky." Speck told Boon
that he could not return to Texas because he had killed a man.
Later, he changed the story to say that he thought he had killed a
man, but later learned that the man did not die. The man, he told
Jane Boon with a wink, was his ex-wife's husband.

Loretta Payne, a twenty-eight-year-old cook at the Elk's
Club in Monmouth, met Speck in the Brass Rail Tavern, and
the two struck up a conversation while playing the tavern's
shuffleboard bowling machine. Loretta could not help but notice
Speck's "funny accent," so she asked him, "What parts do you
come from, honey?" The question set Speck off and running.
Noting that he was originally from Monmouth, he told her that
he grew up in Dallas. To impress her, he said that he had to leave
Texas because of a barroom fight in which he thought that he
had killed a man. Not satisfied with this story, he pressed on to
say that when he was fifteen he was "pushing dope across the
Mexican border." Then, he brought out the photos of Shirley
and Robbie Lynn. Next, he displayed his scars and tattoos and
bragged about all the fights he had survived.

Loretta would see Speck's true colors a few nights later,
when he accompanied a group of her friends on a bar-hopping
trip to Gulfport, Illinois, a Mississippi River shanty town thirty-
five miles from Monmouth. Gulfport's several hundred residents
lived by the river in an area dominated by bars, pickup trucks,
and shanties-on-stilts. During his trip to Gulfport, Speck carried
a knife underneath his sweater in a holster strapped to his chest.
Later, in the saloon's men's room, Speck threateningly flashed
the knife under a man's nose. A report was made and after some
minutes passed, Speck noticed that a Gulfport policeman, aptly
named "Tiny," had entered the saloon. The policeman stood six

feet two inches tall and weighed 300 pounds. Faced with superior force, Speck did the prudent thing and hid the knife in Loretta's purse. Tiny, however, was not fooled by the ruse and packed the whole Monmouth crowd off to the Gulfport jail. Later, at City Hall, Speck explained that he was used to carrying a weapon wherever he went and that he was afraid to go into the "rough" Gulfport taverns without his knife. There was no arrest.

Loretta summarized, "Speck was unable to make friends. He had the kind of personality where nobody wanted to be around him for long. We took him with us to Gulfport because he had just come to town, nobody would make friends with him, and we all felt sorry for him. That night he was happy as a lark but it was like he could not just jive along with everybody else. Since he couldn't really relate to other people, he would just talk about things back in Texas, most of them bullshit. Since he couldn't make friends, he acted tough and was foulmouthed. He was mad at the world and always wanted to fight."

A few days after the Gulfport incident, Speck acted out his signature burglary-rape. On Saturday night, April 2, Mrs. Virgil Harris, a sixty-five-year-old divorcée living in Monmouth, was baby-sitting, a job for which she earned $2.50. She arrived at her home about one the next morning, and, as she removed her coat, a six-foot white male speaking with a strange accent emerged from her bedroom, wearing a dark jacket. Police would later find a chair beneath her bathroom window and a ripped pack of cigarettes. Mrs. Harris, a nonsmoker, noticed that two cigarette butts were on her bedroom floor and that her belongings were strewn about the floor of the house.

Speck grabbed her from behind, covered her face with his hand, and flashed a knife in front of her face. "Don't make a sound and you will not get hurt," he said. He then blindfolded her with a rag and began to slice her housecoat into strips. Walking her into the front room, he softly remarked that he had killed

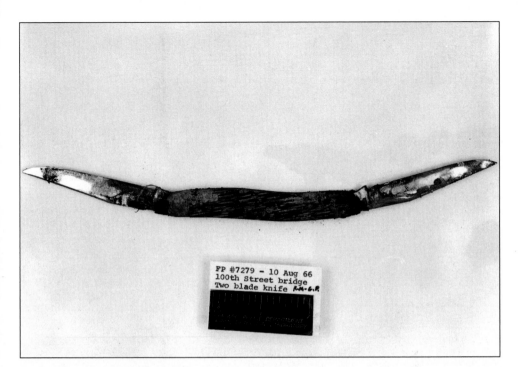

Police photograph of the open two-blade knife recovered from the Calumet River. The blades are long enough and sharp enough to have been the instrumentalities of Speck's brutal murders.

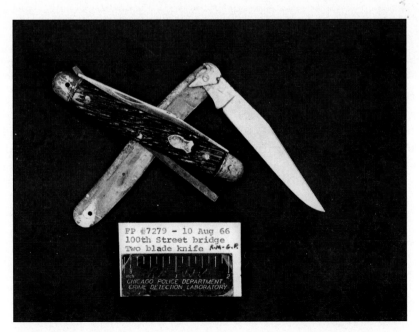

Photograph of the same deadly knife showing its two lethal blades.

100th Street Bridge over Calumet River that Speck had to cross going to and coming from the nurse's town house. Eddie Willow and Byron Carlile dragged the bottom of the river with a magnet and recovered a knife that the police and prosecuters believed was the murder weapon. Not used in evidence because no human blood stains could be detected and no witness could positively identify it.

Screen pushed out of window in Cora's own bedroom which she pushed out to climb on the second-floor deck to scream for help.

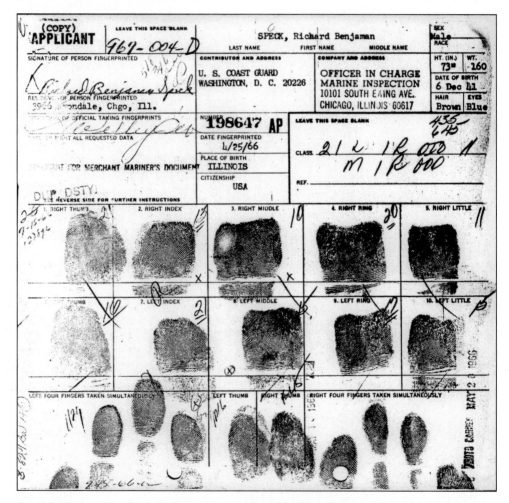

Speck's Coast Guard inked finger prints that matched the three latent fingerprints on the south bedroom door. Flown in from Washington, D.C. by a pilot during an airline strike and given to Lieutenant Emil Giese, who made the positive identification.

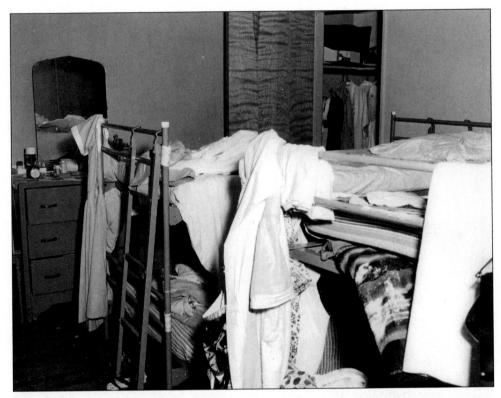

Back bedroom depicting the closet where three Filipino girls ran and hid from Speck until the American nurses talked them into coming out. Two of the three bunk beds are visible in the front of the closet door.

South bedroom bunk bed where Corazon first hid by wiggling underneath the bottom bunk.

Aerial photo of 2319 East 100th Street (far left with crowd in front) and five other adjoining town houses facing East 100th Street. The National Maritime Union hiring hall is clearly visible across the street from 2319. Speck had several opportunities to observe the nurses in 2319 before July 14, 1966.

FBI model of two stories of the 2319 East 100th Street town house. Back bedroom in upper left corner of picture shows the three bunk beds, including the two Corazon hid under.

Speck carved his initials in a tree outside the house of his sister and brother-in-law, Martha and Eugene Thornton, who lived on the North Side of Chicago.

The rear of the town house. Speck entered by jimmying open the window screen and unlocking the back door.

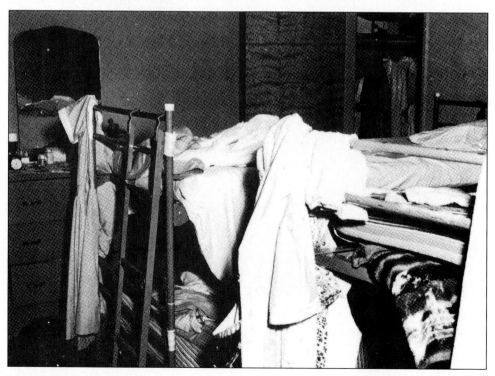

Interior of the south bedroom. The nurses lived in cramped quarters.

The northwest bedroom. The poster on the wall reads: "Sleep well tonight . . . your National Guard is awake!"

Scale model used at the trial showing the upstairs of the town house where Speck held six bound nurses.

Scale model showing positions of the victims' bodies upstairs. The eighth victim was found on the living room sofa downstairs.

Actual photo of Richard Speck on file with the U.S. Coast Guard.

Police artist's sketch of Speck based on Cora's description.

Speck's room at the Raleigh Hotel where he stayed the first night after the murders.

Police Superintendent O.W. Wilson
holding up a photo of Richard Speck,
whom he identified publicly as the killer
before Speck had even been arrested.
© AP/Wide World Photo

Claude Lunsford, Starr Hotel resident. After the murders,
Lunsford testified, Speck repeatedly asked Lunsford to show
him how to jump a freight train to get out of Chicago.

The Starr Hotel, where Speck spent the second night after the murders during the intensive manhunt.

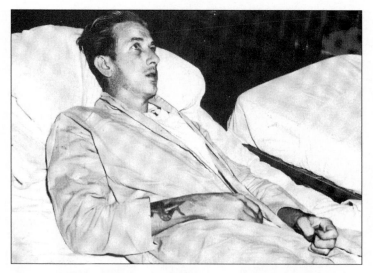

Speck on his hospital cot recovering from a suicide attempt.
His serpent tattoo is visible under his right sleeve. © *Chicago
Sun-Times*

Cora, in nurse's uniform, leaving the Cermak jail infirmary.
She positively identified Speck in his hospital room. © *Chicago
Tribune*

Mrs. Lena Wilkening, mother of the slain
Pamela Wilkening, leaving South Chicago
Community Hospital on July 14, 1966, the
date of the murders. © APAVide World Photo

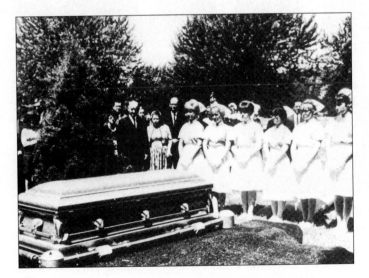

Six student nurses from South Chicago Community
Hospital at the graveside of their classmate Gloria Jean
Davy. © APAVide World Photo

Cora recuperated at the Moraine-on-the-Lake Hotel, where she was safe from reporters and unwelcome visitors.

Corazon Amurao with her police protector, Jack Wallenda.

TEAM SPECK:
Back row, from left to right: John Glenville, Mike Lambesis, Eddie Wielosinski, Byron Carlile, Jack Wallenda, Bill Nellis. *Front row, from left to right:* George Murtaugh, State's Attorney John J. Stamos, Chief Prosecutor Bill Martin, Frank Lassandrella Jim Zagel.

Judge Herbert Paschen.

State's Attorney John Stamos and Bill Martin confer outside the Peoria Courthouse.

Burton Buhrke, Jack Wallenda, and Byron Carlile head to court with a drawerful of files. Courtesy of Bill Scanlon

Relatives of Speck arriving at the courthouse to testify for the defense. *From the left:* Speck's sister Shirley Jensen, brother-in-law Eugene Thornton, sister Martha Thornton, and brother Howard Speck. © APAVide World Photos

Speck being led through the crowd of reporters gathered outside the Peoria County Courthouse on his way to the first day of the trial. © APAVide World Photos

The door from the south
bedroom and the beer can
Gerald Getty claimed was
the real source of Speck's
fingerprint found on the door,
under the theory that Speck had
been framed by police.
Courtesy of Bill Scanlon

Speck, omnipresent cigarette
in hand, sitting with his
attorney, Public Defender
Gerald Getty. © *Chicago Tribune*

Speck's jail cell during the trial. He carved his name on the inside of the door.

© *Chicago Sun-Times*

Speck, wearing handcuffs and dressed for court, smokes a cigarette during a break in the trial. © *Chicago Tribune*

A picture of Bambi drawn and signed by Richard Speck. Psychiatrist Marvin Ziporyn introduced him to painting and drawing. © *Chicago Sun-Times*

Richard Speck in Stateville Prison in Joliet, Illinois, on November 6, 1991, a month before he died of a heart attack at the age of forty-nine. © Lloyd DeGrane

a woman before, adding, "Take off every stitch of your clothes, or I will rip them off."

Trying to reason with Speck, the sixty-five-year-old Mrs. Harris remarked, "You don't seem like a bad man. Why don't we sit down on the davenport and just talk." They both sat down and she held his hand, asking, "Are you a Christian?" Speck was silent.

Then, he blurted out, "I came through the back door, and I'm going to stay all night. How long has it been since you've had any?"

He ordered her to the bedroom and took off his clothes, threatening, "If I don't get what I want, I'll kill you." He then made her remove her clothes, got into bed with her, and completed sexual intercourse. The act took only a few minutes, less time than he would afterward spend using the strips of fabric from her housecoat to tie her hands tightly behind her back and her feet at the ankles. As he did this, he remarked, "I need to go to Springfield." To placate him and to get him out of the house, she offered him the use of her car, but Speck left on foot.

Mrs. Harris was able to get the rag from her face and work her feet loose. Naked, with her hands still tied behind her back, she went to her next door neighbor's house for help. Her hands were tied so tightly behind her back that the neighbor had to use scissors to cut the bindings. The police were called and Mrs. Harris was taken to the hospital, where she was examined by Dr. J. D. Simmons, the same doctor who had delivered Richard Speck into the world on December 6, 1941. She told police that the house had been ransacked and that the $2.50 she earned baby-sitting had been stolen from her purse. She said that her attacker was "very polite" and spoke "very softly with a Southern drawl." She added that he also "perspired greatly."

Speck began to emerge as the leading suspect in this burglary-rape when police also investigated him for the possible murder of an attractive thirty-two-year-old barmaid, Mary Kay Pierce, who worked at her brother-in-law's saloon, Frank's Place, in Monmouth. She disappeared after leaving the saloon at twelve forty-five A.M. on Saturday, April 9. After interviewing 600 people, the Monmouth police determined that her brother-in-law, Frank Nuckles, was the last person to see her alive. Her sister, Ruth Nuckles, found the body on April 13, lying in an empty hog house behind the tavern. She had been killed by a powerful blow to the abdomen that ruptured her liver. The door to the hog house was swinging back and forth in the April breeze. The victim's family did not report her missing until April 13 because they thought that she had left to visit a man in Georgia, and did not find out otherwise until the man in Georgia informed them on April 13 that she had canceled the trip. The body was discovered shortly afterwards.

When Speck came to collect his last paycheck from Oscar Neil on April 15, the police were waiting to question him about the Pierce murder. Neil's construction company had built several of the hog houses—which were intended to be sold to the area farmers—during Speck's brief tenure as one of Neil's employees. One of Pierce's girlfriends had told police that she believed Speck was following her from tavern to tavern. Neil had told police that shortly after the barmaid disappeared, Speck remarked to him, "Do you all know about that woman who was killed? Wasn't that awful? I tried to have a date with her."

On April 15, Police Chief Tinder's two deputies grilled Speck about the murder. Speck gave a typical performance: "No, sir, I sure didn't kill that girl," he said. He readily admitted, though, to being in the knife fight in Gulfport, explaining, "This other guy in a restaurant had a knife and when he pulled his, I pulled mine and he took off." Speck added, "I go to church all the time." Then, the officers tried to goad Speck with a technique straight from Police Interrogation 101, implying that the victim "had it coming" because, as everyone knew, she had previously "dated black men." This ruse, designed to arouse the ire of a hillbilly like Speck, fell on deaf ears. Cunning as ever, Speck replied, "Well, everybody to their own kicks, I say, but I don't like the idea."

The interview was cut short when Speck complained of not feeling well. A second interrogation was rescheduled for April 19, but the detectives arrived at Speck's hotel room only to find that he had bolted town hours before the deputies arrived. Realizing that Speck had fled, the two sergeants searched his room at the Christy Hotel, looking for a blunt instrument that might have killed Mary Kay Pierce. Instead, they found a radio and costume jewelry, and took them into custody. By coincidence, on April 18 Mrs. Virgil Harris had noticed for the first time that her radio and jewelry were missing, and reported it to police as part of the April 3 burglary-rape in her home. The items she reported and the items found in Speck's room matched, providing conclusive proof that Speck was the perpetrator of this bizarre incident.

During this search, the police found several items reported missing in at least two other Monmouth burglaries. Speck was also a suspect in another four break-and-entry cases that occurred during the one month he was in town. At the time he split the scene, Speck had paid his weekly rent at the Christy through April 22. Nevertheless, on April 19, the owner-manager of the hotel saw Speck walking out the door with his two suitcases. "I'm not leaving," Speck said, "I'm going to the laundromat."

Speck was on a bus, once again to find sanctuary in Chicago with his unsuspecting sister, Martha Thornton. He would never be charged with either the Monmouth murder or rape.

He arrived back at the Chicago home of Martha and Gene Thornton on April 19. He had been forced to leave Monmouth, Speck told his sister and brother-in-law, because a crime "syndicate" was pressuring him to "sell narcotics" and he refused to do so. He added that he had been beat up and that he ran away from Monmouth to save his life. Gene Thornton quickly decided that his brother-in-law needed a spell at sea, which led to Speck's shipping out on April 30.

Most of Speck's employment with Inland Steel consisted of recuperating from his emergency appendectomy. In the few days he did spend at sea, Speck did not impress his shipmates, although none found him particularly dangerous. This was the perception despite the fact that Speck's alcohol-induced troubles included two occasions when he exposed his genitals to male shipmates and another time when he threatened a shipmate with a knife.

During his two voyages on the *Clarence B. Randall*, Speck's jobs included pulling lines on the dock, scrubbing the ship down, painting, and cleaning carpets in the pilot house. His roommate, Jessie Blue, proved to be a willing listener for Speck's bragga-docio. Speck related to Blue that one time he and his uncle were hunting, became surrounded by wolves, and his uncle's gun jammed. Speck killed all the wolves with one magic bullet, he said. On another occasion, Speck said that he had once swum the English Channel while entirely under water. Speck read a lot of comic books, Blue thought. Blue found the swimming story particularly farfetched, based on his own experience with Speck. Once, while the *Randall* was tied up at the dock, Speck was work-ing on the side of the ship, scrubbing marks on the rudder, when he lost his balance, fell out of the work boat, and landed in a few feet of water. Speck paddled furiously and screamed for help before being righted by shipmates.

Speck bragged to Blue that he once caught his wife with another man and cut both of them badly with a knife. He said that he cut Shirley in the face and stabbed the man, adding that as a result of the attack he was sent to prison. During Speck's second voyage after the appendectomy, he told Blue about the nurse he had met in Michigan, Judy Laakaniemi, and also showed him

portions of their correspondence. In one letter, Speck wrote to
Judy that he loved her and couldn't wait to get back to Michigan
to go skiing with her (a sport he didn't know in the least). Speck
confided to Blue, however, that he was simply leading the nurse
on. "If you want to pull the wool over a girl's eyes," Speck told
his shipmate, "this is the way you do it. You write her a letter."
He added, "I haven't had sex with her, yet, but I will."

Blue thought that Speck was "intelligent in a sneaky kind
of way. He wasn't too smart, but he could sure get out of work
when he wanted to." Strangely, though, the work Speck usually
avoided was light work. When he worked, he preferred to do
heavy physical work. Blue said that he had several arguments
with Speck, but that afterward, "Speck would always apologize."
Whether aship or ashore, Speck always carried a switchblade
with a three-inch blade, Blue noted. In summary, though, Blue
concluded, "I liked Richard Speck, and I never thought him to be
a potential killer."

Speck's violent nature was also lost on shipmate Raymond
Slope. One day in June, after Slope left his watch as a wheelman
at four P.M., a drunken Speck came to Slope's room and demanded
that Slope take his picture with the Polaroid camera Slope kept.
Speck also demanded a drink. When Slope responded that he
had neither film for the camera nor anything to drink, Speck
got belligerent. Slope replied, "Get the hell out of my room!" As
he retreated, Speck threatened, "I'll get you. I'll cut you up. I'll
beat the hell out of you." As Speck talked, he made a slashing
side-to-side motion with his hand, and Slope saw the flash of a
switchblade. Still, Slope did not take the incident seriously and
never reported it to the ship's captain.

As Speck walked off the *Randall* on the morning of June 15
after being fired, he asked Red Gerrald, thirty-nine, who had
worked as the ship's night cook, to give him a ride to a tavern.
After Speck became mildly smashed, Gerrald recalls, he asked

the bartender for five dollars' worth of change and said, "I'm going to call my nurse friend up in Michigan." In an attempt to win Judy Laakaniemi's affection, the ever-creative Speck was about to transform his being fired from the *Randall* for drunkenness into an act of knightly gallantry on behalf of the nurse. What happened next Laakaniemi subsequently shared with a court-appointed psychiatric panel. In his telephone call from Chicago, Speck told Laakaniemi that he had gotten into a fight with one of his shipmates over a letter that she had sent to him. "This other guy called you a whore," Speck told Laakaniemi, "and I couldn't let him get away with this, so we got in a big fight that got me fired."

Believing that Speck had really lost his job over her, she told him that if he wanted to seek employment on one of the ships operating out of Michigan's Upper Peninsula, she would be glad to try to help him and would show him around her hometown of Houghton, Michigan. At the time, the former Judy Sorensen, twenty-eight, was going through a divorce from her husband of seven years, Waino Laakaniemi. She was a typical upper Michigan Scandinavian woman, blond, with a large, robust frame, fair skin, and a pleasant face. She had a heart of gold and believed in helping people. She had completed two years of college at Northern Michigan University in Marquette and had recently completed a training course to qualify as a nurse's aide. She began working at St. Joseph's in Hancock, Michigan, in March, 1966.

She gave Speck a bath before he went into surgery for his appendectomy on the night of May 3, and chatted with him to get his mind off the pain he was suffering. Speck said that he was out of cigarettes and "sure could use a smoke." Since she was compassionate and was also getting off work at nine-thirty P.M., the nurse volunteered to go out and buy him some. As he recovered, Speck, basking in the attention, joked with all the nurses assigned to him, including Judy. He also studied the hospital's bulletin board intently enough to learn Judy's home phone number.

After he was discharged from the hospital and as he was about to board the train for the trip back to Chicago to continue his recuperation with the Thorntons, Speck called Judy from the train station. He thanked her for the cigarettes and asked her to thank the other nurses for all their kindnesses. Later, from Chicago, he sent cards to all the nurses, telling them that he got back to Chicago, OK and was in fine shape. He also called Judy at her apartment and asked her if she would write to him "as a friend." The nurse told Speck, "I'll write to you as a friend." She made it clear, however, that having just divorced, she was "not looking for a new boyfriend." The two corresponded when Speck resumed his job on the *Randall*, with Judy describing everyday life at the hospital in Hancock and with Speck responding in a girlish scrawl that attempted to describe his adventures at sea.

Now, in his June 15 call from a saloon, Speck was trying to step up the friendship. Reassured that he was welcome to visit her in Michigan, he spent the next week at a Chicago flophouse, the St. Elmo, in the steamy Calumet Harbor world. One afternoon, while Speck was drinking at Pete's Tap, a fight broke out between two customers. To impress two women he had just met, Speck jumped off his bar stool, flashed his switchblade, and told one of them, "If you hit him again, I'll cut your guts out. He's a friend of mine." In fact, Speck barely knew him. When the first man responded to Speck's challenge, saying, "You put that knife down and we'll go outside," Speck refused, answering "I don't play that game." At this point, bartender Ray Crawford broke up the fight.

On June 21, Speck boarded a train that would take him back to Michigan and Judy Laakaniemi. He arrived in Hancock on June 22, and Judy met him at the station and took him to the nearby town of Houghton, where he registered at the downtown Douglas House. She drove him around town, suggesting places where he might work. The next day was her day off and the unlikely couple went to a beach, where they spent ten hours sitting in the sand and talking. Most of the conversation centered on Speck's tour with the *Randall.*

"Don't you think it was kind of silly to get into a fight over what somebody said about me?" she asked. Speck answered, "Well, they didn't have no right to call you that."

Speck said that he liked the water and wanted to get back on a boat. Judy told him that there was a boat that sailed from Houghton to Isle Royale three times a week and suggested that he apply. She offered him the use of the new car she had just bought, but Speck declined. He never followed up on this or any of her other work ideas.

The next night, a Saturday, Speck met Judy at the hospital when she finished her shift at eleven P.M. He had been drinking, and said that he wanted to go to the Mosquito Inn in Toivola, a small town outside Houghton where Judy had lived before she was married. During the drive, Speck appeared disturbed. He told her that he had called his mother in Dallas and learned that his ex-wife had brought his daughter over to visit his mother for the first time since the divorce, and had told her that her new husband had adopted the girl and Richard would not be able to see her again. When Judy explained that this could not happen without Speck's permission, he replied "I'm not going to lie to you. I had been in prison and my rights to my child were taken away."

Again expressing her compassion, Judy said, "Well, you've paid for your crimes, and this doesn't mean that I no longer want to see you."

The two then entered the Mosquito Inn. As they sat at the bar drinking, a man twice knocked Judy's sweater off the bar stool. The first time, Speck politely told him to watch what he was doing. The second time, Speck was more upset, but still in control. Later, Speck shot a few games of pool and the two men accidentally bumped into each other. The other man, U.S. Air Force Staff Sergeant Endean Bailey, was home on leave from West Germany to attend his father's funeral. He grabbed a beer bottle and threatened to hit Speck, who responded by pushing him away with a pool cue stick. Speck then grabbed his switchblade and threatened to stab the man.

Judy stepped between the two men and said, "Look, we don't want any trouble." Speck then put the knife away, shook hands with Bailey, and the two men went up to the bar and had a drink together. It was a typical Speck performance. Once he shifted the balance of power in his favor by flashing a knife, he felt free to become friendly with his intended victim. This pattern of "Like me, or I'll stab you," was a Speck theme throughout his barroom incidents.

After they had left the Mosquito Inn, Judy asked to see Speck's knife.

"Why?" he asked.

"I want to know the reason why you have this to protect yourself," she said.

Speck replied, "Well, I'm chicken to fight with my hands, that's why."

She noted that the blade did not flip out, but had to be handled, and that Speck "had opened it very quickly when he pulled it out in the tavern."

While talking about the knife, Speck asked the nurse if she had seen the scars on his legs when she gave him a bath. Told she had, Speck explained, "Well, someone attacked me with a machete. I need something to protect myself." He then confided that he had hit his wife once or twice, but that "she had asked for it. I don't hit anybody unless they ask for it."

When they got back to the hotel, Judy had to walk Speck back to his room because he was very drunk. She invited him to go to church with her the next Sunday morning, but Speck declined, saying, "I don't have any good clothes." After Judy returned from church, the two had Sunday brunch before she went to work. Speck picked her up after work that evening, and stopped to speak pleasantly with some of the nurses who had cared for him during his appendectomy.

On Monday morning, June 27, Judy called Speck at the Douglas House and invited him to join her for a cup of coffee. Speck declined, saying he was going to the dock at Isle Royale to check on a job in Sault Ste. Marie. He said he needed the money. Although Judy had treated Speck on several occasions, he had paid for most of their outings, "throwing money around like crazy and leaving big tips."

Now, Judy insisted on seeing him, and, still believing that he had lost his job over her, offered to give Speck eighty dollars "to tide you over until you land on your feet." The money had been given to her almost a month earlier by her mother, who wanted to tide Judy over while she grappled with the expense of buying a new car. She told Speck, "You don't have to repay it or any-thing, unless you want to." Speck took the eighty dollars.

When she returned from work that evening, she found a note from Speck stuck to her apartment door. The note said, "I have taken a job and I'll write." Judy Laakaniemi would never again hear from or see Richard Speck, who was off to his sister's apart-ment in Chicago.

In a subsequent September interview with members of the court-appointed psychiatric panel, Laakaniemi said that Speck never talked about sex and never made any passes at her. "I thought that he was a nice person," she said. "When I went out with him, he was a gentleman and he never made any sexual advances toward me. It was like a friendship."

She summed up her feelings toward Speck this way:

"He was strange. He wanted a friend and he was very good to me. He knew I didn't like his drinking and when he was drunk, he would apologize. Was he gentle or tender, did he talk about love? I don't think that he knows what love is. I think that he wants to know what love is, but I don't think that he does know what love is. When he was not drinking, he was very quiet and really had very little to say. I could talk to him, but only about general things. The night he opened up about his prison sentence, well, he probably wouldn't have told me that if he had not been drinking."

She concluded, "I can't believe that he killed eight nurses. Being with him like I was—alone—I can't believe that he did it. It's hard for me to accept, not only because I know him, but because I don't want to accept the fact that any human being could do something like this."

In his own interviews with psychiatrists, Speck would describe the relationship with his usual braggadocio and humor:

"She was a nice girl," Speck said, "and she has a last name longer than a cigarette pack. I was there about ten days, had sex with her four or five times, but she wanted to get married. I didn't want to get married, so I came to Chicago to my sister's. I split Michigan because she kept bugging me about marriage. I told her I'd think about it—and I did. I thought about it and I bought a train ticket out of town."

Speck was partially truthful. On June 27, he left her without saying good-bye and without repaying the eighty dollars she had given him.

Judy Laakaniemi's trip to Chicago to talk to the psychiatric panel gave Martin one final shot at tying the murder weapon to Speck. The passage of time had mended the strained relations between Laakaniemi and the State's Attorney's Office, and, adopting a conciliatory approach, Martin was able to convince

her attorney to drop his slander suit against the Chicago prosecutors and to allow Laakaniemi to come to Chicago to tell the
psychiatrists what she knew about Speck. Her only concern was
that she be protected from the press. Martin made arrangements
for her to fly to Chicago and stay under an assumed name at the
Essex House on Michigan Avenue.

After she had checked in, Martin arrived to take her to dinner. By now an accomplished *boulevardier* in the line of duty, he
escorted her to a corner table at Diamond Jim's, a fashionable but
quiet steak house, and ordered a bottle of wine to help break the
ice. Martin found her to be compassionate, naive, and confused.

Recalling how she had treated Speck as a hospital patient
and subsequently befriended him, she began to cry. The nurse
felt great sorrow for the eight victims *and* their murderer. She
said that she had agreed to talk with the psychiatrists "to help
them understand Richard," and to understand that he had been
"a gentleman" with her.

Martin's hidden agenda was to work the conversation around
to the night Laakaniemi saw Speck pull out his switchblade in
the Michigan bar. Two hours of small talk passed before he felt
the time was right to pose his question. Then, with high expec-
tations, he discreetly took out a photo of the knife salvaged from
the bottom of the Calumet River.

Judy Laakaniemi acted as if Martin had shown her a rattle-
snake and barely looked at the photo. She stared at her plate and
said, "I only saw the knife for a minute. I really can't tell if this is
it or not." The tenderhearted nurse was not going to become an
accomplice in proving Speck's guilt. A disappointed Martin put
the photo back in his pocket.

CHAPTER 28

Speck's biography was strong evidence for what Martin believed: the surest predictor of violent behavior is a history of violent behavior, and this trait correlates most commonly with youth and low levels of education and self-esteem. Violent behavior is usually *not* related to a history of mental illness. Still, his opinion on this point would not carry as much weight as the opinion of the expert panel.

On October 22, a golden fall afternoon, the five psychiatrists and surgeon Norcross met in a private room at the Illinois Athletic Club to vote on their final report. The panelists, who insisted on serving without pay, had previously written extensive individual reports. In an absolutely secret mission, Martin had been chosen by Paschen and Getty to stop by and pick up the report. While the panel met in secret, Martin arrived early and anxiously paced the hallway. The stakes were high.

A unanimous finding of insanity would put Speck on the road toward acquittal, forcing his transfer to a mental hospital and the possibility of an immediate return to the streets. A finding that the killer was incompetent to stand trial would postpone the case indefinitely, which would devastate the prosecution. A long delay would mean that Cora would return to the Philippines and other witnesses would disappear and die, thus eroding the now-solid foundation of the State's case. A split decision by the panel would portend a long and bloody trial, one that could go either way.

Finally, the six men solemnly filed out of the room. Dr. Vladimir Urse, the panel's informal chairman, handed Martin three sealed envelopes marked "Judge," "Public Defender," and "State's Attorney." Then, without saying a word, Urse wheeled about and joined his colleagues at a waiting elevator. When the doctors were gone, Martin, his palms sweating and his heart pounding, tore open his envelope and pulled out a single typewritten sheet of paper. It read:

"Report of the panel appointed and ordered to examine and report on the mental status of Richard Speck:

"The panel is in unanimous agreement that Richard Speck is competent to stand trial at this time.

"Directed to attempt to ascertain the mental status of Richard Speck on July 13–14, the panel is of the further opinion that Richard Speck was responsible for his behavior as of July 13 and 14, 1966.

"The diagnosis established by the panel, in accordance with the American Psychiatric Association nosological classification, is sociopathic personality, antisocial behavior, with alcoholism.

"These opinions are in accordance with legislative standards established by Illinois statutes."

The first two signatures on the report were Gerald Getty's flagship choices: Roy R. Grinker, Jr., and Hervey M. Cleckley. Placing the three envelopes in his inside suit jacket pocket, Martin went directly to his office and locked the envelopes in a file cabinet. On Monday morning, October 24, he delivered them to Getty and Paschen. As Getty read the single page, his eyebrows arched in stunned disbelief. Judge Paschen, expressionless as he read the report, said, "Bill and Ger, be damned sure this doesn't leak out. If it does, there'll be hell to pay." If the

panel's unanimous opinion that Speck was not insane were publicized before trial, neither side would be able to find an impartial
jury. The media would have contaminated the atmosphere with
the pretrial release of evidence devastating to the defense.

Getty had fought to limit all psychiatric evidence solely to
the panel's opinion, and Martin had fought for the right to offer
unlimited evidence. Now, ironically, Martin's strategy had left
Getty with a loophole. Had Martin agreed to Getty's original
proposal, the State would have been in the catbird seat and the
defense would have been behind the eight ball, unable to offer
any evidence to contradict the panel's unanimous finding that
Speck was both competent and sane. Getty was the beneficiary
of Martin's fear of putting all the insanity-defense eggs in one
basket, and now the door was open for him to use other psychiatric evidence to contend that Speck was insane. Martin's first
thought was whether Dr. Marvin Ziporyn would walk through
that open door and testify for the Defense.

Ziporyn, the violinist, and Speck, the drifter, had become
well acquainted by the end of October. By this time, Speck had
converted his basement cell in the county jail into a home. He
had a radio, a TV, a small library of adventure and western magazines, jigsaw puzzles, and a collection of letters from admirers,
mostly women. He also had the fixings to brew homemade coffee
and, like a housewife inviting her neighbors in for a *kaffeeklatsch*,
Speck would often whip up a service of coffee for his closest
friend, Dr. Ziporyn, who had supplied many of the amenities to
be found in Speck's cell.

The psychiatrist not only gave Speck hours of psychotherapy,
but he also brought magazines and books to interest his patient
in reading, art supplies to interest him in painting, and a radio
to entertain him. Ziporyn would also visit Speck's older sister,
Martha Thornton, in Chicago, and his mother and younger sister Carolyn Wilson in Dallas, and provide news for the killer

from his only loved ones. In return, Speck would tell Ziporyn his "life story" and the explanation for what Ziporyn would dramatically term the "Bastille Day Murders."

As their encounters continued, Ziporyn continued to record them in his reports to the warden of the county jail. Some typical entries:

August 19: "Speck is quite garrulous and gave a complete hour-by-hour account of his movements from Monday (July 11) until the time he was in the Raleigh Hotel [excluding, however, the time of the murders]. Still concerned about how he got the gun."

August 26: "Speck much more cheerful and relates better than any previous meeting. Again, goes into detail regarding his movements before and after the killings. Says, 'I would give anything if I could bring those girls back to life.' He feels that he has 'killed sixteen people—those eight girls, his five sisters, his mother, brother, and daughter.' Speck also discussed what happened on the night of July 13. He says that he felt exhilarated when he injected the drug into his veins just prior to the murders. He said, 'It hit me before the needle was out—zoom—and my teeth started to gnash and grind.' Again, he wonders how he got the gun."

August 29: "Speck cheerful and friendly today. Told me that when he was in prison, Shirley (his wife) began to cheat on him. Says that one time he went after her with a shotgun. He frankly admits his grievance against Shirley, saying, 'The Bible says not to hate, but I hate Shirley, if the truth be told.' "

September 9: "Speck is fairly cheerful and communicative. (He was shown) some pictures of the murdered girls. He confirmed the fact that (Gloria Jean) Davy reminds him of his wife, Shirley."

October 10: "Speck in good spirits. Relates past incidents tending to show a pattern of hyperreaction to drugs and whiskey. Gave me anecdotes that tend to confirm my feelings about the underlying dynamics of the case."

October 14: "Speck cheerful and talkative. We had a lengthy discussion, during which he again gave me some insight into the *unconscious* (emphasis added) motivation for the 'Bastille Day Murders.' "

October 24: "We discussed the murders at further length today and Speck finally gave me the information that I had been looking for to put the pieces together."

Both Getty and Martin had obtained Ziporyn's reports by subpoena. Martin noticed that Ziporyn avoided stating his opinion on the two separate and very different psychiatric questions of Speck's competency to stand trial and his sanity at the time of the murders. Martin now felt he had to find out where Ziporyn stood on these issues. On November 2, Martin met with the jail psychiatrist at the State's Attorney's Office. Both men acted unusually deferential toward the other's position. Ziporyn portrayed himself as a completely disinterested and nonpartisan scientist whose findings were for neither side. Outwardly polite and respectful throughout the interview, Martin asked Ziporyn if he agreed with the blue-ribbon panel's finding that Speck was competent to stand trial. "No question," Ziporyn replied. "I think that Speck understands the nature of the charge, and he is capable of cooperating with counsel."

Ziporyn then proceeded to give Martin his opinion that Speck *had been insane* at the time of the murders. "Speck is no sociopath," Ziporyn flatly told the prosecutor. "The panel is wrong about that. Neither the EEG nor the psychological tests are sufficiently developed to detect organic brain damage." Relying upon his extensive contacts with Speck, Ziporyn confidently told Martin, "There's a good deal that he tells me that he doesn't tell the others. I would be forced to testify that Speck was not able to control his conduct on July thirteenth and fourteenth."

Martin recognized the psychiatrist's shopworn standard diagnosis of organic brain syndrome in a criminal, and thought that Ziporyn was being unusually cute in claiming that he was "forced" by his data to conclude that Speck was insane at the time of the murders. Nevertheless, the prosecutor had an obligation to be fair and asked, "Have you given Gerry Getty your opinion?"

Ziporyn answered, "I had one talk with him and I told him nothing beyond the fact that I consider myself neither for the prosecution nor for the defense." More disingenuousness, Martin thought. Yet, in his urbane manner, Ziporyn emphasized his adamant belief that the eminent psychiatric panel had misdiagnosed Speck as a "sociopath." Martin concluded from their meeting that Ziporyn was chomping at the bit for a chance to convince a jury that Speck could not have controlled his murderous actions.

Martin was mindful of the 1963 U.S. Supreme Court decision, *Brady v. Maryland*, and its requirement that prosecutors give the defense any favorable evidence tending either to negate the guilt of the accused or lessen the punishment. First Assistant State's Attorney John Stamos had told his staff to resolve doubts in favor of the defense. Additionally, Martin believed that only inept and shortsighted prosecutors withheld favorable evidence from the defense. If he was able to convict Speck, he did not want the conviction to be reversed on appeal because he did not comply with the duty to give the defense any evidence he had that might help the defendant.

On November 15, Martin walked into Getty's office and handed him a letter. In addition to any defense the inventive Getty might improvise, this letter offered the Public Defender a blueprint for not one but three defenses.

The first was the Ziporyn-based insanity defense, holding that, in Ziporyn's words, Speck's "brain-damaged and alcohol-, barbiturate-, and methedrine-poisoned nervous system could not brake, control, or censor him," on July 13–14.

A second was the alibi defense offered by the unemployed couple who were prepared to testify that the homeless Speck had spent the night of the murders in their home.

The third potential defense was another alibi made possible by statements to the prosecution by a husband-and-wife team, Murrill and Gerdena Farmer, who worked nights at Kay's Pilot House across the street from the Shipyard Inn. Although the name was reminiscent of rustic lodges on Martha's Vineyard, Kay's was a bar, short-order grill, and package-liquor store located on the banks of the Calumet River in the heart of the Southeast Side's gritty steel mill-shipyard area. Like the Shipyard Inn, it catered to the shot-and-beer crowd of hard hat employees from American Shipbuilding, Arco Door, and Garvey Grain Elevator. The owner, Kay Erickson, recalled seeing Speck playing pool in her bar on either July 11 or July 12. Her night bartender was Murrill Farmer, whose wife, Gerdena, was the cook for the same shift.

At Kay's, a customer could grab a drink at the bar, wolf down a hot sandwich, and have time left over to shoot a game of pool. Before leaving, he might buy a half pint of whiskey. All this could be accomplished within the twenty-minute nighttime "lunch" break that the area's laborers were allotted. This meant that Kay's, like the Shipyard Inn, was usually crowded with hungry and thirsty customers because, in 1966, times were good, the factories worked three shifts, and the burgers and booze flowed.

On July 14, as the manhunt for Speck began, investigators went to Kay's as part of their search for any signs of suspicious activity in the neighborhood. Kay told the officers that she would talk to her night crew, the Farmers. That evening, she asked Murrill Farmer if anything unusual had happened on the night of July 13. Farmer told her that a man had come in at about nine P.M. and had lingered over a highball for about an hour while he looked furtively about the room at anyone and everyone. Farmer recalled that he was wearing a red polo shirt and looked like a "German sailor." The same man, Farmer recalled, returned at eleven-thirty P.M. and ordered the thirty-five-cent hamburger, accompanied by a bag of potato chips. During this last visit, Farmer said, the man acted "very nervous." Also, Farmer believed, the man had changed from the red shirt into a black shirt. Farmer told Kay, "He was all in black—black shirt, black coat or jacket, black pants, black shoes," and said that the man had stayed until twelve-thirty A.M.

Kay passed the story along, and after Farmer had repeated it to detectives Carlile and Wielosinski, he and his wife were brought to the State's Attorney's Office on the warm summer night of July 22. Assistant State's Attorney John Glenville drew the assignment of interviewing the two witnesses who potentially offered Speck an alibi for the time of the murders. He ushered the husband and wife into the spacious office of First Assistant State's Attorney John Stamos.

Murrill Farmer was a tall man who wore his greasy hair in a swept-up pompadour and spoke with the trace of a Southern accent. His expression and voice bespoke a carefully controlled and quiet anger. His wife, Gerdena, was a pale, soft-spoken brunette. The couple had four children.

Sitting across from Glenville, Farmer supplied additional details to the story he had told to Kay Erickson and the detectives. The stranger, Farmer reported, had "Shirley" tattooed on his right forearm, and he spoke in a Southern accent. He had allegedly told Farmer, "You know that red shirt I had on? I got beer on it, over there at the Shipyard Inn. I was playing pool."

After interviewing Murrill, Glenville separately interviewed Gerdena, who told the same story. Both husband and wife conceded to Glenville that their estimates of time were guesses and might vary by fifteen to twenty minutes. Glenville patiently went over the story again and again. He frequently cleaned and filled his pipe, since it kept going out when he put it down to take notes. No browbeating, no yelling, just a standard FBI-style interrogation with its emphasis on details. The Farmers did not budge. Speck, or a man matching Speck's description, was in Kay's after midnight. The Farmers were certain.

Over the next month, Glenville painstakingly prepared detailed chronologies of Speck's movements hour by hour, as documented by eyewitnesses who put him in the Shipyard Inn at the time the Farmers claimed he was first at the Pilot House. In late August, Glenville went to Kay's to talk to the Farmers for one last time, in Kay's upstairs apartment. The Farmers told the same story, but this time they were even more inflexible about the times. Murrill Farmer warned Glenville, "If Getty gets my name, it will hurt you." Ominously, he added, "I don't want to see an innocent man convicted." Glenville was not intimidated. "Look," he said, "all we want is the truth. You should tell Getty exactly what you think happened."

Later, Glenville gave a lengthy briefing to Martin and the detectives. The prosecutors were convinced that the Farmers were dead wrong on their times but dead right on Speck's dark clothes. Before setting out for the town house on the night of July 13, Speck had been dressed "all in black from head to toe," just as the Farmers and Corazon Amurao had described him. The Farmers seemed hell-bent to provide an alibi for Speck, and, in his November letter, Martin gave this potential alibi to Getty, who had not previously known about it.

Getty needed all the help he could find. One day, the Public Defender dropped by Judge Paschen's chambers and asked the judge "man to man" if the death penalty would be imposed if he pleaded his man guilty. Paschen replied, "I can't guarantee anything, Ger. If it's like I understand it is from the newspapers and TV, I'd have to give him the chair." Getty was taken aback by this candid statement. Other celebrated Chicago killers had escaped the death penalty through guilty pleas. In 1924, famed attorney Clarence Darrow saved Nathan Leopold and Richard Loeb, the high-IQ "thrill killers" of young Bobby Franks near the campus of the University of Chicago, from the death penalty by pleading them guilty. In 1946, William Heirens, a man who murdered and dismembered Suzanne Degnan, hiding her limbs in several North Side sewers, escaped the electric chair by pleading guilty.

Judge Paschen, however, did not believe a guilty plea should avert the death penalty for Richard Speck in 1967. Getty would have to use everything in his vast bag of tricks to save Speck from the electric chair. From the moment he talked to Paschen, Getty knew that "Speck had nothing to lose by going the whole route."

Going the "whole route" meant that the Public Defender would be filing wave after wave of pretrial motions, hoping to gain winning arguments to exploit upon appeal before the Illinois Supreme Court if Speck were convicted. Death-penalty cases were automatically appealed directly to the state's Supreme Court and Getty knew that the seven justices in Springfield would scrutinize Speck's trial record with extreme care. If Judge Paschen were to make mistakes in denying the defense motions, then Getty might be able to prove reversible error upon appeal.

The pretrial skirmishing began in earnest on November 4. Speck appeared in court wearing his dark blue suit, freshly shined black shoes, and a new ducktail haircut. Unlike previous appearances, he looked alert and occasionally even smiled.

First, Getty went for broke and asked that the charges against Speck be dismissed because of alleged errors in the way the grand-jury indictments had been obtained. Paschen promptly dismissed this request.

Next, Getty baited another trap. He moved that the trial be relocated outside of Cook County because of the massive pre-trial publicity. Paradoxically, Getty wanted to lose this motion and have the case stay in Cook County. However, he knew that Judge Paschen's denial of a powerfully documented request for a change of venue might give the defense a good shot for an appellate victory.

For his part, Martin moved for a formal hearing on Speck's competency to stand trial, noting that Getty had claimed in his August motion for an impartial psychiatric panel that there was a serious question as to the defendant's competence to stand trial. In 1966, Illinois law required that no matter how a question of competency was raised, a hearing had to be held to resolve it. The impartial psychiatric panel's report, by itself, was not enough. Now, however, Getty argued that a competency hearing was unnecessary because of the panel's unanimous finding. Ever cautious, Martin argued that the hearing was still required by law to dispel the "serious question" that had been raised on August 18. Further, he insisted, the issue must be decided by a jury. Paschen agreed.

To avoid press coverage of the psychiatric testimony relevant to Speck's competency, Martin suggested that the press and the public be barred from the hearing. In another paradox, Getty, who had just argued against the effects of harmful pretrial publicity, now objected to this idea. He knew that another blast of media attention would enhance his argument that adverse publicity would prevent Speck from getting a fair trial. Paschen adjourned these issues for two weeks.

Getty believed that the enormous media attention focused on the Speck murders far exceeded that of any other celebrated case. He unleashed his entire staff on the task of assembling all relevant newspaper clips, radio newscast scripts, and transcripts of TV broadcasts. On November 16, Getty presented Paschen with carton after carton of clippings and transcripts, the enormous paper trail of the media blitz that had saturated Chicago. The Public Defender was in rare form as he animatedly paced about the courtroom, arguing that Cook County was the "worst place on earth" for his client to get a fair trial. In truth, Getty knew, the very best place in Illinois for a fair trial was the ethnic and racial melting pot of Cook County. The notoriously conservative law-and-order counties outside Chicago were much more likely to produce jurors determined to convict a mass murderer.

Getty pressed on, saving the full force of his fury for the remarks made to the media on July 16 by Chicago Police Chief Orlando Wilson. Getty told the judge that Wilson "recited about fingerprints, he recited about his record, he held a picture (of Speck) up for all to see on television and in the newspapers and he said that he was the man. And, then, indeed, said that he was the murderer."

Approaching his crescendo, Getty showed the judge a newspaper photo of Wilson holding up the photo of Speck as Wilson told the press conference that Speck was the slayer of eight nurses. "On that day," Getty said, "this man acted as judge and jury by his very statements. And, oh yes! Above this newspaper photo, we have the caption: 'This is the man!' "

Winding down, Getty presented a thorough recitation of the extent of the media reports on Speck's prior criminal record and the statements that he was a suspect "in numerous other crimes." Seldom had the venerable Criminal Court Building witnessed such eloquence in the service of a cause its orator hoped to lose.

The State was not ready to respond to Getty's impassioned plea to move the trial out of Chicago. This was a complex issue and everyone was well aware that even as they argued it in a Chicago court, Dr. Sam Sheppard was being retried in Cleveland for the murder of his wife. His prior conviction had been reversed by the U.S. Supreme Court because of massive pretrial publicity; at the end of this new trial, he would be acquitted.

Since Paschen had granted Getty's request to allow the news media to attend a public competency hearing, Martin argued that the court should first schedule this hearing, because it was premature to decide the motion for change of venue until the publicity from the competency hearing could be evaluated. Paschen agreed, and continued the case for another two weeks to select a jury to rule on Speck's competency. Getty's motion for a change of venue was held in abeyance, pending a decision on whether or not Speck was fit to stand trial.

CHAPTER 29

November was proving to be an eventful month. On Election Day, November 8, Charles H. Percy, bolstered by an enormous sympathy vote over the death of his daughter, was swept into office as a Republican U.S. senator from Illinois by 375,000 votes over the defeated Democratic incumbent, Senator Paul Douglas. Meanwhile, in the Criminal Court Building, the State's Attorney's Office was preparing to prove that Speck was competent to stand trial and was simultaneously embroiled in a heated internal debate over whether the trial should be moved out of Chicago. Also, Bill Martin finally moved to the top of his must-do list the project described, "Interview Cora."

Martin used a yellow legal pad to outline the projects he needed to complete; at the end of each day he crossed out what had been accomplished and prepared a new list for the next day, retaining what was not done. For weeks, "Interview Cora" had been on his list, but was always postponed. Plain and simple, the prospect of interviewing the key to his case frightened Martin, who, mindful of Dr. Haines's advice, often awakened before dawn worrying that he would destroy his own case by ruining Cora's ability to testify. He pictured her sitting speechless on the witness stand, too frightened to speak a word. However, by November, a trial date was fast approaching and Martin knew he could no longer postpone the interview.

One issue Martin wanted to clarify was any discrepancies between Cora's initial description of Speck, as recorded by the police immediately after the murders, and her subsequent description of the killer to a police artist. To prepare for his interview with Cora, Martin first interviewed Otis Rathel, the police artist who had talked to Cora and then drawn a sketch that was eerily similar to Speck. Despite the remarkable similarity of Rathel's drawing to Speck's actual appearance, Martin knew that Public Defender Gerald Getty could still attack Cora's credibility by noting that her tape-recorded interviews with police investigators the morning of the murders had described Speck as having "brown hair, a little longer than a crew cut," and that there was no mention of Speck's conspicuous pockmarks. By contrast, Rathel's sketch, based upon Cora's description *to him*, not to the police, presented the killer in a crew cut and with clear skin.

Martin asked Rathel to describe his encounter with Cora.

"Going in," Rathel recalled, "I was told that I'd have a language problem. I spent forty-five minutes with her in her room at the hospital on the morning of July fifteenth. She seemed somewhat confused as she sat on the side of the bed and described the killer. Because she was obviously so distraught, I tried to do the drawing as quickly as possible. I made only one sketch."

Rathel was empathic about the key points. Cora, he recalled, "told me that the killer's hair was light brown and was *longer* than a crew cut. I never asked her about his complexion, so she had no reason to describe his pockmarks." Martin left Rathel feeling relieved that, under the circumstances, Cora had done a superb job of describing Speck.

That same evening, a new crisis developed—Macario Amurao was admitted to the hospital as an emergency patient. Since late October, Mama had let it be known that her teeth were aching.

Martin asked Assistant State's Attorney George Murtaugh to find her a dentist, and he called upon an old neighborhood friend, Packy Green, a dentist at the Loyola University Dental School Clinic in Chicago. Mama was seen immediately and given VIP treatment while the bothersome teeth were extracted. That went fine.

The trouble came later, after Mama had complained that she felt ill from the effects of the anesthetic. Dr. Paul Foronda rushed to the Sheridan-Surf Apartment Hotel and diagnosed a possible clot in her lung; she was admitted that night to the intensive care unit of St. Joseph's Hospital, which was located only a block away. The admission card described her as "Mrs. Regina Marfil, housewife, 425 W. Surf Street, Chicago . . . Religion: Catholic, Parish: Our Lady of Mount Carmel . . . Nearest Relative: Roger Marfil, nephew." Within twenty-four hours, Mama Marfil was out of danger from what was a clot in her lung and she had been moved from the ICU to a private room on the cardiac ward. Using an alias, Cora moved in with her mother and worked as her around-the-clock nurse, sleeping on a cot in Mama's room. The police detail sat in chairs at the end of the hall, grabbing naps whenever they could. Mama remained in the hospital one month and made a complete recovery. Cora's cover was never blown.

While Mama recuperated, Martin managed another "crisis" with silk-glove diplomacy. A July cover story in *Life* magazine about the murders had erroneously described Cora as having once stuck her tongue out at a bothersome stranger and as having once dated and then spurned a conceited Taiwanese physician who was working at South Chicago Community Hospital. The writer had intended these descriptions, inaccurate though they were, as anecdotal evidence of Cora's spunk and grace under pressure. However, they sounded a sour note with the law student back in Lipa City in the Philippines, who had courted Cora and who was still one of her favorite beaus. Cora asked Martin to intervene and to send an official letter of denial to her peeved admirer.

This was the first time Cora asked Martin to do anything for her of a personal nature, and he thought it was a good sign. Taking pains to craft the most meticulously worded bureaucratic language he knew, Martin used official Cook County State's Attorney's Office stationery and typed a letter to the young man in Lipa City. No, Martin wrote, contrary to reports, Cora was not dating a Taiwanese intern, and no, she had never committed the unladylike sin of sticking out her tongue at a stranger. Martin ended the letter on what was surely an understatement: "The State's Attorney's Office is doing everything possible to keep the Amurao family safe and happy."

Martin's letter was not only unusual but honest. Everything was being done to make the Amuraos happy, and all three Amuraos, especially Cora, appreciated and trusted the detectives who were guarding them. One day, a piece of mail sent from the Philippines to Cora drew the attention of Sergeant Jim Concannon, who thought that it looked like a map to buried treasure. He asked Cora what the coves, mountains, and rivers meant. "Oh, Jeem," she laughed. "That's a tracing of my niece's foot. I'm going to buy her a pair of shoes."

Beginning on November 15, and continuing for the next five days, Martin would wait until the march of daytime visitors and the endless phone calls stopped, and then unlock his office file cabinet to study the twenty-two pages of handwritten notes that Myrna Foronda had made of her conversations with Cora about the murders. Martin wanted everything to be absolutely fresh in his mind when he interviewed Cora. The competency hearing was coming up, and it would be followed by the setting of a trial date. It was definitely time for "Interview Cora."

The night before his visit, Sergeants Concannon and McCarthy casually told Cora during the usual poker game that

Martin was going to visit her the next day. In the early after-noon of November 21, Martin drove to New Town, parked his unmarked squad car three blocks away from the Sheridan-Surf Apartment Hotel, and followed a circuitous route back to Cora's hideaway.

Martin sat across from Cora at a small, dark walnut dining room table in her apartment. Mama was still recuperating at the hospital, cousin Roger was at work, and Sergeants Concannon and McCarthy were on guard in the adjoining apartment. Cora was dressed in a long blue skirt, a white blouse under a navy sweater, dark stockings, and black flat-soled shoes. Her jaw was squared and her eyes were clear and determined. The only noise in the room was the sporadic rattling of circulating steam in the radiators. At Cora's side was a can of Pepsi and a glass of ice cubes. "I just drink Pepsi," she told Martin with a trace of a smile. After declining her offer to serve him a Pepsi, Martin took out a lined legal pad and a ballpoint pen and began to ques-tion the petite, dark-skinned nurse. Still queasy about making a blunder that might force Cora to repress her memories, Martin was somewhat hesitant. Composed and unflinching, Cora gave detailed answers and diagrammed the positions of the girls as they were moved about the upstairs bedrooms. Although Cora and Martin came from very different cultures, they shared one characteristic—the ability to concentrate tenaciously on the job at hand.

When they had reached the point in Cora's narrative where Pam Wilkening was taken out of the bedroom, Martin decided to break for the day. "I'll be back tomorrow, Cora," he said, "and we can finish then. You've really been helpful." Martin was sav-ing the tough questions for the next day.

On November 22, Martin returned to the same small dining room table to resume his questioning. Speaking in a soft voice without moving from her chair, Cora narrated precisely how

Speck carried out his killings. Tears came to her eyes when she recalled Gloria Davy's statement upon awakening: "I dreamed that my mother died." Cora told Martin how she had put her head down on the floor under the bed and prayed furiously as she heard the sounds of Speck raping Davy.

Martin asked Cora for her opinion as a nurse of Speck's mental condition. Her response was immediate: "He was not drunk. His conversation was done in a normal manner. He didn't stagger. He didn't slur his words. I know he was not under the influence of any narcotics or barbiturates."

"How do you know?" Martin asked.

"Because of what I have learned as a nurse. I have given drugs and I have seen people under the influence of drugs. Speck was not."

As he took Cora through a dry run of a courtroom direct examination, Martin was aware of Cora's difficulty with English. For twenty-three years, Cora had spoken Tagalog in the Philippines. Although she had studied English since grade school, learning English in school is not like speaking it as your native tongue. A taught language tends to be literal, stilted, and missing the richness of colloquialisms and slang. This is why, Martin believed, Cora did not recall the precise English she had heard in the town house. For example, she thought that after knocking on her bedroom door, Speck had asked, "Where are your companions?" More likely, Martin felt, Speck asked where her "roommates" were, but in summoning the words she heard from Speck from her memory of English via Tagalog translated back to English, she came up with the somewhat formal, stilted "companions." Even when Cora was speaking in English, she was still thinking in Tagalog.

One of the American girls had asked Speck, "How did you get in?" Cora recalled his answer in the literal sense, "I screwed the door." Similarly, Cora recalled not that the light was "turned off," but that it was "closed." All in all, though, Martin found Cora to be remarkably fluent in English.

After taking a witness through a test run of direct examination, a prosecutor will usually assume the role of his adversary and conduct a mock cross-examination of his witness. Martin, however, decided not to subject Cora to a "mock cross." Having learned poker from his father, Martin knew that you quit while you're ahead. He believed he had pushed her to her limit in having her tell him the complete account of Speck's actions in the town house. Putting her through a mock cross might undo the good he had done. He packed the legal pad into his briefcase and left the Sheridan-Surf. Tonight, for a change, he'd go home early and give his wife and four kids a rare treat—dinner at McDonald's.

Although he removed "Interview Cora" from his list of Speck projects, Martin would not know how she would hold up as a witness until she appeared before a jury. Martin had prepared hundreds of witnesses to testify before letting them take the stand in front of a jury. Some improved in the tense atmosphere of a trial, but many others self-destructed. Martin would have worried greatly about this, but the relentless daily pressure of preparing each part of the case did not leave him time to worry unduly about how Cora would perform before a jury.

Cora's step-by-step narrative of Speck's sober and purposeful actions in the town house gave Martin renewed confidence in the unanimous conclusion of the psychiatric panel that Speck was sane at the time of the murders. His next task was to have Speck declared legally competent to stand trial. Set for late November, the competency hearing would be the first major public event in the case. Martin prepared by interviewing the six experts on the panel.

On November 28, fifty prospective jurors were brought to Judge Paschen's courtroom to be questioned by Bill Martin and John Glenville for the State and Gerald Getty and his First Assistant, Jim Doherty, for the defense. Martin was confident that the jury would not have to render a verdict on whether or not Speck was competent to stand trial. The Illinois test for competency is simple: *Does the defendant understand the nature of the charge against him, and is he able to cooperate with his counsel in defending against that charge?* Speck clearly understood that he was charged with murder, and he was cooperating quite nicely with the Public Defender. Since a competency hearing is a civil, not criminal trial, the trial judge may "direct a verdict"—tell the jury that they must sign a verdict finding the defendant competent because no contrary evidence has been presented.

However, since Martin did not know with certainty that Paschen would direct such a verdict, the State needed twelve jurors with the common sense to recognize Speck's obvious competency to stand trial. If Getty and Doherty were able to choose one contrary juror, the jury would be hung and the process would have to start all over again. To learn if the prospective jurors had had any unpleasant experiences with mental-health professionals, the prosecutors asked each if he or she had had any past contacts with psychiatrists. This was 1966—and none had.

Once a jury of seven men and five women was selected, Martin called as witnesses psychiatrists Roy Grinker, Vladimir Urse, Groves Smith, Edward Kelleher, and William Haines; surgeon Bill Norcross; and neurologist Roland Mackay. Since the press was out in force and Martin feared that a witness might disclose the secret panel's finding that Speck was found sane at the time of the murders, he kept his questions within very narrow limits. Martin did not want a trial jury to be prejudiced by media reports that the panel requested by the Public Defender had concluded that his notorious client was legally sane when he murdered.

Each physician, after testifying to his qualifications and examination of Speck, offered the opinion that Speck was competent to stand trial. Getty, who offered no evidence that Speck was incompetent, cross-examined each expert witness on Speck's alleged abuse of alcohol and barbiturates and his possible amnesia and brain damage. Getty was fishing for answers to use later to try to bolster Dr. Ziporyn's volunteered diagnosis that Speck was insane at the time of the murders. Because Ziporyn agreed with the panel that Speck was competent to stand trial, neither side called him at the competency hearing.

Dr. Grinker testified that he found Speck able and competent. Asked by Getty about "multiple head injuries," the psychiatrist said that Speck had told him about falling out of a tree as a child, but had mentioned nothing of being beaten about the head by policemen or of ramming an awning rod into his head, two alleged incidents that Speck had reported to Ziporyn. Grinker said that Speck told him that he occasionally had headaches, which caused him to "soak his head in cold water" or to drink alcohol.

Getty, referring to Speck's claims to Ziporyn that he had taken a "fix" before the murders, asked Dr. Urse, "Can a combination of alcohol and barbiturates produce hallucinations?" Urse replied, "Ordinarily not, but I presume it could." He added that he did not think that this had happened to Speck.

Dr. Smith told the jurors that he thought that Speck understood the charges against him "very, very well," and that, in his opinion, Speck was not an alcoholic. Smith added that Speck's IQ tested at 80–95, or low normal for an adult, and that his mental age, or level of emotional development, was about ten to twelve. Smith emphasized that Speck had no brain damage or defects and was not mentally ill.

Dr. Haines told the jurors that, based upon his four examinations, Speck showed no evidence of brain damage from either childhood illnesses and injuries or from the effects of alcohol and barbiturates.

Dr. Kelleher, who had administered Speck's electroencephalogram, said that the reading had shown no signs of brain damage. Similarly, the senior neurologist at the Northwestern University Medical Center, Dr. Roland Mackay, said that he found Speck to have suffered no brain damage, to have exhibited normal nerve responses, and to have tested at a mental age of twelve. Answering a question from Getty about Speck's possible mental illness, Mackay looked directly at Speck and replied, "I have seen no signs of neurological impairment. I see him behaving in this room. I haven't seen him rolling around on the floor."

Indeed, Speck was a model of polite demeanor throughout the two-day hearing, chatting amiably with his guards, smiling often, and appearing to enjoy the entire question of whether he was crazy or not.

At the hearing's conclusion, Martin, confident that he was on solid legal ground, asked Judge Paschen to direct the jury to return a verdict of competency. He was still concerned that if the jury were allowed to deliberate, one contrary juror could hang the majority and the entire process would have to start over again, offering Getty another chance to fish for damaging statements and gain more adverse publicity, which would strengthen his request to move the trial out of Chicago.

Paschen agreed with the State's request. "There's no proof to the contrary," the judge said, "and eminently qualified men testified that Speck is competent to stand trial. In the absence of any proof to the contrary, I will direct a verdict."

Stung by this decision, Getty angrily told the judge, "It's the saddest day in this country when a verdict, in the light of this record, shall be directed. I'm ashamed."

This outburst seemed a little extreme to the State. Getty himself had previously said that the court would almost have to direct the verdict. On November 30, the twelve jurors signed a verdict finding Speck competent to stand trial. The next question: Where would that trial be held?

CHAPTER 30

No criminal trial had ever been moved out of Chicago because of pretrial publicity. Now, the request from the Public Defender to move the Speck trial out of Chicago was provoking heated debate and serious disagreement within the State's Attorney's Office. Bill Martin, who favored a move, was in the minority. Although many defense attorneys had asked for a change of venue, the State's Attorney's Office always objected and the courts always agreed to keep the cases in Chicago. This gave the defense an issue to try to exploit upon appeal, but the Illinois Supreme Court had consistently agreed with the decisions of countless trial judges not to move high-profile cases out of Cook County.

Prosecutors have an ingrained belief that murderers should be tried in the county where they have murdered. Besides, agreeing to a change of venue would imply that a trial in Cook County would be unfair, and none of the prosecutors wanted to suggest Cook County voters were unfair jurors.

Waving an unlit cigar, Stamos argued to his assistants, "We've bent over backwards for this guy. He'll get a fairer trial here than anywhere. A lot of publicity doesn't mean that it's prejudicial."

As Jim Zagel went to the law library to analyze cases dealing with pretrial publicity, the internal debate raged on. This was the first and only issue in this highly complicated case upon which a dispute arose among the prosecutors. Zagel's legal research supported the view that the case could stay in Cook County. On December first, the moment of decision arrived. Chicago was in an early deep freeze, with the temperature hovering around zero and a gusting wind blowing flurries of snow, when Martin arrived at the rear entrance of the Criminal Court Building. A stiff wind reddened his cheeks. Waiting inside was the dark-paneled warmth of Judge Paschen's courtroom. The script seemed carved in concrete. The State was expected to file an array of affidavits proving that a fair and impartial jury could be selected right here in Cook County. After all, this was the standard response by the State's Attorney's Office to a defense motion for a change of venue.

Getty began the proceedings by arguing eloquently in favor of getting the case away from the media-poisoned atmosphere of Cook County. He spiced his arguments with a reference to the previous day's directed verdict by Paschen that Speck was able to stand trial, a decision which, Getty boomed, "denied the people the right to decide." Then, having concluded his attack upon the fairness of both Cook County jurors and Judge Paschen, Getty rested his case. In spite of Getty's dramatic arguments, most reporters had already written their stories—describing how the State had objected to the motion for a change of venue and how Judge Paschen had kept the case in Chicago. After all, that's what always happened.

Nattily dressed as always, Getty stood in the center of the courtroom, facing Paschen directly. To his left was Martin, who was in front of and to the right of the judge—the traditional prosecutor's position before the bench. Martin faced the empty jury box, rocking sideways to control his pent-up energy. He looked directly at Paschen and spoke for only two minutes, rebutting the claims of unfair publicity advanced by the defense. Speaking in a measured cadence, he built toward his surprise recommendation:

"We believe, Your Honor," Martin said, "that the defendant can receive a fair and impartial trial in Cook County, but we cannot be assured that appellate courts some months or some years hence will support our views. We must not chance the people's rights. We believe that eventually the opportunity for the fair administration of the criminal process in this case will be enlarged and better ensured by a change of place of trial. It is for these reasons that we interpose no opposition to the defendant's request. Your Honor, to the defendant's motion, we do not object."

Getty, standing only four feet away from Martin, stared in utter disbelief, his mouth agape and, for the moment, speechless. The Public Defender, who had really wanted to keep the case in Chicago, had lost his gamble—and his issue upon appeal. For his part, Martin had no doubts that he had done the right thing. Too much had been done and too much was at stake to take a chance of having the courts reverse a conviction because Cook County jurors had been contaminated by enormous and prejudiced pre-trial publicity.

Although the internal debate in the State's Attorney's Office had been intense, it had not been acrimonious. Martin had fought vehemently for the unheard-of position of *agreeing* with a defendant's request to move the case out of Cook County. He believed that the publicity about Speck's night of terror was far more pervasive than in any prior Illinois case, since never before had one man murdered eight women in one night. Martin had argued that in addition to convicting Speck at trial, the State must also take extraordinary measures to protect the record on appeal. In the end, Stamos allowed his young prosecutor to have his way because Stamos believed that the man trying the State's case should not be stuck with a critical decision that he had so forcefully opposed. Stamos allowed the transfer, saying simply, "If you're going to launch the ship, you should be there for the laying of the keel." Since Martin would be launching the ship, he had been allowed by Stamos to lay the keel the way he chose.

Richard Speck would not be tried in Chicago. The court now had to decide which county in Illinois should inherit this mixed blessing of commerce, notoriety, and publicity.

The State's unprecedented decision to allow the trial to be moved caught many by surprise. Judge Paschen, for one, was disappointed. A transfer out of Cook County meant the end of his stewardship of the case, and a faithful steward he had been. Paschen set about performing his last official task in the case by asking Getty to suggest an alternative to Cook County. Getty refused, shrewdly realizing that for him to suggest any other county would be to imply that he had no objections to the publicity of the murders in *that* county. Paschen adjourned court by stating that he would announce his choice for the trial by December 19. After Getty had refused to suggest an alternative trial location, Judge Paschen asked the State to suggest its ideas to assist the court in determining a new location.

Martin and Zagel immediately launched an all-out telephone survey of the State's Attorney's offices in the 101 other Illinois counties. They asked about the quality of jail, courthouse, and hotel facilities; the quality of local judges; the extent of local publicity about the murders; and the reaction of local citizens to the case. The bottom-line question was this: "Can your county handle this hot potato?"

The responses were mixed. The Madison County State's Attorney said, "You're not serious? We don't want it." The LaSalle County prosecutor was more expansive, noting, "Justice would grind to a halt out here if you stuck us with that case. We have a bad jail, an old courthouse, and no security. Try somewhere else." The State's Attorney in Decatur was more favorable, offering: "We'd love to have it here. Come on down." Asked about press coverage, he blithely assured them, "Don't worry—

I'll meet with the editors and tell them to cool it." The State's Attorney in Tazewell County, a factory town, assured Martin that its jurors would be able to make up any lost pay from their supportive employers. The Montgomery County State's Attorney said, "We have twenty thousand registered voters and every one of them is a damned good state juror."

Ultimately, though, Martin and Zagel decided that it would be unwise for the State to suggest a county, in light of the fact that the prosecution had not requested the change of venue. Judge Paschen would be forced to make the decision by himself.

During the wait, on December 6, Richard Speck turned twenty-five. On the seventeenth, the U.S. Atomic Energy Commission announced that its proposed giant new atom-smashing facility would be built in the cornfields of Batavia, Illinois, thirty-five miles west of Chicago. Illinois Senator Everett Dirksen, Governor Otto Kerner, and Chicago Mayor Richard J. Daley had used their considerable powers of persuasion to convince President Lyndon B. Johnson that this remote location was the perfect choice for the multimillion-dollar project. Soon to be known as "Fermilab," in honor of the University of Chicago's Enrico Fermi, one of the creators of the atomic bomb, the site would become famous as the place where high-energy physicists from around the world searched for the secret of the universe.

On this same day, Sergeants Concannon and McCarthy took Cora, Mama, now fully recovered after her hospital stay, and Roger Amurao to Chicago's Polk Brothers department store to buy a Christmas tree. The Amurao family selected a pretty white tree, in keeping with the white winter wonderland they were encountering for the first time. A child of the tropics, Cora was used to warm weather. In Batangas Province, 70 degrees was a cold day. Now, she was seeing Chicago weather at its worst—bitter cold, blizzards, drizzle, ice storms, mist, sleet, and snow. Sudden thaws would fill the streets with sopping, sooty, gloppy mush, only to have it turn cold and snow all over again. Still, Cora felt at home with her family and police guards always at hand. The nightly poker games had become a ritual.

On December 19, with reporters scribbling furiously in his crowded courtroom, Judge Paschen made his call: Peoria.

The judge said, "On the basis of the media research materials I have studied and of consultations with judicial and legal officers throughout the state, the court has decided to assign the trial in this case to Peoria County in the Tenth Judicial Circuit. The court's selection rests on the fact that Peoria is over one hundred fifty miles from Chicago, that Peoria is not within the Chicago radio or television markets, and that Peoria has virtually no daily circulation and very minimal Sunday circulation of Chicago newspapers. The courthouse in Peoria is of recent construction and all necessary physical facilities are very adequate. In addition, Peoria County has a population in excess of one hundred ninety thousand persons, enabling the court to draw on a large body of jurors. The court orders that the trial in this case be transferred to Peoria County. All further proceedings will be held before the judges assigned to that Circuit."

Paschen spoke this last sentence with a twinge of regret. He was now officially out of the case, and would not be able to meet the challenge of presiding over the most publicized trial in Illinois history. He then directed the prosecutors to hand-carry the court file from Cook County to Peoria County. Despite their long hours and low pay, assistant state's attorneys enjoyed a few fringe benefits. One was the ability to commandeer unmarked squad cars equipped with police radios and sirens. After leaving the courtroom, Martin, George Murtaugh, and Jim Zagel took advantage of this modest perk and, siren blaring, sped off to O'Hare Airport, where they barely managed to catch an Ozark Airlines DC-3 for the short flight to Peoria. They were poorly rewarded for their efforts. In fact, they were greeted at the Peoria courthouse as if they were bringing the plague.

Gritting his teeth, the plain-spoken Chief Justice of the 10th Circuit, John E. Richards, told the Cook County prosecutors that he had a crowded docket and a shortage of judges. He accepted the file on Speck with great reluctance. Next, Martin and company called upon the Peoria County State's Attorney, the sheriff, and the city's chief of police. They, too, shared a litany of laments: they did not have the manpower, space, and time for this hot potato. Also, the city's chamber of commerce did not exactly relish the idea of Peoria becoming home to Richard Speck. For fifty years, Peoria had been trying to live down its reputation as a wide-open Illinois River town featuring a flourishing red-light district and every game of chance known to mankind. In recent years, Peoria had turned things around to become an all-American city featuring a new courthouse, a secure jail, and a growing cosmopolitan population. Ironically, these were the very reasons why Judge Paschen had selected it for the trial. Martin, Murtaugh, and Zagel were impressed by Peoria's urbanity and sophistication—it was not the "hick town" they imagined—but the city's cold shoulder left them with no welcome to wear out. Leaving the court file behind, the discouraged prosecutors quickly left the courthouse for the next Ozark flight back to Chicago.

Getty was no more pleased over Peoria than was Peoria over having his client. The Public Defender knew that by the early 1900's Peoria had richly earned its reputation as the best "hanging county" in the state. Earlier, in 1851, a crowd of ten thousand eagerly watched as self-styled vigilantes ignored a judge's stay of execution for two murderers and themselves carried the men to the scaffold. This set a pattern for several more executions there around the turn of the century. In 1966, there was no doubt but that Peoria was still a law-and-order town.

The Illinois Supreme Court solved the concern of the Peoria judges over their shortage by agreeing to appoint a judge for the Speck case from another county. On December 28, the Illinois Supreme Court announced its selection—Herbert C. Paschen. Reasoning that Paschen had presided over all court hearings since Speck had first been arraigned on August first, the state's highest court ruled that the Chicago judge would continue to preside in Peoria. Like it or not, the trial of Richard Speck was going to play in Peoria under Judge Herbert C. Paschen.

In the meantime, at their regular Monday meeting on December 19, Speck thrust a Christmas card into the hands of Dr. Ziporyn, who had also brought the prisoner a gift—another paint set. Speck excitedly told the psychiatrist that he had received Christmas cards from Dallas from his mother and his sister, Carolyn, and that his sister and brother-in-law, Martha and Gene Thornton, had recently visited him. He said he was thinking about sending a Christmas card to Getty. Then, with a grin, the mass murderer added, "I may even send one to Martin. I like him. He reminds me of my pal from Dallas, Rod Kenney."

Martin, for his part, was busy trying to send Speck to the electric chair. Each weekday evening he worked until nine forty-five P.M., along with John Glenville, George Murtaugh, and Jim Zagel. Then, the four members of Team Speck would adjourn to the nearby Wagon steak house for butterflied filets, baked potatoes, and hot apple pie à la mode. The table talk dissipated the day's tension through the sharing of the black humor known to police officers and prosecutors everywhere. Martin allowed himself to take off only Sunday mornings, a time he spent playing in pickup hockey games. He usually brought his young sons Marc and Pat with him so they could learn the game he loved. He looked forward to the end of the Speck case and a return to spending time with his family and living a normal life, and he thought that the end was vaguely in sight. Until then, the case occupied his waking thoughts—and sleepless nights—to the point of obsession. He was driven by the gut-wrenching knowledge that his colleagues and the nurses' families were counting on him not to screw up.

January 1967

Judge Paschen tentatively set February 6 to start the trial, and ruled that in order to reduce expenses all pretrial motions would be held in Chicago. Getty's first motion was another surprise—he wanted a new judge.

In 1966, any defendant in an Illinois criminal case had the automatic right to substitute away from the judge to whom his case had been assigned. However, the motion had to be made within ten days of the original assignment of the case to the judge.

At a hearing in early January, Getty argued that the case had first been assigned to Paschen on December 28 by the Illinois Supreme Court. "This is crazy," Martin rebutted, pointing out that the case had been assigned to Paschen on August first! "This motion is something out of *Alice in Wonderland!*" Not surprisingly, Paschen agreed with the State, ruling that Getty's request to replace him was too late.

Martin asked Getty if he wanted to try to introduce evidence that Paschen was actually prejudiced against Speck. A defendant has the right at all times to present proof that a judge is, in fact, prejudiced against him. Getty, however, declined to say that Paschen was prejudiced. On several previous occasions, in open court, the Public Defender had complimented Paschen's fairness. Now, Getty was hoisted with his own petard. Judge Paschen would be making the trip to Peoria.

That trip was beginning to worry Martin, though. It was evident from his December visit that Peoria would not be hosting a parade for the prosecutors. A diplomatic approach was needed to win over the Peoria law enforcement officials and to make the necessary arrangements for office and living space for a prosecution staff and over fifty witnesses.

The consensus choice was Sergeant Michael Lambesis, a natural diplomat who was also a logistical genius. Polished and urbane, forty-two-year-old Lambesis looked and dressed like an international banker. The son of Greek immigrants, he had worked in newspaper circulation for eleven years before quitting in 1957 and taking a large cut in pay to fulfill his lifelong dream of becoming a policeman. Enormously good-natured, Lambesis lit up every room he entered with his amiability, laughter, and optimism. During a three-day trip to Peoria in early January, Lambesis, who called everyone "partner"—and meant it—single-handedly turned the Peoria law enforcement community into partners with their Chicago colleagues. He also managed to rent a large office on the first floor of the courthouse; to secure the entire second floor of the nearby Ramada Inn, with access to the rest of the hotel as needed; to set up charges at nine local restaurants; and even to arrange for service at a local laundry and dry cleaners. Most importantly, he convinced the city leaders that the Speck trial was a unique opportunity for Peoria to make a memorable contribution to the history of Illinois criminal justice.

While Lambesis took control of Peoria, Martin and Bill Nellis, the assistant prosecutor who had compiled Speck's biography, flew to Dallas to check on the availability of the Texas witnesses. Concentrating on Speck's prior attempt to fake amnesia after putting a carving knife against the throat of Sarah Wadsworth in a Dallas parking lot, the two prosecutors interviewed Speck's parole officer, the arresting officer, and the detective who had put Speck in a police lineup where Sarah Wadsworth had identified him. Speck had told these three men three different

stories about this knife-wielding incident. He denied the entire
happening to one of them, claiming, "I was at my girl's, I don't
know nothin' about any attack on a woman." He told another
he "couldn't remember" what had happened. He bragged to the
third about his "born to raise hell" tattoo and said that he had
only meant to rob the woman, not attack her.

The prosecutors' main man in Dallas was Chief Deputy
District Attorney Bill Alexander, who looked like a power forward in the NBA, and who sported a wide mahogany-leather
shoulder holster for his pearl-handled six-shooter. He assured
Martin and Nellis that he would personally deliver to Peoria
whatever Texas witnesses might be needed. "You just tell me
who you want," he drawled, "and I'll strap 'em on the plane."

A few days later, Martin and Zagel escaped the Chicago cold
for a quick trip to Georgia to see Hervey Cleckley. The two
prosecutors met the eminent psychiatrist at the famed Augusta
National Golf Club, home of the Masters tournament. The
lunch was pleasant: fresh blueberries and peaches at a window
table overlooking the renowned golf course below. The topics
were less so: feigned amnesia, mass murder, and psychopaths.
The State's preparation to rebut an expected plea of insanity by
Speck had begun in earnest. The witnesses were as disparate as
the genteel, learned Cleckley and the gritty, hard-scrabble former lady wrestler, Nancy Simms of Dallas. Both had observed
Speck and both thought that he was sane.

Elsewhere in the world, on Sunday, January 15, the Green
Bay Packers under Coach Vince Lombardi won the first Super
Bowl by crushing Kansas City, 35–10. Aging, balding receiver
Max McGee, who had not been expected to play, came off the
bench to catch two Bart Starr touchdown passes and help spark
the rout. Afterwards, McGee told reporters that he had been
nursing a terrible hangover from his hijinks the night before
and had been playing in a fog. Jackie Kennedy was reported to

be upset by "unflattering" revelations excerpted from William Manchester's new book, *Death of a President.*

As the trial preparation was heating up, the Amurao clan bravely coped with the Chicago cold and snow. Their loyal police detail, all veterans of Chicago winters, did not let the weather slow the family's adventures in unmarked police cars to Chinatown, department and discount stores, restaurants, and the supermarket to stock up on Cora's supply of Pepsi-Cola. The only change in the routine was the appointment on New Year's Day of Sergeant Renaldo Cozzi to replace Detective Jack Wallenda, who was needed to assist the State's Attorney's Office in its final pretrial preparations. Forty-year-old Cozzi, who was Detective Jim Georgalas's regular partner, became the newest employee of Independent Insurance Adjusters, the fictional company that was being used as a "cover" for the two-day-on, two-day-off comings and goings of the police detail. The soft-spoken Cozzi looked more like a parish priest than a police sergeant and was as comforting as a bedroom slipper. Raised on the city's West Side, Cozzi was the only member of the protective detail who had not done World War II service in the Philippines. He came "on the job" with the police department in 1955. Police officers like this phrase, because, to them, no other job matters.

One great advantage enjoyed by the two two-man teams protecting the Amuraos was their mutual friendship. Working forty-eight-hour shifts through weekends and holidays is the kind of unglamorous security operation that can set a policeman's nerves on edge—and cause friction with his partner. Fortunately, though, Georgalas and Cozzi were close friends, as well as police partners, and Concannon and McCarthy were inseparable both on and off duty. The relaxed camaraderie enjoyed by the officers helped create an enjoyable atmosphere at the Sheridan-Surf both for the police detail and for the family it was protecting. Cora Amurao, the girl from the tropics, was made to feel at home in the middle of a miserable Chicago winter.

When Martin gave his list of potential witnesses to the Public Defender's Office, he listed Cora's address as "c/o State's Attorney's Office, 2600 South California Avenue, Chicago, Illinois." Getty did not have the foggiest notion of where Cora was staying. In mid-January, Martin received a call from the Public Defender, who came quickly to his point: "I'd like to interview Miss Amurao."

Martin's relationship with Getty was always cordial, but never friendly. If Getty remembered having once turned Martin down for a job, he never referred to it. For Martin, that had happened in what seemed like a distant past, almost four years earlier. Martin paused for a beat before answering. He had been nervously anticipating this request.

"OK," the prosecutor said simply. He hoped Cora was ready.

"And I want to have a court reporter present," Getty added.

Again, Martin paused before replying, "OK." Martin told Getty he would arrange a time and place and call back. Back in November, Martin had told Cora that the defense team might ask to see her. Now, Martin returned to her apartment at the Sheridan-Surf to relay the request. After joking with Cora, Roger, and the policemen in the apartment, Martin got down to business. "Cora, Mr. Getty wants to interview you. He wants to take your statements with a court reporter. We think that it's a good idea and we'd like you to do it."

Cora swallowed hard before answering, "If you want me to do it, I will do it."

Martin called Getty the next day to ask, "Gerry, can you take the statement in our office on Sunday?"

"That's fine. I work on Sundays."

"She's frightened of strangers. Do you mind if I'm present with one police officer?"

"No, I want you to be there. You can have anyone you want."

Martin was about to commit heresy. Across the land, the prosecutor's dogma was simple: You slam the door on defense requests to interview your witnesses. Martin, however, disagreed with the dogma and with his colleagues who argued against making Cora available for any type of defense interview, let alone one that would be transcribed by a court reporter. Martin wasn't cocky, but he made decisions and stuck with them. Fond of Shakespearean references, Martin believed that the self-assured Henry V could have successfully prosecuted Speck, but that the indecisive Hamlet could not.

Although he had the reputation of being a dove within the hawkish prosecution world, Martin had his reasons. In civil cases, each side has the right to take a pretrial deposition—a sworn statement recorded by a court reporter—of the other side's potential witnesses. However, Illinois, like most states, does not permit depositions in criminal cases. A defense attorney typically gets his first and only shot at the State's witnesses during cross-examination at the trial. Most prosecutors believed that their witnesses should be told something like this: "You have a right to speak to the defense before trial, if you want to. You also have an absolute right not to speak to the defense. I can't tell you not to talk to them. It's up to you." Most defense lawyers believed that this statement was usually made with a knowing wink giving the prosecutor's real message: don't talk.

Martin was aware, however, that by 1966, legal scholars were beginning to express concern about the fairness of this prosecution-induced silencing of witnesses. If a defendant could establish a concerted pattern of refusal by State witnesses to be "interviewed" by his lawyers before trial, he had an argument—especially in a death-penalty case—that he had been denied a fundamentally fair trial by this orchestrated conspiracy of silence. The record showed that when prosecutors skated near the edge at trial, especially in death-penalty cases, they lost on appeal. This meant, of course, that the case would have to be retried many years later. Knowing that his eyewitness would be leaving for the Philippines immediately after the trial, Bill Martin felt that there was good reason to avoid skating on the edge. Therefore, he gave these instructions to each and every one of the State's witnesses: "The State's Attorney's Office urges that you agree to be interviewed by the Public Defender's Office."

This advice was loathsome to the Chicago police officers who made up most of the list of witnesses. Most police officers instinctively dislike and distrust defense lawyers. Nevertheless, they grudgingly agreed to be interviewed by the platoon of public defenders unleashed by Getty. Unable to completely conceal their contempt, however, the police officers would take out paper and pen and make their own notes of the interview, explaining gruffly, "We want a record of this, too."

Sunday, January 22, ushered in a brief period of unseasonably warm weather for Chicago. The thermometer hit 54 degrees the next day. While Sergeant Steve McCarthy stayed at the Sheridan-Surf to play cards with Mama and Roger, Sergeant Jim Concannon drove Cora to the Criminal Court Building. Parking near the rear door, he quickly escorted her to the second-floor office of State's Attorney John J. Stamos, who in December had replaced Dan Ward after Ward's election to the Illinois Supreme Court. This was the largest office in the Twenty-sixth Street building, bigger by far than any judge's chamber. It took up the entire front corner of the floor facing California Avenue and the House of Corrections. It also boasted a fireplace framed in polished black marble, the only fireplace in the building.

Court reporters do their work either with a stenotype machine or by using shorthand. Believing that the shorthand would be less obtrusive, Martin asked court reporter Paul

Esling to record Cora's statement in his notebook. Cora sat at the head of the large conference table, flanked by the reporter and Martin. Feigning nonchalance, Concannon slouched in a corner leather chair, taking in absolutely everything that was going on. At one-twenty P.M., Getty walked in with Jim Gramenos, a Detroit-born former FBI agent who had been an assistant public defender for two years. Thin and intense, Gramenos, who was in his early thirties, had thick wavy hair and looked out at the world with smoldering dark eyes. He was relentless in the pursuit of evidence. In fact, Getty was so impressed with Gramenos's tenacity and six years' experience with FBI investigations that he named him his top assistant to defend Speck, despite Gramenos's lack of trial experience.

Introductions were quick and formal. The interview began immediately. Getty wanted to size Cora up as a witness, but he didn't want her to size him up as a cross-examiner, so he directed Gramenos to take the statement. Generally, lawyers try to ask simple questions so that the answer is understandable. Asking two or more questions at the same time usually confuses the witness or confuses the answer. It was Gramenos's style, however, to fire away with such machine-gun bursts that he could not save himself from asking complicated, compound questions. He was polite, deferential—and highly verbose.

The interrogation proceeded nonstop for three hours and thirty-five minutes, as Gramenos probed in minute detail for Cora's account of the events in the town house on July 13–14, and her subsequent identification of Speck's photo and of Speck himself in his jail hospital bed. Speaking in a soft voice, Cora unflinchingly answered each and every question, and looked directly at Gramenos the entire time. Never once did she look to Martin or Concannon. Never once did she lose her composure. Martin said nothing; Cora did not need his help. Cora did provide a few details that were new to him, though.

The gun Speck had pointed at her was the first gun she had ever seen. She reported that Speck's conversation with the American girls was "just done in a friendly manner." Cora said that she didn't understand what he and the American girls were talking about because "I am not paying attention to them." She added that Speck was smiling. "Always smile," she said. Martin seethed with anger at the thought of Speck smiling as he methodically tied his victims into fatal helplessness.

When Gramenos finished, the defense had Cora's complete account of the murders, a 133-page uncensored preview of how she would testify at trial. Permitting the State's star witness to be deposed before trial was unprecedented in a criminal prosecution. Martin did not even object to any of Gramenos's questions.

Had Martin's strategy of fairness to the defense been carried too far? He didn't think so. The State, too, had gained from Cora's interview with Gramenos. For the first time in her life, Cora had gone through the frightening ordeal of a cross-examination and her narrative was unfailingly consistent with what she had previously told Detective Byron Carlile, interpreter Myrna Foronda, and Martin. Having been face to face with Speck's lawyers, she would be much less fearful when she faced them again in a Peoria courtroom.

When the interview concluded, Jim Concannon drove Cora back to the hotel and picked up his partner Steve McCarthy, Mama, and Roger. With a sense of relief, the five friends adjourned to Chinatown, where the Amuraos enjoyed a dinner of shrimp with lobster sauce and the Irish sergeants demolished steaming platters of beef chop suey.

CHAPTER 31

Monday, January 23

Public Defender Gerald Getty decided to hit the prosecution with a blizzard of pretrial motions designed to limit the State's evidence at trial and, failing that, to create new issues to contend reversible error upon appellate review. The bombardment began on January 16 with sixteen separate defense motions, and the very first one was pure Getty—he now wanted to move the trial from Peoria. Most of the others asked either to discover or suppress the State's evidence.

Getty also asked that all evidentiary hearings be conducted *in camera,* or outside the view of the press and the public. Both the defense and the prosecution wanted to avoid newspaper and television descriptions of the potential evidence. For example, news reports about the gun seized at the Raleigh Hotel or the knife recovered from the bottom of the Calumet River would have been publicized in Peoria, possibly prejudicing prospective jurors with knowledge of evidence that might not have been legally admissible. Judge Paschen decided to relocate the proceedings from his large, high-ceilinged courtroom to the smaller jury room next door.

The jury room featured a long battle-scarred conference table with twelve stiff wooden chairs, a water fountain, and marble-walled men's and women's bathrooms. The windows looked out over sooty train tracks, the gray concrete wall of the county jail, and a glass-enclosed tower where uniformed guards with shotguns were on duty. Paschen placed the thick stack of defense motions, typed up on blue-backed legal-size sheets, under lock and key in his chambers, and said that he needed four days before starting the hearing. The snowstorm of paper that Getty and his assistants had unleashed from their third-floor offices in the Criminal Court Building piled up in the second-floor offices of the State's Attorney's Office. Team Speck prosecutors Martin, Glenville, Murtaugh, and Zagel were trying to shovel out from Getty's snowstorm when Mother Nature unleashed the real thing—the Big Blizzard of '67.

The weather forecast for Thursday, January 26, called for one to two inches of snow. Beginning at 5:02 A.M. that day, snow began to fall softly all over Chicago. The snow continued to fall for hour after hour after hour, until it finally stopped at three P.M. on Friday, January 27, after dumping a record twenty-three inches. The blizzard completely shut down the "City That Works," as Mayor Daley liked to call it. Transportation came to a standstill and business offices, schools, and stores were closed. The streets were so impassable that buses, cabs, and private cars were abandoned—often in the middle of the street. Police used a toboggan to rush one expectant mother to a hospital. Looting broke out on the West Side.

Team Speck, intent on being in Paschen's jury room on the morning of Friday, January 27, spent the night of the Big Snow napping in shifts on the well-worn red leather couch in the law library and preparing responses to each of Getty's motions. At one-thirty the next morning, hunger pangs overcame them. Martin and Murtaugh were barely able to maneuver a squad car down Twenty-sixth Street to a nearby pizza parlor, open only because the pizza makers could not get home, either. Seldom had pizza tasted so good.

Like everything else in Chicago, the Criminal Court Building was officially closed on Friday, January 27, but room 702—Judge Paschen's jury room on the seventh floor—was open for business because none of the legal combatants had even tried to escape the blizzard. Their biggest fear was that even if they were able to get home, they would not be able to get back to the courthouse. The Public Defender's staff found a couch on the third floor and also slept in shifts, alternated with preparations to argue the motions. By contrast, Judge Paschen was not only able to enjoy an uninterrupted sleep on the large, plush leather sofa in his chamber, but he also had the benefit of the only shower among the group. The next morning, looking freshly groomed, he announced, "All of us are snowbound and can't get out, so we may as well get down to business." The rumpled, unshaven lawyers took their seats at the conference table.

Getty seized this opportunity to file a new motion—to allow a psychiatric examination of Speck by Ner Littner, M.D., a Chicago psychiatrist who specialized in the psychoanalysis of children. Martin found it ironic that the Public Defender, who had initially sought an impartial psychiatric panel to "avoid the spectacle of hiring additional experts in a battle of resources," was now seeking to have yet another psychiatrist try to explain Richard Speck's murderous rage.

Eyeing the growing pile of paper in front of him, Paschen observed, "It's a good thing we all got snowbound so we could get our work done on this." The prosecution was required to file an updated list of the State's trial witnesses and their addresses. The 178 potential witnesses included 80 police officers and 98 citizens. Snowbound at Twenty-sixth Street, both sides dug in for a long weekend of girding for battle. Paschen set the following Tuesday, January 31, as the day to begin hearing arguments on the motions.

People all over Chicago spent that weekend trying to dig out from under the incredible snowstorm. Stunned meteorologists reported that a snow this heavy "would not happen for another hundred years." Aside from the lack of clean clothes and a shave, Jim Zagel, who was single, and John Glenville, whose children were grown, managed the lock-in nicely by concentrating on legal research. However, Murtaugh, who lived with his wife and two young children in a one-bedroom South Side apartment, and Martin, who lived with his wife and four young children in a two-bedroom West Side apartment, both wanted to get home to help their families. On Saturday night, the two fought their way through the snow-clogged streets and managed to spend Sunday building snowmen with their children.

The bad weather didn't shut in Cora and company, though. On Friday morning, January 27, she clomped through the huge snowdrifts with Mama, Roger, Concannon, and McCarthy in time to enjoy breakfast at the cafeteria in nearby St. Joseph's Hospital. On the way back, Mama lost her footing and slowly sank into a huge snowdrift in front of the Sheridan-Surf. Roger ran inside for his camera to record the historic event. When he returned, he got a great photo of Concannon and McCarthy easing a startled Mama out of the head-high snow.

On Monday, major streets began to slowly reopen for traffic despite continued light snow and drifting. On Tuesday, as planned, Paschen was able to resume the secret proceedings in his jury room. Inside, the scene resembled a board of directors meeting. Paschen sat at one head of the table with a court reporter at his right, and Speck, whose weight had ballooned from 160 to 185 pounds during his stay in jail, sat casually at the other, guarded by a deputy sheriff. Speck was not handcuffed and was wearing his dark blue "court" suit; he looked like another participant in the judicial system, no different from the tired young prosecutors and public defenders who faced each other across the beat-up conference table. Outside, the scene resembled the Russia of a Dostoyevski novel—the streets were eerily white and strangely still.

Before the court began, Jerry Wexler, an assistant public defender, remarked to Martin, "This is macabre. One guy is sitting at the head of the table trying to decide if the guy at the other end gets the electric chair. But if an outsider walked in, he'd think that we were trying to decide what dividend our corporation should declare."

Once the arguments began, however, Wexler made an impassioned argument that there was one place in Illinois even more unfair to Richard Speck than Cook County. That place, he said, was Peoria. Carting out boxes of newspaper clippings and radio and TV scripts, Wexler contended that Speck could not receive a fair trial in Peoria. Included in his lengthy inventory of allegedly unfavorable publicity was a front-page story in the *Peoria Journal-Star* that reported on Speck's boyhood years near Monmouth, which was only sixty miles from Peoria. He also cited reports on the crimes Speck was alleged to have committed in Monmouth shortly before fleeing the town for Chicago. Martin was not going to agree to move the place of trial again and he argued forcibly to keep the trial in Peoria.

On February first, the judge issued his ruling: "This case must be tried and it must be tried somewhere," Judge Paschen said. "Yesterday, I asked Mr. Getty where he could get a fair trial, if not in Peoria, and, again, he had no suggestions. . . . This was a horrible crime. Who committed it, I do not know. Speck is presumed to be innocent and I will protect him throughout the trial to see that he gets a fair trial. But it must be tried someplace."

That someplace would be Peoria. When the deputy sheriff took Speck to the adjacent lockup for his lunch—a bologna sandwich on buttered white bread—he jokingly asked the prisoner, "When are you leaving for Peoria?"

"I dunno," Speck replied drolly. "They ain't given me my bus ticket yet."

As the hearing resumed that afternoon, the city was hit with four more inches of snow, compounded by high winds, drifting, and freezing rain. By now, Chicago was snow paranoid. Downtown hotels began to fill up with frightened commuters who did not want to get stuck in another blizzard. Grocery stores were swamped with panicked shoppers.

Paschen adjourned court early on Wednesday and had to cancel Thursday's session because of clogged streets. By Friday, February 3, however, the worst was over and the hearing resumed. On Saturday, Speck got a change of pace when psychiatrist Ner Littner talked to him for three hours and forty-five minutes in the county jail. Getty was trying to bolster a potential insanity defense that would otherwise rely almost exclusively on Marvin Ziporyn.

On the following Monday, the pretrial arguments began in earnest. The snowstorm had forced Paschen to delay the beginning of the trial until February 20. Now, the entire week of February 6 would find the "board of directors" in daily executive sessions in order to resolve the legal issues raised by Getty's motions. On occasion, the drone of legal arguments was welcomingly interrupted by the testimony of live witnesses.

The defense wanted to keep the size 38–40 BVD T-shirt that had been removed from Speck at Cook County Hospital out of evidence. Seven witnesses—four policemen, two nurses, and a physician—testified before Paschen during this attempt to suppress State evidence. Paschen ruled that the T-shirt had not been illegally seized.

Next, the Public Defender made an innovative request for pretrial disclosure of the statements of the State's 178 potential witnesses. Getty's trial partner, Jim Gramenos, told the judge that he had found it difficult to interview many of these witnesses himself, explaining, "We have to go into saloons and taverns." Amused, Martin replied, "Your honor, this is the first time that I have ever heard a trial lawyer complain about having to go into a saloon." Because the Illinois Supreme Court had previously decided that the defense is not entitled to see pretrial witness statements until after the witness has completed direct examination at trial, Paschen denied the motion.

The next evidence the defense tried to suppress was Cora's positive identification of Speck on July 19 at Cermak Memorial Hospital. "That really is him," she had told Detectives Byron Carlile and Jack Wallenda, who were with her. Getty made his request at a time when cases were working their way up to the U.S. Supreme Court toward a decision on whether or not a defendant has a right to legal counsel during a police lineup to prevent unnecessarily suggestive and unfair identification procedures. Getty argued that Cora's viewing of Speck in the hospital was so unfair that she should be barred from mentioning it at trial.

Replying for the State was Jim Zagel, the intense and scholarly assistant prosecutor who had pored over the case law on identification. Zagel noted that Dr. William Norcross had refused to have his patient subjected to the excitement of the usual six-man police lineup. Zagel contended that taking Cora in her nurse's uniform into Speck's room was the only possible way for her to see Speck and still satisfy Norcross's medical concerns. Further, Zagel argued, the circumstances at the time had provided an urgent basis for Cora to see Speck before anything might happen to either one of them. Both the police and Speck himself, Zagel argued, needed to know—right away—if he was or was not the man. Since the Illinois Supreme Court had not yet decided if there was a right to counsel during a lineup, Paschen took the motion under advisement, saying that he would rule during Cora's testimony at trial.

As the second week of the hearing drew toward a close, the record showed that the court had denied every defense motion that was opposed by the State. Getty was coming up empty. Jim Zagel was the prosecutor seated closest to Speck. After Paschen had once again denied a motion by the defense, Speck leaned over to Zagel and drawled:

"Hey, y'all been blowin' that judge?"

Speck resumed his disinterested expression, the hearing droned on, and Getty introduced five new motions. Among Getty's trial fears was his suspicion that the State would use Speck's incriminating statements to psychiatrist Albert Feinerman and surgeon William Norcross at the Cermak jail hospital and to Dr. Leroy Smith at Cook County Hospital. In two complicated motions, Getty challenged the motives of Drs. Feinerman and Norcross, contending that they were "agents of the State" and that any statements Speck had made to them should be suppressed.

This angered Martin, especially because it appeared to invalidate the agreement Getty had made in having surgeon Norcross appointed to the psychiatric panel. Terming the motions "sour grapes," he told the judge, "What is really intolerable to the defense is the fact that their own men—Drs. Cleckley, Grinker, and Kelleher—found Speck responsible for his crimes."

Getty deflected Martin's caustic attack by zeroing in on Speck's question to Dr. Smith—"Say, are you going to get the ten-thousand-dollar reward, Doc?" The question was asked *before* Speck was given powerful surgical anesthesia but after he was given several other preop medications. The State decided to put the "confession" issue to rest, once and for all. "There is no confession in this case," Martin said for the record. "Anything that the defendant might have said to medical personnel during the period of July seventeen to twenty-nine, we do not seek to introduce into evidence at any time." Martin would not risk using the statements, knowing Speck had made them after taking presurgical medications and so believing a reviewing court would find the statements drug-induced and unreliable.

Further demonstrating his resourceful inventiveness, Getty next asked for a two-stage trial—the first to determine if Speck committed the murders, and, if he was found guilty, a second trial to determine if he was insane at the time of the crime. The same jury would hear both trials. Believing that the defense of insanity would require him to admit Speck killed the nurses, Getty wanted two bites of the apple. In the trial for guilt, he could use an alibi defense; if Speck was found guilty, he could then plead insanity in the second trial.

Zagel read the decision in every Illinois Supreme Court insanity case and found that there was absolutely no basis to support a defendant's right to a two-stage trial. On February 9, Judge Paschen denied the motion, which was the twenty-third one filed by Getty during the two weeks of snowbound pretrial skirmishing. Getty had lost every motion opposed by the State.

Martin admired the creativity and scholarship of the Public Defender's growing stack of pleadings. Although he knew that many citizens and taxpayers felt he should roll over and play dead rather than waste resources defending "scum" like Speck, Getty also knew that the public defender system itself was on trial, and this was a system in which he fervently believed. Protecting the integrity of the public defender system, which, like the State's Attorney's Office, was funded by county taxes, required Getty to do his absolute best, and he decided to raise every legal obstacle against a conviction that he could imagine.

Getty carried an added burden, since he knew that all death-penalty cases were automatically appealed and that his legal defense of Speck would subsequently be gone over with a fine-tooth comb by a new set of attorneys who would be looking for lapses, *his lapses*, that might justify a new trial. Getty knew he had to raise all possible defenses, including pleas for a change of venue or change of judge, or face the charge in a reviewing court that he did not do everything possible for his indigent client. So, perforce, Getty continued to dutifully raise motions and Judge Paschen continued to deny them. As Getty kept losing motions, Martin believed that the prosecution was gaining momentum.

Tuesday, February 14

Ironically, it was Valentine's Day. Since dinner with their wives was out of the question, Martin and Murtaugh debated whether to bring home candy or flowers. They decided on candy, then resolved a vexing legal question.

The selection of a jury was scheduled to begin in Peoria in six days, and a very consequential question was yet to be answered: Was the jury to rule on innocence or guilt for one murder or for eight murders?

The return of eight separate indictments against Speck in July 1966 suggested that he would face eight separate trials. None of Getty's previous twenty-three motions mentioned the issue of one trial or eight trials. This was a tricky issue, and previous cases suggested danger for the State.

In a notorious Chicago crime during the 1950's, Vincent Ciucci shot and killed his wife and three children while they were sleeping in their beds and then fled after setting fire to the house. First, the State tried Ciucci for the murder of his wife, and he was convicted and sentenced to twenty years in prison. Ciucci was next tried for the murder of his daughter, and this second trial produced a conviction and sentence of forty-five years. In a third trial, Ciucci was convicted of murdering his son and given the death penalty.

This death-penalty case was reviewed by the U.S. Supreme Court in 1958, and four justices condemned the State's "relentless prosecutions until it got the result it wanted." Although a slim majority, five justices, ruled that the separate trials were permissible, the five-to-four split suggested that there would have been a different result had Ciucci's lawyers been able to prove that the *only* reason for the sequential trials was the State's desire to obtain the death penalty. Subsequent decisions suggested that a second prosecution of a mass murderer might be barred, even if the first trial were to result in an acquittal.

The State faced an excruciating dilemma. If it forced Speck to stand trial on only one indictment, it risked having a second trial barred because of the unfairness of repeated trials for acts that occurred at the same time. On the other hand, if the State moved to consolidate the eight indictments, the defense could claim unfairness because the jury would be overwhelmed by the evidence of eight separate murders. Martin was perplexed. He feared trying the murders separately, but was equally afraid to consolidate them.

Cat and mouse. Could the State entice the *defense* into moving to consolidate the eight indictments? Getty's opening ploy the day before, February 13, had been to try to sucker the State into making the mistake of opting for sequential trials. Feigning innocence, Getty asked, "Which indictment will the State proceed with first?" Martin decided to try to drive a truck through this narrow opening created by Getty. "Since the defense indicates no objection to trying the indictments separately," Martin told the court, "the State would lead off with the indictment for the murder of Gloria Jean Davy."

Getty did not bite on this first effort to have him agree to separate trials. So, Martin baited him further, saying that the State had elected to proceed with the Davy indictment first because the Defense "specifically requested that we elect which of the eight indictments we wish to proceed on, and *therefore indicated that they have no objection* to eight separate trials." With his characteristic folksiness, Getty asked for "time to reflect, so there may be further conversations with the court. So, may we keep this open?"

The next day, February 14, Getty filed a motion to join the eight indictments into one trial. Martin made an intentionally tepid and weak argument in favor of eight separate trials—something he did not want. Judge Paschen approached the issue as a pragmatist. It was "financially prohibitive" to try the case eight times, especially in Peoria, he reasoned. Accordingly, he overruled Martin's objection.

Getty had filed twenty-four motions, and this was the first contested motion he "won." Secretly, the Team Speck prosecutors were overjoyed with Getty's apparent victory. It meant that the defense would not be able to claim on appeal that it had been forced to stand trial on eight homicides at the same time, since the defense itself had requested a single trial for eight murders. Jim Zagel was still seated next to Speck in the spartan jury room. He leaned over and asked:

"Hey, Richard, y'all been blowin' that judge?"

Speck flashed his biggest shit-eating hillbilly grin.

The next step was to select a jury, and the next stop was 150 miles to the southwest—Peoria. However, one last pretrial issue was not yet addressed—what to do with the news media. In addition to determining Speck's innocence, guilt, or insanity, the impending trial in Peoria was shaping up as a morality play between the Freedom of the Press, protected by the First Amendment to the U.S. Constitution, and the Right to a Fair Trial, protected by the Fifth, Sixth, and Fourteenth Amendments. The Fifth Amendment guarantees the accused the right to a fundamentally fair proceeding; the Sixth Amendment guarantees the accused the right to an impartial jury; and the Fourteenth Amendment makes the safeguards of the first two binding in all state criminal trials.

Judge Paschen enjoyed an avuncular relationship with the regular Criminal Court press corps, as well as the expanded corps of reporters assigned to cover the Speck case. He respected the reporters' jobs and asked only that they respect his. After the media riot of July subsided, most reporters limited their accounts to what took place in open court. The police officers involved in the Speck investigation lived with the fear of making a mistake that might damage the prosecution's case; similarly, the reporters were careful not to do anything that might risk aborting the trial.

Despite this happy state of affairs, Judge Paschen knew that once the trial was officially under way, there would be tremendous competition for "scoops." Accordingly, on Valentine's Day, he issued a press order to control the conduct of the news media during the trial in Peoria.

Paschen had solid reasons for doing so. In June 1966, the U.S. Supreme Court had reversed the Ohio conviction of Dr. Sam Sheppard for the murder of his wife because the trial judge had permitted sensationalistic media tactics that had turned the courtroom into a "Roman holiday." Paschen intended to quell any similar media riot before it started, and he asked both the State and the defense to suggest its ideas for the press order.

Taking their guidance from the High Court's opinion on the Sheppard case, Martin and Zagel prepared an order that Getty and his First Assistant, Jim Doherty, approved. Paschen studied it carefully. Although he was sensitive to the enormous public interest in the case, he decided to enter the restrictive order prepared by both the State and the defense to assure the orderly conduct of a cause célèbre.

There were twelve principal provisions in the Speck case press order:

1. No cameras, recording devices, or other electronic equipment shall be used within the courthouse premises.

[All radio and TV equipment was set up outside the court-house stairs.]

2. No drawings or sketches shall be made within the courthouse premises. [Artists' pads distract both jurors and witnesses.]

3. The Sheriff of Peoria County is ordered to search each person entering the courtroom each time that person enters to maintain maximum security and to prevent any prohib-ited devices from being brought into the courtroom. [Sher-iff Williard Koeppel later told reporters that each person entering the courtroom would get "a heavy shake, not a light shake." He meant it.]

4. No teletype machines shall be installed in the court-house premises and no extra telephone lines shall be installed.

5. Witnesses, prospective jurors, sworn jurors, lawyers and their staffs, court personnel, and police officers are for-bidden from making any extrajudicial statements of any kind concerning this case from this date and until such time as a verdict in this case is returned in open court.

6. No photographs of any kind of the jurors as a group or individually shall be taken, nor shall the names and addresses of selected, excused, or prospective jurors be released or pub-lished until after the verdict. [The jurors and their families were entitled to privacy from public harassment.]

7. No release may be made to the news media of any leads, information, or statements from police officers, wit-nesses, or counsel for either side. Nothing except that which occurs in open court will be disseminated. The news media are placed on notice as to the impropriety of publishing material not introduced in these proceedings. The news media must be content with the task of reporting the case as it unfolds in the courtroom—not pieced together from extrajudicial statements. [To prevent the trial participants

from influencing the courtroom atmosphere through news leaks or press conferences, the court reserved the right to hold violators in contempt.]

8. The official court reporters reporting these proceedings are hereby prohibited from selling, giving, or disseminating any transcript of these proceedings to any person other than the lawyers in the case until such time as a verdict is rendered. [The official court reporters recorded not only what took place before the jury but also the confidential arguments in the judge's chambers, known as *in camera* proceedings. If a transcript of them were made available to the media, its publication would potentially expose the jurors to inadmissible evidence.]

9. Attendance in the courtroom shall be limited to the available seating in the courtroom—no standing will be allowed. The first three benches behind the bar railing shall be reserved for accredited news representatives upon presentation of credentials issued by this court. All other seats behind the bar railing shall be available to members of the public in the order of their appearance for each session of court. [In addition to the print and broadcast reporters from Chicago and Peoria, credentials were issued to the *New York Times*, Associated Press, United Press International, *Newsweek*, *Time*, *Life*, *Look*, the radio and TV networks, and other leading media outlets. Paschen issued only twenty-five press credentials, rejecting requests from two hundred others because he wanted to save space for the general public. Among those turned down were reporters from Bonn, London, Paris, and Tokyo.]

10. No person shall be permitted to enter the courtroom after the commencement of the session, nor shall any person be permitted to leave, except during a recess.

11. The bar of the courtroom within the rail is reserved for counsel.

12. No one except the attorneys may handle any exhibit.

Paschen believed that every word of the order had been designed to invest the trial with decorum, dignity, and fundamental fairness. Predictably, however, the rules drew fire from the media.

Stanford Smith, general manager of the American Newspaper Publishers Association, said that a free press was essential to preserve *both* the freedom of the press and the right to a fair trial, and that reporters should have access to court transcripts and jurors' names and that sketches should be allowed.

J. Edward Murray, managing editor of the *Arizona Republic* and president of the American Society of Newspaper Editors, called the press order "ridiculous" and "a travesty." A group representing radio and TV news directors urged that cameras and recorders be allowed inside the courtroom and that sketches also be allowed. The group also wanted access to transcripts, the right to publicize jurors' names, and the right to interview trial participants. The *Chicago Tribune* thundered that the press order constituted a "Star Chamber" proceeding.

For now, however, Paschen was sticking to his guns. He wanted it done right, he said, because "the eyes of the world will be on this trial."

CHAPTER 32

The leading actor in the trial drama that was soon to unfold, Richard Franklin Speck, had adjusted well to life in the Cook County Jail. The "three square" diet of starchy jail food had pushed his weight twenty-five pounds to a paunchy 185, and he had a new hobby, painting, courtesy of Dr. Marvin Ziporyn. Although his first efforts were strictly paint-by-number basics, Speck would soon graduate to freehand renderings. By the start of the trial, Marvin Ziporyn had become the central character in Speck's life. In return, Speck had scrawled a three-sentence written release authorizing Ziporyn to explain "what I am really like." This turn of events, however, had been kept secret from Ziporyn's jail employers and from the State and defense lawyers.

Speck and Ziporyn continued their conversations throughout the new year, and Ziporyn's summaries continued to be made available to the jail warden and the trial attorneys. The record included these reports:

January 5: "Speck was quite talkative today. Enthused about his first efforts at painting and discussed techniques."
January 8: "Speck displays a very fatalistic attitude today. Wishes Getty would not fight too hard for him, since he

feels he cannot face a long prison term. Afraid other prisoners would harm him in the penitentiary."

January 13: "Speck's mood, always volatile, showed a
sharp upward surge today. His painting is going well and
he is proud. All in all, (I) have interrupted a strong movement toward (Speck's) depression."

January 16: "Speck told me that he is 'simply no good,
and should pay for what I did.' I tried to allay this sense
of guilt, but Speck would have none of it."

January 30: "Speck extremely disturbed by the snowstorm and worried about the safety of his family."

February 10: "Speck is extremely relieved today because
his hearings have ended. He is still firmly convinced that
Judge Paschen is prejudiced against him personally and
against his lawyers. Discussed art and thanked me for
introducing him to it."

Ziporyn's last visit to Speck was on February 13. Afterward,
the psychiatrist prepared a four-page "discharge summary."
This document was a blueprint for the diagnosis of insanity
that, if asked by the defense, he was prepared to place before
a jury.

Discharge summary:
"Affect is basically depressed and he repeatedly expresses
feelings of anxiety, shame, remorse, regret, and guilt. These
are general attitudes concerning his total life. Speck has a
deep loyalty for his family and a sincere love for them."

Personality characteristics:
"Obsessive-compulsive personality showing many anal features. Meticulous, concerned with details, rigid, and ambivalent. He is very religious and has an extremely punitive

moral code—he knows right from wrong and is concerned about righteous behavior.

"In dealing with women, he has a Madonna-Prostitute complex, and hostility develops in situations where he feels a Madonna has betrayed him and played the role of a prostitute. This is a cardinal problem related to his ambivalence and explains why he is both loving and antagonistic in dealing with females.

"Speck cannot be understood without reference to multiple cerebral injuries. He has had at least a half-dozen concussions, the two most important being in early adolescence when he fell from a tree and was unconscious for ninety minutes and again at age sixteen when he was clubbed into unconsciousness by a policeman.

"Speck steadfastly denies any recall of the events of July 13–14 after dusk on July 13. He recalls drinking heavily that day (July 13)—a good deal of whiskey and a pint of wine being specifically recalled. He says he had six capsules of sodium Seconal (a barbiturate), plus an injection of a drug into his left-arm vein. He does not know the name of the drug—its effects suggest an amphetamine, but this is conjecture on my part. He states that shortly after receiving the injection he blacked out. Such a reaction is common to him on a combination of alcohol and barbiturates."

Diagnosis:

"Richard Speck has an organic brain defect—chronic brain syndrome associated with cerebral trauma. I reached this diagnosis because of the combination of history and mental-status findings. The differential diagnosis (or other possibility) involves chiefly sociopathic personality disorder. I rule this out because of the presence of depression, anxiety, remorse, guilt, shame, and the demonstration of adherence to religious belief in codes of conduct plus morality. In addition, he displays love, loyalty, and affection for specific individuals close to him."

Dynamics:

"Speck is an obsessive-compulsive personality whose rigidity, ambivalence, and hostility have been accentuated by his organic cerebral pathology. This defect is characterized by intolerance to drugs and alcohol. These agents cause a much more intense response in these cases than in normal people. The basic effect is loss of control over impulsive behavior. The feelings that the person can ordinarily contain explode in a violent and destructive manner. At such times, a patient is not responsible for his conduct and may be completely unaware of what he is doing."

By February 14, 1967, Ziporyn was Speck's therapist, faithful companion, confidant—and biographer. He was also Gerry Getty's best chance to get Speck off the hook on an insanity defense. Ziporyn, in effect, was prepared to tell a jury that since Speck said he had fallen out of a tree as a young boy and now claimed that he often "blacked out" from booze and barbiturates that, ergo, he could not be held responsible for cold-bloodedly murdering eight young nurses.

Getty had been reading Ziporyn's jailhouse reports with growing interest. Also, the Public Defender had been his usual resourceful self in trying to find a biological explanation for the evil of Richard Speck. Back in August, he had sent samples of Speck's blood to Eric Engel, M.D., a researcher at the Vanderbilt University School of Medicine in Nashville. Getty had heard about studies by Dr. Engel and his associates that suggested a possible relationship between abnormalities in the number of chromosome and violent behavior, and he wondered if this might explain Speck. The answer came back quickly: no. The Vanderbilt analysis of Speck's white blood cells concluded that Speck had the normal number of chromosomes. With this avenue closed, Ziporyn appeared to offer Getty his last and best opportunity to argue an insanity defense.

For their part, the prosecutors had a different perspective on Ziporyn. They thought that his diagnosis of chronic brain syndrome, a diagnosis that he had advanced in many previous crminal defenses, was little more than psychiatric gibberish. The State was armed with the overwhelming documentation of how Speck had developed his criminal cunning and skills over the years, how for years he had conveniently lied and copped a plea of amnesia when confronted with his crimes, how he had moved about immediately before and after the murders without any evidence of a "drug fix" or "blackout," and how he had demonstrated consciousness of guilt and had attempted to escape after realizing to his horror that he had left an eyewitness.

The prosecutors were not impressed with the attempt by Ziporyn to explain away Speck's murders with a diagnosis of "chronic brain syndrome." Martin believed Ziporyn's diagnosis was absolutely wrong. Nevertheless, he knew that Ziporyn might make a convincing case to twelve jurors who otherwise found it hard to fathom how one man could kill eight women.

At midnight on Valentine's Day, Cook County sheriff's deputies came to Speck's basement cell to take him to Peoria. Speck was watching *Machine-Gun Kelly* on TV and was upset that the guards interrupted him in the middle of it. He had been looking forward to the violent gangster movie for days. As he was led away from the maximum-security corridor, he asked his buddy in the next cell to write him and tell him what had happened to Machine-Gun Kelly at the end.

It was exactly seven months after the murders. Speck was placed between two armed guards in the backseat of an unmarked squad car, one of three that slipped through the gates of the House of Correction complex into a heavy fog to make their way onto Interstate 55 for the 150-mile drive to Peoria. Among Speck's sparse luggage were his radio, several Western paperbacks, his dark blue "court suit," and his paint set, minus the palette knife. The lead and tail cars of the caravan were filled with more deputies armed with shotguns and machine guns. At three A.M., they dropped their famous prisoner off in a cell on the fourth floor of the Peoria County Jail, across Hamilton Boulevard from the newly built L-shaped five-story courthouse.

The world would soon see Richard Speck's crime reconstructed in a courtroom.

PART IV
THE TRIAL

CHAPTER 33

On Thursday, February 16, Bill Martin and George Murtaugh packed their bags and set out on the three-hour drive to Peoria. A bright but unwarming sun stared down at the frozen Chicago landscape—temperature zero—as the two assistant state's attorneys settled into the unmarked gray four-door Ford sedan that John Stamos insisted they use. The drive ahead of them was a dull stretch of Interstate 55, which cuts southwest from Chicago through miles of flat midwestern farm land until it reaches the Peoria turnoff.

Martin had more on his mind than driving through the hypnotic landscape, and was so engrossed in his thoughts that he nearly tipped over the squad car while swerving at the last minute to make the Peoria turnoff. Specifically, he had Dr. Marvin Ziporyn on his mind, wondering if the psychiatrist would come to Peoria to testify that Richard Speck was not responsible for his crime. Not one to worry idly if something could be done, Martin weeks before had begun a covert investigation of the troublesome psychiatrist.

A minor news item had caught Martin's attention. Herb Lyon's "Tower Ticker" gossip column in the January 16 *Chicago Tribune* had reported that Richard Speck was collaborating with "an unnamed psychiatrist and a pro writer" on a book for New

York's Hawthorn Books, Inc. The title: *Born to Raise Hell*. Martin knew that the unnamed psychiatrist was not a member of the court-appointed panel, and that as of January 16 psychiatrist Ner Littner had not yet seen Speck. That left Ziporyn. The rules of evidence allow a witness to be cross-examined for bias, including any financial interest in the subject on which the witness is testifying. If Ziporyn had a royalty contract with Hawthorn, he had a substantial financial interest in Richard Speck. If this were true, and if Ziporyn were to be called to the witness stand by the Public Defender, the State could explode his testimony by questioning him about the economic profit he stood to make from a Speck book and the conflict of interest between his dual roles as treating psychiatrist and author. Martin needed to pierce the anonymity with which Ziporyn and his coauthor were trying to cloak themselves.

On January 24, Martin turned for help to a close friend from his college days, Bob Ellison, who had the perfect cover for this assignment. Ellison wrote a three-times-a-week bylined arts and entertainment column for the *Chicago Sun-Times*, reporting on books, movies, plays, and television personalities and the young columnist was savvy about the ways and wiles of this world.

Martin asked Ellison to meet him at O'Rourke's, an eccentric and grubby bar in Chicago's Old Town area that caters to journalists. It was located exactly one half mile north of the Cabrini-Green apartments where Speck had alighted with his two suitcases six months earlier after fleeing from the scene of the crime. O'Rourke's strong ales, stiff drinks, and philosophical conversations are all enjoyed under posters featuring the baleful stares and poetic words of the great Irish bards—Brendan Behan, Sean O'Casey, George Bernard Shaw, and James Joyce. Seated at a rear booth, Martin asked Ellison if he could find out the terms of the Hawthorn contract and the identity of the two authors. Ellison's response was quick: "Hawthorn leaked the story to the *Tribune*," Ellison said, "to scare off any other writers from doing a Speck book. I bet that Hawthorn will talk to me because they know that I can give them a lot of ink once the book is published."

Martin asked, "Are you willing to stick your neck out on this? There's nothing I can give you in return, not even a story."

Wiry and intense, Ellison sipped on a stein of Guinness Stout and stared hard at Martin before replying, "I'll help any way I can. I don't want anything."

Martin kept Ellison's identity secret from his colleagues, even Murtaugh, who was his closest confidant on the case, and told only State's Attorney John Stamos and First Assistant Louis Garippo about the secret operation—without naming Ellison.

The morning after his drink with Martin, Ellison called Fred Kerner, the editor of Hawthorn Books, explained who he was, and asked Kerner if he had any interesting projects under way. The columnist explained that the Hawthorn line was of particular interest to Chicagoans because it was owned by W. Clement Stone, one of Chicago's most prominent and wealthiest citizens. Kerner quickly took the bait. Eager to please Ellison so that he could enlist his help in promoting the book, Kerner agreed to speak "off the record." At the time of this conversation, Ellison was in a position to really help an editor like Kerner. His entertainment column was carried by the Field Enterprises Wire Service to newspapers around the nation, and he was doubling up as Chicago's first movie critic on television, foreshadowing the later success of Chicago's Roger Ebert and Gene Siskel. Kerner told Ellison that he had been approached by an attorney-agent on behalf of a book to be written about Speck by two authors whose names he could not divulge. Kerner said that half the manuscript had already been written and that he was projecting an initial press run of at least 100,000 hardcover books. "I don't want the prosecutor to find out about this manuscript," Kerner told Ellison. "If the authors' identities were to become known, the prosecutor would lay a subpoena on them and either they wouldn't finish the book or our sales would be diluted."

Indeed.

As a former working journalist himself, Kerner quickly developed a rapport with Ellison. A week later, he excitedly called Ellison to report that major magazines and paperback publishing houses had been calling Hawthorn about the possibility of purchasing secondary rights to the book. Kerner was very enthusiastic, believing that he had a bombshell best-seller in his grasp.

Kerner's next call to Ellison, on February 15, included the kind of news that Martin had been hoping to hear: the two secret authors were flying to New York on Saturday, February 18, to hand over the first half of their manuscript. Kerner added that the balance of the manuscript was expected to be delivered either during the trial of Speck or, at the very latest, within thirty days after the verdict. He said that he planned to publish the book within sixty days of the verdict. Kerner confided to Ellison that the authors were being given a greater percentage of all book royalties than is normally granted because "they have excellent credentials and, more importantly, they have what no one else has—access to Richard Speck."

On February 15, Martin was preparing to leave for Peoria to begin jury selection. He had only two days to pull together a team to learn the identity of the authors and to prove their delivery of a manuscript. His choices were obvious: Detective Eddie Wielosinski and Sergeant Ken Alexander. Martin had great affection for the two veteran policemen, both of whom were handling the unique assignment of keeping track of the fifty or more State's witnesses that were expected to be called to Peoria to testify. This was a tough job. The characters in Speck's drama were hard to pin down, whether they were seamen, Southeast Siders, or residents of Skid Row. Each week, Wielosinski and Alexander would make location checks at bars, ships, and dangerous street corners to find out which of the nomadic witnesses had changed flophouses or gone to sea. Bald and muscular, Ken Alexander, thirty-five, was a Lithuanian who had worked as an iron worker before joining the police force. He was a dead ringer for TV star Telly Savalas, but his "Kojak" role was for real. He and Wielosinski, the unsung burglary detective whose sharp instincts had cracked the case by linking Speck to the maritime union hall, would subsequently be given the sensitive assignment of guarding and entertaining all State witnesses sequestered in the Ramada Inn in Peoria. They would handle the assignment flawlessly, their only friction being Alexander's locomotivelike snoring. "He snores so loud," Wielosinski complained, "that I have to sleep in the bathtub with the door closed." Martin unhesitatingly gave this odd couple the delicate assignment of zeroing in on Dr. Ziporyn and his mysterious coauthor.

On February 16, as Martin and Murtaugh were driving to Peoria, Wielosinski and Alexander headed for Chicago's O'Hare Field. Explaining their purpose, they were rapidly ushered to a secret office within the bowels of the giant airport and allowed to inspect the manifest lists of all outgoing flights. The American Airlines manifest included a reservation for "Charlotte Ziporyn" on American Flight 324 from Chicago to Newark, New Jersey, arriving at 11:26 P.M. on Friday, February 17. Once the detectives were armed with this knowledge, the chase was on.

Meanwhile, city boys Martin and Murtaugh watched the scenery begin to change dramatically once they made the Peoria turnoff. Slowly rising hills herald the approach to Peoria, a city that rises from a spectacular valley within the otherwise drab Illinois topography. Surrounded by bluffs, lakes, and the Illinois River, Peoria surprised Martin and Murtaugh with its raw physical beauty. Their stereotype of Peoria as just another drowsy, flat Illinois town was dead wrong. As they drove across the majestic four-lane bridge into Peoria over the winding Illinois River, the two prosecutors couldn't resist the morbid reflection that this bridge would be a fitting place from which to jump if they were to lose the Speck case.

The first Europeans to discover the lush Peoria Valley were the Frenchmen Louis Joliet and Père Jacques Marquette, and, in 1673, Marquette exclaimed, "We have seen nothing like this in all our travels!" By 1845, Peoria had been incorporated as a city and, aided by the heavy steamboat traffic plying the Illinois River, its agricultural, brewing, and whiskey trades were flourishing. During the 1920's, Peoria became known as the "earthworm city," in recognition of the international headquarters of the Caterpillar Tractor Company, which in 1967 remained the city's largest employer. As of 1967, fully forty percent of all Peorians were of German descent and, in a real oddity of the saga of American immigration, there was a substantial population of Lebanese living in Peoria—all of whom had migrated from the single city of Itooli, Lebanon, to seek their fortunes on the banks of the Illinois River.

Martin and Murtaugh joined fellow prosecutors John Glenville and Jim Zagel, who had arrived earlier in the week, to begin studying the names on the lists of prospective jurors. The Peoria County sheriff and his deputies went over the lists with the prosecutors and provided personal information about the prospective jurors they knew. The transplanted Team Speck— prosecutors Martin, Murtaugh, Glenville, and Zagel—plus four police officers—Byron Carlile, Mike Lambesis, Frank Lassandrella, and Jack Wallenda—established their headquarters on the second floor of the Peoria Ramada Inn. A makeshift conference room with blackboard, screen, and slide projector was created between two of the bedrooms. Similarly, Gerry Getty,

Jim Gramenos, Jim Doherty, and the rest of the Public Defender's staff set up shop at the downtown Peoria Voyager Inn and enlisted the help of local defense attorneys to give them personal information about the potential jurors.

Back in Chicago, Wielosinski and Alexander plotted their undercover strategy. It was decided that Alexander would fly to New York early on the morning of Friday, February 17 to check out the location of Hawthorn Books, and Wielosinski would shadow Ziporyn on the actual flight that night. Each carried a small publicity photo of Ziporyn taken from his concert violin tours.

On Friday morning, Alexander flew from Chicago to New York, where he met Detective James Harrington of the Manhattan District Attorney's Office, who had been assigned to help the Chicago investigation. He and Alexander drove to the twelve-story white-stone Forbes Building at Fifth Avenue and Thirteenth Street, where Hawthorn Books was headquartered.

Later that night, Wielosinski boarded Flight 324 and took a coach seat in the rear of the aircraft. Alexander and Harrington were waiting at Newark Airport to pick up the surveillance. Friday night, however, was to become a comedy of errors for the undercover operatives. The flight was so turbulent that Wielosinski, who had a deathly fear of flying, became nauseated and worried that he might throw up. And he was amazed at how many bald heads dotted the rows in front of him; he began to despair of ever positively identifying Ziporyn. But after lurching up and down the aisle three times, and carefully studying the photo of Ziporyn he carried in his pocket, Wielosinski was finally sure that he had his man—two seats directly in front of him and across the aisle. Wielosinski couldn't help but think that the briefcase at Ziporyn's side held the manuscript in question.

Meanwhile, Alexander and Harrington were stationed at a bar in Newark Airport, awaiting the arrival of a baldheaded man with glasses. They were confident they would recognize him from the photo. Despite these well-laid plans, Ziporyn stepped off the plane and walked right past Alexander and Harrington, whose attentions were diverted by the four other baldheaded, bespectacled men who had deplaned from the same flight. Nevertheless, Wielosinski subsequently convinced his fellow sleuths that one of the men they had observed was, indeed, Ziporyn. Shortly after midnight, Alexander excitedly called Martin in Peoria to report that Ziporyn had arrived in Newark carrying a briefcase that, no doubt, held the manuscript. Martin, too, was excited. He was on the verge of a cross-examination that lawyers only dare dream about. Martin told Alexander, "Whatever you do, Kenny, be sure that this guy doesn't figure out that he's being followed." No further surveillance was required that night because the sleuths knew that Ziporyn was going to visit Hawthorn Books the next morning.

In Peoria, Judge Herbert Paschen and his wife, Helen, settled into a large suite at the forty-year-old Pere Marquette Hotel, an elegant five-hundred-room brick hotel which described itself as "the largest hotel in southern Illinois." It was located only one block from the courthouse. Paschen was the only participant in the trial able to create a semblance of a normal home life by having his wife with him. On Saturday, February 18, only two days before the trial started, Martin and Murtaugh took a long walk from their Ramada headquarters to downtown Peoria to get a feel for the town and its people. In the afternoon, as they walked past the Pere Marquette coffee shop, they were stopped by a smiling Judge Paschen who insisted that they join him and his wife. The two young prosecutors stayed only long enough to drink chocolate milk shakes and deferentially discuss gardening with Helen Paschen, a gentle and outgoing woman. The judge, more than anyone else, deserved to have his wife with him. Otherwise, he would have suffered the terrible loneliness of

presiding over a death-penalty case while living alone in a hotel
room in a strange town. The lawyers at least had each other for
company.

Meanwhile, at ten this same Saturday morning, Alexander
and Harrington were across the street from the Forbes Building, staking out the scene and waiting for Ziporyn to appear. A
wiry man dressed in a tailored European suit approached the
detectives and politely asked, "Do you know how I can get to
Hawthorn Books on the seventh floor?" The main entrance of
the Forbes Building was closed on Saturdays, and the man, who
spoke with a British accent, didn't know what to do. Harrington
pointed to a side entrance, and the man thanked him profusely.
After the man entered the building, Alexander hurried into the
lobby just in time to see the elevator stop on the seventh floor.
He then returned to the stakeout across the street.

Some forty-five minutes later, the duo spotted Marvin Ziporyn walking toward the Forbes Building. They fell into step
and entered the building behind him. The courtly psychiatrist
stepped aside to allow the detectives on the elevator first. Alexander loudly announced to the elevator operator, "Tenth floor."
Ziporyn said softly, "Hawthorn Books, suite 710." The operator
pulled out a clipboard and asked the three men to officially sign
in. Ziporyn signed his real name and the notation, "7th floor,
10:50 A.M." A "Mr. Anderson" and a "Mr. Moran" signed in for
the tenth floor. Alexander and Harrington watched Ziporyn
step off the elevator on the seventh floor and walk toward the
entrance to Hawthorn Books. Alexander reluctantly fought off
his instinct to flash his badge and take the sign-in sheet from the
elevator operator, fearing Ziporyn might be tipped off as a result.

After Ziporyn departed the elevator, the detectives continued
up to the tenth floor, returning to the lobby after a few minutes
to again take up watching positions across the street from the
entrance. At one-thirty P.M., Ziporyn and the man who asked for

directions were seen leaving the building together. The briefcase that Ziporyn had carried with him both aboard the airplane and in the elevator was no longer in his hand. Alexander had a hidden miniature camera, which he used to take clandestine photos of Ziporyn entering and leaving the Forbes Building. Alas, the film would later come back blank.

Excited by their success, Alexander hurried to a pay phone and called Peoria, where Martin had just returned to the Ramada after his pleasant chat with the Paschens.

"Boss, you've got eyewitnesses to put Ziporyn and his coauthor delivering an attaché case to Hawthorn Books today."

Martin was gratified. He knew that while jurors might have trouble distinguishing between the psychiatric panel's finding that Richard Speck was a sociopath and Ziporyn's theory that he suffered from an organic brain syndrome, that these same jurors would have little difficulty disbelieving a witness whose testimony was discredited by his huge financial interest in that very same testimony. Still, the prosecutor knew that he needed more evidence concerning the manuscript and the terms of the contract.

By now, the prosecutors were settling into their new home. A State's Attorney's Office electronics expert was assigned to check the telephone lines and hotel rooms for hidden listening devices. The prosecutors were not concerned that the Public Defender would tap their conversations, but they had less confidence in the integrity of the journalists who were eager for a competitive advantage. A bug-free private telephone line was installed in Martin's room.

The Speck trial would play out in a brand-new facility. The four-story Peoria County Courthouse had been dedicated in September 1965 by Lady Bird Johnson, and Peorians considered the courthouse's surrounding plaza to be a downtown park. Much to the delight of the nature-loving Lady Bird, the courthouse square featured a small forest of more than two hundred trees, representing seventeen different species. A blue-stone path led to three interlocking circular pools framed by sixteen golden weeping willows. In February, this pastoral square was strangely quiet. The ground was hard and frozen, the trees were barren, and the pool fountains still. In the weeks ahead, however, the trees would bloom, the fountains would bubble, and the blue-and-amber pool lights would form shimmering rainbows.

Inside, the courthouse sported an antiseptic look, sort of a cross between a racquetball court and a cocktail lounge. Speck would be tried in Courtroom A, where the floor was tiled in marbelized gray, the walls were paneled in dark brown walnut, separated by slabs of cream-color pitted marble, and the partially lowered ceiling featured recessed art deco fixtures that spilled soft lighting on the walnut benches reserved for spectators. The well of the court was set off from the spectator benches by a traditional walnut railing and a modern swinging aluminum gate.

On Monday, February 20, at 11:33 A.M., Richard Speck emerged, pale and unsmiling, from a police van that had traveled a circuitous route over one-way streets to bring him from his jail cell to the courthouse across the street. Subsequently, for security reasons, he would be kept locked up in a cell in the basement of the courthouse itself. A raw wind blew through the plaza as a crowd of spectators, including both young kids playing hooky from school and big kids playing hooky from work, elbowed each other aside to try to get a closer look at Speck's greased-back hair and pockmarked face. Handcuffed to two armed guards, Speck followed his convoy of heavily armed policemen, who pushed aside the crowd and quickly led him to a lockup in the bullpen behind the courtroom. The crowd then scrambled to Courtroom A on the second floor and submitted to a lengthy security check before being admitted inside.

Judge Paschen had spent most of the morning in conference, going over the ground rules of jury selection with the lawyers for both sides. Before Speck was brought into the courtroom, he briefed the twenty-five credentialed reporters who filled the first three rows of the spectator benches. Noting that "the world is watching," Paschen said that he was slightly modifying his February 14 press order to respond to the mounting editorial criticism.

Throughout the actual trial, once the entire jury was selected, sworn, and sequestered, Paschen said the official court reporters would be allowed to sell transcripts of the proceedings to reporters. Also, at this time, the judge said the names and addresses of both excused and selected jurors could be published. Still barred was any reporting of the actual questioning of all jurors. Paschen told the reporters that he was afraid that some prospective jurors would be tempted to master the answers required to have them removed from consideration. As an experienced trial judge, Paschen realized that many persons summoned for jury duty try to avoid serving by deliberately giving answers that will cause them to get excused—if they know the answers that can get them off the jury. The longer the expected trial, the more acute the danger of jurors giving "wrong" answers to evade their civic duty.

Unaware of these heavy issues, Speck had spent most of the morning sleeping on the cot in his cell. Now, in the midafternoon, he was led from his lockup into Courtroom A. Minutes later, as the first wave of fifty prospective jurors filed into the room, the slightly built and bespectacled court clerk, Paul Trompeter, arose and, without pomp and circumstance, announced in a flat Midwestern monotone: "The People of the State of Illinois versus Richard Franklin Speck."

The first step in the trial—the selection of a jury—was about to begin. Jury selection is a big bore. For the prosecution, however, this boring procedure is terrifying, because the mistake of selecting one wrong juror can cause a hung jury and undo months of preparation. Whenever Martin lectured on trial techniques, he used a simple question and answer to explain the relative importance of the different stages of a trial:

"What is the most important part of a criminal trial?"

"Whatever part you're doing."

Beginning February 20, selecting the right jury was the most important part of the prosecution of Richard Speck. If a single juror would refuse either to find Speck guilty or to fix his punishment at death, then seven months of preparation was undone. A hung jury was a victory for the defense, because the State would have to try the case again. Martin had to be right twelve times and Getty had to be right only once in this crucial preliminary battle.

The Speck jurors would be selected by a unique process. Normally, each side would be allowed 20 peremptory challenges—the right to dismiss jurors without stating a reason. Getty, however, had asked for 20 peremptory challenges *per indictment,* or 160. Martin agreed to this request, because he believed that the State would obtain both a proper jury and a strong appellate record if each side was allowed to dismiss up to 160 jurors peremptorily. If a prospective juror admitted that he could not be fair or that he had definite preconceived beliefs about the case, the juror was excused for cause. In a death-penalty case in 1966, a challenge for cause was allowed if a juror said that he or she would never sign a death-penalty conviction because of conscientious or religious scruples against capital punishment. There was no limit to the number of jurors who could be challenged and dismissed for "cause," and jurors excused for cause would not count against the 160 peremptory challenges allowed for each side.

The selection of a fair jury requires candid answers from the prospective jurors. This is especially true in a highly publicized case. The usual method of selecting a jury is to put twelve jurors in the jury box, with the remaining thirty-eight in the spectator benches, and to question each of the fifty jurors in the presence of their fellow prospective jurors. Martin believed that the usual method was fraught with danger for the Speck case. If one juror blurted out a prejudicial answer, such as "I read somewhere that he confessed," every other juror in the room would be contaminated by the prejudicial response. Martin was also concerned that jurors are prone to the "herd instinct"—succumbing to the social pressure of giving the same answers they heard from other jurors rather than answering candidly. To avoid these risks, Martin asked Judge Paschen to implement an innovative procedure: interrogate the prospective jurors one by one outside the presence of their fellow jurors; though time-consuming, this process is more likely to allow candor. Paschen quickly agreed and followed these steps:

First, the judge read the indictments and instructed the fifty jurors on general principles of law. This mini-lesson in civics instructed the jurors that the defendant is presumed innocent, that the defendant does not need to prove that he is innocent, that the State bears the burden of proving guilt, and that the defendant cannot be convicted unless the State proves every material element of the indictment beyond a reasonable doubt.

Next, Paschen had all fifty prospective jurors removed from the courtroom and brought back one at a time for individual questioning. The lone juror sat center stage in a swiveled leather chair in the middle of the jury box, facing an array of men sitting in suits behind two long Formica tables. Seated at the prosecution table were Martin, Murtaugh, Glenville, and grizzled homicide detective Byron Carlile. Martin respected Carlile's understanding of human nature and wanted his advice in analyzing the personalities of the jurors. Seated at the defense table, next to their infamous client, Richard Speck, were Getty, Gramenos, and Doherty. The State asked questions first, followed by the defense. If, after both sides concluded their questioning, the juror had not been excused for cause or for peremptory challenge, then he or she was tentatively accepted and sent to the jury room behind Courtroom A. Jurors were accepted and tendered in panels of four. Once the State had found four jurors it was willing to tender to the defense, then the panel of four was presented to the Public Defender to exercise his peremptory challenges. Any juror he bumped was replaced immediately by a new juror, and the questioning of the new juror was started by the defense, followed by the State. The defense would keep at a panel until it was ready to tender the four jurors it accepted back to the State. Eventually, this humdrum routine would produce four jurors found acceptable to both sides.

Speck sat listlessly through it all. When the first panel of fifty jurors was brought into Courtroom A and when every subsequent panel of fifty jurors was assembled, Speck was asked to rise and meet the stares of this group of common citizens who had been called to help decide his fate. On February 20, after rising to meet the first group of fifty jurors, the killer slumped back into his chair by the defense table and stared impassively, as for fifteen highly charged minutes Judge Paschen solemnly read the eight separate indictments of murder with which Speck was charged. The repetition of the eight indictments carried a powerfully hypnotic effect, associating the name of Richard Franklin Speck again and again with "the offense of murder" . . . "intentionally and knowingly" . . . "strangled" . . . "stabbed" . . . "killed."

On Monday, February 20, as Judge Paschen walked back to his hotel suite after supervising the first afternoon of what resembled a slow-moving tennis match, he knew that he was in for a long, grueling ordeal. He found his suite brightened by the arrival earlier that afternoon of a lovely floral arrangement, sent courtesy of the *Chicago Tribune*. The accompanying card wished him well. The plant would turn out to have thorns. The next morning, Paschen received a legal summons, also courtesy of the *Chicago Tribune*, which had filed suit against him before the Illinois Supreme Court, attacking his press order.

In a blazing page one headline on February 21, the newspaper trumpeted, TRIBUNE FIGHTS COURT GAG. An accompanying page one editorial was entitled "The Public's Right to Know." Not content with suing the judge, the *Tribune* asked the Illinois State Legislature to issue a public rebuke of the court order and reported an interview with Illinois Congressman Robert Michel, who obliged the paper by criticizing the judge.

Paschen, in addition to presiding over the most sensational criminal trial in Illinois history, would now have to defend himself in writing before the Illinois Supreme Court. By day, he supervised the selection of jurors; by night, he drafted his response to the *Tribune* suit. Both the State's Attorney's Office and the Public Defender's Office were allowed to file briefs supporting the press order that they had helped craft.

Taking into account the voluntary modifications that Paschen had already made, the Illinois Supreme Court issued a ruling on March 1 from Springfield that upheld his amended court order. Both sides were satisfied. Although no other newspaper, radio, or TV station joined the suit, the *Tribune* took credit for maintaining freedom of the press. Paschen, too, was satisfied that justice would not be obstructed by the modifications. When Paschen allowed the names and addresses of excused jurors to be published, the *Peoria Journal-Star*—the only newspaper for whom this information carried any real news value—still refused to identify the jurors. Often imitated, the Speck press order survives today as the best way for a trial judge to manage a celebrated case.

Despite the sideshow over the press order, the selection of a jury continued to crawl forward. Getty's questioning of the jurors indicated that he intended to keep the State in suspense over his ultimate trial strategy. After describing the three usual forms of verdicts that applied to the Speck trial—not guilty, guilty, guilty with the death penalty—Getty always asked a prospective juror this question: "Now, there may be *other verdicts* in this case, depending upon the evidence that may be developed, and you would consider the not guilty verdict and all the *other verdicts* after you hear all the evidence, is that correct?" There was only one other possible verdict—not guilty by reason of insanity. As Martin slogged through the tedium of choosing a jury, Marvin Ziporyn remained on his mind.

On February 23, as Martin was in his fourth day of jury selection, his newspaper columnist buddy Bob Ellison called again. He was relaying a report from Hawthorn Books editor Fred Kerner, who had just read the first 40,000 words of Ziporyn's manuscript. "It is very, very well done," Kerner had told Ellison and Ellison was now telling Martin. "It has a lot of depth, a great deal of suspense." Kerner added that he had received inquiries about purchasing rights to the book from Britain, France, and West Germany, and that leading U.S. magazines were already bidding for first serial rights. Kerner excitedly told Ellison, "*Born to Raise Hell* will be one of our biggest books, if not the biggest, in 1967. It's a brilliant analysis, incredibly exciting, better than I had hoped for." Kerner told the columnist he would be given an exclusive opportunity to interview the two secret authors immediately after the verdict, adding that doing it sooner would be premature and might burn off sales.

Ellison also told Martin that he had learned that the book's royalties were to be paid to a Chicago attorney who was acting as agent and escrowee for the two authors. Martin was disturbed to hear this. If Ziporyn were to testify and be cross-examined, he might still get off the hook with the dodge that technically he did not have a financial interest in the book. Also, Martin had no proof as to the precise contents of the manuscript, and he was relying on them to prove that Ziporyn exploited the physician-patient relationship with Speck for his own private gain. Martin asked Ellison what to do next, and his friend had another bright idea. "I can go to New York on other business," Ellison suggested, "and I'll tell Kerner that I would like to stop and *read* the manuscript. He really wants to play ball with me because he's convinced that I will do a huge story about the book after the verdict. I think that he'll let me see the manuscript." Martin certainly hoped so, because Getty's behavior during jury selection seemed to presage a plea of insanity.

Meanwhile, Martin was encouraged by the success of his efforts to protect Corazon Amurao from the press, as was amply proven by Edmund J. Rooney's page one report in the *Chicago Daily News* on February 21, the day after jury selection began. The star crime reporter, who was noted for his aggressive sleuthing, wrote that "Cora has quietly been brought back to Illinois. One source says that she has been in California."

Elsewhere in the world, the U.S. Congress was debating what to do about the Vietnam War. On February 23, the U.S. Senate voted $4.5 billion to intensify the U.S. military effort in Vietnam. Georgia Senator Richard Russell, chairman of the Armed Services Committee, strongly supported the new funding, and also asked that selected navy ships be taken out of mothballs to help shell enemy supply routes. While supporting the measure, Maine Senator Margaret Chase Smith added some prophetic words. "The need for this money," Senator Smith said, "shows how wrong the Pentagon guesses on this war have been." The war was also being brought home to Chicago. The *Tribune* reported the names of eight young soldiers from Chicago and its suburbs—all recently killed in the widening conflict. John H. Hammack, director of the Illinois Selective Service Commission, said the state's draft call for May would reach a new high—1,194. "This may signal higher call-ups for the summer months," Hammack added. Another view was provided by Argentinian heavyweight Oscar Bonavena. Referring to his scheduled championship bout with Cassius Clay, Bonavena said, "Cassius Clay is so afraid of me that rather than meet me in the boxing ring he will first go to Vietnam!" Clay would later knock out Bonavena to retain his crown, lose it for refusing to serve in Vietnam, acquire a new name, "Muhammad Ali," and explain his decision with the immortal sentence, "I ain't got no quarrel with them Vietcong. No Vietcong ever called me n----r."

The world inside Peoria's Courtroom A was moving very slowly. During eight long days of questions and answers, a veritable "sea of soul-searching," as *Chicago Tribune* reporter Bob Wiedrich described it, the jury selection process had been both enlivened and prolonged by the performance of Assistant Public Defender Jim Doherty. A barrel-chested, whimsical, red-headed Irishman who also sported a red mustache, Doherty was both an articulate and booming courtroom presence given to spellbinding flights of oratory, and a gifted and poetic crusader against the death penalty. When Doherty wanted to excuse a juror without using up one of the defense's 160 peremptory challenges, he would patiently recite the charges against Speck in gory detail. Then, he would ask in a charmingly slow voice, "Now, Madame Juror, doesn't the fact that this man is charged with the brutal stabbing and strangling of eight beautiful, innocent young women start you off with just an eensie-weensie bit of prejudice?" As he asked this question, he would drive home the point by holding two fingers close together in his upraised hand. If the juror stammered "Yes," Doherty was on his feet, exclaiming, "Cause, Your Honor."

Martin feared that if Doherty continued to sweet-talk jurors into admitting that they had an "eensie-weensie" bit of prejudice, all of Peoria County's 190,000 potential jurors would be excused. Fortunately, though, Getty sent Doherty to Chicago to assist in preparing the defense case. Otherwise, a world record might have been set for length of time required to choose a jury.

Jury selection is a highly inexact science. Some prosecutors believe in certain shibboleths handed down from generation to generation, such as:

Avoid the Irish, Italians, Jews, and other Mediterraneans, because they are too antiauthoritarian.

Be wary of anyone with a college degree.

Never accept anyone who has a Ph.D. or other advanced degree.

Pray for a juror of Middle European ancestry who has lived in the same house and worked in the same job for at least twenty years.

Other prosecutors believe that you can pull any twelve names out of a hat and still have the same chance of success. Believing that the jury should be tailored to the evidence in the case, Martin was looking for jurors whose experience in life would make them comfortable with the prosecution's evidence crucial to convicting Speck—an eyewitness identification, fingerprints, and possibly testimony pitting the impartial panel psychiatrists against Marvin Ziporyn and Ner Littner, the potential defense psychiatric experts. Martin had the additional burden of finding jurors with the emotional strength to vote for the death penalty, if they believed that the evidence against Speck constituted a proper case for it. Saying they would sign a death-penalty verdict was not as significant to Martin as the jurors' body language as they responded. If a juror reacted to the question about fixing Speck's penalty at death with a catch of the voice or a turn of the head or a sudden squirm or a lack of eye contact, he dismissed that juror with a peremptory challenge.

The State's first priority was to choose at least one juror with exceptional leadership abilities. Believing that twelve equally strong-willed people would not end up on the jury, and that most jurors would turn out to be followers of a strong leader, Martin concentrated on finding that strong leader.

On March first, George Weiman, a middle-aged, blond, stocky man, took a seat in the black leather swivel chair in the center of the jury box. The first lawyer to question him was Gerry Getty. The reporters were doodling on their pads and choking back yawns. Getty's approach to questioning was as friendly and informal as a backyard chat:

"Mr. Weiman?"

"Yes, sir."

"I'm going to ask you a few questions. That's George Weiman?"

"Yes."

"W-e-i-m-a-n?"

"Yes, sir."

"And what is your address, Mr. Weiman?"

"One oh six Madison Court, Bartonville."

To show prospective jurors he was an ordinary guy lacking the pretentiousness of the grim-faced prosecutors, Getty fell into his practice of deliberately mispronouncing words.

"Is that Bartville?"

"Bartonville."

"Are you a married man?"

"Yes, sir."

"And what does your family consist of?"

"My wife and a boy of twenty-one years old."

"And what kind of employment are you engaged in?"

"I'm the head foreman of Keystone Steel and Wire Company."

"Well, Mr. Weiman, have you read anything about this case?"

"Yes."

"And, I might ask you, have you discussed this case with anyone?"

"No, I haven't."

"In other words, what I'm trying to ask you is this: from what you have read or heard, have you made up your mind?"

"No, I can't say that I have."

"And you would listen to evidence in this case and make up your mind, is that right?"

"Yes, sir. I think I can."

"Do you have any relatives that are engaged in law enforcement?"

"No, sir. I do not."

"Do you have any relatives who are connected with hospitals or employed by hospitals?"

"No, sir."

"And have you been connected with any hospitals in more or less charitable activities?"

"No, I haven't. I give blood. That's the only connection I have."

Smiling easily, Getty wanted Weiman to realize the Public Defender also gave blood and said, "Well, we all do that. Now, how long have you worked at Keystone Steel and Wire?"

"Twenty years."

"And your boy, is he employed or does he attend school?"

"He attends Bradley University. He's a senior at Bradley."

"Did you attend schools here in Peoria?"

"Yes, sir."

"What schools did you attend, Mr. Weiman?"

"The secondary school, Manual Training High School."

"Did you have any other employment before Keystone Steel and Wire?"

"The United States Marine Corps."

"And how long were you in the Marines?"

"Six years."

"And did you have a commission in the Marines?"

"Yes, sir. I was a First Lieutenant."

"Have you ever served on a jury before?"

"No, sir. I never have."

"Have you ever testified for or against anyone?"

"No, sir. I never testified."

"In any case?"

"No, sir."

"Now, you heard, Mr. Weiman, that it's the duty of the State to prove the defendant guilty beyond a reasonable doubt. Now, if after you hear all the evidence in this case and the instructions on the law, if you have a reasonable doubt, would you return a verdict of not guilty?"

"Yes, sir. I would," Weiman said emphatically.

"And you also heard His Honor state that there is a presumption of the defendant's innocence?"

"Yes, sir."

"And this remains with the defendant all during the course of the trial and until such time as twelve jurors retire into the jury room, and it still remains during their deliberations, the presumption of the defendant's innocence?"

"Yes, sir."

"As you sit here now, do you have any difficulty in presuming his innocence?"

"No, sir, I have none."

"So that anything that you have read or heard, you will not bring that into the jury box with you at all, will you?"

"No, sir. May I explain something?"

"Yes, please."

"We have only one paper in Peoria. I don't always agree with it, and you can't form opinions while reading only one paper."

"Uh-huh. Do you ever read the Chicago papers?"

"No."

"Now, the fact that there are eight indictments here, does that tend to start you off with any prejudice?"

"No."

"In other words, you want to determine from the evidence, number one, has this man been proven guilty or not?"

"Yes, sir."

"And, number two, from the evidence, if you should decide he's guilty, did he intentionally and knowingly murder?"

"Yes."

"Now, there will be various verdicts in this case. And one of the verdicts will be a 'not guilty' verdict. And, of course, you told me, after you heard all the evidence in this case, if you had a reasonable doubt, you wouldn't hesitate to sign that verdict, would you?"

"No, sir."

"And there will be a verdict of guilty in which the court sets the penalty and there will be a verdict of guilty in which the State will ask for the death penalty.

"And I might as well ask you this because, when the State takes over your questioning, they will ask you. Now, part of our law in Illinois is that the death penalty may be inflicted.

"Now, they will ask you, do you have any religious or conscientious scruples against the infliction of the death penalty in a proper case? And, they will ask, do you? And I will ask you that question: do you have any religious or conscientious scruples against the infliction of the death penalty in a proper case?"

"No, I don't. I am a Christian, but I don't have any scruples on that matter."

Getty thought that the "I am a Christian" answer indicated that Weiman had religious qualms about capital punishment. He thought that this was the juror for him, one who had the courage to hold out against the death penalty. However, jury selection is like poker—you don't let your opponent know you have just been dealt a winning hand. Fearing that he might tip off the prosecutors to his belief that Weiman was weak on capital punishment, Getty quickly changed the subject.

"Yes. Now, there will be Chicago policemen testifying in this case, Mr. Weiman, and I will ask you this: would you give their testimony any greater weight than you would another witness, merely because they are policemen?"

"I don't think so, no."

"In other words, you will determine the credibility of each witness, and you will determine that from your own mind, isn't that correct?"

"That's correct."

"And the procedure here, Mr. Weiman, is that the State will put on witnesses first. Now, these witnesses will be subject to cross-examination. And the purpose of the cross-examination is to point out other things that might be an aid for jurors to arrive at a just decision in this case.

"And, then, after that, the defense will put up witnesses, although His Honor told you that the defendant doesn't have to prove anything. And, of course, then there will be instructions on the law. After you have heard both sides of the case, instructions will be given to you on the law.

"Now, you wouldn't make up your mind after you heard some of the State's witnesses, would you?"

"You can't make up your mind until you hear it all."

Getty liked this answer a lot—the Public Defender desperately needed jurors who were open-minded.

"That's right. And that is what you would be looking for in this case—to consider all the evidence and instructions on the law?"

"Yes, sir."

Throughout the questioning of every juror, Getty left the door open to putting in an insanity defense by asking his question about possible "other verdicts."

"And, of course, you would follow the law, as given to you by Judge Paschen. And I recited all these various verdicts. And, as the evidence is developed, there may be other verdicts in this case. But, in any event, you would consider all the verdicts, in arriving at a just decision, wouldn't you?"

"Yes, sir."

"Yes. Have you ever made a study of fingerprints?"

"No, sir."

"Or read anything much about them?"

"No, sir."

"Or know anything much about them?"

"No, sir."

"And, as you sit here right now, you feel you have an open and free mind, is that correct?"

"Yes, sir. I do."

"All right. I submit Mr. Weiman for questioning by the State," Getty said without betraying his enthusiasm for this juror.

Martin, Murtaugh, and John Glenville were alternating the tiresome routine of questioning jurors, and it was now Glenville's turn. Martin whispered, "Keep it short, John. We really want this guy." Martin believed that George Weiman was a tough-minded ex-Marine who had no qualms about the death penalty and whose job as chief foreman at a huge steel company gave him the leadership experience to become the jury's foreman. Glenville, a middle-aged ex-FBI agent with every strand of his thinning gray hair in place, began his questioning of Weiman in a resonant and self-assured voice.

"Now, Mr. Weiman, we are going to be very brief. Mr. Getty has covered the field pretty well. Now, if the State should prove the defendant's guilt beyond a reasonable doubt, would you hesitate about signing a verdict of guilty fixing the death penalty, if you consider this a proper case?"

"No, sir."

"While you were in the Marine Corps, did you in any way have any connection with any court martial?"

"Yes, sir."

"That in no way would affect your judgment in this case?"

"No, sir. As a Second Lieutenant, I was prosecuting attorney for three different cases in court."

Glenville was inadvertently falling into a dialogue that could cause Getty to have second thoughts about George Weiman. Martin, a good poker player, remained expressionless, but scribbled a note to Glenville: "Stop NOW."

Glenville said, "No further questions."

Looking at Getty, Judge Paschen asked, "Are you finished with Mr. Weiman?"

Martin thought that Getty would requestion Weiman about his prosecuting experiences in the Marines and then dismiss him. He was surprised when Getty said he had no further questions and did not use a peremptory challenge to dismiss him.

Paschen said, "Very well. Mr. Weiman, you may retire."

After Weiman left the room, the proceedings were adjourned to Paschen's chambers, where Getty said, "Your Honor, the defense will tender Mr. Semick, Mrs. Tomsovic, Mrs. Mertens, and Mr. Weiman." Jurors could not be selected individually, but only in groups of four. This fact led to a lot of game-playing, as both prosecution and defense tried to come up with panels of four whose chemistry seemed favorable to its side. Now that the defense had committed itself to a panel of four, the State had a choice. If it wanted to be sure of keeping Weiman, it had to accept the entire panel of four, including Mertens, Semick, and Tomsovic. If the State decline the four and "broke the panel," it meant the entire selection exercise would continue and any of the four jurors, including Weiman, could be "bumped" in favor of a new juror selected by either the defense or the State. So, before the prosecutors entered Paschen's chambers, they looked at their notes and debated whether or not to accept the panel.

Frank Semick was the embodiment of stability, a retired painting contractor with five married children who had once lived in Chicago and who had been in Peoria for the last thirty-two years. Adelle Tomsovic, a Chicago native, was a volunteer worker at the state mental hospital in Peoria and had a brother who worked in the pharmacy at Chicago's Cook County Hospital. Martin believed that she would know the difference between feigned and real mental illness. The auburn-haired, blue-eyed Kay Mertens was a twenty-nine-year-old divorced mother of two who worked in the accounting department at the Caterpillar Tractor Company. The prosecutors hoped that her work with the details of accounting would help her understand the details of fingerprint evidence. Besides, it is a tradition among trial lawyers to choose at least one attractive juror for the grueling days ahead, and Kay Mertens was the most striking juror to come to the courtroom. Martin believed that Semick, Tomsovic, and Mertens were solid citizens and good prosecution jurors, but even if they were not he would have taken them to get George Weiman. Expressionless, Martin looked at Paschen and said, "The State accepts the panel, Your Honor."

The empaneling of the first four jurors on March 1 was a milestone of sorts, but Richard Speck, pleading a bellyache, had missed the event. The killer had awakened that morning with stomach pains, and under heavy security had been taken to a local clinic where his ailment was diagnosed and treated as a routine case of gastritis. It was a rare moment of physical activity for Speck, who had been spending most of his out-of-court time painting, reading paperback westerns, and sleeping. In court, he usually appeared indifferent to the details of his own trial. The major exception to this lethargy was Speck's habit of turning and staring at women in the audience. Throughout the six weeks of jury selection, Speck would stare at women in the courtroom as if he were saying, "I'm not afraid of you—I'll stare you down."

He did this frequently with Abra Rockefeller Prentice, a reporter for the *Chicago Sun-Times* who was tall, slender, elegant—and very rich. She stared right back at him, never flinching. One day a prospective female juror appeared in the jury box dressed in her nursing whites. Speck sat bolt upright and stared long and hard at the young woman before she was excused, allowing him to fall back into his own fog.

Late on Sunday night, March 16, Martin's phone rang at the Ramada Inn, where he was up working late. This phone line was checked three times a week to be certain that no one had wire-tapped it. The line was secure. The excited voice at the other end was Bob Ellison, calling from New York.

"I just spent the last two and a half hours reading six chapters of the Ziporyn manuscript," Ellison said. "It's one hundred twenty-two doubled-spaced eight-and-a-half-by-eleven typed pages. It opens with Speck in a jail cell, moves to the crime, then goes into Speck's background, as told to Ziporyn."

Martin now had evidence not only of the existence of a Ziporyn manuscript, but of its contents as well. Ellison had an Irish poet's love of words and spoke rapidly with great animation as Martin tried to jot down notes of the conversation. The columnist had taken a big risk for his buddy.

"I had to read the manuscript right in front of Kerner," he told Martin, "and I could not take any notes. In fact, I was afraid to even leave the room to go to the john. He may have thought that I was taking notes in there of what I had read and would suddenly change his mind and take the manuscript away from me. It was a helluva scene, because, believe me, I was sweating—if not on the outside, definitely on the inside. There was no margin for error. I had your career and reputation on the line in the cause of a life-or-death trial situation. I got the information—accurate and complete. I made notes of the whole story after I got out of there. I'll get them to you when I get back to Chicago."

Martin said, "You did a terrific job, Gordie. I owe you big." Ellison's nickname was "Gordie," because he skated with the smoothness of hockey legend Gordie Howe. Before hanging up, Ellison added, "Kerner and I hit it off. I'll keep calling him to see what's going on."

The next morning was St. Patrick's Day. Although Martin and Murtaugh were not able to have a traditional Irish celebration, they were able to mark another milestone in the case. Both the State and the defense accepted the second panel of four jurors—Donald Albanito, Richard Krause, Mildred Sanders, and Walter Atkisson. Martin broke a sacred prosecutors' rule in accepting Albanito, who was a Ph.D. and chairman of the Department of Business Administration at Bradley University in Peoria. Despite Albanito's advanced degree, Martin liked the fact that he had worked two years for the American Psychological Association and had completed both undergraduate and graduate courses in psychology. He figured that Albanito, too, would know feigned mental illness when he saw it. Krause was a welder for Peoria's Westinghouse Air Brake Company and had served in the Air National Guard for six years. Mildred Sanders was a receptionist for the Peoria Board of Education. Walter Atkisson had worked thirty years as a general laborer for the Hiram Walker Distillery Company after serving in the U.S. Navy. Solid jurors all, Martin thought. Judge Paschen was delighted—two-thirds of a jury had been selected. He encouraged the lawyers to keep working on the final panel, but by week's end the selection process was again bogged down in tedium.

Bob Ellison, however, never lost his momentum. On March 23, the clever and tenacious Ellison made another late-night call to Martin to report that Dr. Ziporyn's financial stake in the manuscript was rising. *Life* magazine was considering paying $100,000 for a portion of Ziporyn's manuscript and had already paid $10,000 just to read it. A few days later, during a recess in jury selection, Martin was approached by Jack Altman, who was covering the trial as an accredited reporter for *Time*. "I'm doing a story on the general topic of selecting a jury," Altman told Martin, "and I'd like to interview you." Although Martin regularly bantered and joked with reporters outside of the courtroom, he was resolute in refusing to discuss the trial. Altman assured Martin that he would not ask him any questions about the Speck case.

Figuring that he might be able to find out if Altman was Ziporyn's coauthor, Martin agreed to have a drink with the reporter that night at the Ramada. Arriving at the Ramada cocktail lounge early, Martin asked the hotel's owner, Roy Demanes, for a favor. Demanes, a big fan of Team Speck, was willing to do anything to help the prosecution.

"Roy," Martin said, "I'm going to meet a gentleman here shortly. Have the bartender do me a favor. Whatever this guy drinks, make it a double; whatever I order, leave out the booze."

Altman arrived shortly, and the two adjourned to a corner table in the dimly lighted lounge. Born and educated in England, Altman wore European suits and spoke with a pronounced British accent. "Gin and tonic," Altman ordered. "Same," said Martin. Altman got a double, Martin a tonic water and lime. Some two hours and six rounds of drinks later, Martin had heard enough from Altman to confirm that he was the coauthor of Ziporyn's book about the psychiatrist's supposedly confidential interviews with Speck. Bright and literate, Altman sprinkled the conversation with speculations about Speck's psychological state at the time of the murders. These speculations sounded to Martin as if they came right from the mouth of Marvin Ziporyn.

"I'm working on an exciting project right now about this case," Altman said with a smile, "but I really can't say anything about it now. It's going to be very, very big." After stepping out of the darkened lounge, Martin went directly to Ken Alexander's room and described Altman to the police officer. "The British accent does it," Alexander said. "That's got to be the guy I saw in New York who asked for directions to Hawthorn Books." The pieces of the *Born to Raise Hell* puzzle were beginning to fall into place, and Martin took comfort in knowing that he would have something very, very big for Marvin Ziporyn if the psychiatrist took the witness stand.

Back in court, jury selection droned on. Winter turned to spring. Easter weekend arrived. On Saturday night, March 25, Martin was the only passenger on the last Ozark Airlines flight from Peoria to Chicago. He wanted to be at home for a family Easter egg hunt the next morning. His four children were as excited about hunting for Easter eggs and jelly beans on Easter as they were looking for presents on Christmas morning. Martin spent Easter Sunday afternoon with Detective Eddie Wielosinski retracing Speck's steps from the Shipyard Inn to the nurses' town house. Then, Wielosinski drove him to O'Hare for the last Ozark flight back to Peoria. Before leaving, Martin happily told his family that he believed that the jury would soon be selected.

Corazon Amurao enjoyed a sumptuous Easter brunch at Chicago's Conrad Hilton Hotel with her family and bodyguards. Oblivious to the proceedings in Peoria, Cora and Mama continued to regularly get out of the Sheridan-Surf for shopping expeditions to Chinatown and department stores and for soothing long rides in the country.

Meanwhile, Ken Alexander and Wielosinski increased the frequency of their location checks on the State's Chicago witnesses, many of whom were brought to Peoria on weekends for pretrial meetings with the prosecutors. Tabs were also kept on the expert medical and psychiatric witnesses, as well as the lay witnesses in Dallas who could testify to Speck's sanity.

Presenting the prosecution case is like building a house, brick by brick, witness by witness. The bricks needed to be ready because the trial was fast approaching.

On March 30, to the relief of everyone in the case, the final panel of four jurors was finally accepted—Clarence Donaldson, Caroline Edenburn, Lawrence Hankins, and Ellen Adams. Donaldson, an elderly retired parking lot operator, had lived his entire life in Peoria. He had sat on a murder jury back in the 1930's, but neither side asked him any questions about this jury's verdict lest it appear that they were invading his privacy by intruding on that jury's deliberations. That jury may have voted the death penalty; if so, Donaldson had more experience in death-penalty cases than the prosecutors. Caroline Edenburn was the mother of four children, ages fifteen to twenty-four, and her husband was a laborer for the Pabst Brewing Company. Lawrence Hankins, the father of three teenagers, was an assistant boiler operator for a Peoria chemical plant. Ellen Adams, another Peoria native, was a computer operator for a department store.

After six weeks of painstaking, individual questioning, twelve average citizens, seven men and five women, had been chosen to decide the fate of Richard Speck. The two alternate jurors, who would also sit throughout the trial in case of injury or illness of one of the other twelve, were George Shamrock and Mary Payne. Shamrock was a machine operator for Caterpillar Tractor, and Mrs. Payne, the mother of five, was a volunteer worker at a Peoria nursing home. Her husband was the foreman of the machine shop at Caterpillar. It seemed to Martin that at least one member of every Peoria family worked at "CAT," the town's major employer.

The final scorecard showed that a total of 609 prospective jurors had been questioned, and 259 had expressed a preconceived opinion about the case and were excused for cause. Their admitted bias was due not so much to what they had read about

the Speck murders as by the brutal nature of the killings themselves, which they had found out about when Judge Paschen read
the indictments. Thankfully, Peoria was not penetrated by the
big Chicago and St. Louis news media and the only newspaper in
town, the *Peoria Journal Star*, had reported the case responsibly.

Among other excused jurors, there were fifteen with personal relationships with either nurses or policemen; twenty-
four who testified that they disagreed with the instructions of
law, namely the presumption of innocence and the right of the
defendant not to offer any evidence; and forty-four who testified that jury duty would be an extreme hardship. Surprisingly
few jurors—only seventy-nine—were excused because they
testified that they would not sign a death-penalty verdict in any
case. By coincidence, the State and the defense had each exercised eighty-one peremptory challenges. Since the defense had
left seventy-nine peremptory challenges unused, it appeared
that Getty would have little chance on appeal to claim that Peoria was an unfair venue.

Service on the Speck jury was not going to be a Caribbean
cruise. During the coming weeks, the jurors would have to get
used to as much security as that enveloping Richard Speck. They
would be sequestered on the fourth floor of the Pere Marquette
Hotel, where the entrance to the floor was guarded twenty-four
hours a day by a Peoria deputy, who, in effect, barricaded the
jurors from the outside world. Both a female and a male deputy were on duty inside the blocked-off complex at all times.
The jurors would take all their meals in the same area of the
hotel's fourth floor, and the same meal would be served to all of
them. Direct telephone calls were barred. Any calls were made
with the assistance of a court-appointed bailiff, who repeated
both sides of the conversation. The jurors would be allowed no
reading of newspaper articles, no viewing of TV news or crime
shows, and no intimacy with loved ones. Their "entertainment"

would consist of a closely monitored trip to the barbershop or beauty parlor and a bumpy Sunday ride in a county-owned bus.

Elsewhere in the world, the alleged conspiracy case in the assassination of President John F. Kennedy was falling apart in New Orleans. District Attorney Jim Garrison saw his star witness, Perry Russo, fall apart when he was forced to admit that his "evidence" linking Lee Harvey Oswald to New Orleans businessman Clay Shaw and pilot David Ferrie in the alleged conspiracy to kill the President had been fabricated. Russo, it turned out, had never even seen Oswald, except on TV.

On March 30, as selection of the Speck jury was finally concluded, New Orleans was again in the news. A Delta jet on a training flight crash-landed into a motel near the New Orleans airport, killing all nine aboard the plane and seventeen others, including nine young girls from Juda, Wisconsin, who had taken their senior high school trip to New Orleans. On Friday morning, March 31, the *Chicago Tribune* ran page one photos of the nine graduating seniors. It was a page eerily reminiscent of the newspaper pages of July 14, 1966, when all four Chicago dailies also ran page one photos of nine young women—the eight nurses who had been stabbed and strangled to death by Richard Speck and the nurse he had forgotten to kill, Corazon Amurao.

At long last, on Friday, March 31, Judge Paschen was able to tell the increasingly restless jurors that the Speck trial would begin the next Monday with opening arguments. In the hardened slang of prosecutors, it was "showtime."

CHAPTER 34

A trial is both a war and a dramatic play. Martin had more than a touch of the playwright in him, and he knew that his opening statement would be the introduction of the plot, the witnesses his actors, their direct examination his script, the exhibits his theatrical props, the closing argument his soliloquy. At the same time, pulling together the witnesses who were now converging on Peoria required the logistical precision of a military campaign.

In preparing the State's case, Martin was guided by the simple principle that had been hammered home to him as a young prosecutor: "Don't gild the lily." The advice comes from the Bard himself, William Shakespeare, who wrote in *King John*: "To gild refined gold, to paint the lily, to throw a perfume on the violet . . . is wasteful and ridiculous excess." In terms of a modern high-profile criminal trial, this meant trim the prosecution to its bare-bones essence so that the defense has a much smaller target at which to shoot.

The prosecution of Richard Speck required understatement. The facts, crisply told, were overwhelming, and Martin would have to resist the temptation to "overtry" the case. For more than eight months, he had lived day and night with the Speck case, and he needed little time to prepare his opening statement. Besides, he was too busy to worry about it. The final weekend before trial would be spent preparing witnesses to testify—conducting mock direct and cross-examinations and selecting and numbering the exhibits each witness would identify. To try to send Speck to the electric chair, the State would rely on a case structured into four parts: taut circumstantial evidence placing Speck near the town house during the three days before the murders; a positive eyewitness identification; definitive fingerprint evidence; and a classic case of postcrime flight culminating in Speck's attempted suicide. The unknown was whether Getty would use an alibi or insanity for Speck's defense.

In following his philosophy of understatement, Martin reluctantly decided to sacrifice much of the State's significant evidence against the killer: Speck's incriminating statements to Drs. Smith, Feinerman, and Norcross; the .22 caliber pistol seized from Speck in room 806 of the Raleigh Hotel; the knife that Speck used to kill and later threw into the Calumet River; the abandoned suitcase of clothes and T-shirts Speck left in room 806 of the Raleigh Hotel; and the clothes and personal grooming articles Speck left behind in room 584 of the Starr Hotel.

Only the gun had been seized illegally. However, each time Martin thought of the other physical evidence, he saw trouble. Though the knife was undoubtedly the murder weapon, no witness could positively identify it as belonging to Speck, and not enough blood had been recovered from it to prove a link to the victims. The "Improved Muskrat" knife was little more than junk dredged up from the sludge of the Calumet River. If Speck's size 38–40 BVD T-shirt recovered from the Raleigh Hotel were introduced into evidence as being similar to the T-shirt found in the living room of the town house and the T-shirt removed from Speck at Cook County Hospital, then the blood on it from Sergeant Vrdolyak's accident in opening the suitcase would have to be explained. This would provide Getty with a golden opportunity to characterize the incident as a police effort to frame Speck. The possessions Speck left behind in his cage in the Starr Hotel proved nothing other than his preference for Noxzema shave bombs.

Martin also struggled over the scientific proof that established Speck's brutal rape of his final victim, Gloria Jean Davy. The crime lab had proven that the rectal swab taken from Gloria contained sperm, as did the cushion from the couch on which the body had been found. This undoubtedly was the sperm of Richard Speck. Placing it into evidence, however, would require the testimony of the police officers who had handled the swab and the cushion to establish an unbroken chain of possession ending with the crime lab chemist's microscopic analysis. The chemist would have to testify to his analysis that the recovered substance was semen. Several hours of testimony, subject to cross-examination at every step, would be required to prove the gruesome fact of Speck's rape. Martin decided that this proof was unnecessary. Corazon's graphic account of having overheard Speck rape Gloria Jean Davy in the upstairs bedroom and the photo of her naked body, lying face-down on the living room sofa, would be more than enough evidence to show Speck had defiled her.

This same philosophy of presenting a streamlined case would keep Ella Mae Hooper off the witness stand. Though Hooper's testimony would have demonstrated that Speck stole her Rohm .22 caliber six-shooter only hours before the murders, the illegal seizure of this same gun at the Raleigh Hotel precluded its introduction into evidence. This would leave Hooper's testimony unsupported, and her drinking problem and prior inconsistent statements seriously devalued her credibility. Hooper's account of having had sexual intercourse with Richard Speck, after he had subjected her to a depraved "Grand Inquisitor" interrogation, would prove Speck's bizarre sexual practices, but did not relate to the murders in the town house. "Bad man" evidence is inadmissible not because it proves too little, but because it proves too much—Speck was not on trial for the separate crime he committed in raping and robbing Ella Mae Hooper.

Proving the "yellow dress" incident would involve a complicated batch of evidence from several sources. According to Cora's account, as Speck was about to lead Patricia Matusek out of the south bedroom to kill her, he asked, "Are you the girl in the yellow dress?" This question proved that Speck had previously seen a girl near the town house wearing what looked to him like a yellow dress. On Tuesday night, July 12, 1966, at about five-thirty P.M., two separate events had briefly intersected: Speck, after being dropped off by another seaman at the union hiring hall, had been walking on 100th Street at the same time that Sherry Finnigan, her boyfriend, and "Mulehead" King—Pamela Wilkening's blind date—were pulling their car into the alley behind the nurses' town house to pick Pamela up to go to Riverview Amusement Park. Nina Schmale, who was wearing a mustard- or yellow-colored nightgown, briefly stepped out of the town house's back door to get a look at Pamela's blind date. Watching from a distance, Speck saw a "yellow dress" and, during the murders, confused Pat Matusek with Nina Schmale. Telling the story of the girl in the yellow dress would have required the State to use Sherry Finnigan, her married boyfriend, and "Mulehead" King as witnesses. The facts of Sherry Finnigan's former residence at the town house and her subsequent expulsion, her sexual relationship with a married man with four children, and the *Daily Calumet* allegations that she had once "dated" Speck, would have been extremely dangerous and unnecessary distractions from the main event. Rather than give Getty a field day in cross-examining this trio, Martin decided, for now, to leave the yellow dress incident unexplored.

At the same time, however, he was holding the yellow dress incident in reserve for a rebuttal of an insanity defense. If Getty gambled with an insanity defense, he would have to tell the jury that Speck claimed he could remember nothing about the night of the murders; Speck had locked himself into this position by claiming amnesia for the night of the murders in all his statements to the six members of the expert psychiatric panel and to Dr. Ziporyn. By using the yellow dress story, Martin would be able to argue otherwise.

Martin thought of the description given by Leo Tolstoy in *The Kreutzer Sonata*, in which the Russian novelist recounts the story told on a train by a man who killed his wife. The murderer says, "When people tell you they don't remember what they did when they were in a mad fit of rage, don't believe a word of it—it's all lies, nonsense. I remembered everything afterwards, and I've never ceased to remember it for one second. The more steam my rage got up, the more brilliantly the light of consciousness flared within me, making it impossible for me not to be aware of everything I was doing."

Similarly, Richard Speck had come very close to a confession in his October 11, 1966, interview with psychiatrist Edward Kelleher in the Cook County jail.

Kelleher: "If people murder, should they be electrocuted?"
Speck: "If I was the father of one of those girls, I would want to see the guy who did it burn." Abruptly, Kelleher changed his line of questioning.
Kelleher: "Which girl had the yellow dress?"
Speck: "Well, that was the one—"
Kelleher reported that Speck suddenly stopped talking, dropped his cigarette on the floor, picked it up quickly, sat back stiffly in his chair, stared hard at Kelleher for a few moments, and then asked, "What did you ask me?"
Kelleher: "I asked which girl had the yellow dress?"
Speck: "I don't know nothing about any girl with a yellow dress."

Later, in the same interview, Kelleher asked, "What do you want to tell me about the nurses being killed?"

Speck: "It all seems like a nightmare. I can't tell you why it happened. I had no reason. I got nothing against them. I didn't even know them. They were such nice girls and pretty girls."

Kelleher: "How do you know about them?"

After stammering, "Ah, ah," Speck finally replied, "Somebody showed me their pictures."

Kelleher: "Who?"

Speck: "I don't remember."

Kelleher: "How do you know they were nice girls?"

Speck: "They seemed to be."

Kelleher: "Were they nice to you?"

Speck: "I told you I never knew them. Other people said they were nice. Don't you think all nurses are nice?"

At this point, Kelleher reported, Speck arose from his slouched seating position, stretched, walked around his chair in a wide circle, and sat back down. Kelleher observed that he now sat "upright rather stiffly."

Kelleher's account of this interview brilliantly pierced Speck's false claim of amnesia, and Martin was prepared, if necessary, to call Kelleher as a witness to rebut any claim Getty might make that Speck was insane at the time he killed.

In the meantime, the State's witnesses were now arriving in Peoria. Weddings, funerals, and trials are the social occasions that bring strangers together for a common purpose, and this applied to the bereaved parents, professional doctors and nurses, and transient residents of Chicago's Southeast Side and Skid Row, all of whom were coming together for the single goal of bringing Richard Speck to justice. Most of the witnesses would be housed at the Ramada Inn, where the police could keep an eye on them and help them avoid certain risks—like getting arrested, drunk, or lost.

The first wave of witnesses arrived on Friday afternoon, March 31, and checked into the Ramada, followed by a second delegation on Saturday. As the witnesses arrived, Martin and Murtaugh reinterviewed them in the makeshift conference room.

On Sunday morning, detective Eddie Wielosinski boarded a Rock Island Railroad train in Chicago to escort a different group of witnesses to Peoria. With Wielosinski were the parents of Suzanne Farris, drawn and sad; a tight-lipped and serious Phil Jordan, who had lost both his sister, Mary Ann, and his fiancée, Suzanne Farris; Otha Hullinger, the desk clerk who had registered Speck at the Raleigh Hotel; and Fannie Jo Holland, the eleventh-floor resident of the Cabrini-Green Apartments who had spotted Speck's arrival by taxi at her parking lot. Wielosinski told the railroad conductor that these passengers were all witnesses in the "Speck case," and the conductor responded by preparing a private rail car for his "guests," complete with coffee, snacks, and playing cards. Since he had begun working on the case the morning of the murders, Wielosinski found that the magic phrase "for the Speck case" prompted the spontaneous, total cooperation of whoever heard it. Once, Wielosinski was sent to Chicago on an urgent mission. Arriving late at the Peoria Airport, he was told that the last Ozark Airlines flight out was full. Wielosinski invoked the magic incantation "for the Speck case" and soon was sitting in the jumpseat of the cockpit with the pilots.

Upon their arrival in Peoria Sunday afternoon, Mr. and Mrs. Farris and Phil Jordan were taken to the Holiday Inn, where they joined the other relatives who arrived by car that day—Mr. and Mrs. Wilkening and their son, Jack; Chuck Davy, father of Gloria Jean Davy; Joe Matusek, father of Pat Matusek, and his daughter, Mary Jo; and Dr. John Schmale, brother of Nina Schmale.

Chuck Davy, an intelligent and forceful executive, emerged as the spokesman for the group. Previously, Joe Matusek's grief had been more publicly displayed than that of the other relatives, and he alone had been willing to speak to reporters and go on TV. A contrast in styles, Davy and Matusek nevertheless turned to each other for comfort. Davy, the dapper, smooth sales executive, tended to keep his feelings bottled up and try to put on a good appearance. Matusek, the burly, rumpled saloon-keeper, was often emotional and teary-eyed. In the days ahead, though, they would frequently reverse their roles, and on any given day the two could be seen together, with Davy wrapping his arms around Matusek's shoulders, or vice versa, depending upon what each had learned that day in court.

It had been almost nine months since the murders, and not one of the parents or relatives had asked Martin to tell them what had happened in the town house on the night of Speck's savage crime. They would learn the horrifying facts for the first time when they listened to Martin's opening statement the next morning. In the meantime, they were under the compassionate care of Detective Byron Carlile, who had comforted hundreds of relatives of murder victims in his long career as a homicide cop. Carlile reserved an entire floor at the Holiday Inn for the relatives and made certain that their privacy was not invaded.

Later Sunday afternoon, five more witnesses arrived, including Dr. Eugenio Tapia, a short, smiling coroner's pathologist who reviewed his findings with Martin that night. Tapia spoke with a thick Spanish acent that gave Martin fits, pronouncing "leever" for liver, "woun" for wound. Tapia looked like the comical TV figure of the day, José Jimeñez, except Tapia was funnier. Martin found it fitting that a pathologist would be a happy-go-lucky prankster.

A more serious concern, though, was the painful decision that Martin had to make without delay, a decision with which he had been wrestling for days: Who should assist him at the State's counsel table?

During jury selection, the allocation of manpower had been equal. Getty, Gramenos, and Doherty for the defense, against Martin, Murtaugh, and Glenville for the State. Having prepared the case nonstop for nine months, Martin decided that he could conduct the direct examination of virtually all of the State's witnesses, and that he needed only one other prosecutor sitting at the counsel table with him. This, he believed, would undercut Getty's expected argument that the State had thrown a vast array of talent against a poor defendant. The question, though, was who it should be—self-effacing, nervously energetic twenty-seven-year-old George Murtaugh, or pipe-smoking, gray-haired, fifty-four-year-old ex–FBI agent John Glenville?

On the one hand, Glenville had been on the Speck case from the very beginning, had diligently completed every task he had been given, had assisted Martin at Speck's competency hearing, and had superbly handled the delicate task of interviewing Gerdena and Murrill Farmer. Glenville's courtroom style was matter-of-fact, his emotions tightly under control, and he had a remarkable ability to see the significance of what appeared to others as minor details. Prosecuting Speck would be the highlight of his dedicated career in law enforcement.

On the other hand, Martin believed that any claims about the State's "superior manpower" would be stopped if the vast resources of the State could produce only two "choirboys"— Martin and Murtaugh—to prosecute Speck. He thought that there would be a distinct tactical advantage to having the jury watch two seemingly inexperienced prosecutors battle the three mature defense veterans—Getty, Gramenos, and Doherty. News stories were repeatedly describing Martin as having limited trial experience in contrast to Getty, who was described by one gushing reporter as "a sly fox at the very height of his physical and mental powers." Having Glenville at the table would even the sides and give the State a veteran appearance. Martin finally decided that the image of the prosecution as the underdog in the upcoming battle would be strengthened significantly if Glenville were omitted in favor of Murtaugh.

This bitter and lonely decision was personally abhorrent and painful to Martin, who knew that Glenville would be heartbroken. *Chicago Daily News* reporter John Justin Smith had described Martin in print as a man who "treats smiles like diamonds and is slow to give them away." Although many casual observers found Martin to be cool and remote, he was underneath a very caring, emotional, warm man, and it devastated him to hurt Glenville. Martin realized that there was no way he could ever make up Glenville's loss of prestige at being removed from the case on the eve of trial and he wished he could have taken himself off, instead. But convicting Speck had to come first.

Sunday night, Martin went to Glenville's room and, without hesitating, gave him the bad news that he would not be at counsel table when the trial opened the next morning. Glenville tried to affect a stoic attitude. "Oh, I'll just have more time to beat Wielosinski at handball," he said, unconvincingly. He was crushed.

In the meantime, Officers Alexander and Wielosinski, acting like a pair of grizzly bears watching over their cubs, visited each hotel room to check on the State's witnesses and to allot that day's ration of goodies. Roommates Claude "One-Eyed Jack" Lunsford and Starr Hotel desk clerk Bill Vaughn, both removed from Skid Row and upgraded to plush king-size beds at the Ramada, were each rationed one six-pack of beer and one half-pint of whiskey each night. Fannie Jo Holland, who was used to a small apartment in her public-housing project, was rooming with Otha Hullinger, desk clerk and resident of the decrepit Raleigh Hotel. Fannie Jo requested a fifth of "good sippin' whiskey," by which she meant "Old Granddad, hundred proof—now don't you bring me that eighty-proof stuff!" Fannie Jo had been so worried about her four children that she had refused to leave them with a babysitter while she journeyed to Peoria. Alexander had visited her husband's employer, invoked the magic phrase, "for the Speck case," and gotten him the week off—with pay—while he stayed home with his family. When Martin put Fannie Jo through the dry run of her direct examination, she became so nervous and intense that she absent-mindedly pulled at the pearls of her necklace until the entire strand snapped.

After completing their witness checks, Alexander and Wielosinski joined Jack Wallenda in the second-floor hallway. Their adrenaline level was so high that the three policemen spent the entire night talking about the case. "It was just such a relief that we knew it was going to finally start in the morning," Wielosinski said. The policemen were not the only ones unable to sleep. Also spending the night quietly talking in their rooms were the victims' classmates, Judy Dykton, Patricia McCarthy, and Tammy Sioukoff. Unconcerned about tomorrow, Richard Speck slept like a baby in his small cell in the courthouse basement.

Monday, April 3

Peorians awakened Monday morning to a crisp, sunny spring day, with the temperature eventually reaching a pleasant 50 degrees. Spectators had begun to gather outside the courthouse at six A.M., and by seven a long line had formed for the nine-thirty opening of the trial. Only thirty-six spectators, and no one under the age of eighteen, would be admitted to Courtroom A.

Arising early, Martin ordered his favorite breakfast from room service—cinnamon toast and a pot of coffee.

A chronic pacer, he circled the small hotel room, silently rehearsing his opening statement. At eight-thirty, Martin and Murtaugh went to their unmarked Ford in the Ramada's basement parking lot for the short drive to the courthouse. Left behind, much to his disappointment, was Kenny Alexander. There was a good reason. Jack Altman, the accredited *Time* reporter at the trial and Ziporyn's coauthor, had asked Alexander for directions during the New York surveillance of Marvin Ziporyn, and the prosecution could not risk the chance that Altman might now recognize the policeman. So, despite his extensive involvement in so much of the pretrial work, Alexander would be confined to the Ramada for the duration of the trial.

Martin and Murtaugh emerged from their car carrying file folders and headed for the front door of the courthouse, walking quickly and silently past the TV cameramen and reporters who lined the sidewalk. Microphones were thrust at their faces, but they said nothing, not daring to risk even a whispered conversation between themselves. Photographers armed with telephoto lenses commandeered the rooftops of surrounding buildings.

In the meantime, Speck was being brought to the rear entrance of Courtroom A. As he was led by guards toward the courtroom door, he flicked his lit cigarette toward a large ashtray outside the door. Handcuffed as he was, Speck missed the tray and then flashed a smart-aleck grin as a deputy sheriff retrieved the burning cigarette. Throughout the trial, this routine would become a little game for Speck, a chance to annoy his guards before being led into court. Speck was wearing his dark blue suit, a white shirt, and a black tie. He was also affecting dark-rimmed glasses. Getty was doing his best to present Speck as being as harmless as the boy next door.

A palpable tension filled the air as Judge Paschen ascended the bench at nine-thirty. "You won't be bored now," the judge told the crowd. The number of spectators watching the jury selection had rapidly fallen off to only a few courtroom stragglers, as word got out that it was a tedious and sleep-inducing process. Today the courtroom was packed. Sitting in the front row nearest the jury box were the families of the American girls—the Wilkenings and their son, the Jordans, father and son, the Farrises, Dr. John Schmale, Joe Matusek and his daughter Betty Jo, and Chuck Davy. Detective Byron Carlile had spent the morning reminding the heartsick relatives that they could not risk disrupting the trial by displaying any emotion in the courtroom, and now they sat next to him, tight-lipped and tense. He prayed silently that they could maintain their composure.

With a kind smile, Paschen looked at Martin and said, "You may proceed." Wearing his dark-rimmed glasses and a navy blue vested suit with red-and-white regimental striped tie, Martin faced the judge and spoke the ritualistic first words of any lawyer's formal argument: "May it please the court. . . ."

For the next seventy-five minutes, Martin commanded the rapt attention of every person in the packed courtroom. Standing at the center of the jury box, shifting his weight slightly from one foot to the other, Martin moved his eyes from juror to juror, as he told the world in graphic detail what he expected to prove that Speck had done. He spoke without notes, having lived with the evidence for so long that he knew it like he knew the names of his four children. However, when he reached the point in the narrative of Cora's description of how each girl was led out of the south bedroom and taken down the hall like a lamb to the slaughter, his mouth began to go dry. He knew that the parents and relatives of the eight slain nurses were hanging on his every word, and that until now, not one of them knew how their daughters and sisters and loved ones had spent the last moments of their lives.

By the time Martin recited Cora's account of how she heard Speck unzip his black trousers to rape Gloria Jean Davy,

Martin's throat was parched and he was almost speaking in a whisper. Looking quickly to his left, he glimpsed the horror frozen on Chuck Davy's face. Joe Matusek and Chuck Davy were seated next to each other in the second row of the spectator benches. Matusek reached over and placed his meaty arm around the shoulders of Davy, who was hunched forward with disbelief. When Martin concluded his opening statement, the world finally knew the facts of the monstrous crime perpetrated by Richard Speck.

One man who was not surprised by anything Martin described was Public Defender Gerald Getty. He knew the State's witnesses, had interviewed most of them, had examined both the demonstrative and scientific evidence, and knew every word of Cora's remarkable account. Getty's defense, however, remained a mystery. Martin was certain that Getty would attack Cora's identification of Speck, but he was less sure of how the Public Defender would try to explain away the three fingerprints Speck left on the south bedroom door. He was even less sure if Getty would use an insanity defense keyed to the testimony of psychiatrists Marvin Ziporyn and Ner Littner. Martin and Murtaugh sat at their counsel table, pens poised, anxiously awaiting any clues in Getty's opening statement.

Getty rose and walked to the lectern carrying a black three-ring notebook. His dark brown suit was buttoned and his reddish hair was neatly slicked back. Facing the jury and speaking in his trademark folksy style, Getty said that Speck had been charged for no better reason than that he had the "misfortune" of being at the union hiring hall around the time of the murders. This was the "shutoff point" of the police investigation, Getty argued. He added, "No one denies that eight beautiful young girls were killed. We all know that. The question is, is this man the killer?"

In discussing the State's fingerprint evidence, Getty referred to the prints on the bedroom door as "smudges without detail, without ridges, without cores, without deltas, and without all this they cannot be classified. The police knew, and I suspect that the evidence will show, that with the identification [of Speck] as it was . . . they needed more evidence. And that is why I expect the evidence to show that fingerprints were *developed*."

With this one word, Getty gave away the secret of his attack on the State's fingerprint evidence. The defense would attempt to confuse the jurors about the two totally separate concepts of identification and classification to support a charge that the prints had been "developed" by the police in an attempt to frame Speck with phony fingerprints found elsewhere. As Getty spoke, Martin's pen flew across his legal pad. Based on Getty's opening, Martin knew that he would have to radically alter how he presented his evidence. In this first skirmish of war, the enemy had unwittingly tipped its hand on where it would strike. But that was all Getty would give away.

Shrewd warrior that he was, Getty had confined his opening to an assault on the State's case. He had not mentioned one word about what Speck's defense would be. Getty still had all his options open. In the meantime, the State had to build its case—one witness at a time.

The two opening statements took all morning, and the jury was recessed until two P.M. Before the trial resumed in front of the jury, Getty and his assistants pleaded several arguments in the judge's private chambers. When the lawyers went in chambers, the reporters stayed out. Judge Paschen, after sitting through six weeks of jury selection, did not want any news stories to accidentally reach the jurors and tell them about evidence that he decided should not be heard or seen by them. If jurors were exposed to media reports of inadmissible evidence and events, the entire process would abort and have to start over.

The defense railed against the introduction into evidence of the FBI-built scale model of the town house, which Getty derisively termed a "dollhouse," arguing that it was inflammatory and prejudicial. After hearing Martin's argument that the neutral-gray scale model was needed to illustrate the testimony of his witnesses, especially one for whom English was not a native language, Paschen allowed the State to use the exhibit. Getty then chided Martin for not giving him the reports and transcripts of prosecution interviews of all the witnesses the State intended to have testify. Martin responded that this information would be supplied six witnesses in advance, so that the Public Defender would have ample time to prepare his cross-examination.

When the trial resumed at two o'clock, Martin put his first brick in place by calling to the witness stand Chicago cartographer Sam Mazzone, who provided the evidentiary basis for two hugely enlarged maps mounted on art board—one depicting Chicago's Southeast Side and the other the city's near North Side. The two blowups were admitted into evidence and placed on easels at one end of the jury box. Martin had decided to give the relevant State's exhibits to the jury at the end of each witness's testimony, rather than follow the prosecution tradition of offering all the exhibits at once at the end of the State's case. By doing this, he let the jurors see the real evidence at the same time they heard the witness's testimony. Bright red stickers on the map of the Southeast Side showed the relative locations of the National Maritime Union, the nurses' town house at 2319 East 100th Street, the Manor Shell Station east of the town house, the Shipyard Inn, the South Chicago Community Hospital, Pauline's rooming house, the Ebb Tide tavern, and Eddie and Cooney's Tap. Similarly, the map of the near North accurately portrayed the locations of the Cabrini-Green housing project at 1160 North Sedgwick, the Raleigh Hotel at 648 North Dearborn, and the Starr Hotel at 617 West Madison.

Martin's second witness began forging links in the chain of eyewitness proof that Speck had been in the vicinity of the town house immediately before the murders. After being shown enlarged mounted photos of 100th Street and Luella Park, a thickly accented Italian seaman marked an X near both the Tastee-Freeze, where he had dropped Speck off on Tuesday night, July 12, at about five-thirty, and the drinking fountain in Luella Park, directly behind the large window of the upstairs south bedroom of the slain nurses' town house.

Day one of the trial concluded with the testimony of a marine engineer who testified that Speck, after being refused a berth on the *Sinclair Great Lakes* on July 12, made the remark, "Oh, hell, I'm going to New Orleans and ship out." The jury didn't yet know it, but this casual remark foreshadowed Cora's testimony of the words Speck spoke to his captives in the town house.

That night, after devouring a well-done cheeseburger and a glass of milk in the Ramada coffee shop, Martin left with Detective Jack Wallenda to meet with Byron Carlile and the relatives of the victims. Judge Paschen had ruled that one member of each family could testify to the fact of life and the fact of death for each nurse—the elemental proof that a homicide had occurred—and Martin had to decide who that family member would be. Choosing the right witness was crucial. Each family member had to endure his or her brief court appearance without breaking down. An overly emotional display could cause the judge to declare a mistrial because the display of a hysterically bereaved parent would prejudice the jury. Martin's burden was to select witnesses who could maintain their composure.

Since two of the Filipino families, the Pasions and Gargullos, were not able to come to Peoria, the life and death of Valentina Pasion and Merlita Gargullo would be established by the testimony of William Moore, personnel director of South Chicago Community Hospital. Although Moore grieved for the nurses, he was not likely to display his feelings when he testified. Carlile, Wallenda, and Martin believed that all of the other life-and-death witnesses would retain their composure, with two possible exceptions—Joe Matusek and Chuck Davy.

Emotionally devastated by his daughter's murder, Joe Matusek could not mention Patricia's name without breaking into deep, wracking sobs. Martin asked Patricia's younger sister, Betty Jo, a soft-spoken and petite interior designer, to testify instead of her father. Chuck Davy was the witness who concerned the prosecution the most. Disturbingly calm on the outside, Davy was seething inside. To enter the witness box, each witness had to pass within a few feet of Richard Speck. Carlile pulled Martin aside in the Holiday Inn lobby and said quietly, "I'm afraid that Chuck might go for Speck. I don't blame him if he wants to kill the son of a bitch." Martin, however, had no alternative. Since Mrs. Davy was too distraught even to come to Peoria, Chuck Davy would have to be his witness. Martin went to a pay phone and called Peoria County Sheriff Willard Koeppel to ask him to alert his deputies to the possibility that Davy might take a lunge at Speck.

Exhausted from meeting with the bereaved and tearful families, Martin left for the Ramada Inn at about ten P.M. On the way, he stopped at a convenience store and bought a quart of skim milk and a box of chocolate chip cookies. Seven weeks at the Ramada had made it his second home; he stored his snack in the coffee shop refrigerator. Then, he went to the conference room, where for the next two hours he and Murtaugh put witnesses through a final dry run. Returning to his room but too keyed up to sleep, Martin reclaimed his snack, nibbling on cookies and milk until he felt drowsy. When his head finally hit the pillow, he was dead to the world.

Tuesday, April 4

As spectators began another early-morning vigil in front of the courthouse in Peoria, Chicagoans were lining up at the polling precincts to overwhelmingly reelect sixty-four-year-old Mayor Richard J. Daley to his fourth term as Chicago's mayor. Hizzoner clobbered Republican challenger John Waner, carrying all fifty of the city's wards.

Meanwhile, the State's first witness on Tuesday was an elderly ship's porter who described how, in the early morning of July 13, Speck had asked him to watch his two bags while he walked from the front door of the still unopened union hall to the drinking fountain behind the nurses' town house. A Manor Shell gas station attendant testified next that Speck had apparently slept in or near Luella Park on the night of Tuesday, July 12, before arriving at the station early on the morning of July 13 to claim the two bags he had left overnight. During his cross-examination of these two witnesses, Getty predictably zeroed in on their recollection of Speck having pockmarks and long hair, in apparent contrast to the police sketch of Speck made on the basis of Corazon Amurao's early description to investigators.

The State then called the recently married Agnes Budak Goze, the owner of the Shipyard Inn, who said that on Wednesday, July 13, Speck rented room 7 from her for one week and that he was in the Shipyard Inn bar early Wednesday night, July 13. Folksy as ever, Getty began his cross-examination by congratulating Agnes on her recent marriage. He also brought out her long career in the hotel business, noting with pleasure that she had once run a hotel in New York and had been head housekeeper at Chicago's famed Edgewater Beach Hotel before drifting to the Southeast Side. Then, he extracted from her the admission that Speck's pockmarks were very noticeable and that, clearly, he did not wear his hair in a crew cut.

Construction worker Patrick Walsh told the jury how Speck had pulled a gun on him in the Shipyard Inn only hours before the murders. Walsh was as tough on cross-examination as he was on the Southeast Side, and Getty dropped him quickly. After the noon recess, Patrick Walsh's new bride told how she had joined her fiancé at the Shipyard Inn shortly after Speck pulled the gun on him. Dressed in a cream-colored jacket and green skirt to accentuate her flaming red hair, which was piled high in a trendy 1960's beehive, she described for the jurors Speck's Jekyll-and-Hyde act at the Shipyard Inn only hours before he left to kill. Speck, she said, had been alternately embittered and polite, as he talked about his ex-wife and young daughter and profusely apologized for pulling a gun on her street-tough boyfriend.

Army Sergeant Richard Oliva took the stand in his full-dress green military uniform, fresh from a tour of duty in Vietnam. He told the jurors that he had seen Speck brandishing both a pocketknife and a hunting knife as he strutted about the Shipyard Inn bar. The combined testimony of Patrick Walsh and Sergeant Richard Oliva proved that Speck was carrying his tools of murder in a public place only hours before he entered the town house. Martin's direct examination of these pivotal witnesses was crisp and pointed, a rifle shot in contrast to the shotgun like queries put forth by Getty upon cross-examination.

The next witness was FBI agent John Dunphy, who was also in uniform—sharply pressed gray suit, white shirt, dark blue tie, and highly polished black wing-tip shoes. Dunphy described the scale model that was being introduced into evidence to help the jurors understand the scene of the crime. Meticulously built on a scale of one and a half inches to the foot, the model featured a removable second floor. Getty had hoped to make points in his cross-examination by pointing out how much money the State had spent on this expensive exhibit, but then quickly dropped

Dunphy when the agent stated emphatically that the FBI had donated the model to the prosecution. The replica of the town house sat in front of the jurors throughout the trial, an unforgettable reminder of the scene of the crime.

The next witnesses were the parents and relatives who would testify to the life and death of the eight nurses. These were the witnesses who would let the jury know that the victims who had lived in the town house were not just names on indictments but young women who had been loved as flesh-and-blood human beings. To foreshadow Cora's testimony, Martin decided to call these witnesses in the order in which the girls had been killed: Lena Wilkening, mother of Pam Wilkening; John Farris, father of Suzanne Farris; Philip Jordan, brother of Mary Ann Jordan and fiancé of Suzanne Farris; Dr. John Schmale, brother of Nina Schmale; William Moore, representing the families of Valentina Pasion and Merlita Gargullo; Betty Jo Matusek, sister of Pat Matusek; and Charles Davy, father of Gloria Jean Davy.

Their testimony took only a few minutes, but it would stay with the jurors and every person in the courtroom for a lifetime. Ironically, it was this life-and-death testimony that, more than anything else, made the victims come alive. The testimony of Pamela Wilkening's mother, Lena, captured the understated emotion of all the life-and-death witnesses. Before beginning his questioning, Martin paused and looked back and forth from Mrs. Wilkening to the jurors, silently calling the jurors' attention to the fact that they were about to hear for the first time from one of the many indirect victims of Richard Speck's crime. Although she was controlled and stoical and spoke in a firm, strong voice, the suffering etched on Mrs. Wilkening's face was not lost on the jury.

Martin: "Would you please state your name?"

The witness: "Lena Wilkening."

"That is L-e-n-a?"

"L-e-n-a."

"Will you spell your last name, please?"

"W-i-l-k-e-n-i-n-g."

"And you are the mother of Pamela Lee Wilkening?"

"Yes, sir."

"And would you please spell her first and middle names?"

"Pamela, P-a-m-e-l-a. Lee, L-e-e."

"When was Pamela Lee Wilkening born?"

"August second, 1945."

"What was her occupation in July of 1966?"

"She was a student nurse at the South Chicago Community Hospital, Chicago, Illinois."

"When is the last time you saw your daughter, Pamela Wilkening, before July fourteen, 1966?"

"July seventh."

"What was her physical condition at that time?"

"Fine."

"When is the next time that you saw your daughter, Pamela Lee Wilkening?"

"July fourteenth, in the Chicago Morgue."

"She was deceased at that time?"

"That's right."

"Thank you, Mrs. Wilkening."

Wisely, Getty declined to cross-examine any of the life-and-death testimony about the American nurses. However, he wanted to make a point with William Moore, the hospital administrator, namely that, in his opinion, Moore could have testified to the life and death of all eight nurses. Getty's strategy was to make Martin appear heart-less and cruel for needlessly subjecting the relatives of the American nurses to the ordeal of testifying. Getty first established that Moore was acquainted with both Pamela Wilkening and Suzanne Farris. He then asked, "Was your relationship any different with these girls [Wilkening and

Farris⌉ than with the girls you just testified about?" He didn't
expect Moore's answer: "Yes, it was. The two Filipino girls were
employees of the hospital, so to speak, and the other six were
student nurses, whom I did not come in contact with, except
by sight." Abruptly, Getty concluded his cross-examination.
He had inadvertently proven that Moore was not a competent
witness to the life and death of the American nurses and that
Martin had no alternative to calling the parents and other
relatives to the stand.

The next witness was a handsome, sad Robert Stern, who
quietly testified to bringing Gloria Jean Davy back to the town
house at eleven thirty-five P.M. Martin had considered gilding
the lily by having Stern name the song—"You'll Never Walk
Alone"—they listened to before parting, and by calling Jay
Andres, the Chicago disc jockey who had played the tune that
night, to establish the exact time Davy entered the town house.
He felt, however, that the flinty Peorians would find this proof
both unnecessary and melodramatic. The final witness of the
day was nurse Pat McCarthy, who described the final carefree
hours she had spent shopping and visiting with Suzanne Farris
and Mary Ann Jordan before her two friends left her room and
the back door of her 2311 town house at one end of the alley to
make their fatal trip back to 2319.

The defense didn't yet know it, but the State's next witness,
due up early the next morning, was going to be one big surprise.
Although he knew she was scheduled among the next several
witnesses, Gerry Getty did not expect to see this early in the
trial the next person Martin would call to the stand:

Corazon Pieza Amurao.

CHAPTER 35

The State's eyewitness had slipped into town quietly. When the trial opened on Monday, Sergeants Jim Concannon and Steve McCarthy, acting with the nonchalance of a family on vacation, drove Cora, Mama, and Roger Amurao from the Sheridan-Surf Hotel in Chicago to Peoria. Sheriff Willard Koeppel had secured a house on the outskirts of town and a borrowed car to be used to conceal Cora from the reporters.

Concannon wheeled his unmarked Ford sedan into the Caterpillar Tractor Company parking lot, where the borrowed car was waiting. The travelers switched to this car and drove to their home in Peoria with a trunk full of fresh groceries brought from Chicago. The fun-loving Gaelic sergeants even brought Ping-Pong paddles and balls and would commandeer a teak dining room table in their borrowed house for a tournament with the Amuraos. The policemen were masters of ways to divert Cora's attention from the trial. The Ping-Pong was in addition to the usual nightly poker games.

On Tuesday night, Sheriff Koeppel picked up Martin at the Ramada and drove him to the hideaway, where he visited Cora, who was calm and smiling. More from instinct than anything else, Martin decided not to take Cora through her direct examination again. Giggling shyly, Cora showed

Martin her neatly pressed blue culottes, asking if she could wear them to court. Sure, Martin said. He played one game of Ping-Pong with her before suggesting that they make a short visit to the courthouse. Martin thought it would help the State's star witness if she had an advance look at the courtroom in which she would be testifying. Under cover of darkness the sheriff drove Martin and Cora to the back entrance of the courthouse and quickly escorted them to the second floor, unlocked the door to Courtroom A, and turned on the lights. Cora got a good look at the witness box, but did not sit in it.

Martin then said to her, "Cora, I'm going to ask you tomorrow if you see the man who knocked on your bedroom door. If you do see the same man, it's up to you as to how you want to point him out." Cora looked at Martin but said nothing. He continued, "You can stand up and point to him from the witness chair. That's all you have to do." Cora nodded but still said nothing. Sensing that she was becoming anxious, Martin suggested they leave. The courtroom visit lasted less than five minutes.

Back at the Ramada, George Murtaugh was dreaming up a scheme so Cora could avoid having to walk past the forest of microphones, photographers, and TV cameras that lined the steps to the courthouse each day. Dr. Leroy Smith, the handsome young County Hospital doctor who had identified Speck in the trauma unit, had brought a guest with him to the Ramada Hotel—a young Argentinian woman who worked in a Chicago hospital. Murtaugh thought that she bore a striking resemblance to Cora, and he suggested that this woman could walk through the front door of the courtroom wearing sunglasses and linking arms with Mama and Roger Amurao, while Cora herself would be slipped into a rear basement entrance. The woman readily agreed to the ruse.

Wednesday, April 5

The ruse worked. Photographers furiously snapped away as Cora's double walked solemnly up the front steps of the courthouse. At the same time, Cora was being escorted to the second floor and a judge's empty chambers behind Courtroom A. She was dressed in her blue culottes, with a yellow blouse, dark stockings, and dark, flat shoes. At her request, there were four men seated in the front row—Officers Concannon, McCarthy, Renaldo Cozzi, and Detective Jim Georgalas. With her trusted and caring bodyguards and friends at hand, the petite young nurse would have no fear of Richard Speck.

When Gerry Getty got wind that Cora was the first witness of the day, he was panic-stricken. He called for a conference in Paschen's chambers to say that the defense wasn't quite ready to cross-examine Amurao. In an artful dodge, Getty added that he had recently bitten his tongue and developed a painful canker sore. "I'm slurring my words—can't you tell?" Getty told the judge. "This jury may think that I had a few drinks or something. I don't feel up to cross-examining this witness."

Paschen said that Getty's speech sounded just fine and, besides, Martin's direct examination was going to take up most of the day. Getty persisted until he was allowed to leave to visit a physician. While Jim Gramenos and Jim Doherty argued vigorously that Cora should not be allowed to testify next, Getty hurried to the nearest doctor, returning shortly with a note saying that he had "an ulcer on the lateral border of his tongue that interfered with comfortable speech." The physician had prescribed a medicated gel that he believed would clear up the condition in a day or two. Getty renewed his plea that Cora's testimony be deferred. After listening to ninety minutes of defense stalling, Paschen ruled that Cora would be allowed to testify immediately but that the cross-examination could probably be deferred until the next day.

At eleven A.M., Cora walked into the courtroom, head held high, and took her seat in the witness box, which was to the immediate right of and slightly below where Judge Paschen sat. The jury box was to her right. Martin stood in front of her, but about sixty feet away, at the far end of and slightly beyond the end of the jury box, which was at his left. There was a small walnut lectern in front of him, on which rested four sheets of paper, outlining the chronology of events he wanted to cover. He was glad that his lectern was this far away, because he wanted Cora to have to speak loudly enough for both him and all the jurors to hear her testimony clearly. This was a distinctly more formal setting than the swimming pool at the Moraine-on-the-Lake, where Martin and Cora had begun their conversations. He thought of the distance between them now as the distance between a baseball pitcher and his catcher—sixty feet six inches. The prosecutor would have little need for his notes, as he and Cora would soon settle into a grooved routine in which Martin would perfectly pitch a question and Cora would perfectly throw back the answer. It was like playing catch, and both were throwing strikes. Before answering, Cora looked at Martin and then spoke directly to the jurors on her right. Occasionally, she looked up and to her left at Judge Paschen.

Shown the FBI scale model of the town house, she said, "That is the same," and described which nurse occupied each bunk bed in the three upstairs bedrooms. Martin wrote a girl's name in blue ink on each bunk bed in the model. As Cora described answering the four knocks "done in a normal manner" on her bedroom door, tears began to form in her eyes.

Getty asked if she wanted a few minutes to compose herself. Martin considered this a ploy by Getty both to pose as a good guy and also to interrupt the growing momentum of her powerful testimony. Since Martin wanted to present Cora to the jurors as a strong, sure witness, the last thing in the world he wanted to do was make her look weak by interrupting her testimony himself so she could "compose herself." Cora shook her head. She wanted to continue. Paschen leaned over and handed her a glass of water, which she sipped and then placed on a ledge.

"I saw a man," Cora resumed, "standing in the center of our door with a gun in his right hand pointed toward me, and I noticed that he had marks on his face, the clothes were dark from the shoulder to the foot, and his hair was blond, hair combed toward the back, and some hair in front."

Martin was about to ask the question he had asked of eyewitnesses hundreds of times in the past. Cora sat alertly in a stiff black leather chair behind a latched door just to the side of Judge Paschen.

"Now, Miss Amurao, if you see that same man in the courtroom today, the man who came to your bedroom door on Wednesday night, July thirteenth, would you please step down and point him out, please." The prosecutor expected Cora to step down in front of the witness box and point toward Speck.

Instead, her response was spontaneous—and electrifying.

Cora stood up, unlatched the door to the witness box, and walked in slowly measured steps directly toward Richard Speck. Without hesitation, she kept walking until she was only a foot from Speck's pockmarked face. Then, Corazon Amurao raised her right arm and stabbed her fingers to within inches of the killer's expressionless eyes, exclaiming:

"This is the man!"

Pandemonium.

While Speck stared back blankly at his accuser, the courtroom buzzed over the startling moment of identification. Despite Paschen's press order, ten reporters jumped from their seats and rushed out of the courtroom to fight over the only two public phones in the building. Getty immediately moved for a mistrial, arguing that the identification had been "ostentatious" and prejudicial. Paschen denied the motion and the courtroom quickly became quiet. Inwardly shocked that Cora had left the witness box and walked within inches of Speck, Martin's dour expression never changed. Without betraying his emotion, he continued to ask questions. "Does the man look any different than he did on July thirteenth?" he asked. Cora, who had walked resolutely back to the witness box, replied, "He is just the same."

It was now twelve forty-eight P.M., and Cora had been on the stand for nearly two hours. Martin was now planning to show her seven figurines representing the seven nurses who had been made to sit on the floor in the south bedroom of the town house. The gray wooden figures were blocks four inches high that had been shaped in the form of a sitting woman. The defense immediately asked for a conference in chambers to object to these exhibits. Martin argued that he needed them to portray the positions of each of the victims in the large bedroom, and he accused the defense of trying to stall Cora's testimony as long as possible. Paschen called a recess until two-fifteen, at which time arguments on the exhibits would resume in his chambers.

During the luncheon recess, Martin asked Murtaugh to join him for a walk. As they circled the courthouse plaza again and again, Martin said very little. He felt as if he was in a trance while questioning Cora, as if some mystical force were guiding him. He thought that being in this zone must be the way a baseball pitcher feels when every pitch is hard and true. Although he knew that the world's press was watching him, Martin had been oblivious to everything in the courtroom except the presence of Cora. Silently, he thanked the Dominicans and Jesuits for teaching him the virtue of unbroken concentration. As Martin and Murtaugh walked in the spring sunshine, Cora sat in the unoccupied chambers of one of the Peoria judges. She had a can of Pepsi and her four policemen for comfort. Although Richard Speck was only two floors below, she felt very secure.

At two-fifteen, the lawyers reassembled in Judge Paschen's chambers to listen to a diatribe from Assistant Public Defender Jim Doherty, who characterized the wooden blocks as "inflammatory little dolls," resembling "coffins" that were worse than "an exhibit in a wax museum." Doherty was a very rugged adversary in the type of hand-to-hand combat that takes place in the privacy of the judge's chambers. He managed to stall proceedings for another forty-five minutes. Finally, at three P.M., Paschen ruled that the figurines were admissible and allowed Martin to resume his direct examination of Corazon Amurao.

Cora's concentration and energy were indefatigable. When asked how Speck had moved from one girl to the next as he tied them into helplessness, Cora volunteered to demonstrate. She left the witness box to move the figurines into the correct positions, then she squatted on the floor, crawling from side to side, to imitate how Speck had moved from nurse to nurse, "always with his gun." Her foresight in wearing culottes and flat-soled shoes made the demonstration possible.

As the amazed jurors watched, she demonstrated how her own wrists had been tied behind her back, with the palms facing outward, and how her ankles were tied with double knots. Martin had emphasized to her how important it was to establish a rapport with the jury. She obliged by looking directly at the jurors as she moved with agility and grace to demonstrate on the courtroom floor how she and her friends had been subdued. Although she spoke with a pronounced Tagalog accent, Cora's voice was clear, even, and firm. The dramatic narrative came to an end with her description of being taken back to South Chicago Community Hospital Thursday morning after the murders. "Then I went to the hospital room and I sleep."

Martin decided not to raise the issues of how she had subsequently identified Speck's photo on July 15 and how she had personally identified him at Cermak Memorial Hospital on July

19. The jurors were left only with the dauntless and unforgettable identification she had made of Speck in the courtroom that morning.

At four-forty, Martin tendered Corazon Amurao for cross-examination, but the defense had successfully stalled the direct examination long enough that Paschen was forced to recess until the next morning. Cora waited in the judge's chambers until the press left the courthouse, and then she slipped through the basement door and was driven over a circuitous route to her hideaway, where she enjoyed a home-cooked meal, courtesy of her mother, and more Ping-Pong, courtesy of her Irish cops.

Getty would be well armed for the next day's cross. Every day, the three veteran and unfailingly accurate Cook County official court reporters assigned to the trial alternated the preparation of testimony transcripts and delivered them that same night to the State at the Ramada Inn and the defense at the Voyager Inn. Getty would have access to Cora's direct testimony of that day, the police reports of the July 14–15 interviews with her, the twenty-two-page handwritten notes of Myrna Foronda, Martin's handwritten notes of his November interviews with her, and the one-hundred-thirty-three-page transcript of the statement that Getty's chief lieutenant Jim Gramenos took from her in January. These kinds of prior statements can prove a gold mine to an astute cross-examiner.

Thursday, April 6

Arm in arm with her mother and cousin, Corazon Amurao walked briskly in the front door of the courthouse on this second day of her testimony. Having already told Richard Speck and the world exactly what he had done to her companions back in July 1966, she no longer had any need for a double. The temperature outside had climbed to an unseasonable 75 degrees and the courtroom was uncomfortably warm. Paschen told the lawyers that they could remove their suit jackets, but only the innately informal Jim Doherty did so. As Cora took the stand to endure Getty's cross-examination, she was wearing her same outfit, except she wore a white rather than yellow blouse.

Gerry Getty, his tongue healed, would be gentle with the State's prize witness. He knew that if he treated her roughly and caused her to break down, the defense would be irreparably harmed. His emphasis was to try to show that she was confused in her identification of Speck as the killer.

Demure but fierce, Cora stood her ground against the sagacious Public Defender. Explaining that during the first police interviews conducted on July 14 in the town house at 2315 she had talked to Mrs. Chan in Tagalog and that Mrs. Chan had translated her remarks back to the policemen, Cora emphasized to Getty that she had described Speck's prominent pockmarks and that, "I did not say the 'crew cut,' sir." Getty persisted in his attack on her description of the killer by asking lengthy textbook identification questions about the shape of Speck's ear, eyebrows, eyes, mouth, and all the other imaginable minutiae of a human face. Cora repeatedly responded, "I can't recall." Although Getty had tried before trial to suppress Cora's identification of Speck's photo and of Speck himself at Cermak Hospital, he now decided to bring these two incidents to the jury's attention. He was trying to show that these identifications and, consequently, the one she made in court were dependent on each other and equally unreliable.

Next, Getty asked permission to introduce into evidence both the sketch of Speck made on July 15 by the police artist, and the photo of a grinning Speck taken by the U.S. Coast Guard. Martin readily agreed to the request. When the two likenesses were juxtaposed on a large art board, the sketch of the killer

Cora had described, though showing him with a crew cut and clear skin, nevertheless pore a deadly resemblance to the Coast Guard photo of Speck.

Quite suddenly, Getty ended his cross-examination. Cora's testimony had so firmly survived the cross that Martin decided that there was no need for a redirect. The State had struck a hammer blow.

Her duty done, Cora walked out of Courtroom A and down the stairs to the front door of the courthouse with her mother, and the waiting photographers captured the moment. Meanwhile, the wordsmiths described her as "unsmiling, graceful, and standing straight." In their bylined account, *Chicago Daily News* reporters M.W. Newman and John Justin Smith wrote:

"Petite and enormously spunky, Corazon Amurao, a blend of steel and lace, stood by her story Thursday under firm cross-examination. The delicate Filipino girl radiated honesty and sincerity on the stand. In a day and age when macabre murder trials clog every TV screen, she projected more vividly than any Oscar winner ever did." Later, Newman, a veteran of many courtroom scenes, would write, "Corazon was the greatest trial witness I have ever seen. Her memory for detail was astonishing and her sincerity couldn't be doubted."

Thursday, April 6

Martin's challenge was to maintain the momentum created by Cora's startling testimony. Following Cora to the stand Thursday was nurse Tammy Sioukoff, mysteriously beautiful with vaguely Asian features, who spoke so softly that she could barely be heard. When she was through, however, the jurors understood why no one had been at the front door when Speck had marched Cora and Merlita Gargullo downstairs to answer the doorbell. Tammy had been standing at the back door. She had nearly paid with her life for the two slices of bread she wanted to borrow.

Nurse Judy Dykton, dressed in a two-piece checked suit, described the poignant and pathetic scene of how she had discovered Cora whimpering on the upstairs window ledge. Before the next scheduled witness, Detective Jack Wallenda, could take the stand, Judge Paschen had to rule on the admissibility of nine black-and-white eight-by-ten photographs taken at the scene of the crime. Arguing that words alone could not describe the force and willfulness with which Speck had killed, Martin fought hard to introduce the photos into evidence.

Jim Zagel had provided him with a comprehensive memo on the admissibility of homicide scene photos compiled from court decisions in every jurisdiction in the U.S., and had also provided a set of grisly crime-scene photos of a nude murder victim that the Illinois Supreme Court had approved in a prominent 1963 case, *People v. Kolep*. Martin knew the *Kolep* case well—it had been his first argument before the Illinois Supreme Court. While Martin used the memo and the *Kolep* photos to bolster his motion, Getty strenuously argued that the photos were inflammatory and unnecessary. Martin countered that if the State really wanted to inflame the passions of the jurors, it would have offered the graphic photos of Valentina Pasion's garroted throat, the photos of the victims taken in the Cook County Morgue, and the thirty-seven colored slides taken in the two blood-splattered bedrooms. After listening to fiery arguments from both sides, Paschen ruled that the nine photos could be shown to the jurors.

Detective Jack Wallenda next took the stand, and in simple and understated language described what he had found when he walked into the town house on the morning of July 14, 1966. Speaking softly, with his emotions in check, the burly detective described the tightly drawn double knots that Speck had tied around the throats of Suzanne Farris, Nina Schmale, Merlita

Gargullo, Patricia Matusek, and Gloria Jean Davy. They were tied so tightly, he testified, that he had to cut them off with scissors. Wallenda provided the evidentiary foundation for the photos, testifying that each picture accurately and truly portrayed the condition of each victim's body when he first saw it. He also laid the foundation for the State's introduction into evidence of Speck's size 38–40 Hanes T-shirt, which Wallenda had discovered two weeks later while closing down the town house. He found the T-shirt wrapped inside Gloria Jean Davy's purple-and-white slacks and her panties, which were lying at the foot of the bottom bunk near the east wall of the large south bedroom. Using a cellophane bag, Wallenda demonstrated to the jurors how the T-shirt had been wadded up into the nurse's clothing.

Getty skillfully avoided cross-examining Wallenda, choosing, instead, to ask only a few simple questions about how Wallenda had prepared his reports. With this technique, Getty hoped to make the jurors think that he had some clever, though invisible, purpose in mind. He would use this same tactic with other police officers when he dared not attack their direct examination. When Wallenda concluded his testimony, the nine photos were passed among the jurors. Martin studied their faces, searching for a glimmer of shock or disgust at the mangled bodies. He saw only that the jurors viewed the photos without outward expression. The next evidence involved T-shirts.

Martin had decided to introduce into evidence three of Speck's T-shirts, the two found in the town house and the one removed from him at Cook County Hospital. He had decided not to use the fourth Speck T-shirt recovered from the Raleigh Hotel, the one stained with blood from a policeman's cut finger. He did not regret this decision, given that the unfolding theory of the defense was that Speck had been framed by a police department desperate to charge anyone with the horrible crime.

The next State witness was a crime lab technician, who was questioned on his finding of Speck's wrinkled and perspiration-soaked size 38–40 BVD T-shirt on the desk in the town house living room on the morning of July 14. Both of the T-shirts recovered from the town house were passed among the jurors. The T-shirt found on the desk, which had a drop of blood on the left rear shoulder and a hole sewn shut in the upper right front panel, may have been tossed into the living room by Speck after he had worked up a sweat killing the first three nurses. Since the nurses had been tied into submission, Speck had the total run of the house and could indulge in his chronic habit of fastidiously changing his shirts. The front of the Hanes T-shirt that Wallenda had found two weeks after the murders wadded up within Gloria Jean Davy's slacks contained three spots of type A blood—which was Speck's blood type—in the area of the T-shirt matching the scratch on Speck's chest. Valentina Pasion had scratched Speck's chest with her fingernails during the brief struggle she had with the killer, a struggle that had preceded Speck's attack on Davy. Finding the Hanes T-shirt wrapped within Davy's clothes strongly suggested that Speck had removed his T-shirt after he removed Davy's clothes and forced her down on the upstairs bed to rape her for the first time.

Only Richard Speck knew why he wore two different T-shirts during the rape and murders. Regardless of Speck's reasons for having left two T-shirts at the scene of the crime, Martin was adamant: both T-shirts must go to the jury. Early in the case, the prosecution had investigated the possibility that one of the nurses owned a size 38–40 Hanes or BVD T-shirt, but inquiries to the eight families eliminated this possibility. Martin was convinced beyond a shadow of a doubt that Speck left both T-shirts behind. Their brands, condition, locations, and sizes proved that Speck was their owner. Even though the State had to expand its proof to put the size 38–40 BVD recovered from Speck at County Hospital in evidence in order to connect him to the brand and size of his favorite T-shirt, Martin believed that this extra evidence was essential to tell the jury the story of the T-shirts in the town house, and, more importantly, to protect the integrity of the prosecution.

By using the T-shirts in his case, Martin foreclosed Getty from exploiting the fact that *two* T-shirts had been found in the town house. If Getty had been able to make it appear as if the State were hiding the two T-shirts, then the defense could seize this opportunity to argue that two men—neither of whom was Speck—had killed the nurses. The Public Defender held the personal belief that several men were involved in the murders. If the State had not introduced the T-shirts into evidence, Getty certainly would have promoted this theory by himself offering the two T-shirts into evidence.

By the time the jury had passed the two T-shirts among themselves, it was four-fifty P.M. Judge Paschen recessed for the day and the courtroom crowd spilled out into the warm April sunshine. By now, Cora was already back home at the Sheridan-Surf, safely back into her routine. She would go bowling on Saturday, have Sunday brunch at Henrici's Restaurant near O'Hare Airport, and begin to plan her flight home to the Philippines as soon as the trial was over. The girl who had "really wanted to help" had kept her promise.

Martin and Murtaugh spent Thursday night preparing the witnesses to Speck's flight from the Southeast Side and his attempt to assume a new identity. This flight and change of identity were compelling evidence of Speck's consciousness of guilt. It was his confession in deeds, not words, of the evil he had wrought.

Friday, April 7

The temperature had dropped 20 degrees by Friday morning and Peorians were being warned of the possibility of a frost by nightfall. Inside, Courtroom A cooled off from the sweltering heat that had prevailed inside the room the day before. The testimony, however, kept the jurors' emotions near boiling point.

The first witness was the short, dark-skinned Eugenio Tapia, M.D., a Cuban émigré and a diplomate of the American Board of Forensic Pathology. A connoisseur of violent death, Tapia had performed more than ten thousand autopsies—half of them on homicide victims. Tapia established the cause of death for each of the eight nurses in clinical language that, nevertheless, did not detract from the brutality with which Speck had killed.

Pamela Wilkening: "Stab wound in the left breast to the pulmonary artery extending to the right ventricle of the heart. Strangulation mark on neck and a contusion to the left thigh."
Suzanne Farris: "Strangulation by neck ligature. Contributing cause—two stab wounds in back puncturing each lung. There were eighteen total stab wounds, indicating repeated knife thrusts—eleven in front, seven in back."
Mary Ann Jordan: "Three stab wounds to chest, one fatal. Stab wound to left eyeball and two abrasions to left side of nose."
Nina Schmale: "Strangulation by neck ligature. Puncturelike stab wounds in neck inside the ligature mark."
Valentina Pasion: "Six-inch laceration of the neck, laying the trachea (voice box) bare. Second stab wound in neck, an abrasion of chin, and contusion on left hip."
Merlita Gargullo: "Strangulation by neck ligature. Partial dislocation of neck and four stab wounds to neck."
Patricia Matusek: "Strangulation by neck ligature. Contusion on left thigh, abrasions on knee. Internal examination revealed a traumatically induced hemorrhage in the stomach caused by a forceful kick."
Gloria Jean Davy: "Strangulation by neck ligature."

Getty did not cross-examination Dr. Tapia.

Tapia's testimony, along with Cora's dramatic eyewitness identification of Speck, the testimony of Tammy Sioukoff, Judy Dykton, Detective Wallenda, and the life-and-death witnesses, and the introduction into evidence of the scene photos and T-shirt evidence, concluded the second phase of the State's case, the first phase having been the circumstantial evidence placing Speck near the town house during the three days before the crime.

The evidence would now shift to Speck's flight from the Southeast Side, a part of the proof tailor-made for a prosecutor's closing arguments. Martin kept thinking how reminiscent Speck's actions after the murders were of the words of British poet Sir Walter Scott: "Oh, what a tangled web we weave/ When first we practice to deceive." Yet, his favorite description of Speck's flight was Biblical: "The guilty flee when no man pursueth."

Only hours after walking away from the wreckage he had caused to grab a few hours of sleep, Speck had wakened on Thursday morning, July 14, to resume his usual pattern of bar hopping. Robert "Red" Gerrald, the night cook on a Great Lakes ore boat and former shipmate of Speck's during the killer's brief tour at sea, told the jurors now he had run into Speck Thursday morning at Eddie and Cooney's saloon a few blocks from the Shipyard Inn. Gerrald spoke in a soft South Carolina accent and employed his own personal idioms to explain his time with the killer. Describing Speck's talk about going to Bond's department store, Gerrald testified, "He was aiming to buy some clothes." Red described his visit to Speck's room at the Shipyard Inn this way: "I had some pretty good booze on me, and my head began to slither around."

About this time, Speck, too, was beginning to slither— away from the Southeast Side. The radio and TV reports of the murders which were blaring in every bar he visited gave him a terrible surprise—he had left a survivor. Bill Olsen of the National Maritime Union testified that when he talked by phone to Speck Thursday afternoon about a ship assignment, the killer, who was standing at the phone booth in the Shipyard Inn, lied and said, "I'm downtown at Ruthie's." Sergeant Mike Clancy testified how he and others had staked out the union hall and waited in vain for Speck to appear. Shipyard Inn bartender Valie Blair testified why the stakeout was unsuccessful. Speck, he said, had checked out of the Shipyard Inn after he got off the phone with Olsen on Thursday, having spent only one night of his seven-day rental in room 7.

The next witness, Commercial Cab dispatcher Larry Beissel, all 350 good-natured pounds of him, cheerfully coaxed his enormous body into the small witness box and testified how a man who called himself "Johnson" had called for a cab at the Shipyard Inn at three twenty-seven P.M. on July 14. Speck, of course, was the caller and he gave as his location "Eddie and Cooney's"—the bar he had just left. Cab driver Matthew Hogan, neatly dressed in a dark suit, his thick gray hair combed slickly back, looked like a shorter version of actor Brian Dennehy. He told the jurors how Speck carried on a conversation with him as they drove to the North Side and 1160 North Sedgwick—the Cabrini-Green apartments. Speck, Hogan testified, made sure that the cab driver heard his alibi. The killer told him that he had only arrived in Chicago at four that very morning and that he and his friend "Red" had spent the early morning hours with two women. Speck said he was scheduled to ship out on the *Sinclair* tanker the next morning and he needed to get some money from his sister. She lived, he said he was ashamed to admit, near the "beatniks."

Speck had intended to lead the police to a dead end, and found the place he was looking for when Hogan dropped him off in the parking lot of a nineteen-story all-black housing project some twenty miles from the Shipyard Inn. Speck figured that if the police he had seen nosing around the Shipyard Inn asked about the stranger who had left in a Commercial Cab, well, their trail would go cold in this project parking lot. They wouldn't have a clue as to where he had really gone. Or so Speck thought.

If the killer had looked up after he patiently waited for Hogan to drive out of sight, he would have seen a woman gazing curiously down at him from her window on the eleventh floor of the housing project. Fannie Jo Holland, demure and very nervous, was in Peoria to tell the jury what she had seen on that Thursday afternoon. While waiting to testify, she pulled still more pearls from her abused necklace. Getty thought that he had scored a point upon his cross-examination of Fannie Jo. He asked, "Is it unusual to see a cab come in there and let people off?" Holland answered, "No, not really unusual, no."

On his redirect examination, Martin gave the soft-spoken witness a chance to explain her testimony.

Martin: "Was there anything unusual about the scene you observed between four-fifteen and four-thirty P.M. on July 14?"

Holland: "Well, the thing that was unusual to me is the fact that where I live is a Negro neighborhood, and the man who got out of the cab was a white man carrying luggage, and it's unusual to see a white person come into that building carrying luggage, because there are no white families in the building where I live. And the fact that the man was wearing a T-shirt and wash pants, and carrying luggage at the same time, looked unusual to me."

Getty tried to repair the damage on re-cross. Displaying the enlarged photograph that had been taken from Holland's window of the parking lot and its surroundings, Getty turned on his most charming and folksy style and asked, "There's a nice-looking church in this photo. What is the name of that church?"

Holland: "I don't know the name of it, but it's a Catholic church."

Getty: "Do white people go to that church?"

Holland: "Yes, they do."

Getty: "That's only a block away [from the parking lot], isn't it?"

Holland: "They go to the church, but they don't live in the church."

Getty: "All right, thank you."

Though genteel, Fannie Jo Holland was one smart, tough lady. When her testimony concluded, the trial was recessed for the weekend.

CHAPTER 36

Cora's powerful testimony had the defense reeling against the ropes. Martin hoped that his next big blow, the fingerprint evidence, would provide the knockout punch. Speck had left his signature on the door to the south bedroom. The problem was finding someone who could explain fingerprints to the jury in such a clear and simple way as to prevent Getty from confusing the issue. The weekend was spent preparing the witnesses to this crucial fingerprint evidence, as well as the remaining witnesses to Speck's flight. Still oblivious to what was going on around him, Speck whiled away the hours in his courthouse cell. He continued to receive "fan mail," mostly from young women, which prompted the killer to tell a guard, "You wanna know something, there's a lot of kooks out there."

Although the energetic and powerfully built Assistant State's Attorney Jim Zagel worked so hard that he developed mononucleosis, he refused to leave Peoria and continued to write scholarly legal memoranda, occasionally stopping to slip down to the Ramada's basement game room to maintain his skills as a "pinball wizard." Zagel, Martin, and Murtaugh continued their regular diet of coffee-shop cheeseburgers.

Monday, April 10

Getty and his deputies tried to slow the momentum of the State's evidence with lengthy arguments in the judge's chambers seeking to suppress Speck's registration card from the Raleigh Hotel and the BVD T-shirt that had been removed from him at Cook County Hospital. Paschen denied both motions. Richard Speck's suddenly acquired dislike of his name was brought home emphatically to the jurors. Raleigh desk clerk Otha Hullinger testified that he told her his name was David Stayton when she registered him at four forty-five P.M. on Thursday, July 14.

Speck's next attempt to escape began on North Clark Street, one block from the Raleigh Hotel, with his encounter early Friday evening with knight-of-the-road Claude Lunsford. Martin and Murtaugh respected the Skid Row day laborer whose down-and-out life had not destroyed his rock-solid integrity. Although Lunsford had originally tried to avoid getting involved, once he was made to understand that he was a key witness to the killer's effort to flee Chicago, he patiently waited without complaint, sipping his daily quota of beer and whiskey in his Ramada Inn room for ten days, until he was finally called to the stand on April 10. During his wait, Ken Alexander took him to a fashionable Peoria men's store and offered to buy him new clothes for court. Lunsford declined the offer, saying, "I don't need no fancy clothes. Just take me to Sears and let me get some wash-and-wear slacks. That's good enough."

Once on the stand, Lunsford described how the "fish-mouthed" Speck questioned him on Friday night about how to hop a freight train to Dallas, and pressured him again early Saturday morning to leave town with him. During the cross-examination, Getty got mildly sarcastic with the hobo, asking him with a sneer, "And do you have a time schedule about these freights and what time they leave?" Lunsford patiently taught everyone in the courtroom something they didn't know about the hobo life: "No. You go in the yard and see a switchman, and he will tell you what track it's on and what time and where it goes. Then, you get out of the yard. When you see the diesel hook on to the train, why, then you move out and you get into a freight car."

Still sneering, Getty asked incredulously, "But the switch-man always tells you about when they're going to leave?" Lunsford replied, "They always tell you, and they always tell you the truth."

Next, Martin quickly presented the evidence of Speck's attempt at the ultimate escape—suicide—and the recovery of his T-shirt at County Hospital.

The State was now ready to introduce its strongest evidence—the three latent fingerprints of Speck's recovered from the town house. Martin intended to compare these latent prints with previously known inked fingerprints of Speck and prove that they were identical. This, Martin hoped, was the linchpin of the State's unbroken chain of evidence. However, none of the three separate fingerprint cards—from the Dallas sheriff's office, the Huntsville branch of the Texas Department of Corrections, and the U.S. Coast Guard—that Lieutenant Emil Giese had used to positively identify Speck could be put into evidence. The two cards from Texas impermissibly established that Speck had a prior criminal record, a fact that could not be mentioned unless he testified. The third card, the Coast Guard prints, would have required the testimony of the Coast Guard clerk who took them, and he was not readily available.

The easy solution was to use crime lab technician Jerry Richards, whose presence that past weekend at the Ramada swimming pool had discouraged police officers from swimming. Richards was an iron-man bodybuilder whose appearance in a bathing suit did not invite comparisons from his less-developed colleagues. Richards had fingerprinted Speck after his arrest at County Hospital, and these prints could be used as Speck's known inked impressions.

However, during Jerry Richards's cross-examination, Getty repeatedly tried to twist the crime lab technician's testimony in such a way as to confuse fingerprint characteristics used to *classify* the inked prints with the totally unrelated science of absolutely *identifying* a latent print left at the scene of crime. Since Getty had tipped his hand about this tactic during his opening statement, Martin was quick to object to the attempted smoke-screen. The long day in court ended with Martin informing Getty that his witness the next morning would take a lot of time, and that his testimony would bring the actual door from the nurses' south bedroom into Courtroom A.

Martin now had only Monday night to put the finishing touches on the State's fingerprint evidence. Making this evidence understandable to the jury was the biggest technical hurdle he faced during the trial. By carefully examining every surface in the town house, police crime lab technicians had ultimately discovered twenty-nine latent fingerprints suitable for comparison. Of these, three had been identified as belonging to Speck.

Putting into evidence the silicon lifts of Speck's latent prints and the photographs of these lifts required tedious proof that there had been an unbroken chain of police custody of the evidence from the moment the prints had been taken from the town house in July 1966 until the day they were shown to the jurors in April 1967. More importantly, it required someone who could explain fingerprints to the jurors.

The State had enlarged photos of the scale model of the town house mounted on art boards to mark the location of the prints. This testimony would be handled by the dean of the police crime lab mobile unit technicians, Bill Scanlon, an ex-Marine and a seasoned witness. Despite his wealth of courtroom experiences, Scanlon was petrified that he would screw up his testimony. By now, however, he and Martin had rehearsed the direct examination for so long that both knew the script by heart.

The final step was to put the finishing touches on Martin's preparation of Burton Buhrke, the Chicago Police Department's senior fingerprint identification expert. Buhrke had made over 500,000 fingerprint comparisons, far more than any other expert in the police department, and his encyclopedic knowledge of fingerprint science commanded national respect. Buhrke had examined the south bedroom door of the town house two days after the murders, and had then removed the door from its hinges and taken it to the crime lab to await the day that it would be used in a courtroom to demonstrate his testimony. For Buhrke, nearing retirement, testifying in the Speck case would be the pinnacle of his brilliant and dedicated career in law enforcement. He had been preparing for this day for eight months. Buhrke's biggest booster was Lieutenant Emil Giese, the forty-two-year-old commanding officer of the identification unit, who came to Peoria to watch the revered veteran testify.

On Monday night, Martin was putting Buhrke through a mock cross-examination, the type of cross that he expected from Getty the next day. Buhrke's answers during this exercise were detailed and lengthy, the kind of scientifically thorough answers that might enthrall an audience of experts. Unfortunately, the "jury" that was now listening to Buhrke—Martin, Murtaugh, and Zagel—found themselves utterly confused by the expert's exhaustive erudition and his inability to express fingerprint concepts in simple terms. Emil Giese was sitting in on the sessions and helping by translating Buhrke's comprehensive answers into everyday language. The articulate and handsome Giese was trimly built and six feet tall, with auburn hair, flashing dark eyes, and a ready smile. He looked like a movie star, except that the impression he created was anything but superficial. The father of ten children, Giese did not own a car, took public transportation to police headquarters, and worked as a security officer to supplement his police salary. By eight o'clock Monday night, Martin had come to the painful realization that he could not give the Public Defender the opportunity to cross-examine Burton Buhrke and to blur the definitions of the terms used by the State's fingerprint experts. Martin recessed the meeting and asked Murtaugh and Zagel to join him in his room. The three prosecutors quickly decided that Giese must replace Buhrke.

For Martin, this was another moment of great sadness, the same sadness he had felt when he took John Glenville out of the case. He knew that Buhrke, like Glenville before him, would be crushed. Martin had to live with the sorrow that he had devastated the lives of two men who, ironically, were both his father's age. Martin clenched his teeth and walked back to the conference room, where he saw Buhrke going over exhibits with Giese, still thinking that he was going to testify. There was no time to beat around the bush. Martin told Buhrke that he was too good a fingerprint expert and that his all-inclusive answers would confuse the jury. Buhrke fought back the small tears that were forming in the corners of his eyes, as Martin asked him to help prepare Giese to testify. Though crushed and stunned, Buhrke agreed, and the intense preparation of Emil Giese began. Martin decided that he would have Giese walk the jury through a basic course in the science of fingerprint identification. If the jury understood fingerprints before Getty got his hands on Giese, then the battle was won. By two-thirty the next morning, Martin, Murtaugh, and Zagel believed that Giese would be able to explain fingerprints to the jury. Then, punchy but happy, as if they had just crammed for a college exam, the three young men danced around Martin's room, jumping on the twin beds and singing jingles about "arches, deltas, loops, and whorls."

Tuesday, April 11

The next morning, the Peoria sky was dark and foreboding, and by noon thunderclaps had erupted and a driving rain was pelting the courthouse. Inside, the jurors were being given Fingerprint Evidence 101 and Gerry Getty was doing his best to fuzz up this crash course in scientific proof. Crime lab mobile unit technician Bill Scanlon vividly explained to the jurors how the surfaces of the town house had been "dusted" to recover the latent prints. On cross-examination, Getty extracted from Scanlon the fact that on July 15 he had also gone to the Shipyard Inn to "lift" a fingerprint from a beer can left in Speck's room. The wily Getty was trying to plant the suspicion in the jurors' minds that the Chicago Police Department could have framed Speck by transferring the print from the beer can onto the south bedroom door.

The next witness was Raymond Heimbuch, who had been the crime lab's chief photographer for twenty-four years. Martin couldn't resist asking him if he had a hobby. "Photography," he replied. Heimbuch explained how he had made enlargements of photos taken of the latent prints, including the ones left by Speck on the door. During cross-examination, Getty arranged for the jurors to see the enlarged photos showing all the latent prints found in the town house. The Public Defender hoped that in the jurors' eyes the prints would all look indistinguishable, both those positively identified and those too smudged for a positive identification.

Lieutenant Emil Giese came up next. The actual door to the south bedroom of the town house stood to the right of the witness and at the front of the jury box. Martin was following a time-tested tradition in putting the door itself into evidence. For decades, fingerprints experts have taken crime-scene objects ranging from panes of glass to entire automobile doors to use in court as the "best" evidence. Using this door as his prop, Giese

demonstrated precisely how Richard Speck had left his fingerprints on the inside of the door. Fingerprints are numbered 1
through 10, Giese explained, beginning with the thumb of the
right hand as No. 1 and counting through the little finger of the
right hand as No. 5; similarly, the thumb of the left hand is No. 6
and the little finger of the left hand is No. 10.

Giese left the witness box and approached the door to reen-
act for the jurors how Speck stood with his back to the bedroom
door and used the index and middle fingers of his right hand to
forcibly shut it. He pointed to the spots on the door where the
latent prints of Speck's No. 2 and No. 3 fingers had been found
and lifted. Giese further told the jurors that the latent print of
the No. 2 finger, the index finger of Speck's right hand, was
found to have ten points of identity with Speck's inked prints
from the card taken at Cook County Hospital; and that the latent
print of the No. 3 finger, the middle finger of Speck's right hand,
was found to have seventeen points of identity. Throughout the
world, Giese testified, "Ten to twelve points of identity are considered absolute proof."

Speck had also left a latent print of his No. 8 finger, the middle finger of his left hand, on the door, Giese testified. He said
that the killer had used his left hand to swing the door shut while
he was on the bottom bunk nearest the door. This was the position he was in immediately before he raped Gloria Jean Davy.
The latent print of this No. 8 finger had seventeen points of positive identity to Speck's inked impressions.

Martin had decided to use Speck's No. 8 fingerprint as the
flagship of the fingerprint proof. During Giese's testimony, four
sets of photo enlargements comparing the latent print on the
door with the inked impression of Speck's finger were passed to
the jurors.

The jurors studied the enlargements as they listened to
Martin take Giese over each point of identification between

the latent print on the bedroom door and Speck's inked finger-print. This technique was designed to maximize the verbal and visual impact of the comparison. Martin's questions and Giese's answers alternated like the litany of a Catholic mass.

Martin: "Lieutenant Giese, would you please explain the enlargement of the inked impression of the Number Eight finger taken from the Cook County Hospital card, which appears on the right of People's Exhibit Fifty-two. What does Point Number One on that inked impression indicate?"
Giese: "Point Number One on the inked impression indicates an ending ridge, which is a particular ridge characteristic."
Martin: "And that is from the Cook County Hospital card?"
Giese: "It's an enlargement of the finger from the County Hospital card."
Martin: "What does Point Number One on the latent impression taken from the door indicate?"
Giese: "Point Number One on the latent impression is an ending ridge."
Martin: "Point Number Two on the inked impression?"
Giese: "Point Number Two is an ending ridge."
Martin: "Point Number Two on the latent impression?"
Giese: "Point Number Two on the latent impression is an ending ridge."
Martin: "Point Number Three on the inked impression?"
Giese: "Point Number Three on the inked impression is a bifurcation."
Martin: "Point Number Three on the latent impression?"
Giese: "A bifurcation."

Unhurriedly, Martin and Giese followed this exchange throughout all seventeen points of identification, until the time came for the climactic questions. Throughout the comparison, the jurors' eyes were riveted on the enlarged photos that showed them what Giese was explaining.

> **Martin:** "Lieutenant Giese, based upon your experience in the science of fingerprints, and based upon your comparison of the Number Eight finger of the Cook County Hospital card and the latent impression appearing at the bottom of People's Exhibit Thirty-five [the door] for identification, do you have an opinion as to whether or not the latent and inked impressions were made by the same person?"
> **Giese:** "Yes, I do."
> **Martin:** "What is your opinion?"
> **Giese:** "After examination as to basic ridge detail in both prints, it is my opinion that these fingerprints or impressions were made by the same individual."

Martin nodded at Giese with an imperceptible smile, then turned his head toward the defense table, saying softly to Getty: "Cross-examine."

To Martin's surprise, Getty didn't move. He left the witness to Assistant Public Defender Jim Gramenos, who bombarded Giese for three and a half hours with nonstop questions. Through it all, Giese remained imperturbable. Gramenos got nowhere. Martin whispered to George Murtaugh, "We couldn't have found a better witness in Hollywood." Getty was unruffled; he was saving himself for Burton Buhrke, whom he expected to see on the witness stand the next morning. The State, however, planned to have a surprise for the Public Defender, his biggest surprise of the trial.

The surprise had its start in a Monday phone call from Jim Boyle, the state's attorney of DeKalb County, Illinois, a hundred miles west of Chicago, to Martin's boss, First Assistant Lou Garippo. Boyle was reporting a rumor he had just heard, a rumor that Getty had asked the director of Chicago's Institute of Applied Science—the foremost fingerprint school in the nation—to testify that the fingerprints found on the door of the nurses' town house did not belong to Richard Speck. Garippo swiftly investigated the tip and found that it was not the director of the institute who had been contacted by the Public Defender, it was the school's head instructor, Andre Moenssens. Within an hour, Garippo served a subpoena on him, compelling him to be in Peoria the next day.

By the time court adjourned at the end of Emil Giese's testimony, Andre Moenssens was in Peoria waiting to meet with Martin. Martin asked the professor to go to the courtroom that night to compare the latent print on the door in the courtroom—Speck's No. 8 finger—with the inked fingerprint card from Cook County Hospital. Moenssens left. When he returned, he told Martin that he was certain that the middle finger of the left hand was the same in both prints. Martin then told Moenssens to be in the courthouse Wednesday morning and to wait in the hallway outside Courtroom A until he was asked to testify.

In the meantime, the prosecution had another high-adrenaline adventure that had to be accomplished Tuesday night—determining whether or not Marvin Ziporyn was in town. If Moenssens were allowed to testify, he would be the State's last witness, with the defense putting its witnesses on the stand immediately afterwards. If Moenssens were not allowed to testify, then the State's last witness had been Giese and the defense would begin even sooner.

Martin frantically wanted to know if Dr. Ziporyn was going to testify. If so, he needed to get Bob Ellison, his columnist friend and secret sleuth, to Peoria, so that the State would be fully armed to attack the psychiatrist on cross-examination. An urgent meeting was called of all the Chicago policemen in Peoria, both those who had been assigned to the case and those who were there only to testify. A standing-room-only crowd jammed the small conference room in the Ramada Inn, as the officers were divided into teams. Each team was given Ziporyn's publicity photo for his violin concerts. Their assignment was to check all arriving flights, the bus and train stations, and all local hotel lobbies to see if Ziporyn or any other defense witnesses were in town.

In 1967, the defense was not required by law to disclose the names of its witnesses, and Gerry Getty had played his cards so close to the vest that Martin still did not know which witnesses Getty intended to call on Wednesday, or even if he intended to use Ziporyn or Littner as the basis of an insanity defense. The Public Defender had left the door open for a defense of alibi, a defense of insanity, or both.

Martin placed an urgent call to Bob Ellison in Chicago. Yes, the columnist was available if needed in Peoria, and he also had more news about the book. Ziporyn's publisher had just returned from London with twenty thousand dollars in his pocket from the sale of the British rights for *Born to Raise Hell*. Ellison added that two of Speck's paintings and several of his sketches were to be included in the book. Most significantly, the columnist reported to Martin that the unknown attorney–escrow agent representing coauthors Ziporyn and Jack Altman had told the publisher that Ziporyn might testify in the Speck trial to "whet the public's appetite for the book." The publisher had relayed this message to Ellison with the unconcerned comment that "the book is a hundred thousand words long and the psychiatrist can't possibly tell the whole story in court."

As the night progressed, however, Martin wondered if Ziporyn were going to show up to tell any of his hundred-thousand-word story in court. The all-out police search of Peoria had discovered only one defense witness—Michael Compateso, Speck's pool-playing buddy from the Shipyard Inn. Compateso was now occupying a bar stool at the Public Defender's downtown Peoria headquarters, the Voyager Inn.

Wednesday, April 12

Dark thunderstorms continued to dominate the Peoria sky on Wednesday morning, but the booming noises erupting in Courtroom A were even louder. Martin had touched off fireworks when he announced that the State's next witness would be Andre Moenssens. Soon, Paschen's out-of-court chambers were crowded, as Martin's team of five gathered to do battle with Getty's team of three in what would be the most volatile argument in the case.

Shocked and angry, Getty charged the State with "the most dastardly move I have ever seen." Martin had never seen Getty display as much emotion as he was pouring into this argument. Martin was equally angry, believing that nothing less than the integrity of the prosecution was at stake. The defense, Martin said, had been claiming since its opening statement that the prints on the town house door were only smudges and that the police had framed Speck. Martin wanted the jurors to know that Moenssens had first examined the fingerprint evidence *at the request* of the defense before offering his opinion that the latent print of the No. 8 finger on the bedroom door was identical to the inked No. 8 finger from Speck's hospital card.

Getty had hoped that his consultation with Andre Moenssens, one of the world's leading fingerprint experts, and Moenssens's damaging finding that the killer's fingerprints belonged to Speck, would never come to the attention of the State. But if it did, he hoped that the consultation would be protected by the attorney-client privilege Getty had with Speck, and that the findings would never be presented at trial. He hoped, in short, that Moenssens's expert opinion would remain a deep, dark secret.

Now, however, the cat was out of the bag, and Assistant State's Attorney Jim Zagel had stayed up all night studying legal decisions that he believed supported the State's argument that Moenssens should be allowed to tell the jury that he had examined the fingerprints on the bedroom door of the town house and had told the defense that the prints on the door matched Speck's fingerprint cards. This, of course, would reveal that before the trial began, Getty already knew the prints belonged to Speck and, yet, had still told the jury in his opening argument that the police had attempted to "frame" Speck by "developing" fake prints. Now, the State had learned about the consultation and was arguing that Moenssens's opinion was not protected by the attorney-client privilege and was fair game for the jury.

The stricken Getty knew that if Moenssens were allowed to testify about this prior consultation, Getty's credibility with the jury would be destroyed and with it anything he said in defense of Speck. Getty's cloak of disingenuousness would be stripped from him, and his prior knowledge that the fingerprints belonged to Speck would be fully revealed to the jurors. This naked truth would demolish his defense. For the first time in the trial, Getty's face was red and his voice strained as he pleaded with Paschen to save him from this catastrophe.

"I practically sat my client in the electric chair," he said, "as a court-appointed lawyer trying to do the best job that I could for an indigent defendant. I have created a monster of a witness. That's what I did for my client. And, I don't get a penny for it, and it will go down in history that I did that. And not only does it destroy me, but I think you're going to destroy the very system of representing the indigent."

Charging Getty with melodrama, Martin responded coldly that Moenssens's finding was not protected by the attorney-client privilege, since "It was not the confidential words of the defendant that had been submitted to Moenssens; it was only the copies of the fingerprints provided by the State to the defense." Martin was not interested so much in having Moenssens confirm the police evidence that the prints were Speck's as he was in driving home the fact that Getty had received Moenssens's evidence long before the trial and knew the prints were genuine, and that, therefore, his claim of a police frame-up was false and Getty knew it was false. In denying that the attorney-client protection applied to the consultation with Moenssens, Martin argued to Paschen that Speck and Moenssens had never met nor communicated, and that the State did not intend to question Moenssens about his conversations with Getty, only establish that Moenssens had first examined the fingerprint evidence at Getty's request. In short, Martin argued, Moenssens should be allowed to take the witness stand and say that the fingerprints on the bedroom door belonged to Richard Speck, enabling the jurors to conclude that Getty had received this same opinion before the trial.

Claiming that the public defenders were being manacled, Jim Doherty, too, moved excitedly about the room as he made an impassioned appeal. "They are going to pull out our claws, Judge," Doherty said. "They are going to say, 'Sit on your ass. . . . Don't investigate cases. . . . Just stand up there like a political hack, but don't seek any real ammunition for your guns, Mr. Public Defender, because if you do, we will have our cops out, looking at night, and we will have them find the men you consulted.' "

Doherty had the consummate trial lawyer's ability to argue passionately for causes in which he had absolutely no interest, but the tough redhead was arguing this one with full-blooded fury. Uncharacteristically, Getty jumped in to add that the only reason the State wanted to bring Moenssens before the jury was to "implant in the jurors' minds that I knew certain things."

In fact, that was exactly what Martin wanted to do.

Sensing that he was on the ropes, Getty offered a compromise: "If they want to put this witness on as a witness who looked at the door, but not refer to me, that would be something else. But what they want to get in this record, which is going to be their downfall, and your downfall, and my downfall, is to smatter me up by having consulted him."

Paschen bought the compromise, ruling that Moenssens would be allowed to testify. "But I don't think," Paschen said, "that he should be permitted to testify that he consulted with you and so forth. I do not want Gerry Getty smeared here. Defending a guy like Speck is rough enough, in a case of this nature, and it shouldn't be blown all over the press."

The ruling, which Martin thought legally wrong, arguably fair, and very protective of the Public Defender, left him a problem: Getty could argue that the State had no faith in the testimony of Emil Giese and had scurried around at the last minute to dig up Professor Moenssens. He asked Paschen not to allow this.

Perpetually crimson-faced, Doherty had taken his suit coat off and thrown it on a chair. His voice reverberated throughout the courthouse as he boomed, "My God, why don't they put a gag on Getty? Put a straitjacket on him, so he can't wave his arms, and put a gag on him and tape him."

Paschen asked Getty if he was going to argue that the State was putting Moenssens on because it had no faith in the prior testimony of Lieutenant Giese. Getty replied, "No, don't you think that I am ever going to say anything like that. . . . [If I do] you just shut me off."

Doherty was not pacified in the least and could not conceal his adamant distaste for his boss's compromise. He yelped, "It's a good thing that I'm not arguing this case, because you would put me in jail."

The debate raged on in chambers for more than two hours, but the compromise had been struck and, at noon, Professor Andre Moenssens was sitting in the witness box, facing the jury.

Martin established the witness's expertise and his independence from the State. Moenssens had begun studying fingerprints
in his native Belgium in 1950, had written fifteen leading articles
on the subject in English, and was the author of the *Fingerprint
Encyclopedia*, to be published in the fall of 1967. He had never
worked for a police department and he had never testified for the
prosecution. Martin then asked Moenssens to compare the latent
print on the door with Speck's inked impressions on the Cook
County Hospital card. As Lieutenant Giese had done before him,
Moenssens followed Martin through the litany of questions and
affirmed the same seventeen separate points of identity.

During his cross-examination, Getty again raised the spectre
that the Chicago police might have lifted a fingerprint of Speck
from somewhere else, say, a beer can, and transferred it to the
town house door. Moenssens told Getty and the jurors that in
theory a fingerprint lift could be transferred from one object
to another. However, pointing at the print on the door, he said
emphatically, "Not that one."

> **Getty:** "By a lift?"
> **Moenssens:** "Not that one, no."
> **Getty:** "It couldn't have been?"
> **Moenssens:** "No."

It was twelve thirty-five P.M. when Andre Moenssens, the
defense's potential Frankenstein, concluded his testimony. Martin stood up, nodded to the jury, and rested the State's case. He
believed in his father's advice about poker. Quit while you're
ahead.

CHAPTER 37

Wednesday, April 12—Afternoon

It had taken eight hectic days and eight frantic nights for the State to carefully put its bricks of proof into place. Now, Martin waited with apprehension to see how Gerry Getty would try to blow those bricks down.

Other than his own wiles, Getty had very few weapons with which to defend Speck. There was no way Speck would testify in his own behalf. The killer had an emotional problem that was as much a part of his makeup as the acne that scarred his face—he had a deathly fear of people staring at him. "Because of this," Getty later said, "he told me one day that he wouldn't take the witness stand to testify in his own behalf. No matter what."

Getty asked for a session in Paschen's chamber to renew his motion for a two-stage trial, the first for his defense of alibi, and, if that failed, a second for his defense of insanity. He wanted to have his cake and eat it, too. Submitting evaluations of Speck from Dr. Marvin Ziporyn and Dr. Ner Littner, Getty told Paschen that these two psychiatrists would testify that Speck was legally insane, *"if in fact he committed the murders."* Getty argued, "I find myself in this dilemma, and I have ever since the inception of this case, that this client has consistently denied any guilt. He cannot tell me how this was done. And he claims he was not there. And he tells me that if anyone identifies him, they are wrong, and that if there are any fingerprints, they're not his."

In fact, Speck had sung a different tune to Dr. Ziporyn. On one occasion, when the psychiatrist was making a hypothetical reference that Speck *might* have been the murderer, the killer cut him short by exclaiming, "Let's just say it was me."

Paschen once again denied the bid for a two-stage trial. So Getty decided to roll the dice and try to save Speck's life by pleading an alibi. First, he would try to gain sympathy for his newly bespectacled client by letting the jurors see that he had a mother, brother, and sisters who loved him and were willing to come to Peoria to help him. Next, he would put on Murrill and Gerdena Farmer, the husband-wife, bartender-waitress team from Kay's Pilot House to offer an airtight alibi that Speck could not have been at the scene of the murders at eleven P.M. because he had been in their tavern until after midnight.

The defense's first two witnesses were Speck's mother, Margaret Speck Lindbergh, and his younger sister, Mrs. Carolyn Speck Wilson. They testified with affection that they had put Richard Speck on a bus bound for Chicago in March 1966. Their testimony proved only that a man charged with mass murder can also have a sweet mother and a pretty sister. Martin saw nothing to gain from cross-examining these two innocent witnesses—the less time they were on the stand, the better.

The prosecutor did cross-examine the next two witnesses, though—one of Speck's older sisters, Martha Speck Thornton, and her husband, Eugene Thornton. From Gene Thornton, Martin extracted the damaging admissions that Thornton had seen Speck playing with a pocketknife in the backyard of his apartment on the North Side of Chicago in the spring and summer of 1966; that he had given Speck a black corduroy jacket on July 11, 1966; and that Speck was wearing black shoes when

Thornton dropped him off at the National Maritime Union hiring hall later that same day. Gene Thornton added that his car was parked directly across the street from the nurses' town house on July 11 and 13, when Speck sat in the car with him trying to borrow money.

To counter the defense impression of a police force hell-bent on charging Speck with the murders, Martin induced Gene Thornton to admit that during the manhunt for the killer, when police had set up a stakeout in his home, "Every one of the police officers was a gentleman—they showed me all the respect in the world." Thornton, in fact, had gone to Area 2 police headquarters to personally thank Officer Carl Edenfield and others for their consideration. "The whole bunch of them had that much coming," Thornton said without a trace of bitterness.

Martha Speck Thornton admitted to sewing her brother's clothes, but the former pediatric nurse did not want to help send him to the electric chair. Martin could not get her to admit that she told Sergeant Mike Clancy during the July 15 stakeout of her home that Speck wore both BVD and Hanes size 38–40 T-shirts.

Four other Speck siblings were on and off the witness stand within a blink of an eye: Howard Speck and Sara Madeline Speck Thornton (married to an uncle of Eugene Thornton) from Monmouth, Illinois; Erma Speck Holeman from Alexis, Illinois; and Shirley Speck Jensen, also from Alexis. The four had nothing to say about their brother except that each had last seen him in March 1966. The jurors were left to ponder the riddle of how Richard Franklin Speck could have come from the same parents as these God-fearing, hard-working people, all law-abiding central Illinoisans.

The last witness of the day was chipper, frenetic, wiry Michael Compateso, who testified that he spent seventeen minutes of his lunch break—from 8:40 P.M. to 8:57—at the Shipyard Inn during the night of July 13, 1966, shooting pool with Richard Speck.

Getty wanted the jury to hear his description that Speck was wearing a red short-sleeved polo shirt, and boots "like the iron-worker boots that I wear." Compateso was the only witness who claimed to have seen Speck wearing ironworker boots on the night of the murders.

Thursday, April 13

Spring thunderstorms shook Peoria, as did the verbal thunder-bolts rattling off the walls of Judge Paschen's chambers. Typical young men refusing to carry umbrellas, Martin and Murtaugh were drenched running from the parking lot to the courthouse. In one final effort to confuse the jurors about the fingerprint evidence linking Speck to the crime, Getty was arguing that the jurors be given copies of sixteen unidentified latent prints from the town house, the fingerprint cards of Gloria Jean Davy and Suzanne Far-ris, and a magnifying glass. In this way, Getty suggested, "The jurors can conduct their own comparisons of all the prints."

Martin objected furiously, the back of his neck turning red as he told Paschen that the only possible purpose for a magnifying glass was to "confuse and deceive the jury."

Looking at Martin's red neck, Jim Doherty asked with feigned innocence, "Are you mad at me?"

"I'm mad," Martin said, "at the defense practice of accusing us of planting phony fingerprints, of accusing us of eavesdropping and snooping, when they went to an expert and they know these prints are Speck's. And if they have doubts in a capital case, and if you, Judge Paschen, have any doubts in a capital case—that these are not Speck's prints—we will submit them to the FBI, to the Institute in London, or anyone or anywhere else. We want the truth in his case, and we are not going to play games and give the jury a magnifying glass and a bunch of these fingerprint impressions and ask them to go back there and get confused."

Paschen ruled that the fingerprint evidence was the proper subject of expert testimony, which had already been rendered, and refused to give the jurors a magnifying glass to conduct their own investigation. The defense was as resourceful as it was desperate, and Martin was relieved that Getty's clever tactic had not worked.

Ironically, Getty's last best hopes to try to save Richard Speck from the electric chair were a bartender and a waitress. Bartender Murrill Farmer from Kay's Pilot House took the witness stand first. His hair greased back in a pompadour, the tall, muscular Farmer was dressed in a dark business suit and smartly coordinated shirt and tie, appearing more like a businessman than a bartender. He spoke with a faint southern accent as he told the jurors that a man he knew to be Richard Speck had been in the Pilot House twice on the night of July 13. The first time. Farmer testified, was between eight and eight-thirty, when Speck was wearing a red polo shirt and drank a highball. The second time, the bartender swore, Speck was in from midnight until twelve-thirty the next morning, sat at the bar, and had a hamburger and a glass of water. During the direct examination, Farmer told Getty that he would "stake his life on it."

Martin knew that he didn't have dynamite to explode Farmer's story. He had learned over the years that false alibi witnesses testify for love or money—a financial stake in the trial or a romantic interest in the defendant. Neither existed here, and Martin was left to grope for the Farmers' motives in sticking to an alibi for a stranger who had murdered eight young women. However, the pretrial investigation had disclosed one possible motive for Murrill Farmer—a motive to which his wife may have later ascribed.

On December 16, 1963, Murrill Farmer met a twenty-year-old Indiana woman at a party. He gave her a ride home and, she later charged, forced her to have sex with him. Answering the complaint, Farmer willingly went to the police station, readily admitted having sex with the woman, and vehemently insisted that it was consensual. Nevertheless, Farmer was charged with rape and prosecuted by the Cook County State's Attorney's Office. He was forced to appear in felony court and, after the preliminary hearing, the case was thrown out.

Martin thought that this prior undoubtedly negative experience with the police and his own State's Attorney office might have given Farmer a prejudice against the prosecution and a bias in favor of the accused. The prosecutor decided, however, not to cross-examine Farmer about his prior arrest. The judge had thrown the case out and Martin felt that bringing it up now would appear both desperate and unscrupulous. He had no way to prove Murrill Farmer carried either a conscious or unconscious grudge against law enforcement.

In the end, all Martin had to work with on cross-examination was the improbability that a busy bartender working late at night in a crowded bar, grill, and packaged-goods store could recall with stopwatch precision the exact times an unfamiliar customer was sitting at the bar.

For the first time in the trial, Martin was nervous. Instead of standing calmly behind the lectern with his hands at his sides, he was squeezing his hands tightly behind his back. Murrill Farmer was a tough witness. He was adamant that Speck had been in the bar after midnight and he pointedly gave the jurors his sobering opinion that the State "must have the wrong man and the murderer is still walking around." Martin could only chip away at the improbability of the alibi and then sit down.

On redirect examination, Getty unwittingly caused Murrill Farmer to provide the jurors with an insight into his view of violence. Farmer told Getty that when he first heard radio reports of the eight murders he didn't pay too much attention, "because murders happen every day, and I must passed it off." Farmer also said, "I just thought that Speck was a German sailor. I don't know why but I just thought he was a German sailor, because we have quite a few German sailors, all kinds."

Lawyers have three kinds of questions: the ones they plan to ask, the ones they actually ask, and the ones they wished they had asked. On July 22, 1966, Murrill Farmer had told Assistant State's Attorney John Glenville that the man who had ordered a hamburger after midnight on July 13 had a "southern accent." Martin didn't think of this inconsistency during his re-cross-examination. When he remembered it later that night, he kicked himself for blowing a scathing question: "What, a German sailor with a southern accent?"

Murrill Farmer was followed to the stand by his wife, Gerdena, graceful and slender, the mother of their four children, and the short-order cook on the Pilot House's night shift. Gerdena was equally adamant that she had seen Speck in the Pilot House until twelve-thirty A.M. on, Thursday, July 14, 1966. If she were believed, the jury could not convict Speck, because Corazon Amurao's testimony placed the killer in the town house at eleven P.M.

When Martin stood behind the lectern to cross-examine Gerdena Farmer, he continued to fidget with his hands behind his back. His focus was the improbability of her being able to recall the exact times of a customer's entry and exit from the tavern. He got her to admit that she had been very busy cooking hamburgers for the workers on break from Arco Door and Garvey Grain Elevator. These workers had come in between ten and ten-thirty P.M. and Martin was suggesting that, perhaps, the Farmers had seen Speck during this period instead of after midnight.

Martin believed that it was probable that Speck, a notorious shirt-changer, had exchanged his drink-stained red shirt for the black shirt after saying good-bye to the engaged couple and

Vietnam vet Rich Oliva at the front door of the Shipyard Inn at about ten P.M. Speck might easily have then ducked into the Pilot House for a quick drink, before returning one final time to the bar at the Shipyard Inn. Alternatively, the Farmers might have seen Speck at their bar after midnight on a night other than Wednesday and simply confused the dates. Gerdena Farmer was not as intractable as her husband, and Martin got her to admit that Kay's Pilot House was a hotbed of nighttime activity.

After Murrill and Gerdena Farmer gave testimony that, if true, meant Richard Speck could not have been the killer, Getty stood, smiled knowingly at the jurors, and told Judge Paschen in a triumphant voice, "The defense rests."

The State's rebuttal was short and sweet. Martin decided to call only one witness—Sergeant Mike Clancy—to prove that the State had accurately and honestly recorded Speck's preference for BVD and Hanes T-shirts exactly as his sister had described them. Clancy told the jurors that he had interviewed Martha Speck Thornton during the stakeout of her home on Friday, July 15. At this time, Clancy was aware of the fact that police had discovered a size 38–40 *BVD* T-shirt on the desk of the living room. However, as Martin led him through the questioning, the jury learned that Martha Thornton had told Clancy that Richard Speck preferred BVD and Hanes T-shirts almost two weeks *before* Detective Jack Wallenda had found the size 38–40 *Hanes* T-shirt wadded up with Gloria Jean Davy's slacks. Since Clancy had written and dated his report on July 15, there could be no doubt that Speck had been linked to Hanes T-shirts some thirteen days before the Hanes T-shirt was found in the town house. When Sergeant Clancy stepped down from the stand, the jury had seen its last witness.

In his most grandfatherly manner, Judge Paschen announced that a conference with lawyers to discuss the instructions to the jury would be held the next day, Friday, April 14. The jurors would be given the day off, the judge said, so that "you all can get a good rest" and "you girls, if you want, can get your hair done."

The next day, while the "girls" were getting their hair done, the State and defense lawyers argued over the written instructions that Paschen would give to the jurors on Saturday morning, April 15—the last day of trial. Each side had submitted its version of how the written instructions to the jurors should read, so that the judge could then decide precisely how he would explain the law to the jury. Zagel and Doherty argued over the instructions, while Martin and Getty argued over the forms of verdicts. Martin and Getty agreed, and Paschen ruled, that there would be three possible verdicts for each of the eight indictments:

Not guilty. Guilty. Guilty with the death penalty.

The lawyers' courtroom work concluded late Friday afternoon, and Paschen wished everyone a good night. Martin joked to Murtaugh, "It's all over but the shouting." The shouting would be the closing arguments.

CHAPTER 38

Inseparable for nine stress-filled months, Bill Martin and George Murtaugh had become closer than brothers. Each was fiercely loyal to the other; neither jealousy nor envy clouded their alliance. The two men had much in common: an Irish immigrant ancestry, the relentless discipline of a Catholic education, their youth, their young and growing families, a fiery combativeness nurtured on basketball courts and hockey rinks, a shared initiation into the rough-and-tumble world of crime and justice in the Criminal Court Building, and, at this moment in their lives, an inexorable determination to convict Richard Speck. They were about to have their first argument, a shouting match in Martin's Ramada room over how the summing-up for the prosecution would be done.

The Cook County State's Attorney's Office had one unwritten rule: the two assistants trying a case split the State's closing arguments. Martin favored the traditional approach, but Murtaugh, blunt as ever, insisted that Martin should give both the State's opening argument and the rebuttal. "This is your case," Murtaugh said. "You've worked on it day and night for nine months and you've put the whole case in. You should have both arguments."

Martin countered that their contrasting styles would have much more impact on the jurors. "If I give both," Martin said, "this jury will be damned sick and tired of me before I get to the end of the rebuttal. That jury has looked at you for a long time. They expect to hear from you, too. They don't expect me to be a goddamn egomaniac."

Murtaugh continued to resist and was, in fact, becoming inflexible. "I'm just glad you picked me to try this case with you," he said as he sat sprawled on the bed. Martin agitatedly straddled a wooden chair next to the desk. "Look, George," he said, "we've been together since the first day of the case and we're sticking together now."

Murtaugh sat bolt upright, his eyes burning like hot coals, and said, "I've never argued a death-penalty case before. I might commit reversible error. I don't want to screw up and ruin all the work you've put into this case. It's too risky." Martin, now on his feet and pacing near the windows, was quick to reply: "You've never argued a 'chair' case? Well, if that's the test, then I can't argue myself. I've never tried a chair case before, either."

Both men stopped talking. Murtaugh thought of his uncle's advice to him before the trial started: "If you lose this case, kiss your career good-bye and move to Keokuk." Martin thought of the jury. He believed they would think that he wanted to be a big shot if he hogged both arguments. Murtaugh had assumed throughout the trial that Martin would give both arguments. Martin had thought that custom should be followed; Murtaugh would give the opening argument and he would give the rebuttal. By this time Murtaugh was beginning to realize that Martin, too, was intractable. To be sure his younger partner understood, Martin invoked seniority: "Look, Duke," Martin told him, "I'm in charge down here and I'm telling you you're gonna argue. You open. I close. Here's the transcript. Dammit, go to work."

The two high-strung combatants then retired to their rooms to review the transcript of the trial. Martin sat down and began making detailed notes of the two weeks of testimony, soon filling up an entire legal pad with summaries of what the forty-one State and eleven defense witnesses had said. This was the easy part. Then, he went into his pacing routine, stopping occasionally to jot down an idea that came to him. His thoughts came in waves, but without any coherence. Martin was distressed to realize that his notes of ideas took up parts of only two sheets of paper and were unintelligible. One entry began, "If he be innocent. . . ." Never before faced with drafting a summation in a trial of this magnitude, Martin decided he would give it without notes. Having thought of little else but Richard Speck for the past nine months, he hoped the right words would be there when he needed them.

Rattling about in his head were the words of Richard Speck himself on the death penalty. The killer had once told Dr. Norcross that he was in favor of capital punishment. "Anybody who is opposed to capital punishment is silly," Speck had told the surgeon. "How else are you going to control people?" After Norcross had countered with the traditional anticapital punishment argument that the death penalty is not a deterrent to criminals, and had patiently explained the meaning of "deterrent," Speck shot back: "That's a joke. It sure as hell stops the guy that's electrocuted. He won't kill anybody again."

Suddenly, there was a knock at the door, and Martin feared that yet someone else wanted him to help them attend the final arguments. Admission to the courtroom for closing arguments was only by special judicial ticket, and Martin had already received several calls from colleagues and friends, requesting one. The bellboy at the door handed him a telegram from veteran Assistant State's Attorney John Gannon in Chicago. Martin ripped the envelope open and read a message that sent a chill down his spine:

"Your alma mater, associates, and superiors will be thinking of you tonight and praying for you tomorrow."

Martin hoped so.

Saturday, April 15

Martin awoke at six-thirty A.M. and called room service for his usual cinnamon toast and large pot of black coffee. By the time he had taken a long steaming shower and dressed, George Murtaugh was knocking on his door. "Show time?" Martin asked. "Show time," Murtaugh answered with a smile, his jaw set with determination. Murtaugh had stayed up all night preparing his argument, but his face was alert and fresh, his shoes were highly polished, and his off-the-rack suit hung on his athletic frame as if it were custom tailored. The two men drove in silence to the courthouse. The thunderclouds that had held Peoria under siege all week had disappeared, leaving behind a clear, blue, windless sky. Without saying a word, the prosecutors walked past the gauntlet of cameras, microphones, and reporters lining the sidewalk to the entrance of the courthouse and up the one flight of stairs to Courtroom A.

State's Attorney John Stamos was there, remaining unobtrusive, not wanting to interfere with his assistants. Ken Alexander was not there. Martin had told Detective Alexander that he could come to court now that the case was over and Marvin Ziporyn was no longer an issue. However, Alexander's wife, Barbara, was nine months pregnant and about to go into labor. Alexander had his priorities straight. While everyone else went to the courthouse, he drove to Chicago to be with Barbara.

Tension filled the air as everyone settled into their seats. The brothers, sisters, and parents of the victims once again sat in their reserved seats. These family members had been in court for the opening arguments and for their testimony as life-and-death witnesses. They had accepted Martin's suggestion that they not stay in Peoria for the balance of the trial because of the increased difficulty he was having in maintaining their privacy after they had testified and reporters recognized them. Martin's real reason was that he did not want them to have to sit through graphic and emotionally draining proof of how their daughters had been murdered. He figured that at least one of the families would ignore his advice and stay throughout the trial, but none did. Now, he wanted them back in court for the closing arguments.

Paschen sensed the electricity in the air as he ascended the bench. After thanking the press for their cooperation so far, he admonished one and all: "We will have no showing of emotion during this final argument by anybody in this courtroom. Let's all understand that."

George Murtaugh stood to give what prosecutors call the "opening close," which is typically a low-key summary of the State's proof. Old-timers referred to this opening by gesturing to an imaginary piano keyboard and saying, "Once over, lightly."

Up to now neither Martin nor Murtaugh had displayed any emotion in front of the equally emotionless Peorians on the jury. Up to now the young prosecutors had held their fiery intensity in check. Murtaugh was about to review the evidence, but instead of using a low-key delivery, he unleased a passionate torrent of words weaving Speck into an inescapable web of guilt. Murtaugh gave the world what it was waiting for—a no-holds-barred condemnation of the killer. The twenty-seven-year-old prosecutor characterized Speck as a cowardly and lazy man who had turned into a murderer, not by booze and pills beating against a brain-damaged mind, but by the mere acquisition of a gun and a knife and the fact that he could both sweet-talk and strong-tie nine trusting nurses into utter helplessness. Employing a riveting stream-of-consciousness technique, Murtaugh brilliantly captured Speck's evil by reliving the evidence, witness by witness. His remarks were powerfully articulated and passionately emphasized. He spoke without notes. As he excoriated the killer, Murtaugh moved fluidly about the room, stopping frequently to point at Speck, who stonily stared back.

"This man has the face, the mind, the heart of a murderer," Murtaugh declared. "Death stalked the hallway that night, and it wasn't with a sickle, and it wasn't with a skull and cross-bones. Death that evening carried a small black pistol and a three- to four-inch knife. Eight girls against me, I better have some insurance, so I have a knife and I have a gun. And, brother, if you move, you're in trouble."

A college basketball player and a scratch golfer, Murtaugh moved in front of the jury box with athletic grace, his voice dripping with sarcastic indignation. When he turned toward Speck, Murtaugh's face filled with revulsion at a man who didn't have the courage to fight men and who used a gun and a knife to subdue helpless women. He believed that Speck was as ugly as his crime.

After demonstrating to the jurors how Speck, "the tailor of death," had cut the bed sheets to create a "suit of death" for the girls, Murtaugh again looked directly at the pockmarked Speck and said, "Now, he's ready to go to work, Mr. Richard Franklin Speck. He's got what he needs. He's got the binds, he's got the gun, he's got the knife, and he's got the innocents. So the march of death begins.

"'You, my friend, Miss Wilkening, I've chosen you to die first. Me, Richard Franklin Speck, self-ordained judge, jury, and executioner. There is no trial for you. There never will be. There is no justice. I will do what I feel, when I feel, and how I feel.'"

Referring to the rape without mentioning it, he said, "Gloria Jean Davy was the defendant's choice. 'I've got something special for you.'"

"Merlita Gargullo wrote a letter that night. There's the man who took the pen from her, and she will never return to write another letter or to utter another word." Murtaugh was abandoning logic in favor of raw feelings that invested the dead girls with life.

"Corazon Amurao testified—eighty-five pounds of flesh, two tons of hardened steel. She was a breath, a cough, a sneeze away from extermination by that man right there. Tammy Sioukoff—well, that slice of bread almost put her name on one of these indictments. She was about fourteen steps, from the top to the bottom of the town house, from being wiped out—fourteen steps.

"Do you realize what it takes to strangle somebody? Do you have any idea? It's not just a slight movement, it's a pulling until there is no breath left, there is no life, and you're dead—you'll never get up."

Murtaugh pointed at Speck's heart, observing, "There he is. The executioner. Nothing else."

Describing Speck's behaviors and flight, Murtaugh noted, "The man's a great shirt-changer . . . he wanted new clothes, he told Red Gerrald, 'I've got to go to Bond's, got to buy some new clothes.' He's short of money, he's carrying two suitcases, but he's got to buy some new clothes. This murderer has the unmitigated gall to tell Matt Hogan that Red Gerrald is 'all right.' Who is Richard Speck to say that anyone is all right? Here is a man who's killed eight people. Here's a murderer with the heart and mind of a murderer. The unmitigated gall to tell Matt Hogan that Red is all right. And the murderer lies to Hogan, like he lied to William Olsen at the union hall. What's one lie, two, three, four, five?"

Murtaugh built to a crescendo: "Are we going to sit here and permit, in 1966, what wasn't done in 15 B.C.? This was a crime not only against those eight girls, but a crime against the peace, the dignity, and the law and order of this whole country. In the interest of self-preservation, remove a cancer. Give this man the death penalty."

During Murtaugh's peroration, Speck had leaned across to Getty and whispered, "I'd like to get George out in the hall!" No wonder. Murtaugh had more than risen to the occasion, and his irresistible flow of words created a firestorm of outrage that were now crackling beneath the surface of the stunned crowd. Paschen declared a recess.

About thirty minutes later, Getty walked to the table in front of the jury and placed a large three-ring notebook in front of him. Dapper and unflappable as ever, Getty knew that defending Speck did not lend itself to passion. He would be at his folksy best and try to reason with the jurors, shrewdly talking to them as if he were the village barber—an older man with common sense and uncommon wisdom, expressed softly.

"You know," Getty began, "sometimes young men, well, they think light of what they are doing. They think light of taking the life of a person. But there were many people that passed through this box—your neighbors, citizens of this state, who said that they would not give the death penalty."

Without attacking Cora personally, Getty challenged her description of the killer as being different from Speck. Noting that neither the first officer to interview Cora at the scene nor the police artist had been called as witnesses, Getty implied that the descriptions Cora gave them of the killer did not resemble Speck. "But, I tell you," he argued, "it was a haste of judgment in this trial, in this case, a haste of judgment by the higher-ups in the Chicago Police Department."

He moved on to attack the credibility of Patrick Walsh and Richard Oliva and to claim that it was unlikely that they would have noticed a man carrying a knife and a gun in the crowded bar of the Shipyard Inn on Wednesday night. He attacked the fingerprints as "smudges" and the expert fingerprint testimony of Emil Giese and Andre Moenssens as mere "opinion," noting, "If there were one point of dissimilarity in the smudge, the print would have to be disregarded."

Standing absolutely still directly in front of the jurors, occasionally turning the pages of his notebook, Getty continued to try calmly to dissect the State's case. "Now, these people don't want to talk about it, but it seems that the right killers could not be located. The other Hanes T-shirt, up in Davy's bed where these acts took place, that the police never found until some two weeks later. How many killers were there? How many were there? They want you to believe that Richard Speck wore two T-shirts on July 13, on a hot day. They want you to believe that he also had a black jacket over the two T-shirts."

Getty rationalized Speck's attempted suicide as a reasonable response to hearing his name blared across the land as the killer of eight women. This had a "mental effect" on Speck, Getty argued, noting that "most people" would have done the same thing. Gathering momentum for his ending, Getty extolled the virtues of Murrill and Gerdena Farmer as witnesses. "I have tried over four hundred murder cases," Getty told the jurors. "I have seen many witnesses and Murrill and Gerdena Farmer are the best alibi witnesses I have ever encountered, because they came to Gerry Getty from the State."

Finishing with the contention that the "killer or killers" had been in the nurses' town house for an hour and a half "before Richard Speck left Kay's Pilot House," Getty ended with the words: "I commit you to make a proper decision in this case."

Martin found it odd that Getty could not bring himself to say the final words of every defense summation: "Find him not guilty."

Judge Paschen declared a short recess, and as spectators milled in the corridor, Martin arose and walked quietly about the courtroom, trying to develop a sense of the impact the Public Defender had had on the jury. He had listened attentively to every word that came out of Getty's mouth and he knew that his job during the rebuttal was to do just that—rebut Getty.

Getty had gambled Speck's life on the testimony of the Farmers. His gamble was not so much that the Farmers' alibi would acquit Speck but that it might generate just enough doubt to cause the jury to refuse to sign a death verdict. It was Martin's job to dispel those doubts so convincingly that the jury would fix Speck's punishment as death. Prosecutors cannot "prepare" a rebuttal. They can only hope that the right words are there when the time comes. For Martin, the time had come.

The jury reassembled in the courtroom and Judge Paschen ascended the bench. Martin stood up and walked slowly to the center of the jury box. He was wearing a dark gray vested suit, a white tab-collared shirt, and a red-and-white striped tie, and carried no notes. The prosecutor promptly went to the heart of Getty's defense and dismissed the Farmers' alibi because of its inherent improbability—"The human mind is not a stopwatch!"

After analyzing the many reasons why the Farmers' estimate of time was apt to be off, Martin contrasted their fleeting opportunity to observe Speck with the long, lingering opportunity afforded the only nurse to escape Speck's murderous rage—Corazon Amurao. Martin took the jurors through Cora's testimony, reminding them of the many times she had been face to face with the killer, beginning with the moment he stood in the light of her room, gun in hand, and demanded to know where her "comrades" were. Recalling the many minutes that had passed before Speck began his death march, Martin said that Speck's face was "indelibly imprinted" in the mind of the State's star witness. He also didn't let the jurors forget that Cora had chosen Speck's photo out of 104 others. She did this, Martin noted, *before* talking to the police artist.

Holding aloft the enlarged juxtaposed photos of the police artist's sketch and the Coast Guard photo of Speck that Cora had chosen as "most similar," Martin told the jurors: "And we're not ashamed of this"—he indicated the sketch—"either, because, boy, take a look at this"—indicating the photo—"and add that to the fact that she picked out the picture with the pockmarks and the swept-back hair. That's her identification. And it wasn't shaken one inch on cross-examination. Compare that with the Farmers, who thought he looked like a German sailor, and they were so sure of the time."

Martin wanted to rebut every insinuation that Getty had planted. Turning his attention to the credibility of army sergeant Rich Oliva, who testified that he saw Speck drop a pocketknife in the bar of the Shipyard Inn less than two hours before he broke into the town house, Martin asked the jurors: "Did he come from Vietnam to stain his hands with the blood of an innocent man? Or did he in fact see the pocketknife on the floor? And did he in fact see Richard Speck slowly reach down and pick it up and put it back in his pocket? And is it so ridiculous for an army sergeant to tell you that the blade was three or four inches long, when he had looked at the handle?"

At times, Martin's voice would drop so low that the jurors could barely hear him. At others, it would reverberate off the paneled courtroom walls. He moved back and forth from the front of the jury box to the well of the court, and occasionally held up exhibits. Turning to the question of the extra T-shirts, Martin told the jurors: "Sure, he got a room at the Shipyard Inn. You know that it is easy to enter and leave that room without being seen by the patrons in the bar. And when he walked down 100th Street and when he went to that town house, is it unreasonable to assume that he took clothes with him?

"There is a park behind the town house. You have seen the park. You know it is there. Where did he sleep Tuesday night? What did he see? What idea was implanted in his mind on that Tuesday night that bore fruit on that evil Wednesday?

"Is it so unusual to find [extra] shirts from a man like that, who might again contemplate being in a park and needing a change of clothes? And when you kill eight people you must perspire very, very much. And if you are, as he has been shown to be, a person who likes to change shirts even without perspiring a lot, is it so unusual that he left two T-shirts in that house? And the black jacket is not only the testimony of Corazon Amurao, but also of Gene Thornton, who told you that when Speck left on Monday he took a black jacket with him. Is that another coincidence? Like the knife? Like the gun? Like New Orleans? Like Cora identifying this picture? Can that be only a coincidence? He had the jacket. He had the shirts. And, reasonably, we can assume, he even had the bag.

"And, sure, his bed was slept in that night. He went back to the Shipyard Inn. He went back there the same way he came to the town house, down 100th Street. . . . He went back to that room a murderer, a murderer who had snuffed out eight lives. And he still slept in that bed."

After describing the many ways Speck attempted to lie and run and escape, Martin turned his attention to the south bedroom door, which sat directly in front of the jurors. His oratory in full flight, he continued: "Not only," he said, "does Corazon Amurao get down from the witness stand and say, 'This is the man!', but this door also sits in this courtroom and says just as forcefully, just as dramatically, for now and for all time, 'This is the man!' "

Having finished with the evidence of Speck's guilt, Martin turned to the need for the death penalty. Reminding the jurors that each and every one of them had sworn an oath to inflict the death penalty, if they believed this was a proper case for it, he concluded this way:

"We submit to you that this is a proper case. And if this is not a proper case, then there never will at any time or any place be a proper case. But the whole burden of determining a proper case does not rest on your shoulders. There's one extraordinarily significant fact in this case that I ask you to bear in mind when you soon go into that jury room to deliberate. The supreme and ultimate irony of this entire case is that before you ever came into this courtroom, before this case was ever assigned to Judge Paschen, before Mr. Getty was ever appointed to defend Richard Franklin Speck, before we ever sought to prosecute it, there was a man who knew that this is a proper case for the death penalty.

"And that man sits before you, the accused, Richard Speck. And he told you and he told the world that it was a proper case when he slashed his arm and he slashed his wrist lying in that cubicle at the Starr Hotel, because he could run away from the Southeast Side, he could run away from his name, but he couldn't in the end run away from his conscience. And he knew, and he knew well that there can only be one penalty for a crime of this magnitude. There can be no other.

"He, who had the strength in his hands, in his wrists, in the sinews of his arms and shoulders to bind those seven girls, didn't have the strength to take his own life. In the end, it was nurses and doctors who saved his life—nurses like the very ones he had killed.

"He, who had the strength to plunge that pocketknife into the heart of Pamela Wilkening, didn't have it when it came to taking his own life. But he knew his own life should be taken.

"He, who had the strength to plunge that knife eighteen times into the body of Suzanne Farris, knew this was a proper case. He, who with the nurse's stocking strangled every breath out of her body, didn't have the strength to take his own life.

"He, who with that same knife that Oliva had seen on the floor, smashed the left eye of Mary Ann Jordan and plunged it three times into her chest, didn't have the strength to take his own life.

"He, who with those bindings choked the life from the body of Nina Schmale, didn't have the strength to take his own life.

"He, who could take that knife and slit six inches of the throat of Valentina Pasion, didn't have the strength to take his own life.

"He, who could strangle every breath from Merlita Gargullo and puncture her four times and dislocate her neck with those strong hands, didn't have the strength to take his own life.

"He, who could take Patricia Matusek into that bathroom and tell her, 'lie down, lie down here,' while her hands were knotted behind her back, he who could then kick her in the stomach and with those same strong hands, with a double knot, strangle the last breath from her innocent body, he didn't have the strength to take his own life. But he knew this was a proper case. He knew it long before anyone else. He knew it after he had done it.

"And after he had defiled the body of Gloria Jean Davy while she was still alive, he, then, with those strong hands, with a double knot, squeezed the last breath of life from her and left her lying nude on the couch. He had that strength. But not the strength to take his own life. . . ."

The words had come easily to Martin because for nine months his whole life had been invested in this moment. He was building to his conclusion:

"The law must exact pain. And, in this case, the law must exact another human life. And we don't stand here and with arrogance tell you that this is any great pleasure, to take a life. But we face that duty which descends upon society to protect itself. We must protect ourselves from killings like this. Ladies and gentlemen, it is your responsibility to this county and to this sovereign State to say that a man cannot murder eight innocent girls in their beds and expect to spend the rest of his life in a prison cell. You cannot say that. That is easy. But courage is what is demanded of you, the same courage that Corazon Amurao had that made her survive. . . .

"Ladies and gentlemen, there is no doubt about the defendant's guilt. If you doubt his guilt, send him home tonight, if you will. But if you find him guilty, this is a proper case. He knows that it is a proper case. And when you are alone sometime, when this is all over, and, perhaps, you see an early morning sunrise, or, perhaps, you walk alone in the rain, or, perhaps, you are alone somewhere in your own house, and you examine your conscience, don't let it be said that on April 15, 1967, you fled from that duty and that moment of responsibility that society has entrusted to you. You are paid a very small sum, and you are taken from your families, and you are placed here to decide life and death. This is your moment of responsibility. Don't do the easy thing and simply say, 'Guilty.' This is a proper case for you to live with your conscience for the rest of your life, for you to sign the verdict finding him guilty and fixing his punishment at death."

The final words came straight from Martin's liberal conscience:

"And write it not with vengeance toward Speck as a man, because the law doesn't bear vengeance toward men. The law is here to control society and to deter crime in the future. Write that verdict not in hatred, write that verdict not with any sense of animosity. But write it in truth, because this is a proper case. And write it because this is the only just verdict that can be returned in this case. Find him guilty and fix his punishment at death."

Finally drained of emotion, Martin sat down next to Murtaugh and both prosecutors stared at the jurors as Judge Paschen read the instructions of law in a monotone. The bailiffs then took the jurors out of the courtroom for a box lunch in another jury room. Considerate to the end, Paschen wanted the jurors to be able to eat in peace before having to take the written instructions of law and the actual forms for the three possible verdicts into the jury room of Courtroom A to begin their deliberations.

It was now high noon. Martin believed that waiting in the courthouse for the return of a verdict was a sure way to an ulcer. The lawyers from both sides left for their hotels. There were no reporters to avoid because they had all already heard everything that everyone had to say and had left to file their reports of the closing arguments. The next big story would be the verdict itself.

The verdict could take hours or it could take days. In the meantime, the State's team sat down at a large table at the Ramada Inn and ordered lunch. Before their lunch arrived, however, court clerk Paul Trompeter put through an urgent phone call to Martin. After only forty-nine minutes of deliberations, the jury had reached its verdict.

CHAPTER 39

It did not take long for everyone to reassemble in Courtroom A. The jury filed in, led by foreman George Weiman, the ex-Marine who had once prosecuted courts-martial. Weiman handed the eight separate verdict forms to a bailiff, who gave them to Paul Trompeter. The courtroom waited in hushed anticipation as Trompeter began to read:

"We, the jury, find the defendant, Richard Franklin Speck, guilty of the murder of Gloria Jean Davy, in the manner and form as charged in the indictment, and we fix his punishment at death."

Trompeter then read seven additional verdicts, all identical to the one for Gloria Jean Davy. He concluded the reading of each verdict by saying, "Signed by the foreman and the other eleven jurors." There were ninety-six signatures affixed to the eight separate verdict forms. The jurors were then individually polled by Judge Paschen with a single question: "Were these and are these now your verdicts?" Without hesitation, each of the twelve jurors responded, "Yes, sir." Paschen thanked the jury, asked them to retire, and then cleared the court.

Bill Martin felt numb, as he slowly made his way downstairs to the prosecutors' large office on the first floor of the court-house. A bailiff guarded the door, allowing only lawyers, police officers, and family to enter. Despite the gathering crowd, the large room was strangely quiet. To Martin, everything in the room seemed to be moving in slow motion. He spotted Murtaugh and Zagel in a corner, and the three prosecutors unashamedly hugged. Detective Jack Wallenda soon joined them, tears streaming down his face. By now, the families of the nurses were in the room and rushed over to the members of Team Speck—to shake their hands or to kiss them affectionately on the cheek.

Zagel later remarked that being in that room at that time created a "physical sensation of knowing that you are present at an occasion that is both sad and momentous. Somehow the victims had remained alive during the trial of their murderer; the end of the trial, however, is the final part of their deaths."

State's Attorney John Stamos pulled Martin aside and asked if he'd be able to write a statement for the press. The reporters were in force outside the courthouse door and would not leave without some comment from the prosecutors. Martin excused himself and went to a desk to try to jot something down. After every brief attempt, he would stop and throw the paper away. Finally, he said, "John, I don't think that I can write anything out. Can we just go outside and get this over with?"

Team Speck—prosecutors and police alike—walked out to the top of the courthouse steps to face a sea of reporters and Saturday spectators. Standing in the spotlight, Martin looked out at the plaza fountain, quietly splashing in the spring sunshine, and spoke two sentences:

"The enforcement of the criminal law, particularly in a capital case, is certainly something that doesn't leave us any cause to rejoice or to celebrate. We came here to perform a duty that is imposed upon us by the statutes, we presented the evidence to the citizens of this county, and we believe that they did their duty in returning a verdict."

CHAPTER 40

Technically, the twelve jurors had only *recommended* that Speck be sent to the electric chair. It would be up to Judge Herbert Paschen to actually impose the death sentence, and he had the option of rejecting the jurors' recommendation. Getty not only could move for a new trial; he also would be able to present evidence in mitigation of the jury's recommended sentence as a final effort to help his client avoid the electric chair.

A brief session was convened by Judge Paschen Monday morning in Courtroom A of the Peoria County Courthouse. Much like a pin deflates a balloon, Saturday's verdict had taken all the emotion out of the proceedings. Everyone—the judge, the prosecution, and the defense—was spent from Saturday's passion and, in an anticlimactic gathering, it was agreed that all posttrial motions would be heard in Chicago and that Richard Franklin Speck would be transferred back to his death row cell in the Cook County Jail.

The papers of Sunday, April 16, had trumpeted the news from Peoria. The banner headline in the *Chicago Tribune* proclaimed DEATH SENTENCE FOR SPECK. Both the *Tribune* and veteran *Chicago Sun-Times* crime reporter Ray Brennan had obtained copies of the jailhouse interviews conducted with Speck by Dr. Marvin Ziporyn. Both papers reported extensive summaries of

Ziporyn's reports, and it was disclosed that Brennan had enjoyed access to the reports during the trial, but had withheld publication in order not to violate the press order issued by Paschen. This was strong proof of the effectiveness of—and necessity for—the press order.

That same Sunday night, the Amurao clan—Cora, Mama, and Roger—and their police friends enjoyed a celebratory dinner at Arnie Morton's Restaurant in Chicago and reminisced about their days at the Moraine-on-the-Lake months earlier. The happy days of this odd extended family of Filipinos and police were drawing to an end.

Once the trial had concluded, reporters learned where Cora had been staying and police were now afraid that kooks might begin harassing her. A few days later, Cora and her police bodyguards moved out of the Sheridan-Surf and relocated to Chicago's famed Edgewater Beach Hotel.

On April 20, Ziporyn was fired from his $8,100-a-year, part-time job as the Cook County Jail psychiatrist. Sheriff Joe Woods told reporters, "He has too big a mouth." The official reason was that he had exploited his position and used county time to pursue a private project—his interviews with Richard Speck for the purpose of writing a book for financial gain. In the uproar over Speck's conviction, Ziporyn also lost his publisher, Hawthorn Books. The publishing house was owned by W. Clement Stone, the Chicago insurance magnate and Republican fund-raiser, and Stone decided that he could not be associated in any way with Richard Speck. The publishing rights were subsequently sold to Grove Press in New York, which published Ziporyn's book, entitled *Born to Raise Hell,* in the summer of 1967. The *Saturday Evening Post* paid $25,000 to excerpt portions.

On April 28, Martin accompanied the four-man police detail as it escorted the Amuraos to O'Hare Airport for their trip home to the Philippines. The Amuraos' cover was retained right to the very end, as Martin leaked erroneous information to the press that Cora would be leaving Chicago on April 29—one day later.

Invoking the magic talisman, "for the Speck case," the police also managed to get Cora and her family pre-boarded on the plane, a move that foiled a *Tribune* reporter who got a belated tip that Cora was leaving a day earlier than announced. By the time the photographer arrived at the airport gate, Cora, Mama, and Roger, who was anxious to get home to his wife, had already exchanged warm hugs and handshakes with their Chicago protectors and had settled in for the long flight home. The U.S. State Department had been notified of the Amuraos' departure, and had made sure that Japanese security police would provide all amenities for their overnight stopover in Tokyo. One day later, the Amuraos touched down in Manila and were greeted with open arms by the Philippine government. The Philippine consul-general in Chicago, Generoso Provido, proved to be a politician to the end, sending Martin a florid telegram congratulating the State's Attorney's Office on its successful quest for justice. That quest, however, was not over.

On Monday, May 15, Getty filed a fifty-five-page motion for a new trial, alleging multiple errors by Paschen during his conduct of the trial. Arguing for more than two hours, Getty cited everything from Paschen's denial of a trial judge other than himself to Paschen's refusal to move the trial out of Peoria after it had already been moved from Chicago to Peoria. Only Paschen could judge Getty's motion because, as the trial judge, he was the only judge familiar with the entire record of the trial. However, Paschen was mindful that his decision would be reviewed by appellate courts and that any errors could lead to a reversal. Paschen was confident of his prior rulings. When Getty stopped talking, Paschen denied his motion for a new trial.

Richard Speck would be held guilty of the murders of eight nurses. The only issue remaining was an eleventh-hour effort by Getty to seek mitigation and mercy for his client—to help Speck avoid the electric chair. Paschen set this hearing for May 25. Getty was investigating the possibility that his client was suffering from an "epileptic furor" at the time he took his gun and knife, put on his black jacket, and walked to the town house to kill.

Getty's extensive postverdict maneuverings were keeping Martin busy six days a week, but at least he had escaped from his cinnamon toast and cheeseburger diet at the Ramada Inn and was back home in Chicago, able to enjoy home-cooked meals and get reacquainted with his four children—Marc, age five, Patrick, four, Colleen, three, and Victoria, one. Sundays, he and his wife took the family to Brookfield Zoo, Kiddieland, and the Museum of Science and Industry. Since the older children understood what Speck had done, Martin frequently had to reassure them: "No, honey, he's not going to get out of jail and try to kill you." Martin also had time to go to his parents' house and notice that the paint job remained to be done. He assured them he would get to it—soon.

George Murtaugh was overjoyed that he could return by day to his assignment in felony trial court and by night to his wife and two young children. John Glenville also returned to felony trial court, sad that he had not been able to participate in the Speck trial. Only Jim Zagel remained with Martin as a full-time member of Team Speck. The remaining phase of the case involved psychiatric testimony, which was Zagel's specialty.

In the middle of May, the four prosecutors were briefly reunited at a meeting with their boss, State's Attorney John Stamos. The meeting was a surprise and the four men wondered if, perhaps, something had gone wrong. Cigar in hand, Stamos arose majestically from behind his huge polished desk and nonchalantly handed each man an envelope. The four were stunned and speechless; each envelope contained a bonus check from the county board for a thousand dollars. Bonuses were unheard of in the State's Attorney's Office, and Martin's entire salary was only ten thousand dollars a year. Observing the bewilderment on the faces in front of him, Stamos said laconically, "Shit, it's the least we can do for you, after all you have done for us."

On May 25, it was back to court to hear Getty ask Judge Paschen to authorize additional brain-wave tracings or electro-encephalograms (EEG's) of Speck to determine whether or not he had been suffering from an alcohol-induced "epileptic furor" on the night of the murders. The defense was desperately trying to find a biological reason to explain Speck's evil. The feisty and loquacious Jim Doherty argued that it was absolutely impera-tive that additional EEG's be taken of Speck both while he was in a deep sleep and while he was under the influence of alco-hol. Doherty said that the new tests would show whether or not Speck might have been prone to epileptic fits when drinking.

In response, Martin filed the formerly confidential eleven complete examinations of Speck by the six-member psychiatric panel and its five consultants, plus the reports of Drs. Feiner-man, Haines, Littner, and Ziporyn. The reports had not been part of the court record previously in order to prevent their contents from being reported by the media. The fear was that if jurors were aware that the panel unanimously found Richard Speck sane, then they could not fairly judge an insanity defense, if one were presented. Martin also filed the original EEG taken of Speck on September 29, 1966, at the Psychiatric Institute and subsequently analyzed by the panel's consulting neurologist and electroencephalographer.

Martin argued that fifteen medical experts had already examined Speck without finding any trace of epilepsy, and that the defense had not stated sufficient grounds that the new tests they were proposing would in any way affect the court's deci-sion on the mass murderer. Paschen adjourned the session by telling Getty to be prepared to proceed the next day with any evidence that he had mitigating against the death penalty. The judge said that he would rule on the advisability of the proposed new EEG's at that time.

The next day, the defense called Dr. Frederick Gibbs, a prominent electroencephalographer from the University of Illinois Medical Center, to testify in favor of the new tests. Dr. Gibbs said that alcohol-provoked and deep-sleep EEG's would "complete" the brain tests of Speck. He added that the additional tests could be performed upon ten-channel EEG machines, compared to the "limited" eight-channel machines used during the earlier tests.

Martin stood on the scientific reports that the State had already filed with the court and argued that the additional EEG's were not required medically, scientifically—or legally. However, since the State had no standing to oppose a defense request to test the defendant, all Martin believed he could do was make a strong push with Paschen to expedite the proceedings.

However, Martin changed his position when he learned that the two new psychiatrists Getty was proposing examine Speck were planning to use the new EEG results for a "treatise" on violence, and that the Chicago lawyer who represented them was the same lawyer who had represented Dr. Marvin Ziporyn in negotiating his book, *Born to Raise Hell*, and the Hollywood rights for it. Believing that the Public Defender and his client were being unwittingly used to further another scheme to profit from the sensational case, Martin adamantly opposed the new tests. To bolster his position, Martin interviewed the members of the court-appointed panel. Their response was unanimous: the proposed EEG's were "neither essential, indicated, nor necessary." Martin also enlisted the testimony of Dr. John R. Hughes, the Northwestern Memorial Hospital electroencephalographer who had read Speck's EEG for the court panel. He said that deep-sleep EEG's are "not as reliable" as the light-sleep readings he had previously analyzed, and that "alcohol-provoked EEG's had been discredited as a diagnostic tool twelve years ago."

Judge Paschen had heard enough. He denied the defense motion for the new EEG tests, noting: "I am not interested in making Richard Franklin Speck a guinea pig for history." Adding that the proposed tests would not have any bearing on mitigation for the mass killer, Paschen continued the case until June 2—at which time, he told Getty, he wanted to hear *actual* evidence arguing for mitigation.

The only thing left between Richard Speck and the death penalty would be the testimony of Dr. Ner Littner, an urbane, Freudian analyst and child psychiatrist who had interviewed only one other murderer in his professional life. For reasons only hinted at previously, Getty had decided not to use Dr. Ziporyn as a witness in the presentencing hearing. Marvin Ziporyn, the man who had spent more than a hundred hours with Richard Speck and become his closest confidant and his biographer, would never take the witness stand to try to save his patient's life.

Martin was determined that neither the distinguished Freudian psychiatrist nor the final impassioned arguments of Gerry Getty, who had never lost a client to the electric chair, would help Speck avoid his just punishment.

With the case winding down to its final days, Getty and Martin were still able to walk into Judge Paschen's majestic seventh-floor courtroom accompanied, as usual, by several colleagues, and appear civil to each other. The ordeal of the eight-week trial, however, had taken its toll, and now the two lawyers were about to get personal. The flash point was reached on June 2, when Getty told the judge that the State had previously agreed to allow Speck to undergo the new EEG tests. Martin termed this "an absolute falsehood," prompting Getty to blast back, "Well, I'm just sick and tired of being accused of falsehoods by this angelic altar boy."

The only witness of the day, the energetic and trim Dr. Ner Littner, dressed and looked more like the CEO of a major accounting firm than a psychiatrist. At the time, there were 18,000 psychiatrists in the U.S., and only 1,100 psychoanalysts like Littner. He took the stand looking confident and unconcerned about his lack of courtroom experience. Littner had interviewed Speck for two hours on the morning of February 4 and for another two hours that same afternoon. He had also studied the reports of the court-appointed psychiatric panel and the inquiry into Speck's Dallas years that had been compiled by the Assistant Public Defender Jim Gramenos.

Littner told Judge Paschen that Speck suffered from a "serious mental disease," which he termed "chronic personality disorder, with neurotic features." He observed that Speck used a number of neurotic and self-destructive behaviors to try to cope with the "excessive anxiety" and "unbearable tension" in his mind.

He explained that this anxiety was due to Speck's sense of guilt and inadequacy and that it caused him to have no control over his impulses, especially when he was drinking. Littner said that Speck had been suffering from this mental disease from at least age thirteen and possibly as early as age six. He then enumerated seven broad patterns of behavior as examples of Speck's mental illness. Littner's explanation of these seven behavior patterns tripped off his tongue as fluently as if he were lecturing a seminar of graduate students. Judge Paschen turned toward the witness with great interest and took notes rapidly.

First, beginning at age six, Littner told the court, Speck had developed various phobias, including a fear of closed spaces; an irrational fear of being stared at by strangers and an excessive anxiety about reciting in front of classmates; a fear of swimming because of the possibility that water moccasins might be lurking in the water; a tendency toward nightmares in which he was buried alive; and a fear of spiders. Littner termed these fears as being all part of one cluster of symptoms—using phobias to deal with inner tension. Second, Speck used hysterical, or bodily symptoms—throbbing headaches, blurring vision, dizzy spells, and sexual impotence—to try to deal with the tension in his mind.

Third, Littner said, was Speck's long history of self-destructive behaviors—auto accidents, falling from trees, running into poles, acquiring gonorrhea on five separate occasions and syphilis on two—which were Speck's way of handling his great surges of guilt. Fourth was Speck's pattern of abusing alcohol and drugs and seeking out violence, especially knife fights, a sign of unbearable tension in Speck's mind and a symptom of his mental disease. Fifth was Speck's trouble-proneness, including thirty-six arrests in Dallas and two stays in prison. He needed to get into trouble and get caught by the police, Littner said, because of his anxiety and tension.

Sixth, the analyst said, was Speck's inability to be close to people, preferring the company of older beaten-down men and bad-news women to people his own age. Littner said that Speck's association with prostitutes proved his basic difficulty in forming close relationships with women. Seventh was the fact that Speck had been proven inadequate to the "major tests of maturity"— school, jobs, marriage, every aspect of growing up that implies independence. Pointing out that Speck was the "family deviate," Littner suggested that the cause of the difference from the rest of the law-abiding, church-going family was Speck's mental illness.

Littner maintained a detached professorial air as he began to address the burning question of why Speck murdered eight women:

On Wednesday, July 13, 1966, Littner theorized, Speck was "living in a pressure cooker in his mind," and drank all day, one of his favorite ways to relieve tension. Further, Speck took a lot of pills he got from a stranger and also injected himself in the arm with an unknown drug. In Littner's version, Speck paid for a prostitute but was unable to perform, and turned her over to the men with whom he had been drinking. Littner saw Speck's entire Wednesday as a means of trying to cope with the overwhelming tension in his mind.

The erudite psychiatrist was an impressive witness. He did not refer to notes and displayed a mastery of the evidence. Littner concluded with his opinion that Speck should be confined and given intensive psychoanalytic treatment so that "society can learn something to prevent the Richard Specks of tomorrow. I think that it would be a great disservice to psychiatry if we pretended that there are no reasons to explain a Richard Speck, if we pretend to ourselves that he is just 'bad' and explain his crime away on that basis."

Based upon what he had heard about and from Littner, Martin thought that the psychiatrist was both brilliant and honest and that his only motive for testifying was his sincere view that psychoanalyzing Speck was a way to prevent future mass murderers. At the same time, the prosecutor thought that Littner's theory was fatally flawed, because it assumed that Speck had told the truth—and Speck was a world-class liar who had manipulated the Freudian analyst as easily he had the nurses. In an effort to burst what he considered a hot-air balloon of Freudian jargon, Martin did a mildly sarcastic cross-examination.

Littner was the only witness of the day, and Paschen adjourned the hearing until two-fifteen P.M., at which time he said that he would hear the final arguments on whether or not he should impose the death penalty.

During the luncheon recess, Martin was left alone to ponder the fact that Getty's hope for an insanity verdict after a two-stage trial probably would have failed, anyway, because it was now apparent, after Littner's testimony, that his two experts—Ziporyn and Littner—were in irrevocable conflict.

Ziporyn said that Speck was an "obsessive-compulsive personality who demonstrated guilt, remorse, and shame." Littner testified that Speck was suffering from a "severe chronic personality disorder with mixed neurotic traits," and that he had found "no evidence of guilt, remorse, or shame."

Ziporyn found that Speck totally had no control over his impulsive behavior because of his "organic brain syndrome" and "alcohol-, barbiturate-, and methedrine-poisoned nervous system that cannot brake, control, or censor him." Littner emphasized how Speck's inner anxieties and tensions led him to impulsive behaviors.

Most significantly, Ziporyn based his diagnosis on Speck's ability to "have loving relationships with members of his family," while Littner testified that one of the killer's basic problems was "a chronic inability to form close relationships with others."

The essence of Ziporyn's thesis had been that "Speck cannot be understood without reference to multiple cerebral injuries," and that "Speck has an organic brain defect—chronic brain syndrome, associated with cerebral trauma." Littner considered this alleged cerebral trauma, but concluded that Speck "shows no evidence of neurological physical disease."

Clearly, Getty could not have presented these two "experts" to the same jury without incurring the substantial risk that each of their contradictory diagnoses would be disbelieved and rejected. Martin felt better—the Illinois Supreme Court could not logically find that Judge Paschen had erred in denying the Public Defender's motion for a two-stage trial.

It was time for the final task—to convince kindly Herb Paschen, gardener and grandfather, that the twenty-five-year-old Speck should be jolted to death by electricity.

In his final argument, Getty made an impassioned personal plea to Paschen not to inflict the death penalty. Part of his

argument included his reasons for not using an insanity defense
for Speck.

Getty began by estimating that the six court-appointed panel
physicians had spent a total of twenty-one hours and fifty minutes trying to fathom the depths of Richard Speck's mind. He
continued: "Many people have suggested that I should have had
a psychiatric defense, although I have reiterated again and again
that I could not have used a psychiatric defense. The defendant
has never admitted his guilt to me, nor has he been able to tell
me how the murders were done. So, there isn't any lawyer who
pleads guilty a client who cannot tell him that he is guilty or
how the murder was done. And that is exactly what a psychiatric
defense is—you are pleading your client guilty and saying, 'Yes,
but this is the mental condition of this man at this time.' " Getty
added that even if Speck had told him that he was guilty that the
odds against an insanity defense "were too great—one (Littner)
against seven (the six panel members, plus Dr. Haines)."

Referring specifically to Ziporyn, whose financial involvement in *Born to Raise Hell* had been publicized widely after the
verdict, Getty told Paschen, "I could have had two witnesses for
the defense, but I have not called one in mitigation because I
do not think that he would have any influence on Your Honor
because of reports of his writing a book for personal gain, and I
would not bring that kind of testimony before Your Honor."

There had been a great amount of armchair quarterbacking
questioning Getty's choice of an alibi defense over the defense
of insanity, especially since the alibi kept the jury out for only
forty-nine minutes. In truth, though, this was an unfair and
uninformed criticism of Getty. For an insanity defense, all he had
to work with were the conflicting theories of a psychiatrist with
an enormous financial interest in the defendant and a Freudian analyst with no experience in dealing with criminals. Had
Getty tried an insanity defense, he knew he would face as many

as thirteen experts who found Richard Speck sane at the time of the murders.

Speaking with passion and conviction, Getty turned his attention to why Paschen should not inflict the death penalty. Pointing out that the abolishment of capital punishment had occurred in thirteen states and was "knocking on the door in Illinois," Getty said that the judge should heed the temper of the times. Getty knew that Paschen was not a "hanging judge," and he tried to appeal to his humanitarianism and sensitivity. He offered him the compromise of giving Speck, instead, eight consecutive life sentences. "This would be a greater punishment," Getty concluded.

It was Martin's turn. He knew that Paschen found it personally distasteful to take a man's life. It would take a strong argument to convince him, and this was Martin's final assignment during the Speck trial. Standing at the lectern with Murtaugh and Zagel seated to his left, Martin's voice rose and fell with emotion. He gave the same argument to the judge he would have given to a jury, comparing Speck's evil to that of the Nazis and noting, "We know that there is evil in this world and that it does not masquerade as insanity. This is the nature of man." Speck had shown no mercy to the nurses, Martin argued, and the law could now show no mercy to Speck.

There was nothing more to be done or said. Paschen took the case under advisement, saying that he would return to Peoria the next Monday, June 5, to pronounce sentence. That Sunday, Martin and Murtaugh, once again, set out in their unmarked squad car for the Peoria Ramada Inn. This time, though, they traveled light.

CHAPTER 41

Monday, June 5, 1967—11 A.M.
The Peoria County Courthouse

It was a beautiful day in late spring. Outside, in the courtyard plaza, trees and fountains sparkled in the morning sun. Inside, Courtroom A was crowded with the news media, police, and families of the nurses, as everyone awaited the final act in the dark drama of Richard Franklin Speck.

Unsmiling, Judge Paschen ascended the bench. He would remain unsmiling when he left—only minutes later. The clerk called the case, and Paschen asked, "Is there anything counsel wishes to add before I pronounce sentence?"

Gerry Getty stood, his eyes betraying how tired he was from the ordeal that had begun eleven months earlier. He said stiffly, "On my behalf and on behalf of the defendant, there is nothing more that we can say and there are no further motions at this time. I have also conferred this morning with the defendant, Richard Speck, and he advised me that he has nothing to say himself personally." Richard Speck, the master of barroom braggadocio, was never to utter a single word in the courtroom.

His voice raspy but polite, Judge Paschen said, "Very well. Will you bring the prisoner before the bench, please?"

Getty curtly told Speck, "Step up." Speck's face betrayed no emotion as he stood and shuffled up to the front of the bench, standing next to Getty. Paschen looked away from Speck to the typed sheets in front of him and declared that he was about to read the judgment and execution order. He coughed and began. Although his voice was steady, he read the archaic language in a monotone that was hurried enough to suggest that he wanted this case over and done with. He read:

"And now neither the defendant, Richard Franklin Speck, nor his counsel, having anything further to say why judgment and sentence should not be pronounced, thereupon, it is the order and judgment of the Court that the defendant, Richard Franklin Speck, upon the verdicts of the jury as aforesaid is guilty of the crimes of the murders of Pamela Lee Wilkening, Suzanne Bridget Farris, Mary Ann Jordan, Nina Jo Schmale, Valentina P. Pasion, Merlita Gargullo, Patricia Ann Matusek, and Gloria Jean Davy, in the manner and form charged in the indictments."

Paschen paused to adjust his dark-rimmed glasses before reading the last dramatic words:

"Therefore, it is ordered and adjudged by the Court that the defendant, Richard Franklin Speck, be and he is hereby committed to the custody of the Sheriff of Peoria County, Illinois, to be taken from the bar of this court to the common jail of Peoria County from whence he came and from thence by the Sheriff of Peoria County forthwith to the Illinois State Penitentiary and be delivered to the Warden or keeper of said penitentiary, and the said Warden or keeper is hereby required and commanded to take the body of the defendant, Richard Franklin Speck, from and after the delivery thereof and confine him in safe and secure custody until the 1st day of September, 1967, and that the defendant, Richard Franklin Speck, be on that day, at the Illinois State Penitentiary, put to death by causing to pass through the body of the defendant, Richard Franklin Speck, a current of electricity of sufficient intensity to cause death, and the application and continuance of such current through the body of the defendant until such defendant is dead. . . ."

Like a giant balloon, the word "dead" hung suspended in the air. Motioning toward Richard Franklin Speck, who had stared ahead in icy silence throughout the brief proceeding, Paschen told the bailiff:

"Take him away. Court is adjourned."

PART V
THE AFTERMATH

Richard Speck died of a massive heart attack on December 5, 1991. The nurses and doctors of the Silver Cross Hospital in Joliet, Illinois, struggled for six hours in an unsuccessful attempt to save him. He was one day short of his fiftieth birthday, and had spent more than half his life at Stateville, the nearby correctional center. A long and sedentary prison life had transformed the once-lean killer into a pasty middle-aged man with a prominent paunch and a deeply lined, puffy face. He was seldom seen without a cigarette dangling from his hands or lips, and he was known to be a fan of jailhouse "hooch," or homemade alcohol. The autopsy disclosed that he had an enlarged heart and that his left anterior descending artery, one of three supplying the heart with oxygen, was one hundred percent blocked. He also suffered from emphysema, and his weight was a hefty 220 pounds. The coroner duly noted his collection of tattoos, including the inscription "Shirley" on the back of his right shoulder and "Carol" on the front of his right calf. On the front of his left calf was the image of an erect penis with wings, a tattoo Speck had referred to as his "West Texas Dickie Bird." The tattoo on his right forearm of a snake encircling a knife was blurred but still visible. The emblematic "Born to raise hell" tattoo on his left forearm had been burned off with a cigarette. Speck's brain was removed and preserved for possible additional study.

Dr. Alvin Ring, the pathologist at Silver Cross who performed the autopsy, removed Speck's brain and sent it for examination to Jan Leetsma, M.D., a neuropathologist and highly respected member of the Chicago Institute of Neurosurgery.

After the conclusion of the autopsy, Speck's body was not claimed. The Will County Coroner, Duane Krieger, spoke with one of Speck's sisters. She told Krieger that the family was afraid people would desecrate the grave if they knew where Speck was buried. Since no one claimed the body, Speck was cremated (except for his brain) and Speck's ashes were scattered in a location known only to Krieger, his chief deputy, a pastoral worker, and a Joliet newspaperman. Their secret about where the ashes were scattered in the Joliet area has never been revealed.

By this time, Dr. Leestma had received Speck's brain in formalin. He has an exemplary resume and served as neuropathology consultant to the Cook County Medical Examiner. After performing a gross examination of the brain, he photographed it. Dr. Leestma was struck by what he perceived as a strange anatomy of the hippocampal formations—the medial temporal lobe area involved in memory formation and located close to the amygdala which controls aspects of mood and aggression. When the doctor showed gross photos to other experts in neuropathology (without telling them the photos were of Richard Speck's brain) they agreed that there might be structural abnormality in the hippocampus and possibly the amygdalas.

Dr. Leestma had performed over twenty thousand brain examinations at the time he examined Speck's brain and he had not previously seen the anatomical abnormality he observed in Speck's brain. There has been a large body of scientific literature on the hippocampus and amygdalas and their relations to aggression and epilepsy since 1991. Case studies have been published regarding possible lesions in these areas that may be responsible for aberrant behavior in man and higher-functioning animals. "The literature is all over the place," Leestma told Martin in an interview for the updating of this book. "The structural abnormality may mean something and may mean nothing. That is why I wanted to send it to Dr. Marcel Mesulam at Harvard, the best expert in the world on the hippocampus," he said.

Dr. Leetsma did not complete sectioning the brain because he decided to send it to Dr. Mesulam and he did not want to damage the brain in any way so as not to interfere with further examination. For all Dr. Leestma knew, the Harvard expert might have wanted to do special studies he could not do. He very carefully packaged the brain to send to Harvard. What happened next is startling and frustrating. A secretary placed the brain and other packages in the anteroom of an office that was not secure. When the commercial courier came to pick up the items, they were gone. As best we know, someone stole them. Leestma searched in garbage cans all over the neighborhood and a reward was offered. Speck's brain had vanished and has never been recovered. The perversity of fate had prevented further scientific study of Speck's brain. In closing, Dr. Leestma said, "This seriously unfortunate occurrence is just one more enigma which surrounds Speck. Very, very frustrating and embarrassing." Speck had narrowly escaped the death penalty. After his death, he escaped having science study his brain.

Dr. Leestma authored the third edition of *Forensic Neuropathology* published by CRC Press in 2014. In chapter 9, titled Forensic Aspects of Complex Neural Functions, he wrote a section on the Richard Speck case. He wrote that Speck's "hippocampal formation appeared somewhat unusual in that there may have been a malformation of the Ammon's horn with a somewhat smaller than expected, possibly firm and gliotic, right hippocampus. The left temporal lobe appeared somewhat larger than the right, and there may have been a slight ventricular asymmetry, with the left lateral ventricle slightly larger than the right, an observation noted in the CT and MRI scans taken during Speck's life." He further found that "if a demonstrable abnormality in Speck's hippocampus could have been found, it would have added to the body of knowledge in which hippocampal lesions apparently can have behavioral effects; however, in a specific case, such correlations remain elusive."

Speck evaded the electric chair and lived to die of natural causes because the U.S. Supreme Court changed its philosophy on capital punishment. His 1967 date with the electric chair was automatically appealed to the Illinois Supreme Court, which affirmed his death penalty on November 22, 1968. However, on June 28, 1971, the U.S. Supreme Court reversed the affirmation, ruling that potential jurors opposed to capital punishment had been improperly excluded from Speck's and forty-one other death-penalty cases. In June 1972, the nation's High Court went a step further and ruled that the death penalty was unconstitutional. Accordingly, on September 20, 1972, the Illinois Supreme Court voided Speck's death sentence.

Speck was delighted at his continued good luck in evading the legal consequences of his murderous actions. On July 13, 1971, five years to the day from the time Speck had knocked on the nurses' town house door, the killer was evaluated by a prison psychiatrist. Although he was still locked up on death row in the separate Joliet branch of Stateville, Speck was well aware that only two weeks earlier the U.S. Supreme Court had rescued him from the electric chair. Speck had no complaints for the psychiatrist, who reported Speck to be "friendly, outgoing, and without psychosis or need of psychiatric intervention." Speck said, "Things are fine. I get along with everybody. They have a good bunch of guards working here. I'm in A-one shape." The killer spoke of boozing, blockbusters, redbirds, and yellowjackets, but with characteristic drollness added, "I've quit drinking lately."

Speck's resentencing was scheduled for November 21, 1972, in Courtroom A of the Peoria Courthouse. At one-thirty A.M. on November 21, Stateville Assistant Warden George Stampar went to Speck's cell on death row and awakened him for a special night flight on a single-engine plane to Peoria.

Speck, however, stubbornly refused to go, exclaiming, "I've never been on an airplane before and I'm not going to get on an airplane now." Stampar called for advice and was given an unequivocal order: "Get him on the fucking airplane!" Stampar decided to try diplomacy. "You'll be able to brag about riding in the governor's plane," he suggested. Speck flashed his hillbilly grin and agreed to board the plane for the short low-altitude flight.

When the two arrived at the Peoria County Jail, Speck announced, "I'm not going to eat any shit they try to feed me. They'll poison me." Anxious to accomplish his mission, Stampar agreed to go to an all-night restaurant and fetch Speck's requested order for a hamburger and Pepsi. At lunch the next day, Speck renewed his distrust of jail food and Stampar again obliged him with a hamburger and Pepsi from the same nearby grill.

By November 21, 1972, both Martin and Getty had left public office for private practice, and Judge Paschen had died. Getty, however, returned to Peoria to speak for one final time on behalf of his most infamous client. Speck sat impassively throughout the hearing, wearing a black suit and open white shirt and resting his head on his left hand. Presiding Judge Richard J. Fitzgerald of the Cook County Criminal Court imposed the new sentence—eight consecutive sentences of not less than 50 nor more than 100 years, for a total sentence of 400 to 1,200 years. The sentence ended with Speck's heart attack.

The killer had adjusted well to the numbing routine of life behind the walls. Retired Stateville warden Vernon Revis, who saw Speck daily for fifteen years, describes him "as just a big nothing doing time. All I've ever known him to do is paint walls and eat. He was a total loner who could have cared less if the sun rose or not. He just shuffled along, never in a hurry. The other inmates let him alone. I never saw him in the gym or the recreation yard or taking any classes. He'd talk forever to me, just shooting the breeze, if I'd let him. Most of the time he had a request—'Warden, can you get me a new shirt? Warden, can you get me a new radio?' He was never a threat to go over the wall and try to escape. It was impossible to get mad at him or he at you. Of course, all that might have changed if you gave him a six-pack and a knife." A prison guard once said of Speck, "If a tornado had blown this place down, Speck would have been the last man to leave."

Unsatisfying as it is, neither police work nor psychiatry ever fully penetrated the mystery of Speck's evil. Speck was not insane. Plain and simple, he was a sociopath, or psychopath—a man who acted out his hostility toward other people with no feelings of remorse. The American Psychiatric Association formally refers to this character trait as "antisocial personality disorder," but this label can only *describe* a person's past behavior; it cannot *explain* it. John J. Stamos, who headed the team of prosecutors who brought Speck to justice, says bluntly, "Who gives a damn about Speck's mental condition? He was simply a bad seed—a total rotter, a pig. He was bad when he woke up in the morning." Bill Martin and his colleagues never had to concern themselves with why Speck did it; they simply had to prove that he did. In his presentencing argument for the death penalty, Martin described Speck as a supremely selfish killer "who did what he wanted when he wanted, without regard for the consequences . . . we know this as the kind of evil that does not masquerade as insanity."

The preceding portrait of Speck's "numbing routine" in prison, his life as a "big nobody doing time," and as a man who steadfastly refused to confess his murders, a portrait widely believed at the time of his death in 1991, would be proven to be only part of his story.

In a video made by Stateville inmates in 1988 and smuggled out of prison as part of a money-making scheme, Speck was shown on camera as a long-time jailhouse queen who willingly offered himself as a sex object to the black gangbangers who ran Stateville, in return for protection and drugs. He also made, on camera, an absolute, unequivocal confession to his crime —without a trace of remorse or compassion for his victims and their loved ones.

The 1988 video, which eight years later found its way to Chicago TV anchor Bill Kurtis, would be seen by millions of stunned viewers in May 1996, on Chicago's WBBM-TV and on the A&E cable channel. It would also be shown to the Illinois State Legislature and would lead to prison reform in Illinois and an end to the inmates running the prison.

For the full story of Speck's prison video confession, see the special report following this section.

For twenty-five years, Corazon Amurao had a recurring nightmare: that Speck would come back and kill her. After the killer's death in 1991, she broke her self-imposed silence and spoke briefly about her night of horror.

"I think there was somebody up there who was hiding me from him," she said. "God was so nice." She dismissed Speck this way: "It seemed like he died so easy. I thought he should have died a long time ago . . . I feel relieved now that he is gone. I am OK now. Speck's death has lifted a great burden." In 1993, during an Oprah Winfrey show that launched the original publication of this book, Cora was on stage with prosecutor Bill Martin and her police friends and bodyguards from the time of the investigation and trial in 1966–1967. It was her only extended public interview. During a commercial break, she turned to Martin and said, "Oh, Bill, I don't know why God spared me!" She would later call her good fortune a "special gift from God."

In 2016, Cora is the spunky, happy matriarch of a loving extended family of more than one hundred relatives who live in the US, most of whom are in Virginia. Cora married her husband, Bert Atienza, an attorney, in the Philippines in 1969 and the couple and Cora's entire family came to the US that year to live. Cora initially worked as a critical care nurse at the Georgetown University Hospital in Washington, DC, and Bert started his own business as a real-estate broker. The couple settled in suburban Woodbridge, Virginia.

Cora is now retired and is the mother of two and grandmother of six. She and Bert, who now practices immigration law, split their time between their long-time home in Virginia and, since 2012, a new vacation home in Nevada.

Cora and Bert's son, Christian, a certified public accountant, is a senior director of finance and accounting for a large telecommunications company in Virginia. He and his wife have two sons and one daughter. The Atienzas' daughter, Abigail, is a nurse practitioner in family practice in Virginia at one of the nation's largest health networks, Kaiser Permanente. She married an American man, a high school classmate, and the couple has two sons and a daughter.

In a phone call from Bill Martin, followed by an exchange of emails, Cora recalled her long career as a nurse in intensive care at Georgetown University Hospital and later a similar high-pressure job in intensive care at the Veterans Administration Medical Center in Washington, D.C. She wrote that she babysits her grandkids once or twice a week and visits relatives in the Philippines every three years or so. One favorite relative in the Philippines is her cousin, Roger, who came to stay with Cora in Chicago in 1966–1967. One of Roger's daughters lives in Arizona and his eldest sister, also a nurse, and her family live in Chicago, giving Cora a reason to occasionally return to the city where she came to work in May 1966. She has never forgotten the prosecutor who helped her bring Speck to justice and honor the memories of her friends.

In one email, Cora wrote, "Bert and I have more than one hundred relatives living in Virginia—sisters, brothers, nephews, nieces, grandchildren. Most were born here in the US. My mother, father, and brother-in-law all died in Virginia. My father-in-law is alive at ninety-four—in good shape and still walking."

One email flashed back to 1966, before the murders. "I have a good memory of the nurses, when Merlita (Gargullo) cooked *adobo filipino and pancit*, and they came home from the hospital and smelled the food and they say it's good, so we invited them to join us to eat and they really like it. That was a good time that we had." The prosecution's star witness, who has outlived Richard Speck by twenty-five years and counting, wrote, "I have a normal healthy and happy life with Bert. As you know, I want to be happy all the time. Life is short and you do not know when you are going to die. It has been a long time since Speck died, but I still have some nightmares. . . . I guess I will not be able to forget that for the rest of my life. Every time I wake up in the morning, I thank God that I am still alive." She has fond memories of her slain classmates, "who were very nice and helpful to us, especially Nina (Schmale) and Pat (Matusek)."

Cora and Bert now escape the Virginia winters to stay at their vacation home in Nevada. Occasionally, the seventy-two-year-old Corazon Amurao Atienza can be seen with her husband in a Nevada casino, playing the penny slot machines and, especially, penny-ante poker, the game she learned while in protective custody back in 1966–1967 with her beloved police protectors—Steve McCarthy, Jim Concannon, and Jack Wallenda. The girl who beat the fatal odds fifty years ago can be recognized by her ready and unmistakable infectious laughter—and, whether she wins or loses at penny-ante poker—a smile that seldom leaves her face.

To honor her survival and mark the fiftieth anniversary of the crime, Cora agreed to have photos of her family taken in Virginia during Thanksgiving 2015 to be included in this book.

Immediately following this section, there are photos of Cora, her husband, their two children and their children's spouses, and their six grandchildren. It is the first time a photo of Cora, who values her privacy, has appeared in the media since 1966, when a photographer with a telephoto lens captured a shot of her as she left the Cermak Memorial Hospital after identifying Speck during hospital rounds she made with the medical team caring for the killer.

By the time of Speck's death in 1991, historical forces had transformed many of the key scenes in the killer's dark drama. And many of the key actors in the story and those most affected by the mass murders had for twenty-five years been trying to come to terms with the consequences.

Jeffery Manor is now a black neighborhood. The water fountain is still there in Luella Park, just behind the town house at 2319 East 100th Street. Young players practicing their moves on the nearby asphalt basketball court often stop for water and, straightening up, see exactly what Speck must have seen fifty years ago: the large picture window of the back, south-facing upstairs bedroom where four of the nurses slept. In one of the many ironies of the case, there is today a sign at the town house's back door reading: "Warning: We call police. This is a neighborhood watch area." In 1966, people did not think this way.

The former National Maritime Union Hall is now the Greater Morning View Church, and its front facade has been redone with swirls of inlaid stone. A mile to the east, most of the steel mills and ship repair yards have been closed.

The Shipyard Inn is now the Golden Shell, renamed by the new owner after a famous restaurant in her native Serbia. It is one of the few things on the Southeast Side that has actually improved with time. Asked recently about the building's notoriety, the owner promptly volunteered, "Oh, sure, Richard Speck slept here." She then conducted a tour of the upstairs narrow corridor and small rooms and pointed out room 7, the room where Speck had obtained his black pistol from Ella Mae Hooper on July 13, 1966, and the room from which he had walked out later that night, dressed in black, to kill.

The Raleigh Hotel, its insides gutted by a fire in 1983, has been restored and is now a complex of retail and commercial offices. A fashionable Mary Walter boutique occupies the two ground floors. The nearby Pink Twist Inn, where Speck spent the night after the murders drinking and whoring, has long since been torn down to make way for an enormous parking lot for the young people who flock to this area to visit the Hard Rock Café, the Rock 'n' Roll McDonald's, and the popular restaurants named after Chicago Bears coach Mike Ditka and former star player Walter Payton.

The Starr Hotel was torn down in 1982, and the former Skid Row neighborhood has been replaced by the three Presidential Towers—high-rise rentals for yuppies. Across the street is the Harold Washington Social Security Administration building—named in honor of the man who broke Richard J. Daley's political machine and became Chicago's first black mayor.

The Moraine-on-the-Lake ended up in bankruptcy and was torn down in 1971 to make way for a public park. Though the beach is in good condition, swimming is prohibited because of pollution. The Ramada Inn in Peoria, where the Cook County State's Attorney's Office set up shop in 1967, is now the Peoria Methodist Medical Center School of Nursing and its second- and third-floor rooms—where the prosecutors worked and slept—are now dormitory rooms for nursing students.

South Chicago Community Hospital remains, but it has been bought and absorbed by the Evangelical Health Systems chain. In 1966, the hospital's neighborhood was almost one hundred percent white, most residents being employed by the nearby

South Chicago steel industry, which had fifteen thousand workers. Today, the steel mills are a ghost town and the neighborhood
is fifty percent black, thirty percent Hispanic, and twenty percent white, mostly Polish and Serbo-Croatian.

The ten-thousand-dollar reward offered by South Chicago
Community Hospital for the capture of the nurses' killer was
awarded a few months after Speck was sentenced to death in
1967. Corazon Amurao received the lion's share—five thousand
dollars.

In 1967, Cora and the families of the eight slain nurses sued
the hospital for breaching its "custodial" responsibility. Attorney Casimir Wachowski, now retired, represented the families.
The hospital, fearing the emotionalism of a jury trial, settled
out of court for a figure that Wachowski, as a condition of the
settlement, swore never to divulge. However, it was, he says,
"very substantial."

Wachowski's legal theory was that since the hospital provided
a housemother, it had in effect assumed a custodial responsibility
for the nurses' safety, and because of the presence of the union
hiring hall and its rowdy types, should have provided better
security. He also sued the Shipyard Inn and Kay's Pilot House
under the Dram Shop Act, which holds tavern owners liable for
the actions of intoxicated patrons. Both suits were settled out of
court. Finally, he sued Speck himself, "from whom we got not a
penny." Wachowski allowed as to how he had written a "terrific
brief," but acknowledges, "You couldn't really blame the hospital. Who would ever have thought this would happen?"

Not the hospital. Retired hospital president Harlan Newkirk,
who in 1966 was an associate administrator, says, "We were all
completely devastated by what had happened. We were terribly
hurt by the lawsuit. These were our nurses and our friends. But
at the same time I can understand that the hospital was one of
the few targets at which the families could lash out."

Marvin Ziporyn, the psychiatrist who had been prepared to testify that Speck was insane, was expelled in 1992 from the Illinois Psychiatric Society and the American Psychiatric Association by vote of the APA Board of Trustees for "an ethical violation." The expulsions followed the action of the Illinois Department of Professional Regulation, which revoked Ziporyn's license to practice medicine and to prescribe medication.

Martin's former adversary, Public Defender Gerald Getty, appraises his most famous case by concluding, "Justice was served. The defendant got a trial that went all the way to the U.S. Supreme Court. During my nineteen years as a public defender, I made it a practice never to judge my clients. You have to represent all comers, and if you judge them, you cannot defend them. Speck told me that he didn't do it, or that if he did, he didn't remember it. I tried to prove that he wasn't at the scene on the night of the crime. Speck and I had a good relationship. He refused to come out into the courtroom unless he could first see me sitting there, waiting to defend him. Oh, sure, I got a lot of phone calls at three A.M. and a lot of threats by phone and mail, but it all went with the territory."

Detective Jack Wallenda remained enraged as long as Speck was alive. "If we had found him on the streets," Wallenda said, "he never would have come out alive. As for his attempt at suicide, well, hell, there wasn't enough bleeding for a blood test. Speck never showed any remorse. In fact, he was kind of cocky about it; he fancied himself a great stud. A jailer at Peoria told me once that Speck had told him, 'I hit those girls so fast that they never knew what happened.' On the wall of his cell he had pasted photos of the eight nurses. He may not have been proud of what he had done, but he sure as hell didn't appear to feel bad about it."

Until Speck's death, the people who had brought Speck to justice and the classmates and families of the slain nurses had to endure the agony of the killer's parole hearings. In 1976, Speck became eligible for parole and made his first and only appearance before the parole board. He was denied. Speck waived his right to appear at the annual hearings in 1977 and 1978, and the board denied parole each time. In 1978, it was decided that Speck's case would be reviewed every three years rather than annually, and the board subsequently denied parole in 1981, 1984, 1987, and 1990. The hearings were always held in early September, as the hot days of summer began to fade, and they always stirred up strong emotions.

For the bereaved classmates and relatives of the slain nurses, the parole hearings were an extended wake and an opportunity for minireunions. At the 1990 hearing, Judy Dykton Radzik, speaking for the South Chicago Community Hospital Class of 1966, told the parole board that she and the others were "living victims" who felt "insulted" by Speck's right to a hearing. Representing the State's Attorney's Office, Cook County prosecutor Wayne Meyer reminded the board that Speck "remains the yardstick by which all crimes are measured." Without comment, the board announced on September 10, 1990, that it was denying parole for Speck. His next hearing would have been in September 1993.

Speck's death changed all of that. "There's nothing to celebrate," Dr. John Schmale, brother of Nina Jo Schmale, told the *Chicago Tribune* after the killer's death. "There's no argument. There's no anything anymore. It's over. The families can finally relax." Jack Wilkening, who was fifty-four in 1991, was the brother of Pamela Wilkening, who at the age of twenty had been one of Speck's first victims. "It's morbid to say that you are glad someone is dead," Wilkening told the paper, "but I am relieved it's all over. It closes the door on a major portion of our lives. At least once a day I think about what happened. It never leaves you." When Wilkening called his mother, Lena, to give her the news, she responded, "Praise the Lord." She added, "If he had

gotten the electric chair, I would have pulled the switch myself."
Betty Jo Purvis, sister of victim Patricia Matusek and daughter
of the late Joe Matusek, said, "I'm sorry my father is not here to
see that he's gone. It certainly doesn't seem a bad enough end."
Joe Matusek had been a fixture in opposing parole for Speck,
attending the hearings even after he became too ill to walk and
had to be wheeled into the hearing room.

The people most directly affected by Speck's evil remain horrified by what he did to their lives. Marilyn Farris McNulty, the
older sister of Suzanne Bridgett Farris, lives with her husband
and three daughters in Oak Park, a suburb immediately west of
Chicago. In 1986, she and her family agreed to an extraordinary
interview published in the *Chicago Tribune Sunday Magazine* as
part of a cover story on the twentieth anniversary of the crime.

"I've never talked about this before," she said during the
interview, "and I'm not doing it now to simply say, 'Hey, world,
something terrible happened many years ago and some of us
are still alive to talk about it.' No, I want some good purpose to
come out of it. I want people to know that we were all totally
destroyed by this and that he—I still cannot bring myself to
say his name—that he killed more than Susie and the other
nurses. It should never be forgotten that he killed a little bit of
all of us."

The family—Marilyn Farris McNulty, her husband, Bob,
and daughters, Beth, then eighteen, and Peg, twenty—were
discussing the crime for the first time as a family. The oldest
daughter, Patricia, twenty-one, was at work. It was a very emotional time, and Marilyn Farris McNulty, who is tall and thin
like her younger sister was, and undoubtedly looks very much
like she would today, spoke in a grave, sad voice that dominated
the room. Her daughters and husband hung on her every word,
as for the first time they heard the raw feelings that had been
deeply suppressed.

"I didn't believe it then," she began, "and I still have trouble believing it now. Other than husband and wife, I think that the relationship between two sisters is one of the closest in the world. Susie was only a year younger than I, and we both were very well loved and very well protected by our parents. The first time I ever left Chicago was when I accompanied my husband, Bob, to an army base in Ohio. The first time Susie ever left home was when she moved into the town house in 1965. By 1966, Bob had just gotten out of the army and we were living in an apartment in Riverdale, Illinois.

"A neighbor had heard the news on the radio, and she told me, 'You'd better call your folks. Something's happened to Susie and the other nurses.' I had no idea what she was talking about. Then, I called Mom and Dad."

Momentarily, she broke off the interview. The memory of calling her parents and learning what had happened was too painful—even twenty years later. Marilyn McNulty allowed herself a good long cry and a chance to be comforted by her family. The reporter offered to end the discussion, but she wanted to resume.

"You know," she continued, "I used to have a photo of Susie in her nurse's cap that I kept in the living room. But visitors would always ask, 'Is that you?' I would say, 'No, that's my younger sister, Susie.' Then they would ask, 'Oh, at which hospital does she work?' And I would break down in tears. So, now I keep the photo up in the bedroom. It's easier that way.

"I'm still devastated. One year later or twenty years later, it's all the same. I guess I'll feel this way when they bury me in Mount Carmel. And my parents, I know that it shortened their lives. My mother always used to say, 'A mother should never live long enough to bury her children.' My mother was very stoical and could never talk about what had happened. Everyone said, 'What a brave woman.' She wasn't brave; she was totally destroyed. My dad died three and a half years later on the first day of his retirement; he was sixty-three. Mother died ten years later; she was sixty-six. They both died of a broken heart.

"When Susie died, my little girls were only eighteen months and six months. I had a job to do, but I was in a fog. For months, I couldn't seem to slip out of it. One day I was ironing and watching television, and somebody said something stupid about the murders, and I began to scream at the TV. Bob, who is about one thousand times stronger than me, turned off the TV. Patty was crying, and she needed a bottle. Life had to go on."

Her family of 1986 was now grown and raised—and sympathetically sitting beside her. Like his wife, Bob McNulty is tall and thin. He has graying hair, and at the moment, a worried expression. His main concern on that day was comforting his wife, but he had some definite memories of his own, too.

He said, "I was determined that this thing was not going to break us. We had our own family to raise. I was working shift work at Republic Steel, including some nights, and I took a cut in pay and transferred to days because Marilyn needed me home at night. We both were pretty broken up. The day of the murders I went down to the morgue to help identify Susie's body. The reporters were waiting for us, and I found it very difficult to fight my way through. Once inside, I saw a detective who was an old friend. He could tell that I was pretty shaken and he took me aside for a cup of coffee. This man has seen a lot, but on this day he appeared to be in a state of shock. . . . People simply did not know how to comprehend what had happened."

Bob McNulty paused at this remembrance. He tapped his feet, lit another cigarette, and resumed: "As for Speck, what a shock! I went down to Peoria for the trial thinking that I would see a man who was ten feet tall. What I saw was an ordinary jerk. He was transparent. You could look right through him—a man who was a loser and a jerk. He looked like the kind of guy who is a loser in work, a loser in love, a loser in life. He simply looked noninterested, as if he were always off somewhere else. There did not appear to be anything in him that was human or normal. In a way, it was a letdown. If he had looked like Darth Vader, I might have been able to focus my anger."

Other memories did anger him. "Right after the murders," he recalled, "some people were heard to say, 'Well, they—the nurses—must have been having a wild party or something.' How ironic. I don't think that I have ever seen nine young women who were any more committed or clean-cut than these women were. The unnaturalness of the crime is striking. I'm sure that the nurses must have thought, 'Hey, we have a drunk here and we need to quiet him down and get him out the door.' I'm sure that the women did not feel a sense of danger, until it was too late.

"During the trial, I lost interest in Speck. He just sat there with a glassy stare, a million miles away. I kept my eyes on the jurors. These were hard-nosed midwesterners and you could tell by the looks on their faces that they were horrified by what was being described."

Marilyn McNulty listened to her husband with great interest, nodding in sad agreement. She added, "When you've been hit by a billion-to-one shot, it scars your life. Ask my daughters. If they're ten minutes late coming home, I get very upset. When I took Patricia and Peg down to Charleston, Illinois, to begin college, I was a nervous wreck. On the ride home, I cried. We were raised in a loving, protective family in which our parents probably did not raise their voice at us more than two or three times. And then for Susie to run into someone like him. We were all destroyed, simply shattered. My brother, John, was only fifteen at the time, not quite a man but no longer a little boy. He was a youngster of few words and he's a man of few words, but one morning he simply woke up and broke down. He couldn't keep it inside any longer."

Beth McNulty, who in 1986 was about the same age as Suzanne Farris had been in 1966 and who also resembles her more than a little, was planning a career in pediatric nursing. She said, "I wasn't even born when Susie died, but still I miss her. It really makes me mad that this man took her away from us." Her older sister, Peg, concluded, "Mom and Dad are very strong people and they've weathered this. They've come through it stronger than ever, and I'm very proud of them. But we all cry for Susie and for what it did to us. The nurses were looking forward to a life of marriage and family and helping the sick, and it was all taken away from them."

After Speck's death, Marilyn McNulty reflected, "I'm grateful that I outlived him, but he had twenty-five more years of life than my sister had."

Members of the nursing Class of '66, now middle-aged women with daughters of their own who are as old as their slain classmates, always made it a point to attend the parole hearings—both to keep Speck in prison and to help their own healing. The memories of their slain classmates remain strong.

Judy Dykton Radzik says, "When my father walked me down the aisle for my marriage, when my husband took me to the hospital for the birth of our first child, I found myself crying and thinking, 'Why were my classmates deprived of these joys? Why did they have to die so young?' "

Karen Besida Geronovich says, "What really disappoints us is that the hospital never established a memorial for our friends. They are the forgotten ones, since all the attention goes to the killer. If it's the last thing we do, we want to see that a suitable memorial is created for our eight friends who died so young."

Tammy Sioukoff, now a nursing supervisor, shivers when she recalls the night of the crime. "How can I ever forget it?"

she asks. "Every time July rolls around and the weather turns hot and humid, I try to work overtime at the hospital to keep my mind off what happened. But it's so hard with all the talk about Bastille Day—July 14—and the publicity over the crime and so on. In 1966, we knew nothing about crime. There was no counseling provided to help us grieve—absolutely nothing.

"I still get very anxious in the summer. I like the short winter nights, but when the long hot summer nights roll around, I get very nervous. I refuse to sleep without the lights on. I don't even trust my husband—he sleeps too soundly. My own daughters think that I'm silly, that this type of thing could never happen to them. Well, people can sympathize with what happened, but you cannot empathize unless you went through it. Our friends were so very, very innocent and, yet, they suffered so dearly."

The president of the Class of 1966 is Ellen Harnisch Stannish, who is now a happily married mother and nurse in Florida. In 1986, after reading the *Chicago Tribune* article on the twentieth anniversary of the murders, she wrote a letter to the editor, explaining:

"I sat in my living room reading the article as if it were the first time I had read about it. I was crying, and I went to my bedroom where I sobbed until I was emotionally drained. I got up from my bed, looked at myself in the mirror, and said, 'My God, you look like you just got back from the funerals.'

"It was the first time that I had read such a detailed, intense account. It was too painful and too shattering and too scary to read twenty years earlier. As I read in 1986, I hurt so badly for my friends, imagining and feeling what terror they must have been experiencing at that time. I thought it odd that I was suffering for them . . . here it was twenty years later and I was still suffering for them. Their suffering is over and I'm still suffering. It was at that time that I really did my grieving for the 'town house,' as I refer to 'it.' Of course, I had profound grief at the time 'it' occurred, but I was so numb, so dazed, so confused, so lost.

"We understand things on one level and then we come to another level of understanding twenty years later. Now, I am forty and have children about as old as I was back then. Now, I have this maternal part of me that is grieving for my friends from a maternal point of view rather than as a peer. I was also grieving for myself—for my young twenty-year-old former self who had been so traumatized. We were so young, so innocent.

"Looking back, we were kind of like the 'forgotten children.' We were trained to be strong, competent, confident. Our leaders weren't equipped to deal with our emotional distress. As I look back, I realize that I had walked around in a fog then, going through the motions of life. I have mental snapshots of myself doing so, trying to figure out what the hell happened. We had to stay in class and do nursing work until September . . . I was consumed with grief and fear and confusion. I would look for my deceased friends in a crowd to confirm that this had just been a nightmare.

"I describe it as being 'shot out of a cannon.' One minute, I was a happy-go-lucky woman, on top of the world. I loved being in nurses' training. I loved my friends, the 'sisterhood,' the camaraderie. Time passed very slowly back then. Three years was a lifetime, and we went to class together, studied together, worked together, ate together, talked intimately about our families, our lives, our feelings. We shared our pains and our joys. It was a rather sheltered life, and most of us had minimal contact with friends outside of school, other than boyfriends. It was a time when we had to live in the dorm and abide by curfews.

"And, now, here we were, about to graduate and become R.N.'s. Cars were a privilege, and my parents had just got me my first car which I would pay for after graduation. I had a job at the University of Illinois with Sue Farris. I was being cut loose and I was ready to fly! I was already soaring, then—boom!—it was all over. All the excitement and joy were gone. Nothing had any meaning. My new car, my job, my plans, my life—all were irrelevant. One of my classmates told me, 'You know, I never told them I loved them.' I guess the only thing that seemed important anymore were the people in our lives, having been made grossly aware of this by our losses. So many of us clung to each other and the other people in our lives.

"A number of us, myself included, got married soon there-after. Would we have done so had our lives not taken this turn? We needed protection, security, nurturing, and understanding. I was afraid to sleep alone, to drive, or to go out at night. While we were still in school, a number of us would all go to one person's house after school and wait there until our parents came home from work before we would go home. One year later, when I was living in an apartment building, I would be terrified when I heard other tenants enter the building, or people walk outside. When I had children and saw their dolls on the floor, I would see them as bodies.

"Did I ever talk to anyone about this? Of course not. One night, when I heard someone talking outside, in the midst of my crazed fear, I said to myself, 'You have got to get a hold on yourself or you are going to go crazy.' By now, it was not only myself I had to protect, but also my baby.

"And, so, I got a hold on myself. I took a deep breath, broad-ened my shoulders, got stronger and harder and marched through life. What did I do with all that fear? I denied it and repressed it. That's the only thing I knew how to do. And, so, for years it rolled around in me and recycled itself.

"When I read the *Tribune* article, it triggered my need to ventilate, to be heard, . . . I work in a psychiatric-related field of nursing that facilitates and necessitates personal growth, healing, and awareness of our emotional and spiritual natures in connection with the physical. So, I am fortunate to have the opportunity for counseling and growth groups. There was nothing of this nature available to us back in 1966. When something horrible of this magnitude happens today, the corporation or the university or the community responds immediately to the victims by sending in therapists. Our hospital sent in a psychiatrist once to talk to our class as a group. I don't remember what he said. I think that someone told me later that he invited us to come back to him individually if we needed help. But who would see a psychiatrist back then? It just wasn't a part of our consciousness.

"In 1987, I had some therapy to help grieve. After the parole hearing that year, a group of our classmates got together for a minireunion. I surprised myself and broke into tears and felt foolish about doing it, but, still, I seemed to be much more healed than many of my classmates. Their emotions were so raw, and many of them still cannot talk about it at all. After the 1990 parole hearing, a small group of us had a 'process group for closure' to deal with our feelings. One month later, I entered therapy with a diagnosis of 'posttraumatic stress disorder.' This counseling has been very helpful. . . .

"Somehow in tragedy we 'middle-aged women' have become survivors together and we have sealed a permanent bond. No wonder Mr. Wilkening didn't recognize me when I spoke with him at the 1990 parole hearing. He told me, 'Pam was so young when she died.' I didn't realize that I had become middle-aged. What a rude awakening! Two months later, we held a 'middle-aged class reunion' in Florida, wondering, 'Is that us?' "

A long overdue memorial to the eight nurses was created in 1999 when producer Greg Kolack and playwright Rebecca Gilman presented the world premiere of Rebecca Gilman's *The Crime of the Century*, a three-act stage play adapted from this book. It played before sold-out audiences and received rave reviews from November 3—December 12, 1999, at the Circle Theatre in the Chicago suburb of Forest Park.

Kolack, who conceived, developed, and directed the play, wrote in his director's notes:

"In 1966, mass murder was practically incomprehensible. We slept with our doors and windows open. We trusted strangers. We felt safe in our own neighborhoods. In four and a half hours, Richard Speck changed all that in a neighborhood where a major crime might be a cat stuck in a tree. Speck chose eight women who had totally dedicated their lives to helping mankind and murdered them in the safety of their own home.

"I was nine years old in July 1966, yet I remember many of the details as if it were yesterday. However, it wasn't until I read Dennis and Bill's book that I realized the remarkable dedication of hundreds of people to bring Speck to justice. More importantly, though, the book gave faces and lives to the victims. They were no longer the eight nurses; they were someone's daughter, sister, fiancé, friend. That is the story that is rarely told."

The retelling of the story on stage made a powerful impression on the entire cast and crew, Kolack reflected in an interview with Breo.

On a visit to the warehouse that stored the physical evidence of the crime, Kolack notes, the cast saw the bloody clothes and personal possessions of the nurses, including a simple fortune-cookie fortune in the wallet of Valentina Pasion which read, "You will live long and enjoy life."

During rehearsals that night, he continues, Seema Sueko, the actress who played Corazon Amurao, burst into tears. Kolack and the stage manager comforted her with hugs. "It was a poignant moment," he recalls. "The experience was too much for her."

Several cast members and even Kolack's brother, Stephen Kolack, who helped re-create the town house model, had nightmares after the intense rehearsals. "What are you doing to me?" Stephen Kolack asked his brother.

On another occasion, Kolack said, he had to cope with a phone call from a very agitated Dr. John Schmale, who is very protective of the memory of his sister, Nina Schmale, and was concerned about the impact of the developing play.

"I assured him our treatment would be respectful to the memory of the nurses," Kolack said, "and invited him to attend our rehearsals. Not only did he come to Chicago from his home in downstate Urbana, Illinois, but he attended a rehearsal and, afterward, cried and hugged the actress who portrayed his sister. We all went out for pizza and beer that night and he became a good friend of mine—we've stayed at each other's homes—though he could never bring himself to sit through an actual performance."

Helping the actors develop the right feel for playing the key figures in the manhunt, investigation, and trial, Kolack noted, was welcome coaching from the actual participants in the case, who attended multiple rehearsals to demonstrate the body language, mannerisms, and voice inflections of those being portrayed.

For example, Martin spent several rehearsals with Seema Sueko, explaining Cora's demeanor and movements during her trial testimony; he also worked with the actor who played him to rehearse how he presented the closing arguments. Co-prosecutor George Murtaugh demonstrated the mannerisms of various trial witnesses. Jack Wallenda and Jim Concannon imitated the voices and speaking patterns of several cops and detectives. Federal judge James B. Zagel did the same for the Speck trial judge, Herbert Paschen, and defense attorney Gerald Getty.

These same real-life actors in the drama, plus many of their colleagues, attended many performances of the play, never without tears.

Kolack said the play enjoyed a "perfect storm" of success: "We had this incredibly famous crime, set in Chicago, that featured a script by the internationally acclaimed playwright, Rebecca Gilman, who was just beginning her rise to fame, and it was being staged at the newly prominent Circle Theatre, and would receive great reviews. The pre-opening buzz was tremendous."

Playwright Gilman kept Speck nearly invisible and used each of the nurses, in turn, as the narrative voice. Kolack and the actresses meticulously re-created the women's appearances from photos that were projected at the rear of the stage.

Theater critic Chris Jones wrote in the *Chicago Tribune*: "All of the performers are excellent. So, even though the nurses talk to the audience about such typical preoccupations as boyfriends, engagements, and family members, the lost potential of their lives hits you like an oncoming train." He adds, "Since every event in the investigation takes place under the watchful eye of one of the nurses, the play makes a very powerful statement about accountability to victims."

Critic Hedy Weiss, writing in the *Chicago Sun-Times*, praised the performance of Seema Sueko as the heroic Corazon Amurao. "Seldom has an actress had the opportunity to seize the stage . . . as Sueko, who for close to twenty minutes stands beside a large model of the town house and leads us minute by minute through her night of unimaginable horrors. And we follow her—riveted, mesmerized, revolted."

As the stunned audience filed out on opening night into the theater's lobby, surrounded by a large gallery of enlarged photographs showing key locations of the crime, conversations could be heard about the nurses and their haunting faces of loss. The play received four Joseph Jefferson Awards in 2000 for outstanding achievement for production (the play itself); director (Greg Kolack); actress in a principal role (Seema Sueko); and new adaptation (Rebecca Gilman).

Classmate Judy Dykton Radzik, the nurse who first heard Cora's screams of terror and led her back from the ledge of the town house, commented after watching the play, "I finally have closure."

Kolack adds, "We had a record two hundred actors audition for a role and everyone in the cast told me that this play was their greatest experience as a performer. And, every year on the July 14 anniversary, we all post on Facebook about our memories." Every anniversary, Kolack himself places flowers on the graves of the nurses who are buried in the Chicago area and on the lawn of the town house, where the owners have no idea what happened on July 14, 1966.

In his director's notes, Kolack concludes: "For us, this has been much more than a theatrical experience. It has been a profoundly human experience. We present this story in memory of Pat, Nina, Valentina, Pam, Suzanne, Mary Ann, Merlita, and Gloria."

Recently, to mark the fiftieth anniversary of the crime, family and friends of the eight nurses established a Facebook page at Ournursesmemorialassn.com to honor their memory. Readers are invited to post comments.

● ● ●

On a hot sticky day in June 1991, Bill Martin and his coauthor Dennis Breo drove to a dark county building on the West Side of Chicago. There, in a small dusty, stale locked room on the sixth floor, is kept some of the evidence from the Speck prosecution. The killer's trusty tan vinyl suitcase is still there, looking as good as new. A pink handwritten inventory slip records the suitcase's overflowing contents—the remnants of Speck's traveling wardrobe. The suitcase was opened and sitting right on top, neatly folded, was the black corduroy jacket with rayon lining, still ready for fresh wearings. Holding it up for a moment, Breo observed, "He must have been hot wearing this on that July night."

Martin and Breo left the small room and walked out into the waiting sunlight. A child was skipping through the spray of an open fire hydrant, the same event that had helped set off the racial riots in 1966. Martin was glad to be out of the dusty room. While there he had the eerily uneasy sensation of feeling he was in the presence of the killer. It was the same feeling that he had experienced back in 1966 when he had stood in the upstairs bedrooms of the tiny town house and stepped around the congealed blood on the floor. Seeing the artifacts of Speck's monstrous crime, now locked away in this dumpy warehouse, brought home the banality of a man whose incredibly evil deed on a hot summer night some twenty-five years earlier had murdered the American sense of innocence and had redefined forever the landscape of crime. The forces that drove Speck remain unfathomable.

Marilyn Farris McNulty has the last word: "Nothing will bring Susie and the others back. The passage of time helps, but what happened on July 14, 1966, turned our worlds upside down. I wish that we all could have stayed the way we were on July 13, 1966."

PART VI
A PORTRAIT OF EVIL: SPECK'S CONFESSION

During the trial, the State had proven Speck's guilt by introducing four classic principles of proof: *circumstantial evidence*—Speck was near the town house before the murders; Corazon's *eyewitness identification*; the irrefutable *physical evidence* of Speck's three fingerprints on the second-floor south-bedroom door; and his *flight* from the southeast side culminating in his attempted suicide, all evidence of a *consciousness of guilt*.

The only gap in the state's proof, though not necessary to prove a criminal case, is that the prosecution lacked a valid, voluntary *confession*. A statement by the defendant that revealed evidence only the killer would know is the gold standard of proof. An uncoerced, voluntary confession, free from the medications administered to Speck at Cook County Hospital, would offer a dimension to the case that answered unresolved questions about the killer's actions in perpetrating the crime.

Before the trial, Speck told his lawyer, Gerry Getty, and jail psychiatrist Marvin Ziporyn that he had taken drugs at the Shipyard Inn. He claimed he "blacked out" and had no recollection of going to the town house and murdering eight young women. His persistent account to Ziporyn was that he had no memory of the murders.

Everyone, including those closely involved in the case, knew Speck never confessed to the crimes. When his ashes were spread across the Joliet countryside during the Christmas season of 1991, all hope of a confession floated into the winter air.

At various times after the trial ended, acclaimed Chicago TV anchor Bill Kurtis interviewed Bill Martin about the case for news broadcasts and for the A&E cable network. In 1996, Kurtis called Martin and asked if he could film an interview with Martin in his law office. Although Speck had been dead for five years, he still was an object of public interest. Martin agreed. After the interview was filmed, Martin walked Kurtis to the elevator. Kurtis said casually, "When you have time, I'd like you to come to my office. I want to show you something." Martin assumed Kurtis was being a nice guy and would treat Martin to spectacular footage Kurtis had filmed of an obscure part of the world he had visited during his exotic travels. Kurtis's studios were at the north end of downtown, an area Martin had no professional reason to visit. He forgot the invitation. A week or two later, Mike Harvey, then Kurtis's producer, called Martin. "Bill would like you to drop by our office. He would like to show you something." Martin said he would try to visit the studio.

The demands of his practice distracted Martin from the Kurtis invitation until Mike Harvey called a second time. Martin realized that there must be more to the visit than an interesting display of Kurtis' world travels. He and Harvey agreed on a date and Martin went to Kurtis' office. It was well-appointed with striking artifacts from around the world. Martin did not have a chance to examine the memorabilia. Kurtis quickly stood up and said, "I want to show you something and then ask you a question. There is something we have to be sure about." He walked Martin down a corridor to a door that opened into a large room as black as a coal mine. Martin glimpsed a series of chairs leading up to a projection booth in the dim light. He was in a movie theater. Kurtis and Harvey were in the room.

Immediately, the first image appeared on the large screen. There sat Richard Speck, much heavier than he was in 1966, dressed in paint-smeared clothes. His face was ugly, puffy, and pockmarked, his ragged blond hair disheveled, and his eyes, as always, revealed nothing. He was sitting in a chair, leaning forward, and seated next to him was a slender, younger black man wearing aviator sunglasses, his arms akimbo, slouched backward against a wall. His name was Ronzelle Larimore. The third person in the room was not visible and remained anonymous. He was operating a hand-held black-and-white video camera with audio capability.

In a sick parody of *60 Minutes*, the off-stage cameraman asked questions that Speck and, occasionally Larimore, answered. The video was slightly grainy but clearly visible. The audio was very good. The angle of the camera made it impossible to determine what kind of room the three prisoners were in. It had no bunk beds and was too large to be a prison cell. For the prisoners to have a video camera, a "studio," and all the time they wanted to produce a "show" suggested that the inmates were running the asylum. They displayed no fear of detection by guards. At Stateville, in December 1988, it was a case of "anything goes."

Kurtis had prepared a summary transcript of the interview and, subsequently, gave Martin a copy. The "interview" is highly disorganized. Questions and answers jump from subject to subject, back and forth, up and down, without rhyme or reason.

This partial transcript of the video has been edited by Martin, insofar as possible, to group subjects together so that the interview is as easy to understand as possible. Under the best of circumstances, the failure of the interviewer (marked as "I") to stick with a subject makes it difficult to follow the audio in a logical way. "I" is off camera, asking questions like a Stateville parody of Charlie Rose. "S" is Speck, and "L" is Ronzelle Larimore, another inmate and Speck's gay lover, or, in prison vernacular, "main ride." The off-camera interviewer, another black inmate, was also one of Speck's "rides." The dialogue began. All quotes in boldface were so typed in Kurtis's original transcript.

The comments in italics interspersed throughout the interview are Martin's critique of the Speck interview, sorting out the truth from the lies, the true confession from the macho boasting. Martin also cites the evidence that proves when Speck is untruthful and the evidence that corroborates the truthfulness of his full confession. The parts of the interview not included here are, in Martin's informed opinion, either excessively pornographic or irrelevant to Speck's account of the crime and his confession. The sections of the interview that have been omitted are marked in the following transcript with a series of xxxxxxxxxxxxx which indicate that an unnecessary portion of the Kurtis summary transcript has not been reproduced.

I: What is your name?
S: Richard Speck.

Speck's slow southern drawl was unmistakable. Martin had not heard it often, but he had heard it before the trial and it was unforgettable.

L: Ronzelle Larimore.
I: You all in love with each other?
L: Yeah.
I: Are you, Rich?
S: Absolutely.
I: Where were you born at?
S: Kirkwood, Illinois.
I: When was you born?

S: December 6, 1941.

I: How old are you now?

S: Forty-seven.

I: How long have you been locked up?

S: In July (1989), it will be twenty-three years.

What followed was a discussion of why Speck and Ronzelle loved each other. The interview contains several colloquies in which Speck brags about how many homosexual encounters he has had in Stateville. Speck frequently boasted about how much he enjoys having sex with black men and how he wants to have sex every day.

I: About how many people have you had sex with since you have been locked up?

S: Oh God, I can't count that high. (Laughter)

I: If you were going to kill yourself, what would you do?

S: Get (expletive deleted) to death. (Laughter) It would take him two weeks to get the smile off my face . . .

I: Someone said you have real titties. Do you?

S: Yeah.

I: Let me see them.

A grotesque visual spectacle followed. Speck stood up and removed the layers of his house painter clothes, stripping down to blue silk women's panties. His naked chest revealed that he had grown nearly full-size women's breasts. They were saggy and unnatural. The cold-blooded killer had found a way to turn his flabby body into a monstrosity, a sickening ersatz imitation of a woman.

Why would a white man from Dallas transform himself into a constantly available sex object for prison-hardened black gang-bangers? Some who have seen the video feel that Speck was punished in prison by being constantly degraded as a sex object. Martin disagrees.

Speck was as shrewd as an alley rat. He knew that he was the most likely target in the prison to be shivved, or stabbed to death with a prison-made knife. Richard Loeb, of the infamous murdering duo of Leopold and Loeb, who killed fourteen-year-old Bobby Franks in 1924 for the thrill of it, had been shivved in Joliet in 1936. His killer became a hero and was found not guilty in less than an hour. Speck cleverly morphed himself into a corruption of a female body so he could trade sex for protection. Speck's primitive instincts paid off. The black brothers protected him every day as "the drunken painter of Stateville" ambled about the prison, painting walls. No one harmed him.

How did he change his flaccid male body into a freakish "woman" whom the gangbangers who ran Stateville would want to have sex with?

How was Speck able to pervert nature? In 1988 Stateville, contra-band of every kind was not hard to sneak into the institution by visitors and bribed guards. If the interviewer could get a hand-held video/ audio camera into the joint and find a room to film a video without fear of interruption, how difficult would it have been for Speck to get the hormones that would enable him to sprout female breasts? The video also showed Speck snorting large amounts of cocaine. Cocaine and pot and ingredients for making prison hooch were regularly smuggled into Stateville.

I: Can't stand them titties.

S: No, I love them. I pet them every night before I go to sleep. I got nothing I'm ashamed of.

I: Do you use drugs?

S: No.

L: You lying (expletive deleted). He uses all types of drugs. He'd snort up a root. He even snorted up some Sudafed one time trying to get high. But when you stop bullshitting, he's the best wine-maker around.

I: Do you like your step-father?

S: No.

I: Why?

S: I hated him.

I: Do you enjoy sex with blacks or whites?

S: I haven't had sex with too many whites. I think about three whites in my lifetime. That should answer your question.

I: What year was you locked up?

S: July 1966.

I: What that date today?

S: 19 of December 1988.

I: About how many people have you had sex with since you've been locked up?

S: Oh God, I can't count that high. (Laughter)

I: What's you locked up for?

S: Eight counts of murder.

I: Did you kill them?

S: Sure I did.

I: Why?

S: It just wasn't their night.

xxxxxxxxxxxxxxxxxxxxxxxxxxxxx

Speck's heartless and spiteful blood-curdling words betray the monstrosity of his evil. It is beyond comprehension that a human being could be absolutely devoid of contrition or remorse. For once, he has told the truth and unequivocally admitted that he killed the eight nurses. He jettisoned his phony blackout excuse so that the truth would make money for his rides and protectors in prison.

I: Is he crazy?

S: No.

L: He told me somebody spit on him.

I: What happened?

S: That's what set it all off. I was on acid, drugs. At one point I was spit on in the face. She said she was going to pick me out in a line up. I went off and hit her in the chest with the knife. There was two more there, so I offed them. Wound up trying to kill off all the witnesses.

Mary Ann Jordan and Suzanne Bridget Farris, who had been out shopping and then looking at bridal books in the town house down the alley, walked into the northeast bedroom of the townhouse at 2319 East 100th Street at 12:30 a.m. Speck was preparing to rape Pamela Wilkening, whose hands were tied behind her back and whose mouth was plugged by strips of bed sheet to prevent her from screaming during the sexual assault. Unless there is physical corroboration, it's impossible to tell whether Speck is lying or telling the truth throughout the video. The physical evidence showed that Suzanne Farris had eighteen stab wounds in her chest and back and was strangled with a nurse's stocking. Lying next to her was Mary Ann Jordan, who was on her back and had been stabbed three times in the chest, once in the left eye, and once in the neck. The manner in which the two nurses were murdered strongly indicates that Speck suddenly and viciously killed them without first tying them up. He had begun his murderous frenzy to eliminate witnesses.

I: Did you carry a gun on the street?

S: Yeah, a .25 automatic.

I: Did you have a gun on the night of the killing?

S: Yeah, the police got it.

I: Why didn't you use the gun? Why did you use the knife?

S: Cause it makes too much noise. I was in no shape to run and the knife was quiet.

I: Did you go into the door with the gun?

S: Yeah, I went to the door with the gun and the knife.

L: He was going to steal some shit.

S: All I wanted to do is just a burglary. It started off as a burglary. Then all hell broke loose.

Speck's claim that all he wanted to do was a burglary is contradicted by several facts. After he herded all the nurses who were home at the time of his entry into the back bedroom, he ushered each one at gun point to go to their purses and give him what money they had. Were it his intention to steal their money, Speck had already completed that crime and could easily have left the townhouse. Instead, he tied up the six nurses in the south bedroom and then tied up Gloria Davy when she entered the second-floor bedroom where the six nurses were being tied. Speck now had what his sex-crazed mind desired: a group of women whom he could rape.

Speck is lying when he claimed that he was only going to commit a burglary. He knew there were young women in the townhouse from watching it when he was outside of the union hiring hall earlier in the week. If all he wanted to do was commit a burglary, he could have done it a lot closer to the Shipyard Inn. Speck was lazy and it would have taken him much effort to walk over a mile and back to and from the crime scene. He deliberately made this trip because he knew there were unprotected women in the town house. He took the gun, the knife and the extra T-shirts because he had sexual assault as his ultimate objective.

I: Have you ever tried to commit suicide?
S: No, that's bullshit. That's propaganda stuff that Gerald Giddy (sic) used in the courtroom to try to get sympathy from the jurors so they wouldn't give me the death sentence.

I: Were you high on drugs when you caught your case?
S: Yeah. But it was no excuse. I'd a done it sober. That bitch spit in my face. Hey.

Speck said he wasn't drunk yet claimed he was high on acid and drugs. Speck's modus operandi throughout his prison confession was to intersperse the truth with lies. When he tied up Corazon, a trained nurse, she looked at his eyes. She was familiar with the appearance of the eyes of people under the influence of drugs. Speck's eyes were normal. He had walked over a mile to get to the townhouse. He had pried off the screen to get in the kitchen door. He was able to calm the nurses with his steady demeanor. He handily tied up all the nurses in the back bedroom. He was able to cut bed sheets into strips and carefully tie each one while keeping his gun and his knife close to him. His behavior was consistent with a person who was not high on drugs. His actions were purposeful and consistent with sobriety. Speck cunningly chose what parts of his jailhouse interview would be truthful and what would be lies. Many of his lies occurred when he indulged in his trademark macho boasting. He wanted to impress his audience on how tough he was. Take away his gun and his knife and he was a quivering coward.

I: How far did you go in school?

S: Tenth grade.

I: Is it true you were born the day before Pearl Harbor?

S: Yeah.

I: Now you know Pearl Harbor is when the Japs bombed. You think that affected you in any way as far as the bombing is concerned. Make you insane or something?

S: I was born up here in Illinois and they blew the hell out of Hawaii. The day I was born all hell broke loose the next day. Hasn't stopped since.

xxxxxxxxxxxxxxxxxxxxxxxxxxxxx

I: Do you have panties and a bra in prison?

S: Yeah.

L: You got lots of that shit.

xxxxxxxxxx

I: Do you believe in God?

S: I'm God.

I: Do you believe in the devil?

S: I'm the devil. I believe in myself.

I: What's your religion then?

S : Mine. Hypocrite, Baptist, all that bullshit that people's in. All church is something people afraid of dying think they are going to heaven.

XXXXXXXXXXXXXXXXXXXXXXXXXXX

I: How do you feel after killing those ladies?
S: Like I always felt. Had no feelings. If you're asking if I felt sorry . . . no.

XXXXXXXXXXXXXXXXXXXXXXXXXXX

I: How you made 'em strip.
S: How I made them strip! I stuck the (expletive deleted) pistol underneath her jaw and cocked it and said, "Get naked, bitch." (Laughter)
L: Did nine (sic) of them get away?
S: One did, that's why I'm sitting here.
L: That's the one you didn't see, huh.
S: Yeah. If none of them got away, I wouldn't be sitting here. I mean it's a hell of a thing. Goddamnit, I ain't going to cry or feel ashamed, sorry, or all that crazy shit. What's done is done.
L: I can understand that shit.
S: Life goes on.
L: According to society they gonna put you in for life. They figured you gonna pay, huh?
S: Yeah, but if they only knew how much fun I was having. They'd a turn me loose.

Among the depraved combination of truth and lies, Speck, always the macho and unrepentant murderer, told the interviewer that it takes three minutes and much strength to strangle a person. This was more bragging by Speck's about his supposed strength and revealed his complete lack of conscience, recorded forever on the video. His persistent previous claims of amnesia were false, as the prosecutors always believed. He knew everything he did in the townhouse and he had absolutely no sorrow for the lives he had ruined.

At one point during the viewing of the video, Kurtis asked Martin. "Is that Speck?" Without hesitation, Martin replied, "Yes, that's Speck. No one else on earth looks like him." Martin now knew why Bill Kurtis was anxious to have him come to the studio. Kurtis had to be certain Speck was the man in the video. Martin had no doubts in confirming Speck's identity.

The video did not surface publicly until 1996, when Kurtis came into possession of it, eight years after it was made and five years after Speck's death. It has never been revealed how he acquired it. A logical inference is that the anonymous lawyer who got the tape from an inmate as a fee was never able to sell it. For eight years, no one knew about the prison confession except the participants in the money-making scheme.

After the validation of the prison video by Speck's chief prosecutor, Bill Martin, things moved rapidly. Kurtis's production company repackaged the prison-made video into a polished presentation. Parts of it were broadcast on Chicago's WBBM-TV over six nights during sweeps week of May 1996, followed by a longer version of the video on A&E's *Investigative Reports*. All these broadcasts were heavily hyped to millions of stunned viewers.

The *Chicago Tribune* described the jailhouse confession tape as a "bizarre mixture of talk show, freak show, and hardcore pornography." Having been made unmistakably aware of the sordid culture of Stateville, the Illinois State Legislature promptly invited Kurtis to show the tape before both houses in Springfield.

Kurtis came prepared to screen the full two-hour prison video before a packed audience. The legislature stopped the show when Speck began to have oral sex with his lover, "Honey Bun" Larimore. The lawmakers had seen enough.

Subsequently, the legislature ordered a severe crackdown on the Illinois Department of Corrections (DOC). The pressure put on the DOC by the state legislature led to major reforms which, when implemented, ended the years of allowing an inmate-run prison system.

So, beyond the hoopla over the prison video, two meaningful things were clear. Finally, Speck had made an absolute, unequivocal confession to his evil murders. And, ironically, the mass murderer had contributed to a much-needed and long-overdue reform of the Illinois prison system.

Bill Kurtis's typed note at the end of the first page of his summary transcript states that the prison video was clandestinely removed from Stateville in an attempt to raise money for a lawyer for a gangbanger's legal fees. Kurtis further wrote, "A book was contemplated and the video was created to prove Speck's total cooperation in the venture."

The entire venture was too horrific to lead to a book. If such trash had been written, it would have been comprised of Speck's confession, his lies and complete fabrications, his perpetual boasting, and his cold-blooded lack of remorse. Despite his lies, Speck had said enough to make a full confession to the murders. The final chapter of the evil story had been completed by Speck's voluntary confession. The magnitude of his total lack of a conscience showed the world the full reality of the evil man who slaughtered eight nurses, eight young women who had dedicated their lives to helping others. The Speck case had come to its terrifying close.

Martin's reaction to Speck from the first time he saw him at County Hospital on July 17, 1966, and throughout the investigation and trial, had been one of professional detachment. He could not have done his job if he allowed himself to react to Speck emotionally. He could not afford to hate the killer. He had to take a neutral position to avoid having his feelings interfere with the job of trying the case. Not until his closing argument could he release his feelings about the twentieth century's first mass murderer.

After he watched the prison video twenty-nine years after the end of the trial, Martin was appalled by Speck's total lack of contrition and his inhuman braggadocio, spoken without one word of regret. Indeed, Speck was pleased with himself for his consummately evil murders.

Previously, Martin had never had an emotional reaction to Speck. He couldn't afford to. Martin had prosecuted and defended hundreds of criminals. He never encountered one who didn't have at least a single socially redeeming trait, no matter how slight. Speck's heartless confession sickened him. This was the first time he had reacted to the killer viscerally, the first time he encountered a murderer who lacked a single ounce of humanity.

He dreaded the realization that the families of the nurses would have to watch this revolting pornography. And pornography it was. Bill Kurtis thanked Martin and was grateful because Kurtis, for the first time, was able to obtain a positive identification of Speck on the screen. Martin quickly left the studio, shaking like he had never shaken before. His hands were shaking, his legs were wobbling, and his insides were churning. He couldn't wait to get away from the chamber of horrors he had witnessed, and to step outside and breathe the fresh air.

POSTSCRIPT

Expert commentary
by William J. Kunkle, chief prosecutor of serial killer
John Wayne Gacy

Robert Piest was a fifteen-year-old sophomore at Maine West Township High School on December 11, 1978. His home was in Des Plaines, Illinois, but his part-time job was located in Park Ridge, Illinois. He worked evenings at a pharmacy owned by the Torf brothers. He was trying to save money for college and especially, for a car. Since he had none, his mother Elizabeth would pick him up at the end of the school day and drive him to his job in Park Ridge.

December 11 was Elizabeth Piest's birthday. There was to be a big family dinner and birthday celebration at their home when Robbie got home from work. Elizabeth drove to the pharmacy a little early, at about nine o'clock, to bring them home as early as possible. At about nine-fifteen, Robbie ran out the front door of the pharmacy throwing on his jacket and hollering to his mom that she should wait for him. He said he was going to talk to a contractor about a job.

He never came back.

Over the course of the first twenty-four hours after Piest's disappearance, the Des Plaines Police Department learned that the "contractor" was John W. Gacy, a general light contractor who had previously done remodeling work at the pharmacy and was present there just before Piest left. During the next week they received oral and written denials from Gacy that he had met or talked to Robert Piest. They obtained a warrant to search Gacy's house and vehicles on December 13, 1978, and executed a search on that date. They recovered evidence linking Robert Piest to Gacy's home at 8213 Summerdale Avenue in the unincorporated Norwood Park Township. They also found evidence regarding a young man named John Szyc, who had been an employee of Gacy's and had disappeared on January 20, 1976. Also seized were handcuffs, ropes, chains, other restraint devices, as well as sexual and drug paraphernalia. They took numerous photographs inside the house that proved extremely useful in witness preparation and as evidence at trial. They even photographed the dirt crawl space under the house, plainly showing the lime that had been spread over the area, which was very muddy from poor drainage and had a musty odor. There was no evidence of recently disturbed soil and they had no authority in the warrant, or otherwise, to dig for evidence of Piest's possible abduction.

Gacy was put under twenty-four-hour surveillance from the 13th until his arrest on December 21, 1978.

Much more was learned about John Gacy over that week. In addition to John Szyc, two other young men working for Gacy's construction crew had gone missing. John Butkovitch had disappeared July 31, 1975 and Gregory Godzik on December 12, 1976. Gacy had been interviewed by officers from two different Chicago Police areas and Park Ridge, Illinois, and had not been regarded as a suspect in any "foul play."

The Des Plaines investigation and Gacy's interaction with the surveillance officers was beginning to paint a picture of a man who was much more than the gregarious and workaholic contractor known for his self-promoting summer theme parties, his roles as a democratic precinct captain, and a trustee of the Norwood Park Township Lighting District, and his entertaining at parades, picnics, and other events as "Pogo the Clown."

Gacy had been convicted in Blackhawk County, Iowa for sodomizing a sixteen-year-old boy in 1968. He was sentenced to ten years in the penitentiary, but was paroled after serving eighteen months. Sadly, his parole was transferred to Illinois.

He had a penchant for hiring young men, even teenagers, to work on his crew. Some of his neighbors were aware of the constant parade of young men, employees, and others through 8213 Summerdale for parties that ran late into the night. During his short second marriage, he had told his wife that he would remain bisexual, but that he would exercise his preference for males in his expanded garage, which contained mattresses, red lights, and mirrors among other things. The garage area was "off limits" to his wife and daughters.

During his surveillance, he told the officers that when he was a clown at parades, he could walk right up to women at the curb and squeeze their breasts and everyone would just laugh because he was just a clown. "In fact," he told them, "a clown can even get away with murder."

On December 21, 1978, under the watchful eye of a surveillance team, Gacy passed some pills and a packet of marijuana to a young gas station attendant in Park Ridge. As Gacy pulled out of the station, the attendant brought the contraband over to the officers, who confiscated it.

That day, Gacy was being driven around by one of his employees, David Cram. When Gacy went into DeLeo's restaurant for a meeting, his driver excitedly approached the surveillance officers and told them Gacy had said he had killed over thirty people for the "outfit" and feared he was going to be arrested shortly. He said he was going to the cemetery to visit his father's grave.

Gacy was pulled over and arrested for delivery of controlled substances. While in custody in Des Plaines, he had one of his signature phony "heart attacks," and was taken by paramedics to Northwest Hospital for diagnosis and treatment.

During the same time period, a second search warrant was being prepared and authorized to search the crawl space by excavation for human remains. This was based on the products of the first warrant and subsequent investigation, as well as the specific averment of a surveillance officer who had been in the house, in the bathroom, when the furnace in the crawl space kicked on and sent a flood of warm air up into the bathroom. He had experienced the odor of decaying flesh on forty or more occasions and immediately recognized the smell coming up from below.

By the time Gacy was returned to the lockup from the hospital, investigation of the crawl space was begun and Cook County sheriff's police evidence technicians discovered human remains in two separate areas. Gacy was formally arrested and charged with murder.

He then proceeded to give a series of oral confessions, mostly with his attorneys present, albeit over their objections and noted advice. He named four of his victims and described the circumstances of the first (January 3, 1972), and last victim (Robert Piest), and gave the circumstances and nickname for a seventh.

During his description of the last murder, he stopped talking, then began again in a changed voice, saying, "Who are you and what am I doing here?" When told he was describing the murder of Robert Piest, he stated that he was not the murderer. The killer was "the other John." Even the defense psychiatrists would agree this was "malingering." His attempt to mimic a multiple personality disorder was purportedly rejected even by the queen of multiple personality disorders, Dr. Cornelia Wilbur.

Gacy had described in gory detail how he had used his "hand-cuff trick" to subdue his victims and his "rope trick" to strangle them. The exception was his first victim who had been stabbed twice in the chest (confirmed by postmortem examination). He also indicated he had buried the victims in his crawl space and when that became full, he put the last four or five bodies in the Des Plaines River.

The next day, he had a voluntary conversation with assistant state attorney Larry Finder and a policeman during which he demonstrated the rope trick using his rosary beads and also drew a sketch of the crawl space on the back of a police telephone message slip, showing the location of trenches and individual bodies in the crawl space, hoping to avoid unnecessary damage to his premises.

Also on the 22nd, he was taken to the bridge to show where and how he had dumped the bodies in the river, and to his house where he spray-painted a stick figure showing the exact location and orientation of the body of John Butkovich under the concrete floor of his garage addition.

Late in the afternoon, I was back in my office at 26th Street, looking through the stacks of paper already being generated by the several law enforcement agencies already involved. I had already enlisted a number of Chicago homicide detectives, through the chief of detectives and the superintendent's office, to immediately canvass the neighborhood around Gacy's house and interview every relative, employee, or friend of Gacy's they could find and "get them on paper." When interviewed by experienced detectives, they are usually as factual as possible. But if the media or, worse yet, a defense investigator, gets to them first, memories may get a lot less factual and more colorful.

There was no doubt that this was going to be an insanity defense. The defense of last resort. I had handled a number of such cases. I was prepared to immerse myself, with the help and guidance of those experts who would ultimately side with the prosecution, into the study necessary to present the factual evidence needed to support our experts' opinions. My objective was to destroy the opinions of the defense experts. My other difficult tasks would be presenting our experts on direct examination and cross examining the defense experts.

But this would be a huge media case, with defense motions for delay, change of venue, jury sequestration, and any other twists the defense could imagine based on claims of prejudicial pre-trial publicity. Just like *People v. Speck*.

I had handled "specials" and "heaters" before. But this would be the biggest pressure cooker yet. I had seen everything 26th Street could produce, first as a public defender and then as a state's attorney. I had seen the breadth and depth of the inhuman acts evil people had committed upon their fellow citizens and it was staggering. You learn to deal with anything. But this would be different. There would be not one, but dozens of victims' families to try to comfort, deal with, and prepare for "life and death" testimony. There were already not one but several police agencies involved. Des Plaines, Park Ridge, Chicago, the Cook County sheriff's office, which had jurisdiction over the crime scene at 8213 Summerdale because it was in unincorporated Cook County. There would no doubt be more, as bodies might be recovered from the river in different counties or municipalities. Getting court-worthy identifications of the recovered remains would be a monumental task. And, we might very well have wound up trying a few, or many, indictments based on unidentified victims' remains and possibly even prosecute based on a murder of a known victim with no remains ever recovered. Would there be one trial or many? This would be a death case. As the Speck trial had shown, the jury would have to meet the stringent standards of the U.S. Supreme Court as those standards stood at the time of the trial and as those standards might be defined in the future.

What had I gotten myself into? How did I get to this once-in-a-lifetime opportunity and once-in-a-lifetime burden? It is often said that to get by in the felony trial division of the Cook County state's attorney's office you had to win the cases that should be won. If you wanted to be a star, you had to win a few that were expected to be losers. But if you wanted to be viewed as an utter failure, just lose a big case that's supposed to be won.

This case was supposed to be won. Gacy had the bodies on his property and made oral admissions. How could you lose?

To win, twelve ordinary citizens, who no doubt would start the trial thinking that anyone who could kill thirty or more victims and then go to sleep so close to their bodies over a period of six years would have to be "crazy," would have to be convinced that the killer was legally sane during every murder. Indeed, seven of the twelve selected jurors who ultimately signed the guilty verdicts and the death verdicts expressed the "crazy" opinion during *voir dire* examination.

I had arrived at this life-altering place and time by a circuitous and fortuitous route.

I attended Northwestern University School of Law after working three years with Union Carbide Corporation as an engineer. My initial purpose was to become a corporate and/or patent lawyer and return to the company significantly higher up the corporate hierarchy with engineering and production experience and a law degree. Several criminal law and trial practice classes and some successes in moot court competitions had instilled in me an interest in both criminal and trial law. But I stuck with the plan, taking Securities Regulation, Corporate Financing II, and Antitrust Law.

Then I met Professor William Martin.

I took his Criminal Evidence Seminar. The curriculum involved assignments as either a prosecutor or a defense attorney, preparing and presenting live witnesses and evidence before a real criminal court judge on various pre-trial motions using actual Chicago police reports, evidentiary materials, and real narcotics and homicide detectives, crime lab personnel, and evidence technicians. Complainants, defendants, and other witnesses were played by other law students.

There was no other practical course in the curriculum anything like it. I was hooked. I spent more time preparing for these exercises than I spent studying for finals. I was learning how to do something that mattered. As the late Hon. Earl Strayhorn, a superb, practical, street-wise, and fair 26th Street criminal felony trial court judge once said, "The true meaning and application of the United States Constitution is not decided in the Supreme Court of the United States by and for legal scholars. It is decided every day in the well of this courtroom by trial judges and trial lawyers for the victims, complainants, defendants, and the people of Illinois."

This experience taught me many critical lessons. One, that Bill Martin was one of the most intelligent, most compassionate, and most diligent felony trial prosecutors in the history of the office of the state's attorney of Cook County. That, if he would have me, he would be my mentor for a forty-four-year legal career as an assistant Cook County public defender, as he had first wanted to be; an assistant state's attorney of Cook County, as I had first wanted to be; a private practitioner in both civil and criminal trial practice; and, in my case, a criminal division judge in the circuit court of Cook County.

It was often said that a good trial prosecutor was usually a frustrated jock looking for another arena in which to compete. It is no surprise that Bill Martin played competitive hockey throughout his life.

Bill Martin taught many good lawyers the supreme importance of out-preparing your opponent. Every legal issue must be anticipated and researched, with a written brief or memorandum ready for the judge before the argument arose. Every witness must be thoroughly prepared and comfortable with giving his or her testimony and being cross examined. A prosecutor must be able to think like a defense lawyer in order to anticipate every move and tactic of the defense and either preclude it in the state's direct case or eliminate it in cross examination of defense witnesses. Finally, it is often effectively done in the state's case in rebuttal. A prosecutor must also be able to think and speak like a juror when a jury is deciding the case.

Just as we learned these lessons in the Criminal Evidence Seminar, you have learned them from the prosecutor/defender professor in this book. You have come to understand that Bill Martin did not become the best by trying and winning the "Case of the Century." But rather, he was chosen to be the "first chair" for the biggest heater case anyone had seen out of a pool of talented and experienced trial prosecutors. Prosecuting Richard Speck did not make Bill Martin the best. Giving him the case demonstrated clearly that he was already the best.

The investigators, detectives, and prosecutors assigned to assist Martin knew and shared that belief, and state's attorney John Stamos and first assistant Lou Garippo were aware of that fact and entrusted him with being the chief prosecutor of the case.

The crucial points where Bill Martin followed his gut shine through in this case; his knowledge of the trends being applied to change rules written in stone by years of law or practice was proven correct time after time. Not opposing the defense motion for a change of venue, agreeing to a court appointed panel of experts to provide expert opinions on the issues of fitness for trial, his sanity at the time of the offense, and providing the defense access to a protected and concealed key witness, not just for an interview, but for a court reported or recorded cross examination (essentially a criminal pre-trial deposition) were unprecedented, hotly debated, and ultimately all were correct. *The Crime of the Century* has given the reader a detailed, accurate, and fascinating account of the behind-the-scenes strategies employed in the celebrated case.

Indeed, these and dozens of other obvious or subtle tactics and procedures would become crucial to the successful prosecution of serial murderer John Gacy in 1980.

As luck and prescience would have it, two critical assignments brought the lessons of Bill Martin and the wisdom and experience of one of his superiors into direct contact with the prosecution and trial of the man who would become the serial killer with the most murder convictions (thirty-three) in the history of the United States.

On December 22, Cook County State's Attorney Bernard Carey appointed me to lead the investigation and prosecution of John Gacy. On January 10, 1979, in the criminal court building at 26th Street and California Avenue in Chicago, chief judge of the Criminal Division of the Circuit Court of Cook County, Richard J. Fitzgerald, assigned Judge Louis B. Garippo as the trial judge for the matter of *The People of the State of Illinois v. John Wayne Gacy*, then consisting of Indictments No. 79 c 69 through 79 c 75. These first seven indictments charged the defendant with the murders of seven identified victims, including Robert Piest, whose body had not yet been recovered.

Lou Garippo was the chief of the Criminal Division of the Cook County State's Attorney's Office during the investigation and prosecution of Richard Speck. He had agreed with Bill Martin's appointment and was directly involved in providing personnel and other resources to the trial team, as well as serving his sage counsel. He gained first-hand knowledge of the issues and problems associated with the prosecution of Richard Speck.

Garippo's experience with the Speck case led directly to his masterful and error-free trial of John Gacy. He warned the defense attorneys to "be careful what you ask for" with respect to filing a motion for change of place of trial due to allegedly prejudicial pre-trial publicity. He was well aware of the reality of leaving a jury from a big city in favor for a jury from a rural area. Publicity for a case like these reached everywhere. Particularly in a case where the defense of last resort, the defense of insanity at the time of the offense, was sure to be raised, the defense had a better chance in a large metropolitan area than in rural, "downstate" Illinois. Nevertheless, the motion was filed. As in Speck, the defense motion was granted. Also, as in Speck, the state did not object. I felt that we would get a more state-minded jury pool elsewhere, and if Judge Garippo wanted to protect the record on appeal and eliminate a potential defense issue on appeal, so much the better.

However, unlike Speck, where Judge Paschen had a free hand at selecting the place of trial, in Gacy, the defense wanted to have a very extensive and expensive media survey of potential venues done by experts of their choice, as well as studies of the potential jury venires. Again. following the examples of Judge Paschen, Judge Garippo began with his own survey of potential venues with adequate jury pool populations, jail and courthouse security, courtroom availability for a lengthy period, access space for public and media spectators, housing for lawyers and witnesses, and the willingness to take it on. He did not put Peoria on the list, as he felt Peoria had already paid its dues in full. While the Court's search was going on, we were doing our own. I was talking to prosecutors in likely locations to get a feel for their jury pools, local media, and court and jail personnel.

Judge Garippo ruled that the defense proposal was overbroad and unnecessary. He chose six possible venues, including Winnebago County, to assess, using a more limited media survey involving inches of written media reporting on the case to-date. The report came back with a significantly lower level of publicity in Winnebago County. It was believed that Rockford was the best venue. The county seat of Winnebago County, it was Illinois' second-most populous city and was located farther from Chicago than most of the other contenders, had more citizen focus on local newspapers, and local television and radio, than smaller counties, which relied on Chicago-based media more heavily. We were delighted, as our research had suggested that Winnebago County jurors would be just what we were looking for.

Judge Garippo's additional ruling was even more appreciated. I knew him well by reputation and through personal contact. As a public defender, I had second-chaired my first murder defense before him. He was a true product of the great Chicago neighborhoods, a real trial lawyer himself, a superb judge of people, street-wise, a legal scholar, and was a man who always found a way to do the right thing and protect the record at the same time. Many who knew him, but not well, viewed him as a defense-minded judge. Much like Bill Martin, he had been a competitive and successful prosecutor, but never lost his sense of fairness or his compassion. As he put it, he just couldn't get overly excited about the "routine" drug, auto theft, or other less serious cases, which he called the ninety-five percent. On those cases, he didn't give anyone a free pass, but he didn't take all police traffic stop or narcotic surveillance testimony as gospel if it didn't stand up to cross-examination or common sense. However, he had fair but intense focus on the five per centers. He issued the death penalty on more than one occasion and well understood the seriousness of the armed robberies, rapes, and murders that were the basis for most jury trials at 26th Street. Richard Speck and John Gacy were at the very top of the five per centers.

We had not worried about losing him in a change of place of trial, because we knew he was going to remain the trial judge. His plan was to ask the Supreme Court of Illinois to transfer him to sit in the Seventeenth Judicial Circuit Court of Illinois, which included Winnebago County, for the purposes of selecting the jury. Once the jury was selected he would be transferred back to the Circuit Court of Cook County to attend to the trial and his court call as necessary. Since the defense had filed a motion to sequester the jury during trial to protect them from any and all publicity during trial, which was granted, it mattered little whether they would be locked up in a hotel in Rockford or a hotel in Chicago. The Judge implemented a six-day-a-week trial schedule. We were to have witnesses ready to keep working steadily from nine to five on week days and nine to four on Saturday. He arranged for dinners out and sometimes a play or other event for Saturday nights and gave the jurors the option of being bused to and from their homes near Rockford on Sundays, or meeting with families in the hotel in Chicago. None of this was objected to by the defense. They knew they would never get a fairer judge in Cook or Winnebago Counties. Although this was a first in Illinois, none of these procedures ever created an issue on appeal. Lessons were learned from the "Trial of the Century."

Also, by holding the trial in Chicago, experts and other out-of-state witnesses had easy transportation and lodging access, other judges were available to handle any emergencies on Judge Garippo's regular court call, physical evidence in the custody of the medical examiner was properly maintained a short distance away, the families of twenty-two known victims could travel easily from home to testify or observe. The huge volume of physical exhibits and the large size of some of them were easily accommodated in areas very close to the courtroom.

Judge Garippo also took charge of modifying the courtroom itself. The "hard seats" for spectators were altered to create more room in the well of the court and the jury box was modified to accommodate four alternate jurors. Special passes for media and families of the victims and the defendant were prepared and a "first-come" process was set up for passes for the public. Front row seats were available for the media's courtroom artists.

Because of the large media presence, Judge Garippo met with representatives of the media and made an agreement whereby the media pool on any given day was to select a single representative to be given access to all "side-bar" conferences, including those conducted in chambers, and to then report back to all reporters present during the next break.

Again, more lessons learned from Speck.

Like the Speck team, I did not want to create an appearance of unfairness, or piling on, by having too many lawyers at the prosecution table. As first chair, I would have the ultimate last word on any procedural or strategic decisions. But, as was always my practice on trial, the rest of the team would be expected to have a large share of the burdens and the exposure. I would direct the overall trial strategy and "order of proof." I would handle my share of the "routine" witnesses, but my focus would be on the direct examination of six of our seven psychiatric witnesses, the cross examination of five of the six defense experts, and the direct examination of Dr. Robert Stein, the medical examiner of Cook County. I would give the last or "rebuttal" closing argument for the people in both the guilt phase of the trial and at the end of the separate penalty phase.

The second chair, Robert Egan, would focus on the testimony on the recovery of the remains from the Gacy property, which he had personally viewed from beginning to end, the dental and radiological identifications of the known victims, the direct examination of one of the prosecution psychologists, and the cross examination of one of the defense psychiatrists. Bob would make the opening statement for the prosecution, which all jury research and most trial lore regards as critical. The jury must begin hearing of the evidence already knowing that the people can and will prove the defendant guilty. He would also give the people's opening closing argument during the death penalty sentencing hearing.

The third chair, Terry Sullivan, would focus on the majority of the Des Plaines Police testimony, the largest portion of the "life and death" testimony of the identified victims' family members and friends, and certain Gacy employees and friends. Terry would also give the people's opening closing argument in the guilt phase of the trial.

The fourth chair, who did not sit at counsel table unless presenting a witness, was James Varga. Jim was a "Rule 711" law student clerk, practicing under our direct supervision pursuant to Supreme Court rules. He was our legal researcher, the same task carried out by Jim Zagel on the Speck team. He also presented several witnesses at trial, including "life and death" witnesses and others.

All of us would direct or cross examine many other witnesses. In our case alone, I think approximately eighty witnesses were presented.

To fulfill my central role as the architect, some might say the cinematic director, of the evidence and arguments to prove Gacy legally sane at the time of all thirty-three murders, I had to take up the study of psychiatry, at least to the extent defined by the diagnoses and opinions of thirteen experts. To understand what legal insanity entailed, I had to come to my own understanding of this insatiable killer.

I had known Dr. Robert Riefman of the Psychiatric Institute of Cook County and Dr. James Cavanaugh of the Isaac Ray Center at Chicago's Presbyterian Saint Luke's Hospital for several years from prior cases. Both were appointed as court's witnesses and were in no way "controlled" by either party. The Psychiatric Institute evaluation was requested by the defense and the Isaac Ray Center's team was requested by the prosecution. Both found Gacy fit for trial and sane at the time of the offenses.

Both men and their supporting staff or team would be called to testify by the prosecution. However, because they were court appointed, and owing to their fair nature, they were all readily available to both sides for interviews and to us for preparation. Therefore, I did not need a separate, non-testifying expert to assist my preparation. Particularly, Dr. Cavanaugh became my tutor and adviser regarding my effort to win the battle of experts. As the defense of insanity had to be raised affirmatively by the defense, they had the burden of going forward with evidence to support their theory. Therefore, all of our psychiatric expert witnesses would be offered in rebuttal to individual or groups of defense experts and were given copies of the transcripts of the testimony of the witnesses I would ask them to rebut or refute and we would prepare in detail for their own testimony.

I compiled files on all of the expert witnesses including their reports and notes all psychological testing materials and other documents, their testimony in prior relevant cases, their professional history, their articles and publications, and any "expert treatises" they relied on in their reports.

The people's experts were very uniform in their diagnoses. All agreed generally that Gacy was not suffering from any psychotic illness, had no neurological or relevant physical problems, and was not suffering from any mental disease or defect which would excuse him from legal responsibility for his crimes. They regarded him as suffering from personality disorders, such as antisocial personality disorder, psychosexual personality disorders, and some added narcissistic personality disorder as well. Illinois law did not recognize personality disorders as a "mental disease or defect" sufficient to constitute a valid basis for an insanity defense.

The defense experts were all over the map. Their Freudian-oriented diagnoses included consistent paranoid schizophrenia for the entire time period or only during the murders and body disposal, psychotic rage attacks induced by stress and/or drugs and alcohol, and a borderline personality disorder which expanded into florid psychosis at the time of the murders. Two of the defense psychiatrists did not give any legal opinion at all, but rambled on about their diagnoses, using old European Freudian terms and definitions not mentioned in the current *Diagnostic and Statistical Manual of Psychiatry*, the "bible" of psychiatric diagnosticians as adopted by the American Psychiatric Association.

The most significant difference was that the people's experts relied heavily on the *facts* of the crimes and on Gacy's life during the relevant period in reaching their opinions, while the defense experts relied on psychoanalytic theory, Gacy's self-serving statements to them and, in essence, that his upbringing, failure to accept his homosexuality and abuse of alcohol and drugs was at fault. Dr. Reifman said it best for the prosecution: "John Gacy denying he is a homosexual is like Bruce Sutter (a star with the Chicago Cubs in 1980) saying he is not a ball player" and "John Gacy has no remorse because John Gacy has no remorse."

My personal conclusion was that John Gacy is simply evil. In reading this book, I have learned in painful detail that Richard Speck was simply evil.

The defense witness testimony and the defense arguments to the jury repeatedly alluded to Gacy having a condition or psyche depicted in Robert Louis Stevenson's *Dr. Jekyll and Mr. Hyde*. In rebuttal argument I told the jury that Gacy had a base of morality. The kindly Dr. Jekyll had sought to study evil. Not external evil, but the evil that lurks under the surface in all of us. He sought to study the evil buried within him. He devised a potion which would release that evil and he made a conscious decision to take it. It worked. He was transformed into the evil Mr. Hyde. He was now capable of awful brutality, of the worst of crimes against his fellow humans. And he committed them. And he learned that he enjoyed committing them. He learned to love what he believed was the god-like power to decide who would live and who would die. And when the potion wore off, and he turned back into kindly Dr. Jekyll, he *remembered it all.*

And then he made a conscious decision to do it again, and again, and again.

Just like Dr. Jekyll, John Gacy made the conscious decisions to have the handcuffs ready, to have the rope and handle ready, to have trenches dug for use as graves, to assault and immobilize his potential victims and then to take their lives for his own conscious pleasure.

But I told the jury that they must not forget the moral balance at the end of the story. Dr. Jekyll paid for his crimes with his life.

Trial preparation took just over one year. The trial was originally scheduled to begin in November 1979, but another Gacy phony heart attack delayed us until January 28, 1980. The jury was selected in Rockford, Winnebago County, Illinois. Judge Garippo's superb process for selecting the jury completed the process in less than a week. Opening statements followed by a full day of evidence began the trial on February 6, 1980. Working full days, the trial was completed in six weeks. The jury's guilty verdicts in the guilt phase were returned on March 11, 1980 after deliberations lasting one hour and forty-five minutes. The jury returned twelve death verdicts on March 13, 1980.

John Gacy was ultimately convicted of thirty-three murders of young men and boys. Twelve of those murders were committed during the time that Illinois had reinstated the death penalty. Gacy was sentenced to twelve death sentences and twenty-one life sentences without possibility of parole. Although he never won a new trial or significant hearing on appeal, Gacy was not executed by lethal injection until May 9, 1994. That he was convicted and executed without need of a second trial, or in legalese, "without reversible error," is in no small measure due to the caliber and character of my trial team and the legacy of the lawyers in the Felony Trial Division of the Office of the Cook County State's Attorney and their wise supervisors in the 60s, 70s, and 80s, and in particular to the courage, character, and intellect of Bill Martin and Lou Garippo.

The Crime of the Century is a comprehensive and spell-binding account of what goes into the preparation and trial of a celebrated case. I set forth the strategies applied in Speck that were utilized, in part, for the preparation of the Gacy prosecution. There are differences, mainly attributed to Gacy invoking a full-fledged insanity defense and Speck not raising an insanity defense at all. Another crucial factor is that Gacy gave pre-trial confessions to certain elements of his murders whereas Speck did not confess to anything. A substantial number of mental health experts testified and were cross-examined in detail in Gacy. No psychiatrist testified in Speck's trial. In order to use an insanity defense, the defendant must admit that he committed the crime. Speck was shrewd and admitted nothing. He did not want to trade admitting the crime for raising an insanity defense. Moreover, the Speck defense was locked in by the impartial psychiatric panel that the public defender requested and received. Their unanimous finding that Speck was sane at the time of his murders left Speck no experts to testify to an insanity defense, as opposed to Gacy, who used multiple mental health experts.

The problem of dealing with a frenzied media was identical in each case and solved the same way. Neither case was turned into a media circus nor sensationalized because the prosecutors kept their mouth shut.

I strongly recommend *The Crime of the Century* as a compelling, comprehensive, and fully documented account of one of the worst crimes ever committed. I know of nothing else like it.

During Thanksgiving 2015, the sole survivor of Speck's murderous rampage, Corazon Amurao Atienza, agreed to a worldwide publishing first—posing for family photographs with (*from left*) son, Christian Amurao Atienza; Cora; husband, Bert Atienza; and daughter, Abigail Atienza Phillips, outside Abigail's home in Virginia.

This photo of the entire family, also taken at Abigail's home, includes Cora's six grandchildren: (*front row, from left*) Jadon Atienza, Bailey Phillips, Bert Atienza, Cora, Jasmin Atienza, and Abigail Atienza Phillips; (*back row, from left*) Christian Amurao Atienza; his wife, Maria Atienza; Jacob Atienza; Tyler Phillips; Steve Phillips, Abigail's husband; and Jordan Phillips.

ABOUT THE AUTHORS

DENNIS L. BREO, a Florida author and journalist, is the former national correspondent of the *Journal of the American Medical Association* (JAMA). His cover story on the Speck murders, published in the *Chicago Tribune Magazine*, won an award for exemplary journalism from the Chicago Headline Club. His work has also appeared in *Parade, People, Reader's Digest, Chicago* magazine, *Chicago Sun-Times*, Los Angeles Times Syndicate, and New York Times Syndicate. This is his fifth book.

   WILLIAM J. MARTIN, the assistant State's Attorney who led the prosecution of Richard Speck, has been a criminal defense attorney in Chicago since 1970. An editor of the *Loyola Law Times* and a former Northwestern University law school professor, Martin is a member of the Order of the Coif, the American Academy of Forensic Sciences, and is named in *The Best Lawyers in America*. He has lectured nationally on the Speck case and is a Fellow of the American College of Trial Lawyers.

AUTHORS' NOTES

First, we want to thank the thoughtful and energetic Skyhorse team for publishing the fiftieth anniversary edition of this infamous true crime:

Publisher Tony Lyons was an early and enthusiastic champion of the authenticity and appeal of our account of the crime that murdered American innocence and ushered in the era of mass murders that plagues us today. Assistant editor Alexandra Hess adroitly, unflappably, and enthusiastically handled the myriad details required to revise and update the manuscript of a twentieth century crime for readers in the twenty-first century, offered helpful insights for our many rewrites, and wove the many changes into a seamless story. Director of editorial operations Dean Notte provided timely assistance to secure the use of exclusive photographs of Corazon Amurao Atienza, the sole survivor of the murders, and her happy family. For fifty years, Corazon never posed for a public photograph. The pictures she agreed to have taken for publication in this book are a worldwide publishing first.

The impetus for this book came from our collaboration in 1986 to produce a cover story published in the *Chicago Tribune Magazine* on the twentieth anniversary of the murders. *Tribune* editor Mary Knoblauch provided invaluable help in preparing this anniversary article for a new generation of readers.

Special acknowledgments must go to the slain nurses' classmates and relatives, many of whom agreed to be interviewed for our book. Classmates Karen Besida Geronovich, Judy Dykton, Kathy Donzalski Emmons, Pat McCarthy, Tammy Sioukoff, and Ellen Harnisch Stannish gave generously of their time and thoughts. Marilyn Farris McNulty, older sister of Suzanne Bridgett Farris, allowed an extraordinary interview to be conducted in her home in the presence of her husband, Bob McNulty, and daughters Peg and Beth. Other helpful interviews were granted by Mary Jo Matusek Purvis, sister of Patricia Matusek, Dr. Leroy Smith, attorney Casimir Wachowski, hospital administrator Harlan Newkirk, Public Defender Gerald Getty, and retired Stateville warden Vernon Revis.

Among the publications we consulted were the four Chicago newspapers thriving in 1966—*Chicago Tribune*, the *Chicago American*, *Chicago Sun-Times*, and *Chicago Daily News*; and two books, *My Life as Public Defender*, by Gerald Getty (1974), and *Born to Raise Hell: The Untold Story of Richard Speck*, by Jack Altman and Dr. Marvin Ziporyn (1967). The 1966 article in *Life* magazine "The Nine Nurses," written by Loudon Wainwright, was very helpful in providing quotes from letters written home by Filipino nurses Merlita Gargullo and Valentina Pasion and in providing descriptions and quotes from the South Chicago Community Hospital Class of 1966 about their slain colleagues and friends.

Mostly, I want to thank my wife, Julie, for first envisioning the idea of expanding a magazine article into a book; for helping with all the necessary marketing and sales of the original book proposal; for reading *every* word of the many revisions of this manuscript, usually within hours of the writing; and for offering unfailing encouragement and unflagging good cheer. She was the perfect elixir to transform the writer's pessimism into productive work.

D.L.B.

This book is based upon primary sources: the 10,000-page trial transcript; the Abstract of Record and Books of Exhibits; the complete case reports of the Chicago Police Department; dozens of verbatim statements of witnesses taken by prosecution investigators; detailed internal memoranda describing the extensive prosecution pre-trial investigation throughout Texas, upper Michigan, New York, and in Chicago and Monmouth, Illinois; Detective Byron Carlile's comprehensive personal investigative file; Richard Speck's lengthy psychiatric, psychological, medical, employment, school, arrest, jail, and prison records; voluminous scrapbooks filled with the era's press clippings; and interviews with most of the living participants, including Corazon Amurao. There are no reconstructed quotes or other artificial contrivances in this true story of a true crime.

W.J.M.